THE RENAISSANCE AND
REFORMATION IN SCOTLAND

Frontispiece

THE RENAISSANCE AND REFORMATION IN SCOTLAND

Essays in honour of
GORDON DONALDSON

edited by
IAN B. COWAN & DUNCAN SHAW

SCOTTISH ACADEMIC PRESS

1983

Published by
Scottish Academic Press Ltd,
33 Montgomery Street
Edinburgh EH7 5JX

SBN 7073 0261 7

© 1983 Scottish Academic Press Ltd

Printed in Great Britain by
Clark Constable (1982) Ltd, Edinburgh

Contents

Preface

Following his retiral from the Sir William Fraser chair of Scottish History in the University of Edinburgh, the opportunity has been taken to present a *Festschrift* to Professor Emeritus Gordon Donaldson, Historiographer Royal in Scotland, in appreciation of his dedication to the furtherance of his chosen subject. The studies in this volume are by former students, colleagues and friends and their wide-ranging contributions to an understanding of the sixteenth century reveal the continuing influence of the professor's teaching and inspiration in this field.

The editors, one, as undergraduate, research student, and, for a time, a colleague in the university of Edinburgh, and the other, a former research student and friend of forty years' standing, both bear witness to his kindness and encouragement during his distinguished career. Gratitude is expressed to the volume's contributors and to Mr Douglas Grant, managing director of the Scottish Academic Press.

IAN B. COWAN
DUNCAN SHAW

December 1982

Abbreviations

ADCP – *Acts of the Lords of Council in Public Affairs: Selections from Acta Dominorum Concilii*, edited by R. K. Hannay (Edinburgh, 1932)

AHCAG – *Archaeological and Historical Collections relating to Ayrshire and Galloway*

APS – *The Acts of the Parliaments of Scotland*, edited by T. Thomson and C. Innes (Edinburgh 1814–75)

AT – Argyll Transcripts made by 10th Duke of Argyll (Originals at Inverary; copies at Department of Scottish History, University of Glasgow)

BM – British Museum

Calderwood, *History* – D. Calderwood, *History of the Kirk of Scotland* edd. T. Thomson and D. Laing, 8 vols (Woodrow Soc. 1842)

Cowan, *Parishes* – *The Parishes of Medieval Scotland* ed. I. B. Cowan (SRS 1967)

CPL – *Calendar of Entries in the Papal Registers relating to Great Britain and Ireland:* Papal Letters, edited by W. H. Bliss and others (London, 1893–)

CPP – *Calendar of Entries in the Papal Registers relating to Great Britain and Ireland: Petitions to the Pope*, ed. W. H. Bliss (London, 1896)

CSPD – *Calendar of State Papers, Domestic* edd. R. Lemon and others (London, 1856–72)

CSP Ireland – *Calendar of State Papers Relating to Ireland* edd. H. C. Hamilton and others (London, 1860–1912)

CSP Scot. – *Calendar of the State Papers Relating to Scotland and Mary, Queen of Scots 1547–1603* edd. J. Bain and others (Edinburgh, 1898–)

Diurnal of Occurrents – *A Diurnal of Remarkable Occurrents* (Bannatyne Club, 1833)

Donaldson, *James V–James VII* – G. Donaldson, Scotland: *James V to James VII* (Edinburgh, 1965)

EHR – *English Historical Review*

ER – *The Exchequer Rolls of Scotland*, edited by J. Stuart and others (Edinburgh, 1878–1908)

HMC – *Reports of the Royal Commission on Historical Manuscripts* (London, 1870–)

I.R. – *Innes Review*

James IV Letters – *The Letters of James IV*, 1505–13 edd. R. K. Hannay and R. L. Mackie (SHS, 1953)

James V Letters – *The Letters of James V* edd. R. K. Hannay and D. Hay (Edinburgh, 1954)

L.P. Henry VIII – *Letters and Papers, Foreign and domestic of the reign of Henry VIII* ed. J. S. Brewer and others (London, 1864–1932)

Melville, *Memoirs* – Sir James Melville, *Memoirs* (Bannatyne Club, 1827)

NLS – National Library of Scotland.

Pitcairn, *Trials* – *Criminal Trials in Scotland from 1488 to 1624* ed. R. Pitcairn (Edinburgh, 1833)

PRO – Public Record Office

Prot. Book Cuthbert Simson – *Liber Protocollorum M. Cuthberti Simonis Notarii Publici et Scribae Capituli Glasguensis 1499–1513* (Grampian Club, 1875)

PSAS – Proceedings of the Society of Antiquaries of Scotland

RCAHMS – *Royal Commission on the Ancient and Historical Monuments of Scotland*

RSCHS – *Records of the Scottish Church History Society*

Reg. Supp. – Vatican Archives, Registra Supplicationum

RMS – *Registrum Magni Sigilli Regum Scotorum*, edited by J. M. Thomson and others (Edinburgh, 1882–1914)

RPC – *The Register of the Privy Council of Scotland* edd. J. H. Burton and others (Edinburgh, 1877–)

RSS – *Registrum Secreti Sigilli Regum Scotorum*, edited by M. Livingstone and others (Edinburgh, 1908–)

Scots Peerage – *The Scots Peerage*, edited by J. Balfour Paul (Edinburgh, 1904–14)

SGTS – *Scottish Gaelic Texts Society*

SHR – *Scottish Historical Review*

SHS – *Scottish History Society*

SRO – Scottish Record Office

SRS – *Scottish Record Society*

SS – *Scottish Studies*

TA – *Accounts of the Lord High Treasurer of Scotland*, edited by T. Dickson and J. Balfour Paul (Edinburgh, 1877–1916)

TCD – Trinity College, Dublin

TDGAS – *Transactions of the Dumfriesshire and Galloway Natural History and Antiquarian Society*

TGSG – *Transactions of the Gaelic Society of Glasgow*

TGSI – *Transactions of the Gaelic Society of Inverness*

Watt, *Fasti* – *Fasti Ecclesiæ Scoticanae Medii Aevi ad annum 1638* (SRS, 1969)

Vat. Arch. – Vatican Archives

Vet. Mon – *Vetera Monumenta Hibernorum Historiam Illustrantia* ed. A. Theiner (Rome, 1864)

I

Gordon Donaldson

(i) *An Appreciation*

The historian in Gordon Donaldson appeared early. At the Royal High
School of Edinburgh, where in the 1920s he went to school, the scope and
exactness of his knowledge of European and British history were acknowledged by his class-mates. He and they were twelve and thirteen years old, yet
here was one of their number who knew incomparably more history than any
other boy in the entire school. It was not merely an outstanding feat; it was
something phenomenal, unique; and they knew it. Schoolboys in that decade
were not particularly interested in anything beyond necessary class-work
and all-engrossing rugby and cricket. Contemporary political and social
troubles did not disturb them unduly. The General Strike of 1926, when
men stood around in throngs all day at the GPO and the boys were
cautioned about their journeys to and from school, certainly invaded the
consciousness of them all.

To Gordon, the past was explanatory prologue to the present, and
infinitely more interesting. On one occasion, a year or so after the General
Strike, he astonished an interested group of class-mates by tracing the genesis
of the Great War back in a causal chain to the capture of Constantinople by the
Turks in 1453. Such knowledge, such confident logic, such striding over
continents and centuries, to the other youngsters eating their lunch-rolls, had
something uncanny about it.

In those days the High School was still a classical school. Science had a
place, but it wasn't a place in the sun. Pre-eminently the school still purveyed
the centuries-old European tradition of education – Latin and Greek, above
all Latin being the means whereby a gentleman became educated. Under a
rector convinced of the virtues of classical languages in the education of
young people, this tradition was maintained largely undiminished in
Gordon's time. Every year as a senior, his schooldays were given over to
grappling with the languages and literature of Greece and Rome. Of course,
other subjects were included – it was a broad general curriculum. But the
rector, William King Gillies, saw to it that every boy over eleven was taught
Latin every year, with Greek added in the second year for those who showed
they could juggle with the inflexions and syntax of Latin. Gordon's class were
given the elements of physics and chemistry, with astronomy replacing these

in the third year before the final abandonment of science. If science appealed to a boy more than classics, or if he needed it for a medical course later, the rearrangement was made at this point.

Gordon was entirely happy with the Arts curriculum of which the study of classical texts in the original languages was the core. With all that, his reading in English literature and history meshed easily. Although he never bothered with the proceedings of the history class – it was too slow for his tempo, too narrow for his scale – in the upper reaches of the school he was out in front alone, receiving from the master, W. C. A. Ross, separate and different attention and borrowing books in plenty.

The school motto – *Musis respublica floret* – proclaims the supremacy of the Arts for the well-being of the community. It was Clio, the Muse of history, that laid her bewitchment on Gordon Donaldson at this early age.

On his paternal side, Gordon is of Shetland stock. In the seventies of last century his grandfather, George Donaldson, left his native island, Yell, the second most northerly of the Shetland group, and, found his way to Edinburgh. The circumstances are unclear – his plans, his motives, the details of his sea-passage; but the young man settled in Edinburgh and soon married. When a son was born, he was given a name common all over the northern islands, Magnus. To the father the infant's name must have brought something like Home Thoughts from Abroad. Certainly the name Magnus, with its hints of the islands and their turbulent history, appealed later to Gordon. He far prefers it to his own name. He is the first Gordon in the family and cannot explain why the name was given to him.

The infant Magnus grew to manhood in Edinburgh. In due course he married, his wife being Rachel Hetherington Swan, whose family connections were with Fife. They set up their home in the capital (where Magnus had started his career in the postal service) and there on 13 April 1913, their son Gordon was born.

But to our tale of his schooling: when the time came to leave school, he found that the only university bursary that the school had to award to sixth-formers would not be available until the following year. Needing financial help and being still only seventeen (the youngest boy in the year), he stayed, won that school bursary to cover his next three years and added another bursary by the university's own competition for freshmen. In view of his outstanding record in classics and in the general work in class over the past years, culminating in his being named 'dux of the school' in the year he left, he received much advice and persuasion from the rector and masters to go for a classics degree. But – not for the last time at crucial points in his life – he struck out for himself. The 'idea of history', to borrow Collingwood's phrase, had already captured him.

Going up to Edinburgh University in October 1931, Gordon threw himself into the four years course in the department of history. In 1935 he emerged with a brilliant First. On the way, with every sign of ease and enjoyment, he took the medal in each of the history classes which made up the course. The one exception serves to give an extra polish to the apple. The lecturer in charge of one of the classes made it a matter of principle not to award his medal to a student who had won a medal in another class in the department. A not wholly indefensible policy! Anyway, it was clear that a *stella nova* of unusual brilliance had appeared in the firmament.

This was no bookish swot or recluse. Although – as at school – games and sport had little appeal for him (tennis was his game), his incurable modesty, bright spirit and amusing company made him as well-liked a companion in the Old Quad as he had been at the High School. And yet he was not a 'joiner' or a 'mixer'. Things military did not attract him – neither at school nor at university did he enlist in the Officers Training Corps. Nor did he join any of the numerous societies flourishing in those days. Presumably, of course, he attended the Historical Society from time to time.

At that time, and for a long period previously, Scottish history was in a sadly neglected state. The reasons need not detain us here but it had something to do with the pre-eminence which English history and historians enjoyed. Professor Robert Hannay, although personally a distinguished figure in the university and beyond, was regarded as presiding over a dull backwater. His department was small, attracting few students when it came to selecting among the available options. The time for selection came in the third year. It was standard practice to choose Economic history on the ground that the work could be overtaken – so it was believed – by mugging up the lecturer's text-book and thus making attendance at his lectures unnecessary.

It was Scottish history that Gordon chose. And in that class which covered the years 1542 to 1567 he first experienced the satisfaction of linking fact with source, source with fact and drawing inferences. This was the rule of research that was to control his mind and teaching from that day forward.

With his First in his pocket, Gordon considered the next stage. What was it to be? The brilliant papers he had written in the final honours examinations, not to mention the quality of his whole performance over the preceding four years, had aroused the interest and expectations of his teachers. Professorial advice was unanimous: he should go off to Oxford or Cambridge and add a BA to his Edinburgh MA. That course seemed to everyone a *sine qua non* for anyone hoping to pursue historical work. But once again Gordon decided on a different line. On a hint from one of the lecturers in the history department, David Horn, he elected to go to London, to the Institute of Historical Research of London University. There he would work for a PhD under J. E. Neale, the Elizabethan historian. Once again his independence of judgment was to prove fruitful.

Fortuitously the way opened for him. Now, just as at the time when he was contemplating the move from school to university, a bursary to help to pay his living expenses was the *unum necessarium*. The Gray bursary, which rotated annually among the various faculties, by chance was available that year in the Arts Faculty. This bursary was awarded to him, enabling him to act as he wished to do.

From the very first interview, Neale received the young Scots scholar hospitably and with encouragement. He shrewdly saw, beneath the nervousness and tentativeness, something of his underlying confidence and self-reliance. Gordon began work on the study of Anglo-Scottish relations in the religious field.

London soon showed itself to be an inspired choice. Its reputation as a centre for research in historical records was in the ascendant. Experts from the Records Office and other institutions gave lectures at the Institute on palaeography and similar subjects. Neale taught research methods and of course maintained a friendly oversight. The common-room allocated to postgraduate workers was naturally a place of stimulating interchange. Oxford or Cambridge would have given Gordon an experience of collegiate life which he would have enjoyed and benefited from. But his natural proclivity is towards detachment rather than the group; and in any case, Oxbridge had nothing to offer comparable to what London was able to provide through the Institute of Historical Research. Gordon's choice of London was amply vindicated and opened into a further productive stage in his *cursus*.

In 1938 London University awarded him a PhD for a thesis entitled 'Relations between English and Scottish Presbyterian and Episcopalian movements to 1604'.

Towards the end of his research in London, a vacancy for an assistant in the Records Office in the General Register House in Edinburgh was advertised. Gordon applied; but another was preferred. Disappointment and dismay: it seemed to close cut the chances of a job dealing with the records of Scotland. But quite unexpectedly in the same department a woman assistant resigned to be married. This time the vacancy was not advertised but was offered to the applicant who had been the reserve choice on the previous occasion. Thus Dr Donaldson, as we may now call him, came home. All the education, training, interest, self-awareness of his life to this point had prepared him for this work. He seemed to have found the path thither by following some inner star that he alone could glimpse.

Dr Donaldson's work on the Scottish records forms the subject of one of the essays contributed to this *Festschrift* and so need not be described here. It was of course the best possible place to be for one who wanted to understand Scotland's past. What a chance to open up the wealth of original sources, to make fresh discoveries about the story of the nation and people, to throw shafts of light into the dark places in publishing the findings. Enthusiastically the new assistant started in.

But international tension and the threat of war filled the horizon in his first year at the Register House. In an interesting article which he contributed to the *Scottish Historical Review* many years afterwards (vol. liii, pages 211–19, October 1974) Donaldson tells the story of the war-time adventures of the earlier records. He recounts entertainingly how he and others shared the sojourn of the volumes and documents in a Perthshire shooting-lodge where they were sent for safety. As a consequence he is able to claim that he has read the Register of the Privy Seal in bed!

Some time later, however, when a health problem threatened, Dr Donaldson was ordered back to Edinburgh for medical treatment. It was judged imprudent for him to return to Perthshire afterwards. When he then offered himself for war-service, he was turned down on account of his medical category. Thus he continued his work at the Register House for the remainder of the war.

With the coming of peace, followed by the return of the records to the place where they had been preserved since the end of the eighteenth century, the universities came alive and Scottish history (to focus on the study that concerns us here) picked up momentum. At this point Donaldson's fortunes took another decisive turn; again 'time and chance' in the biblical phrase came together and an unexpected opportunity presented itself to alter the direction of his life.

One day in 1947 Professor W. Croft Dickinson, of the chair of Scottish History at Edinburgh, was engaged on some piece of work in the Historical Room at the Register House. During conversation with Dr Donaldson it emerged that he was restive at the Register House, where, among other things, various war-time stringencies had not been relaxed. The professor at once glimpsed a possibility: 'Do you mean to say that you would leave this job for something else?' A vacancy was promptly created on the Scottish history staff at Edinburgh and Donaldson was appointed lecturer. He remained there as a teacher of Scottish history until his retirement thirty-two years later. He became reader in 1955 and eight years later, on Dickinson's death, he was appointed to succeed him in the Sir William Fraser chair.

Leaving aside administrative details, the work of an academic is two-sided: teaching and research, a process of cross-fertilisation linking the two. Donaldson pursued both with zest. But first he had to apply himself to learning something about lecturing and communication. For some years he was plagued with nervousness while lecturing and speaking in public. From the beginning he seems to have been able to conceal his efforts to subdue his nerves. One of his former students, whose experience of his powers of communication covers all the stages from ordinary class to postgraduate seminar, in recalling the impact made by the new teacher and his lectures, spurns any suggestion that he was nervous, but mentions two impressions that remain: complete mastery of his subject and an amusing style of presentation. But in truth it was some years before the last of the diffidence subsided.

Donaldson's amusing style of lecturing and conducting seminars – indeed the easy, friendly atmosphere that pervaded the whole department – was the first thing to be mentioned by the former students who were asked for their impressions and comments for the purposes of this biographical sketch. This good-humoured tone in lectures and seminars was matched, according to the testimony of them all, by every sort of helpfulness to students and indeed by an instinctive sympathy with young people. With the passing of the years, this sympathy seems to have become even more sensitive.

The style of Donaldson the author in writing history is in keeping with the lightness of touch he showed in lecturing. At the time of his retirement the Senate of the university adopted a special minute in which his 'attractive, incisive style' is particularly mentioned when the number and variety of his publications are referred to. A just comment indeed; it is not uncommon to find history written in an unsmiling manner.

As the Senate's special minute records, 'even before he joined the Scottish history department he had a formidable list of publications, articles in learned journals mainly, which showed not only his meticulous scholarship but also his wide range of interests'. He was obviously well-equipped to take up the task that his predecessor in the chair had left unfinished, namely to bring Scottish history back into repute both in the academic community and in a wider context. Two of Dickinson's achievements had made a significant contribution: with Professor Pryde of Glasgow he wrote a text-book suited to undergraduate needs, thus filling a serious gap, and, secondly, in 1947 he revived, under his own editorship, the *Scottish Historical Review* which had been allowed to lapse nearly twenty years before Gordon took up the uncompleted work. In his unaugural lecture he called attention to some of the circumstances that underlay the imbalance between the esteem enjoyed by English history and the lowly place accorded to the story of Scotland's past. He had no difficulty in showing the one-sided and unfair nature of this state of affairs. He attributed the universal regard for the history of the nation south of the border to the clear-cut and comprehensible way in which its institutions have developed and can be studied. This is assumed to be what history is about, with the further assumption that the Scots have no such institutions and no such development. Donaldson's inaugural demonstrated the falsity of these delusions and established the history of Scotland as a valid, indeed attractive field for study and research in its own right.

Following these pointers, the lecture plots a course to be pursued in the department in the future. The professor's plans are unspoken, implicit; his words are restrained and without passion – or rather with a passion that is under stern repressive discipline. But it was abundantly clear that the new man knew what he was doing and where he was going.

With its course thus clearly set, the department soon began to expand. The ordinary class increased its numbers. For many years it never fell below seventy and on one occasion a figure of over one hundred was attained. By the time of Donaldson's retirement, the framework of the honours course in Scottish Historical Studies seemed to some to be rather narrowly conceived. Yet it increasingly attracted postulants. Postgraduate workers too in a steady stream beat a track to the department's door. During Donaldson's time in the chair the university awarded fifty degrees with honours in Scottish Historical Studies; in addition, for theses in Scottish history, PhD degrees were conferred on twenty-eight graduates and five MLitt degrees. At Donaldson's retirement in 1979, twenty postgraduates were on the department's books.

Clearly Scottish history has come in from the cold. By his conduct of the department and with the help of his lecturers (soon up to four in number),

Donaldson was the architect of this expansion. His published work, his growing reputation as a palaeographer and his editorial work on the early records combined to bring the department, its staff and the courses it offered to the attention of a very wide public.

The inaugural lecture had briefly sketched a reasoned statement of the claims of the institutions of Scotland, their stability and continuity, the absence of social unrest and the degree of religious freedom when comparison is made with other countries. This became one of the binding threads in the work of the department. The lecture was a declaration of intent as well as an indication of outlook.

Something of the atmosphere prevailing in the department in the Donaldson years has already been suggested. Mrs Auld, the only secretary the professor ever had (her time in the job was co-terminous with his in the chair), testifies to the pleasant relationships which always existed. There was never any desire or demand among the students for any formal channel of communication between staff and students. 'My door is open', the professor would say, and that was all anyone asked. As an administrator – and this is the kind of evidence a secretary is in the best position to give – Professor Donaldson was brisk and efficient, suffering no delay in dealing with incoming letters, confident and clear in dictating, making few alterations in the resulting typescript and when the office was under some pressure, even helping out with the typing himself. Enthusiasm gave a yeasty touch to the life and spirit of the whole department. If all this sounds too idyllic, too good to be the whole truth, then it must be said that there is some evidence from independent sources that things were indeed so in the Scottish history department.

Since the Fraser chair was founded, record scholarship has gone hand-in-hand with teaching. As we have seen, Donaldson had published many learned articles and had achieved a high reputation for his exact scholarship and profound historical knowledge, chiefly in the sixteenth century, above all in the decades where he had 'first cast his anchor' when a student under Hannay in the early thirties.

The first significant notice of his work from a quarter quite outside Edinburgh, and indeed Scotland, came in the form of an invitation to deliver the Birkbeck Lectures in Ecclesiastical History for 1957–8 at Cambridge University. His subject was the Scottish Reformation 1560. The book based on the lectures and with the same title appeared in the quater-centenary year of the Reformation and was thus in time to contribute a thoroughly researched and documented basis for informed discussion. It was a period in which Donaldson by this time was entirely at home. His knowledge of the record evidence was unrivalled. For the first time, by means of this book, he attracted to himself and the department in Edinburgh (of which he was not yet head) the attention and interest of a much more extensive readership than he had so far reached. This book, his first original work of substance, made him an internationally known scholar.

The book was widely noticed by the learned journals. 'Objective treatment of a subject which has too often been distorted by bias', said the *Journal of Ecclesiastical History* review. 'A good deal of new information' (on the Reformation in Scotland), the reviewer in the *Scottish Historical Review* pointed out. 'It also challenges all the traditional interpretations.' The writer in *The Scotsman* put his conclusion simply: 'The history of the Reformation in Scotland will never be quite the same again'.

A bibliography of Gordon Donaldson's publications is given in a separate contribution to the present volume. Here we may mention in particular two publications because of their importance in facilitating the study of the subject at universities and by other serious students. Back in the 1930s, the absence of printed source material in handy form and the lack of a suitable, up-to-date text-book had been two of the features associated both as cause and effect with the debility of Scottish historical studies. In collaboration with Dickinson, Donaldson compiled a *Source Book of Scottish History*, published in three volumes. To meet the need for a text-book the 'Edinburgh History of Scotland' was planned under Donaldson's editorship. When the first of the four volumes was published, covering the period from James V to James VII and written by the editor himself, it was met with a chorus of acclaim. The review in the *Scottish Historical Review* saluted it as 'an event of major importance', while in the New World, where the study of Scottish history had taken root and was flourishing, Professor Maurice Lee in the *American Historical Review* spoke of 'the stylistic grace and wit, the profound scholarship, the many originalities of interpretation on specific points, the clarity and balance of the narrative'. Donaldson's two major publications so far mentioned are concerned with the period of Scottish history in which his researches have given him a special authority. But in numerous monographs, he has written on the long reach of Scotland's past, from the Dark Ages down to as recently as 1970. His books number thirty to date, with more promised. As author and public lecturer (for over the years he had been much in demand), he has touched the story of the Scottish people and nation at a great many points. His work has well served both the serious student and the general reader. But his editing of records for publication, especially the *Register of the Privy Seal of Scotland* (volumes v–viii) is his most important contribution to scholarship.

To Donaldson the author, historiography is an art. It is much better to practise it than to speak or write about it. He does not seem to have written anything about historiography. His historical writings and the artistry he brings to their composition speak for themselves. 'The eye is not satisfied with seeing', says the book of Ecclesiastes, 'nor the ear filled with hearing.' But not for Donaldson; he seldom strays from what the evidence will support.

He has not concerned himself, in print at least, with the questions and problems usually subsumed under the heading 'the philosophy of history'. The algebra of ideas, either on the historical plane or on any other, seems to make little appeal to him. Pursuing speculations, hunting ideas, chasing hypotheses – these intellectual exercises are not the way his mind works.

But wait! A children's story by Gordon Donaldson has recently appeared. Privately printed, personally distributed rather than published. Its title 'There's a Lad Here'. A new career – in fiction – for the academic? Yes and No. Yes: because this brief tale suggests what he might achieve if he were to give himself more time and space to develop the technical aspects of historical novel-writing, given his mastery of the history involved. No: because this little book was written for one specific purpose, to reward some boys for services rendered. It appears that when Donaldson went to live in an historic house near Preston Tower in East Lothian, three local boys came to offer help with the vast amount of work waiting to be done in the garden. Eventually the grateful householder wrote this story for them. The plot is centred on Preston Tower, visible from the house, in the time of the battle of Pinkie. Of course a group of boys are the effective instruments in making things happen and these boys are given the names of the author's band of helpers.

This *jeu d'esprit* has carried our attention away from academic to Gordon's private life. From his early manhood his religious faith has been a declared and influential element in his life. In his late twenties he was attracted by the worship and liturgy of the Episcopal Church in Scotland. The ministry of J. R. Kennedy, the rector of Christ Church, Trinity, where he worshipped, had a far-reaching influence on him through his evangelical preaching. To this day Gordon is an evangelical Episcopalian – a lay reader who has often supplied pulpits when the services of a priest were lacking – for years a member of the Representative Church Council and the Edinburgh Diocesan Council. In recent years he has participated as one of his Church's representatives in the ecumenical discussions that have been taking place among the Churches in Scotland. In this area of churchmanship he has shared the frustration that comes with deferred hopes, preferring unconsidered spontaneous action in localities to unfruitful talk at the top.

Have his Episcopalian sympathies imparted some degree of bias to his understanding of Scottish history? This has been insinuated, but never with chapter and verse. The judgment of the goodly company of historians throughout the world is strongly in his favour. He was erudite in the ways of Presbyterians and Episcopalians alike long before his private predilection declared itself. After all, look at the subject of his London PhD thesis: it ante-dates by some years his confirmation in the Episcopal Church.

Shetland is in truth the *fons et origo* of this story. Gordon can date exactly the time when in his own experience he first became acutely aware of the spell of the islands. The summer holiday of 1929. No doubt his genetic inheritance brought a pre-disposition, something like a tincturing of the blood-stream with the salt water of the Voes. Edinburgh born, educated and employed for virtually the whole of his life in buildings erected at the city's finest cultural flowering, yet he ever turns in mind and spirit to the sea and the islands of the farthest north. The hold that Shetland – its way of life, its crofts, its boats and fishing, its history – laid upon him in his teens strengthened with the years. He paid his sixtieth visit in 1980. He has written two monographs on aspects of Shetland's past. He has many friends among the islanders. Yell, the second most northerly of all the islands and the place where his family came from, is for Gordon an *alter focus*, a hearth away from home. There he is as familiar a figure as he is in George Square.

The sea has been a vivid element in Gordon's experience. He is never happier than when he is afloat. For many years he has owned a boat – he still has a dinghy. Soon after he entered academic life he bought a house at Benderloch in Argyll, to provide himself with a country home now that he was able to be away from Edinburgh for longer spells. This west coast retreat offered ample opportunities for messing around in boats. When in 1963 he became head of department, he found himself with ever-diminishing vacation time to spare, and gave up the Benderloch house.

Not unconnected with Gordon's delight in Shetland and the sea is his interest in the salt water communications which link the northern islands and connect them to the east coast ports of the mainland. The network of trade relationships between the northern and east coast ports of Scotland and Scandinavian, Baltic and German ports came into the picture. Long before oil was discovered under the North Sea, he traced the affinities of race and outlook between Scotland and the lands of the north: 'A northern land in a northern setting.'

At this point an important aspect of Donaldson's considerable output of writing about Scotland's history and culture may be identified for separate mention. A certain detachment characterises his work. Interest in Scottish affairs, past and present, is always evident, and something like affection is occasionally a traceable implication. But he seems to be able to stay at a certain distance when surveying the scene. In his inaugural lecture, which had the title 'Scottish history and the Scottish nation', he remarked that the subject suggested an emotional approach at variance with the standards of austere scholarship associated with the chair; only one of his predecessors, Dickinson, an Englishman, had ever given something like a nationalist interpretation to the history of Scotland, and had written with considerably more emotion than either Hume Brown or Hannay had done. Throughout the entire *corpus* of his writing on Scottish affairs, this air of distance, this coolness of tone is one of the contents. It is not the same thing as scholarly objectivity. Donaldson doesn't see Scottish affairs the nationalist way. He himself believes that this element of detachment in his work may be attributed to his Shetland background.

Although an excellent administrator, Donaldson is not an ardent committee man. He endured this side of his professional duties with fortitude but no great pleasure. Not that he dislikes or eschews polemics; his inaugural lecture gives ample evidence of his ability to present a challenging case with trenchancy. Both in the university and in Lothian Region Education Committee (where he was for three years the university's representative), he had much experience of what Bagehot called 'government by discussion'. In the Education Committee, decisions reflect the party political structure of local government, the ruling party councillors normally agreeing in advance what the final decision of the whole committee will be. The debate at the full committee meeting tends to be a public relations exercise. Gordon found this kind of government by discussion frustrating and disheartening. He much prefers the university's method of seeking the largest attainable measure of agreement so that the most widely acceptable decision may be reached.

Two occasions may be recalled when he spoke out publicly in downright terms about controversial issues of the day. In 1972 when Lothian Region Education Committee, of which he was a member at the time, announced their plans for comprehensive schools, he addressed a public meeting in the Usher Hall, criticising the nonsensical nature of the scheme and pointing out, with scorn and irony, the hypocrisy of the ruling faction which had imposed it. The second occasion was in 1969 at a Town and Gown lecture in the City Chambers when he considered the recently published Wheatley Report on Local Government. His criticisms were directed at the crude way in which its proposals had been framed without regard to existing real living communities and their relationships. The fabric of social connections – some obvious to any observer, others gossamer-fine – was to be torn asunder. In the event, under the pressure of public opinion, the grossest of these mistakes were prevented; but still much injury was done.

Donaldson was naturally drawn to the learned historical and similar societies and to the various national and local bodies concerned with the nation's past. His interest in preserving the heritage was specially active. In time he became president of most of these bodies – the Scottish History Society, the Scottish Record Society, the Scottish Church History Society and the Old Edinburgh Club being prominent cases in point. For some fifteen years he has been a member of the Royal Commission on the Ancient and Historical Monuments of Scotland.

Distinctions and honours came with fame and the years. The university of Aberdeen conferred on him an honorary doctorate of Letters in 1976. This gave great pleasure far and wide. In the same year he was elected to a fellowship of the British Academy, the highest distinction which can come to a literary or historical scholar. The designation FBA is awarded on the sole criterion of the quality and integrity of the person's scholarship over a lengthy period, the judgment being made by peers in the branch of scholarship concerned. In 1979 came the culminating mark of honour for a Scottish historian – he was appointed Historiographer to the Queen in Scotland.

The man himself, the man among friends, the man surrounded by students or colleagues, the man whose door is always open to everyone who cares to come for help or advice, whether students or American scholars – what of the man?

Direct, unassuming, honest, light-hearted without loss of sincerity or seriousness. A kind of *sancta simplicitas* underlies all. In matters such as architecture and everyday artefacts he prefers the vernacular to the out-of-the-way. In general he finds the minor key more pleasing than the major, plain modes more congenial than the showy. To a degree that is seldom suggested, he is a wonderfully adaptable person. Not having married, he has long ago acquired a variety of domestic and culinary skills which have enabled him to dispense hospitality most agreeably. Two pointers: he is an adept at joinery and he makes his own jam! His writing style is an index of the man: no rhetoric, no display, no stridency, straightforward workmanlike narrative, always readable, with a smooth and limpid flow, like plain chant.

A former postgraduate student whose first degree was from London University, may be allowed to speak for all who studied in the department with Gordon Donaldson at one time or another during his thirty-two years. With pardonable hyperbole, he claims 'it is impossible to exaggerate the esteem he is held in outside Scotland, especially in England and America'.

In the summer of 1979, a few years before the regulations required it, Gordon acted on a plan he had long considered. He retired from the Fraser chair. Sixteen years before, it had given him the greatest satisfaction to become the fourth in the distinguished succession, Hume Brown, Hannay, Dickinson. He has added fresh lustre to the legacy bequeathed to him.

How will he spend his time in retirement? What will he do with 'the diminished king', in Robert Frost's fine phrase? His first act on freeing himself from the collar of necessity was to buy a house on the north shore of the Firth of Forth where he is close to the sea and has a panoramic prospect from his windows from May Island in the east to the familiar profile of Edinburgh to the west. Writing takes up much of his time. If advance hints are to be trusted, more than one book may be expected. On sixteenth century subjects, of course. Factual – not fictional!

THOMAS LOTHIAN

(ii) *Gordon Donaldson and the Records of Scotland*

In his Inaugural Lecture,[1] delivered on 4 May 1964, the fourth holder of the Fraser Chair of Scottish History and Palaeography in the University of Edinburgh spoke of his earlier service in the Register House (1938–47[2]), and of his work on editing record publications (from 1952 onwards) 'as a kind of associate of the Register House staff'. Another link in an association which has proved of immense value to the Scottish Record Office and to the public had been forged in 1963 when Gordon Donaldson was appointed to the Scottish Records Advisory Council.

[1] Gordon Donaldson, *Scottish History and the Scottish Nation* (University of Edinburgh, Inaugural Lecture, no. 20).
[2] For the story of the years 1940–2 when Donaldson was in exile at Morenish Lodge on the north side of Loch Tay with the earlier records, see his article, 'The Second World War: Further Adventures of the Records', *Scottish Historical Review*, liii, 211–19.

Over the years all relationships inevitably have their ups and downs. In 1963 Donaldson spoke of the time he had spent in the 'congenial surroundings' of the Historical Room. A year or two later, as the pressure on space in the Register House began to pinch, he had some truthful, and therefore unflattering, things to say about the accommodation and facilities provided for editors of record publications. But he has always retained an affection for his old department. As joint editor of *The Scottish Historical Review* he promoted the Register House Bicentenary Number in 1974, and as Chairman of the Scottish Records Association he took an evident pride in the reception held at the Register House in September 1979 for the members of the joint conference with the British Records Association.

The 'Register House connection' has given Gordon Donaldson a knowledge in depth of pre-1707 Scottish records,[3] which in modern times at least has only been rivalled by that of his contemporaries in the Register House, H. M. Paton[4] (Curator of Historical Records, 1936–46) and C. T. McInnes (Curator, 1946–61). This knowledge pervades all his published work. And it is this knowledge – particularly of the great public registers of private rights, which he rightly describes as 'the peculiar glory of the Scottish records'[5] – that makes him one of the most humane of Scottish historians in his judgments on the past. It also makes him a formidable reviewer – Mr Bruce Webster's very good study of sources, *Scotland from the Eleventh Century to 1603*,[6] received praise for sections on charters and exchequer records, which was however rather dampened by the general qualification that the book 'came from an author who simply did not have enough knowledge of the records'.[7] Little escapes Donaldson's eye. In 1971 the present Keeper of the Records received a merited rebuke for certain errors and obscurities in a descriptive list of commissary court records, which might have been thought reasonably submerged in an appendix to his 1970 Annual Report. But, as he himself admits, there is an idiosyncratic touch to Donaldson's approach to the records and he is sometimes open to the criticism of misleading which he has levelled at others. For example, he is fond of coining descriptions, such as 'Quia dedimus' and 'Compertum est'

---

[3] Modern departmental records have not so far engaged his full interest. They receive rather perfunctory treatment at page 24 of his *Sources of Scottish History* (privately produced, 1978), and indeed narrowly escaped being relegated to the 'Miscellaneous' section. In discussions at the Scottish Records Advisory Council Donaldson has not displayed any marked enthusiasm for reduction of closure periods applying to modern government records. On the other hand in 1972 he supported a project for indexing the records of Scottish departments and made an unsuccessful application to the S.S.R.C. for funds.

[4] In *Sources of Scottish History* readers are reminded (at page 9) that use can still profitably be made of Mr Paton's pamphlet, *The Scottish Records: Their History and Value* (Historical Association of Scotland, 1933).

[5] *Sources of Scottish History*, 20.

[6] The Sources of History Ltd., 1975.

[7] *Sources of Scottish History*, 10. For his detailed review, see *S.H.R.*, lv, 74–6.

for precepts,[8] and while he prefaces these with the words 'what I call' his less experienced readers may not always observe this distinction. In indexing the *Register of the Privy Seal* he sometimes forgot that others would not share his own great knowledge of sixteenth-century ecclesiastical offices. When, in 1967, a reviewer criticised the omission of certain parsonages and vicarages from the index of offices, his reaction was one of pained surprise that the nature of appropriation should be misunderstood. As regards the index of offices, the reviewer should not have instanced items 'which no-one would expect to find there'. They did in fact appear in their 'proper place', namely the index of places.

In fact the criticism of the *Privy Seal* index was an oblique tribute to Donaldson as a record editor. The *Register of the Privy Seal* has been the backbone of the Scottish Record Office's modern publications programme. The assiduity with which it has been edited and published means that it has been the only regularly reviewed publication in the programme. And since it was difficult to fault the impeccable scholarship of text and introduction the reviewer had inevitably been driven back on reviewing the index. From the Scottish Record Office's point of view Gordon Donaldson is the ideal editor. He has accepted cheerfully the process whereby increasing responsibility for the index has been taken by the permanent staff, while making a stand about the introduction which he quite properly regards as peculiarly the editor's own product. At the same time he has experimented with further abridgment of the entries where this can be achieved without omitting points of substance.

There was a stage, during the accommodation problems of the mid 1960s, when Donaldson seems to have sometimes felt that he was in the way of the full-time staff, and he once even spoke of giving up work on the *Privy Seal*. However he suggested at the same time a way out of the difficulties whereby he was provided with photocopies from which he could work without attending in the Register House. The Register of the Privy Seal is obviously a congenial source for him, reflecting as it does so many aspects of the life of sixteenth-century Scotland. And the fact is that record editing has always been something of a relaxation for Gordon Donaldson. When, in 1972, as a matter of principle, he raised the question of the rate of payment, which indeed had not risen very much from 1952, he prefaced his 'protest' with an admission fatal to any pay negotiation: 'I do it because I like it, and constantly apologise for not being able to do more'.

While on holiday in Argyll in the 1950s he corrected galley proofs and prepared index slips, at least on rainy days. On 24 July 1954 he wrote to the Curator of Historical Records: 'The first fortnight of July was good here but the last ten days or so have been mostly bad, with a climax yesterday when I think the weather did its worst, even by West Highland standards. I have made good use of the rainy days, partly in working on the house, but partly, you will be glad to know, in indexing the 300 or so entries in R.S.S. v. . . . '

[8] *Sources of Scottish History*, 13.

Other letters of the period reveal him spending the fine days in bricklaying, painting his boat and cutting peat in the moss near the house. Bad weather in July 1956 was reported as 'very healthy for the historical work, which had been sadly neglected on the fine days' but an improvement in August 'tended to hold up my work on R.S.S.'.

Of him it may truly be said, as Cosmo Innes said of Thomas Thomson, 'To correct a proof-sheet was a favourite occupation of his time; to spell out a hard passage of old writing an actual enjoyment'. Fortunately for scholarship in Scotland, he has not suffered from Thomson's 'grand defect' – 'a morbid reluctance to commit his opinions to paper'.

When Gordon Donaldson was appointed to the Scottish Records Advisory Council in 1963 he naturally took a keen interest in matters affecting publications policy. He was prominent in discussions on the vexed question of prices of record publications, which (although unsuccessful in bringing about any change in the pricing policy for these volumes) did lead to changes in publishing methods and to improved publicity which at least did something to encourage foreign retail sales. In 1972 his influence was important in maintaining a balanced publications programme. While accepting the arguments, based on trends of historical research, for including post-1707 records, hitherto inadequately represented in Scottish Record Office publications, he cautioned against any assumption from search room statistics that interest in the earlier period had diminished, making the valid point that extensive publication of pre-1707 records rendered access to the originals less necessary. But his most important contribution to the work of the Advisory Council probably lay in the discussions concerning the custody of local records, which followed the publication in 1967 of the report of the McBoyle Committee on local authority records.

Having served in the Register House at a time when in the words of his contemporary Henry Paton centralisation was the 'keynote of modern Record policy, at least so far as regards Scotland', Gordon Donaldson might reasonably have been expected to have endorsed the views which Paton expressed in 1933 on the convenience of that policy for the historian interested in comparative studies. 'When a scholar settles down in his sanctum to the study of his subject, he naturally finds it convenient to have around him and near to his hand all the resources available. It is irksome to be always under the necessity of leaving his comfortable chair to explore it may be some dusty recess for the requisite volume.'[9] Donaldson, however, partly perhaps because of his Shetland background, was able to take a more detached view. In looking for a remedy for the neglect of local records in Scotland he turned rather to the philosophy earlier expressed by J. Maitland Thomson. 'Centralisation would be a cure; but it would take local records out of the reach of those who would be their most capable and ought to be their most interested students.'[10] In 1967 he greeted the McBoyle Report with the words,

[9] *The Scottish Records: Their History and Value*, 37.
[10] *The Public Records of Scotland* (1922), 160.

'The feature of this Report which I especially welcome is the concern it shows for the local custody of local records in order to serve the interests of scholars up and down the country'.[11]

While Donaldson considered that the McBoyle Report made a good case for a scheme providing for local custody combined with central control, and was particularly impressed with the arguments for regular liaison between the Scottish Record Office and local repositories, he was not altogether convinced by the proposal that the custody of local archives should in general be combined with the library service, 'especially as we are almost certainly going to be faced with larger units of administration, the records of which could not appropriately go either to a County Library or to the Register House'. Even in 1967 he felt that there was a stronger case than the McBoyle Report allowed for regional repositories and, as the future pattern of local government became clearer, he advocated a system of regional record offices. Throughout, however, he retained an essentially pragmatic approach. He supported the proposal made in 1968 that the Keeper should undertake a survey of the volume and nature of existing local authority records before general consideration of long-term repositories. Since the division of functions between regions and districts was not to be wholly uniform in other respects he saw no objection in principle to a lack of uniformity for record offices. He had a particular sympathy for the retention by the cities of their own repositories if they wished – he had of course played an important part in the appointment of a city archivist in Edinburgh in 1967 – and he hoped that there might be provision for the retention of some material in museums and libraries under the supervision of the regional record office. In general he thought that the solution of all problems would be facilitated if the Keeper of the Records were given responsibility for the supervision of the regional record offices and that it would be best if all records were formally vested in him. On the other hand should regional offices be instituted he hoped that local records held in the Register House would be transferred to them so that the archives could be re-integrated.

In the event the ideas advanced by Donaldson and others for statutory controls of the archive system foundered, mainly on the relationships, as they were seen at the time, between the two tiers of authorities and between the new local authorities and the central government. Otherwise, however, the very open system which has emerged in the wake of section 200 of the Local Government (Scotland) Act of 1973 reflects much of his own philosophy and, despite the slow and in many respects disappointing progress, he has professed himself as encouraged by the general situation. At a meeting of the Scottish Records Advisory Council held in November 1975 he described what had already been established in local archive services, starting almost from nothing, as 'a very great achievement'.

While basically in sympathy with a regional system Donaldson recog-

[11] Letter to the secretary of the Scottish Records Advisory Council, 21 August 1967.

nised throughout the discussions that accumulations of papers were already in the possession of museums and libraries. Writing in 1971 to the secretary of the Advisory Council, he thought that official records could, and probably should, be transferred to regional offices, but he saw no moral right to remove formerly private papers from the repositories to which they had been donated or loaned. 'Behind this lies the fact that people are often more ready to deposit their papers in their own locality, and they might be no happier about seeing them in a regional office than in a central office in Edinburgh.' Behind it also lies an understanding, not always found in scholars, of the problems faced by the owners of archives. Speaking, at the first Scottish Records Association Conference, held in November 1977, of the respective roles of archivist, owner and user of records, from his experience of changes over forty years, he described the owner as 'the most unselfish'. This was no empty statement, for Donaldson had been actively associated with the National Register of Archives (Scotland) from its inception in 1946.

In its first pioneering days the Register, possessing no whole-time staff of its own, was heavily dependent on the unpaid work of a small number of outside scholars. In this connection no-one made a greater contribution in time or in skill than Gordon Donaldson. Between 1947 and 1952 he carried out a large number of surveys of manuscripts held in private houses and in lawyers' offices, located for the most part in the counties of Angus and Perth. These included collections of major historical importance. In some cases his surveys led to the deposit of collections with the national archives. The Dalhousie muniments at Brechin Castle are the outstanding example. More often, as with the muniments at Glamis, his visits represented the initial step in cordial long-term relationships which still subsist between the Register and the private owners concerned.

In 1952, as calls on his time increased and as the Register began to acquire a professional staff of its own, Donaldson withdrew from the front line and became a member of the Register's advisory directorate where his direct practical experience of archival fieldwork proved to be of the utmost value to his colleagues and to the Register's staff. As a director his major contribution to the Register's work was unquestionably the remarkable scheme which he devised and initiated in 1966 for the calendaring of large sections of the muniments of the Dukes of Hamilton. This scheme represented a unique exercise in co-operation between the Department of Scottish History, the Scottish Record Office, and the owner of the muniments. Sections of the Hamilton muniments were brought into the Scottish Record Office where they were calendared by postgraduate students and others under the general direction of the Professor and with the day-to-day supervision and assistance of the staff of the Record Office. The core of the end product of the exercise was the six-volume calendar of the Hamilton correspondence from 1563 to 1716 compiled by Dr Rosalind Marshall. This remarkable series of letters covers the period in which the Hamilton family played a major role in national affairs and represents perhaps the major historical source for the period outwith the national archives. These six volumes were subsequently supplemented by a series of other calendars covering many of the estate and financial records of the family as well as a variety of ancillary series. The exercise continued to operate up to the time of the Professor's retirement.

As part of his concern for the safeguarding of the national archival heritage as a whole Gordon Donaldson has been an advocate over the years of the need to provide financial and other assistance to private owners of archives. At a meeting of the Scottish Records Advisory Council in 1978 he confessed to a dread that the dispersal of the Warwick Castle collections might be repeated in Scotland. A decade earlier, in 1967, he had urged the Advisory Council to provide a test case for assistance from the Historic Buildings Council for Scotland for private muniment rooms, 'since archives were as integral a part of a house as furnishings'. Some years later the valuable principle was accepted that the cost of restoration of family muniments of proved importance could be added to an application for assistance with repairs to an historic house. Donaldson has also been involved in discussions over manuscript trusts, and in some ways his ideas can be seen to have anticipated features of the National Heritage Act of 1980. It was no doubt a source of particular pleasure to him when the Scottish Records Association under his chairmanship played an important part in ensuring that the heritage legislation preserved both Scottish and archival interests.

Gordon Donaldson would probably be the first to admit that his concern to protect owners' interests has not always extended to the rights of copyright owners. When, early in 1979, the Scottish Records Association decided to prepare a datasheet on copyright as affecting records and archives, their newly-appointed Chairman made a far from contrite confession: 'There cannot be many people of my generation who have pillaged and plundered the records for publication as I have done, and I have done it with hardly a thought for copyright'. He continued, 'Now that I do give copyright a thought, I see that my work has been sufficiently varied to conclude that the whole position is very complex indeed and that generalisation is dangerous if not impossible' and proceeded, partly with tongue in cheek and with an eye cocked towards the Keeper of the Records, to particularise at length on cases where copyright might cause problems – at least in theory, for in the case of the *Court Book of Shetland* the complications which he foresaw extended even to the *de jure* sovereignty of Shetland in 1602–4. Perhaps it is a testimony to the links forged over the years that his four-page letter, and the nine-page reply (ignoring the sovereignty of Shetland but mentioning the Berne Convention) which it elicited, caused no strain in an agreeable relationship. But the episode illustrated Gordon Donaldson's dedication to the dissemination of historical information. As regards restrictions (albeit largely formal) on the reproduction from official publications of material still in copyright, he observed, 'I am almost inclined to ask what is the purpose of publishing records at all (at the public expense) if it is not to make them available to the public'.

For the same underlying reason he has sometimes been critical of the gaps in the official publications programme and is apt to use the phrase 'private enterprise has come to the rescue'.[12] This may seem a trifle unfair when it is considered how much 'private enterprise' in this field has owed over the years either to the active support and assistance of the Scottish Record Office and other national institutions or to the spare-time activity of their staffs.[13] The criticism should however be read against his Inaugural Lecture of 1964, in which, after paying tribute to the great improvement which had been made in the care of the national records, he declared, 'But much work has still to be done on the records before we have anything which can properly be called a history of the Scottish nation and, I may say, a history of the Scottish nation which will be worthy of the Scottish nation'.[14]

Writing in exile in California, in 1880, Robert Louis Stevenson sought for the origin of what he called 'some ready-made affections' which join the Scots in a nation. Gordon Donaldson has suggested on more than one occasion[15] that the answer to Stevenson's question is to be found, at least in part, in the fact that the varied peoples who make up Scotland share a common heritage in the past and acknowledge a common history – or what they conceive to be history. His imaginative gesture, in connection with International Archives Week in 1979, in offering a prize to the school pupil who could find the most interesting document not already printed or listed was in a sense an expression of his belief that it is still history which maintains the identity of the nation. But he is aware that the history absorbed by the average Scot is not yet purged of legend and has worked to bridge what has been called the 'incredulity gap' between popular ideas of history and the discoveries of scholars. In his own publications he has shown a willingness to use informal methods and to experiment with new techniques (including an essay with the present writer into the field of audio learning in 1971, which has hardly ranked as a best-seller); and he has directed an increasing proportion of his work towards a national rather than a limited professional readership. The books, *Who's Who in Scottish History* (1973) and *Dictionary of Scottish History* (1977), which he produced in collaboration with Mr R. S. Morpeth, are aimed at the growing number of people who want ready access to essential facts.

To many in Scotland the greatest proof of Professor Donaldson's success will no doubt be the volumes he has written or edited and on this score alone there was universal welcome for his appointment as Her Majesty's Historiographer in Scotland in 1979. But one of the reasons why that office

[12] E.g., in *Sources of Scottish History*, 10.
[13] This kind of help still occurs today. Professor Donaldson has drawn attention in books and articles to the value of the inventories in testaments for social history and has called for similar studies on a more serious scale. But the material is intimidating in its bulk, and it is a voluntary group, mainly of Record Office staff, working in their own time, who are exploring means of extracting from the inventories the information which will enable social historians to form a fuller picture of society in the past.
[14] *Scottish History and the Scottish Nation*, 11-12.
[15] E.g., in *Scotland: The Shaping of a Nation* (1974), 25.

has survived in Scotland, when the English post has disappeared, is that it has been consistently bestowed on an historian not only distinguished for past achievement but likely to give continued encouragement to investigation and research into the history of Scotland. Gordon Donaldson remains active as a record editor and on a range of advisory bodies concerned with the national heritage, and one hears of further books to come. Moreover he has been remarkably successful in training successors and inheritors who are already making a notable contribution to record scholarship.

Like his own teacher Robert Kerr Hannay, to whose influence he has attributed both his abiding interest in the sixteenth century and in church history and his whole approach to Scottish history and the work of the Fraser Chair, Gordon Donaldson possesses the quality of interesting others in aspects of Scottish history which need further study and in impressing his approach upon them. This is particularly true of social history, which he described in his Inaugural Lecture as 'the very core of the history of the nation yet . . . unquestionably the most unsatisfactory field in Scottish historiography', since politics and ecclesiastical history had been too much divorced from society. The call which he then made for studies which would reveal the structure of society and the classes in society has been answered, partly from his own pen (as in the analysis of the legal profession in Scottish society in the sixteenth and seventeenth centuries presented in his Wilson Memorial Lecture delivered in the University of Edinburgh in December 1975[16]) and partly by others inspired and in some cases directed by him, to an extent which makes his dream of a 'history of the whole nation' less remote than it must have seemed to many of his listeners eighteen years ago.

Donaldson's influence has also extended to the care of records in Scotland. One of the points at which he found himself in disagreement with the McBoyle Committee was over the proposition that training in England was essential for work in Scottish archives. 'I should have thought', he wrote to the secretary of the Scottish Records Advisory Council in August 1967, 'that an academic course which gives a thorough grounding in Scottish history, some knowledge of its sources and some acquaintance with the main types of Scottish documents and records would be a more important foundation than a mere qualification in archive administration. I feel it would be easier to add to that foundation by a period of practical training in Scotland than to add experience in Scottish history etc to an archive qualification acquired in England.'

In part he was probably reacting, as in his Inaugural Lecture of 4 May 1964 and elsewhere, against the common tendency to regard the institutions of

[16] *Juridical Review*, 1976 (Part I), 1–18. His growing appreciation of the significance of genealogical work is based in large part on the contribution it can make to the solution of central problems in Scottish social history, notably the links between 'the kin' and 'the name' and the question of the stabilisation of surnames (*see* 'The Significance of Genealogy to the Scottish Historian', *The Scottish Genealogist,* xxi, no. 3 (August 1974), 59–64, in which he also refers to studies of Scottish institutions in their social context carried out by his postgraduate students).

Scotland as somehow inferior and second-rate when compared with those of England. The 'Scottish Record Office' has not escaped his censure in this regard. In 1965 he was moved, as editor of Volume viii of the *Register of the Privy Seal,* to 'put on record' his reasons for objecting to the popularisation of the term 'Scottish Record Office'. His reasons were two-fold: first, 'If a stranger to Edinburgh were to ask his way to the Scottish Record Office I doubt if one person in ten thousand would know the answer, whereas nine thousand nine hundred and ninety-nine could tell him the way to the Register House (even although I am well aware that the two are not identical)'; and secondly, 'the usage . . . seems to me to reduce this ancient kingdom to the level of an English county . . . just one of those provincial record offices'.

But it is also true that the kind of 'foundation' which he described in 1967 was provided by his Edinburgh course which has proved of the greatest value for work in archives in Scotland. It is understandable that his students should have found a natural home in the Scottish Record Office; but they are also to be found in archives throughout Scotland. Not least among Gordon Donaldson's contributions to Scotland and Scottish history lies in the progress which has been made towards achieving Maitland Thomson's prescription for the safety of the records – 'a body of men and women students in every record centre'.[17]

[17] *The Public Records of Scotland* (1922), 160.

JOHN IMRIE

2

The Early Scottish Notary

The earliest Scottish notaries public occur in the thirteenth century, but there are only four or five, so far discoverable; and in the fourteenth century only thirty-five. The reason for the increase around 1400 is not clear. Of the five notaries before 1300, one is an apostolic notary, one imperial, two unidentified, and another of 1231, Robert de Lambden ('my notary who carries and keeps my seal'), not necessarily a notary public. Of those traceable between 1300 and 1400, a dozen are apostolic and as many imperial, eight are both, and three unidentified; thus the impression that the majority are imperial notaries has not been verified, nor does there seem to be any difference in the business transacted. For these early times there are no records of creation, though visiting papal nuncios may have had temporary faculties. For long delegation to create notaries was sparingly given and for limited numbers of creations only. For instance in 1287 the bishop of Dunkeld got the power to make a single papal notary. The diocesan organisation of Scots notaries is not evidenced in the earliest instruments, for diocese and clerical status are generally omitted. The villages of origin, mostly south of the Forth (Lambden, Garvald, Horsburgh), may appear instead: one of these notaries was previously recorded as chapter clerk to the Glasgow cathedral chapter, William de Horsbroch. The earliest notary to record his diocese is found in 1328.[1]

Shortly before that Rome tightened up its rules with regard to the employment of married clerks. The earliest papal legislation of Innocent III in 1211 merely excluded priests and deacons from notarial practice, so presumably married clerks and even laymen were freely admitted, though the latter would have difficulty in gaining access to church records, and only clerks had guaranteed access to education. Though the title 'magister' may at times be honorific, it is likely that some had academic training involving studies in the notariate at Bologna or Avignon: some certainly are included among Scottish law students. Thereafter, though growth was sluggish, in

[1] J. Raine, *North Durham* (London, 1852), appendix no. 129; *CPL*, i, 491; D. E. R. Watt, *A biographical dictionary of Scottish Graduates to A.D. 1410*, henceforward Watt, *Scottish Graduates*, (Oxford, 1977), 215 (Garvald), 271 (Horsbruk), 318 (Lambden); *Registrum Episcopatus Moraviensis* (Bannatyne Club, 1837), henceforward *Moray Reg.*, 153.

the fourteenth-century diocesan organisation of notaries clearly emerges, and there are notaries, not only from St Andrews and Glasgow, but also from Aberdeen, Moray, Dunkeld and Ross, and although no Galloway notary appears till 1413, a bishop of that diocese, Adam of Lanark had authority to create two in 1364.[2]

In the fifteenth century there was a great increase in notaries. When the monastic prelate, James Haldenstone, prior of St Andrews, arrived as papal nuncio in 1419, his creations were nevertheless limited to six, none to be in holy orders, though Rome itself had begun to depart from the rule.[3] The notary's register, to which the name protocol book came to be annexed, may originally have been in the form of rolls of parchment; the clear evidence of the diversity of notarial acts has to await the arrival of the protocol book. The earliest survivor, James Darow's, is as late as 1469, followed by that of John Kerd of Dumbarton in 1471. Notaries in this period varied in status and qualifications, though internal evidence would suggest that Kerd was a schoolmaster.[4] In their docquets some describe themselves as bachelors or licentiates in decreets, one as a licentiate in civil or Caesarean law, while many claim to be masters of arts: developments connected in part with the new university foundations at St Andrews and Glasgow. One arts master added proudly that he was a graduate of Paris, Robert de Hopprew in 1423, while another notary could claim to be no more than a humble bachelor of arts.[5] The title 'professor of arts' is limited to notaries with a north-eastern connection; where this may not seem to be so at first sight, generally closer scrutiny reveals the link. For instance, John Robertson of Dunkeld diocese, first exercised his art in Aberdeen and there he was created notary in 1550.[6] The creative period in notarial teaching, during which the instrument was

[2] Watt, *Scottish Graduates*, records at least 17 fourteenth century notaries; *Liber Cartarum Prioratus Sancti Andree in Scotia* (Bannatyne Club, 1841), henceforward *St A Lib.*, 18; *CP*, i, 476.

[3] A convenient, if far from complete, list of notaries is given in *Calendar of Laing Charters 854–1837*, ed J. Anderson (Edinburgh, 1899), henceforward *Laing Chrs.*, 1041; *CPL*, vii, 2.

[4] SRO, B66/1/1, Protocol Book of James Darow; Protocol Book of John Kerd is in NLS, Notarial Protocols Dunbartonshire, Advocates MS 19.2.23, fos. 2–19v.

[5] Some samples: B. Dec. William Clerici, plate in *National Manuscripts of Scotland, Facsimiles* (London, 1867–71), ii, pl. lxxii; Lic. Dec. Gilbert de Galbraith, Adv MS 15.1.18, no. 90; Lic. in Caesarean Law, Henry Spital, W. Fraser, *Memorials of the Montgomeries, earls of Eglinton* (Edinburgh, 1859), ii, 88; Robert de Hopprew, M.A. Paris, *Charters of the Abbey of Inchcolm* (Scottish History Society, 1938), 49; George Alain, BA in 1518, *Registrum Episcopatus Brechinensis* (Bannatyne Club, 1856), ii, 73, henceforward *Brechin Reg.*

[6] For the Aberdeen connection of professors of arts, *Fasti Aberdonenses: Selections from the Records of the University and King's College of Aberdeen* (Spalding Club, 1854), 76. The first such notary on record is John de Gardin in 1514, *Records of Aboyne MCCXXX–MDCLXXXI* (New Spalding Club, 1894), 43, who as parson of Tyrie was readmitted notary in 1540, *Registrum Episcopatus Aberdonensis* (Spalding Club, 1845), ii, 323. For John Robertson's creation, SRO, NP1/6, Protocol Book of Robert Lumsdane, fo. 16v; he describes himself as professor of arts, General Register House Charters, RH6/1677.

perfected in close contact with the social requirements of a new age, was a short one and it acquired a standard form from which it seemed scarcely to evolve.

The clerical status of notaries is a more complex matter. The earliest Scots notaries did not refer to themselves as clerks, and when later they did so were not necessarily unmarried. In the first post-Reformation register of admissions of notaries, as many are described as married as unmarried. In 1395 one imperial notary, William de Cranyston, openly acknowledges he is 'clericus coniugatus' but others merely kept their heads down. James Young, the Canongate notary, was a married clerk. A layman graduate from Dunkeld diocese acted as notary, and in an instrument of creation for Mr Andrew Wilson 'laicus' he is entitled 'clericus idoneus' where 'clerk' refers rather to the candidate's literacy than to any special status as churchman. A burgess of Inverness is notary in 1440 at Dingwall, but as his surname was Clerk the evidence is ambiguous.[7] Again the title 'clericus' in its broad sense refers to priests as well and there are two examples, at least, where notaries design themselves as both clerk and priest in their docquets. Legislation itself was not uniform, though about 1320 it was laid down that married men and ministers of the altar were excluded; whether from the dislocating effects of the Great Schism or otherwise, there were so many priest-notaries in the following century that their occurrence is almost normal; an ancillary determining factor must have been the lower age-limit of twenty-five on creation.[8] Recruitment was local in most cases, often from remote villages: for instance, Alexander Thomson in 1436 describes himself as 'de Kyndrochat.'[9] In the fifteenth century also notaries are recorded in the remoter dioceses: in Lismore in 1411, in Dunblane in 1427 (in the person of Robert Gardiner, a St Andrews law graduate of some notoriety), in Caithness in 1450, in Orkney in 1457 and in the previous year in the Isles (in the person of Duncan Obrolchan, witnessing, not in the chapel of St Finlay in Canna, but of St Finlagan in Islay).[10] By the thirteenth century the notarial act had

[7] Laing Chrs., no. 82; Protocol Book of James Young 1485–1515 edd. H. M. Paton and G. Donaldson (SRS, 1952), vi; SRO, St James Hospital Perth Writs, GD79/6/87 (creation of Andrew Wilson, layman); SRO RH6/305, Ranald Clerk, witness at Dingwall.

[8] Fraser, Montgomeries, ii, 64; Registrum de Panmure, ed J. Stuart (Edinburgh, 1874), ii, 239; CPL, vii, 389.

[9] Brechin Reg., i, 78.

[10] W. Fraser, The Lennox (Edinburgh, 1874), ii. 60 (Lismore: Celestine Macgil-lemichael, in sacris ordinibus constituto); Registrum Monasterii S. Marie de Cambuskenneth (Grampian Club, 1872), 116 and regarding Gardiner's academic troubles, Acta Facultatis Artium Universitatis Sanctiandree 1413–1588, ed A. I. Dunlop (Scottish History Society, 1964), 39–41; D. Laing, Adversaria (Edinburgh, 1867), 12–15 (Caithness and Orkney). For the Isles, The Mackintosh Muniments 1442–1820, ed H. M. Paton (Edinburgh, 1903), no. 4, give the location as Canna mistakenly; the original reads 'in capella insule sancti finlacani in yle' (i.e. Islay), SRO, GD176/4, Moy muniments; Obrolchan was parson in Islay, Munimenta Alme Universitatis Glasguensis (Maitland Club, 1854), ii. 61.

acquired its definitive, foolproof form to which these subsequent notaries adhered.

What was this standard form? Most notaries faced with their clients preferred to consider themselves the subjects of a solicitation (*rogatio* or *requisitio*) rather than of an order (*mandatum*). The instrument invariably opens with solemnity, invoking the one God, the Trinity or Christ specifically.[11] A Renaissance form was used by a Banff notary in 1530, Thomas Wallas of Aberdeen diocese, who invokes high Olympus, 'Summi Olympi invocato nomine.'[12] Maximum precision was the aim in the dating procedures, but also the maximum solemnity as these rolling phrases were read off to clients many of whom were illiterate. There follows the year of the Lord, or of the Lord's nativity or incarnation (the last the official Scottish style). No Scottish notary used the imperial year. If a notary was hired by a bishop merely to add force to his personal 'subjective' document, then he might vary from his usual style to conform with that of the client. The 'millesimum' method of dating was a medieval introduction; the pontificate method actually preceded it in time, though the earliest notaries, Robert de Garvald and Nicholas Campion, omitted it.[13] These also use the incarnation style, though thereafter for a time the nativity style predominated, the result perhaps of influence from Bologna or Avignon. The Bologna form 'exeuntis' for the end of the month appears to be rare, a variant being employed by Nicholas Campion, but the nativity style appears in an Argyll deed of 1433. The incarnation formula is sometimes varied with 'year of grace,' 'year of the annunciation' or 'year of Christian salvation'.[14] Occasionally to the reader's confusion, both styles appear in a single document.[15] The indiction, a relic of Roman antiquity, may break up the 'millesimum' date, the day and month frequently following and not preceding it. The actual weekday may be recorded as well as its date, and even, though seldom in the preamble, the actual hour. The notary in a cathedral could be guided by the divine office and use, for instance, 'the hour of terce' (*hora terciarum*). Notarial practice made the increase of timepieces desirable. The clock of Abernethy collegiate kirk figures in 1555, where redemption money was offered at the high altar, the

[11] Of these, the last is rare, *Inchcolm Chrs.*, 52.

[12] NLS, Adv MS 20.3.5, fo. 79.

[13] Garvald's first recorded instrument was drawn up at Carlisle in 1284, Watt, *Scottish Graduates*, 215. He was at Edinburgh in 1287, SRO GD45/13/287, Dalhousie writs (printed in *Carte monialium de Northberwic* (Bannatyne Club, 1847), 24–5) and at Scone in 1298, SRO RH6/66 (printed in *Liber Ecclesie de Scon* (Bannatyne Club, 1843), 89); for a facsimile of a 1305 deed, see *National MSS Scotland*, ii, no. xii. Nicholas Campion is printed in *Liber S. Marie de Melros* (Bannatyne Club, 1837), i, 315, hereafter *Melrose Lib.*

[14] For the 'consuetudo Bononiensis' see M. del Pazzo, *Manuale di Cronologia* (Fonti e Studi del Corpus Membranarum Latinarum iv: Rome, 1969), 42–5. Scottish History Dept., Glasgow University, Argyll Transcripts, ii, pt. 1, 212. Fraser, *Memorials of the Family of Wemyss of Wemyss* (Edinburgh, 1888), ii, 22; Fraser, Montgomeries, ii. 17; *Liber Collegii Nostre Domine* (Glasgow, Maitland Club, 1846), 259.

[15] *Registrum Episcopatus Glasguensis* (Maitland Club, 1843), i, 231–2, hereafter *Glas. Reg.*

offering party in the absence of his opposite number 'remanand still at the said hie alter wythin the forsaid college kirk fra ane efternone quhill the down passing of the soune that four houris war surlie strikin be the knok of the forsaid kirk.'[16] The indiction referred to the imperial decree fixing the total sum contributable in tax, and each indiction lasted fifteen years; it is used in papal documents as far back as the eighth century, and its usual opening date, the eighth kalends of October (24 September), was employed in the imperial chancery, though subsequently at Rome fixed on Christmas day in the late eleventh century. A Dumfries notary wrote the mnemonic,

> 'In festo Sancte Trele indictio incepit
> Mensibus Octobris indictio sit nova semper,'

(read 'Tecle' for 'Trele', which gives the 24 September). The Glasgow notary, Cuthbert Simson, in his memoranda gave the date precisely.[17] Since 1 A.D. was reckoned the fourth indiction, the indiction for subsequent years was found by adding three to the current Christian year, dividing by fifteen and counting the remainder as the indiction; notaries occasionally got their sums wrong. Finally, also borrowed from papal documents, came the dating by pontificate. Here remoteness from Rome led to occasional inaccuracy, but the rule, given by Cuthbert Simson, was to start from the new pope's coronation. As in 1379, at the start of the Great Schism, there was sometimes uncertainty as to who was pope. John de Waryne, imperial notary, Glasgow diocese, is found noting in his docquet that he was unsure of the pontificate and had omitted it. The customary formula was used in 1563 by Henry Young at Dysart, 'the see of Rome being deprived of the solace of a chief pastor or otherwise vacant'. Another notary in 1550 cited the fifteenth year of Paul III 'regarding whose death a rumour is spreading' (*de cuius morte fama volat*).[18] After the act of Parliament of 1469, purging civil, though not church, courts of imperial notaries, the new royal creations often used the regnal year after the pontificate, and its usage was revived in post-Reformation times. However, the Dysart notary already cited employed in July 1564 a Reformation reckoning, 'Anno Reformationis ecclesie Jesu Christi in Scotia quinto' prior to the regnal year.[19]

The body of the act or declaration followed these opening solemnities. Some, however, were postponed till the instrument's close or even entered in the docquet. Although the whole developing trend was for notarial documentation to replace the testimony of witnesses, yet witnesses were a vital part of its public nature and an added guarantee of authenticity. The separate docquet or eschatocol was not just the addition of an extra witness,

---

[16] *Moray Reg.*, 172; SRO NP1/19 Protocol Book of Thomas Dalrymple, no. 15.

[17] *Protocol Book of Mark Carruthers*, ed R. C. Reid (Scottish Record Society, 1956), 4; *Prot. Book Cuthbert Simson*, ii, 507.

[18] Ibid., 337; NLS, Acc. 3142, Wigtown Papers, vol. i. no. 4 (Waryne); SRO B21/1/2, Protocol Book of Henry Young, fo. 11v; *Antiquities of Aberdeen and Banff, Illustrations* (Spalding Club, 1848–69), henceforward *A.B. Ill.*, ii, 260–3.

[19] *Prot. Book Henry Young*, fo. 25.

but a final legal validation by the notary who may not have drawn up the protocol personally, but employed a substitute scribe (*manu alterius*). Therefore he generally used the nominative 'Et ego' form of subscription, though at times, as if merely an additional witness, he has the ablative, 'Et me,' an instance being provided by Henry Barry, who incidentally designated himself notary by apostolic, imperial and royal authority.[20] Such triple designations are rare. After his creation as notary by apostolic authority, Cuthbert Simson, a practitioner hitherto solely by royal authority, subjoined a memo under an earlier protocol that it should be extended under royal authority only.[21] In his docquet or elsewhere the notary may use a Latinised form of his name. With Johannes Lapideedomus the reason is clear; John Stenhouse had been enrolled and matriculated in the writing office of the Roman curial archives. For others, such as the Dunfermline schoolmaster-notary, Johannes de Montefixo (Moffat), Aurifabri (Goldsmith), de Janua (Porter), the effect is to underline the international acceptability of the instrument, already guaranteed by imperial or papal (but not royal) authority.[22] If the notary has an alias he may insert it (sometimes in the form 'Nicholaus dictus Campion') or if a patronymic, use that, as in Johannes Symonis or Thomas Johannis Boner, whose father, John, was also a notary. Another type of subscription was where the notary's village of origin was accompanied by his *alias*, for instance, in 1428, 'Johannes de Carnbe dictus Barry.'[23]

In preparation of the instrument the notary would use his shears to cut a suitable size of parchment, and his knife as an eraser. His sign manual was personal to himself, like a seal in pen and ink instead of wax, yet though each is unique there are families of these hand-drawn signs. A common one is a star or monstrance-shaped design rising from a stem above a pedestal of one or more steps, doubtless signifying the public nature of the act. In Robert de Garvald's case the text was positioned sometimes to make room alongside for the upper part of his sign manual. In one Garvald specimen a circular knob on this stem formed the initial letter in the 'Et' of the eschatocol. He also wrote his Christian name into the star section of the sign, but it was

---

[20] *Panmure Reg.*, ii, 252. For a specimen of Barry's secretary hand, G. G. Simpson, *Scottish Handwriting 1150-1650* (Edinburgh, 1973), pl. 11. His sign-manual is in monogram form, a vertical 'h' intertwined with a horizontal 'b'.

[21] *Prot. Book Cuthbert Simson*, 89–91, creation (by George Symontoune) and 'regali solum auctoritate' in deed placed later, though earlier in time.

[22] In Registrum de Dunfermelyn Ms, Adv MS 34.1.3A, Moffat in the same document uses de Montefixo in his eschatocol and Moffat in his sign manual, fo. 108v; Burgh Records of Dunfermline, ed E. Beveridge (Edinburgh, 1917), nos. 255 (Stenhouse), 279, 298; *Collegiate Churches Of Midlothian* (Bannatyne Club, 1861), 28 (de Janua); *Registrum Monasterii de Passelet* (New Club, 1877), 262 (Aurifabri). For 'at Dysart' Latinised to 'apud Desertum,' Prot. Book Henry Young, fo. 40, but Latinised place-names are rare.

[23] *Bamff Charters A.D. 1232-1703*, ed Sir J. H. Ramsay (Oxford, 1915), 60, gives David Jak alias Anderson; Symonis, clerk of Dunkeld diocese, at Falkland, 1412, SRO, GD297/195, J. and F. Anderson collection; *Moray Reg.*, 153, 156–7 (Boners); *Charters of the Abbey of Coupar Angus* (Scottish History Society, 1947), ii. 19 (Barry).

commoner to add merely the initial of the Christian name or both initials. John Knox, when notary apostolic, worked his full name into a sign manual which was little more than an elaborate flourish. In time, the notary's monogram became the most usual form, though William Schevez had the family heraldic symbol of three wild cats *passant*, with Peter's keys standing for apostolic authority superadded, and Walter Chepman the saltire of his family arms with what appears to be a Chi-rho symbol surmounting it. A form picturing the contractual nature of much notarial business is that of intertwining elliptical shapes.[24] A notarial sign in stamp form was envisaged in the 1549 Provincial Council's deliberations; the earliest surviving appears to be that occurring about 1557 on James Nicolson's protocol book. Mottoes, generally in Latin, are in frequent use, Knox's being 'Non falsum testimonium perhibeto.' One notary, Duncan Nevay, used Greek.[25]

The first form of the act recorded by the working notary was an abbreviated note or minute, which at first would have as much authority as the extended instrument being its source and ultimate basis. In 1549, 'Jok Finlay requirit ane noit' that the late vicar of Kilbarchan had left his black gown to himself and his wife. John Foular's Latin entries varied from curt memoranda to what approximated to full instruments. Some Dumbarton notarial minutes get to the heart of the matter in a few lines.[26] How valid were such minutes in law? Probably, their acceptability varied with the passage of time. Certainly in 1535 the earl of Huntly had problems with a notarial minute recording the fact of his being retoured to lands in Badenoch before 'ane famous notar', one overtaken by sudden death before making a perfect protocol. Having made 'bot ane mynute alanerlie,' with his last breath he asked another notary to extend it, the minute by itself having insufficient proof value in court. Yet contrariwise when a minute was extended or a document transumed, the onus of fidelity to the original was on the notary, who often added that nothing had been added or removed that might change the sense or vary the understanding of it, 'unless it chanced to be in a point of syllable.'[27] Protocol books of dead notaries could be used as working models by their inheritors, and styles were copied into their own books. Some notaries must have had Rolandino Passaggeri's *summa* of the notarial art or

[24] SRO RH6/66 (Garvald); W. Fraser, *Memorials of the Earls of Haddington* (Edinburgh, 1889, i, pp. xl–xliii (with plate) for Knox; NLS Adv MS 20.3.6, unfoliated (Schevez); SRO GD1/661/18 (Chepman). Examples of contractual signs in SRO RH1/4/3 (William Cryne, notary, 1416); in Adv MS 34.1.3A, fo. 115v (Feldeu: with Peter's keys also) and James Darow (ill. 3), Richard Cady (ill. 21), John Lauder (ill. 29, combining keys, contractual and monogram features) in G. F. Browne, *Echt-Forbes Family Charters 1345–1727* (Edinburgh/London, 1923), plates.

[25] *Statutes of the Scottish Church*, ed D. Patrick (Scottish History Society, 1907), 117–8; SRO NP1/10 P. B. James Nicolson, fo. 49v; SRO NP2/1, Register of Admission of Notaries i, fo. 66.

[26] SRO NP1/8 Prot. Book Sir John Craufurd, fo. 26; *Protocol Book of John Foular, 1501–1503*, i (SRS, 1930), pt. 1, later parts do not give Latin text (useful topographical introduction by Marguerite Wood); Dumbarton minutes included in Adv MS 19.2.23.

[27] *ADCP*, 434; *Melrose Lib.*, ii, 457.

similar guide, perhaps the *Speculum Judiciale* of Gulielmus Durandus which made ample use of Passaggeri. John Stenhouse had the Roman curia's *Formulare Advocatorum* and John Crauford had parts, at least, of *Regiam Maiestatem* under his eye.[28] An Edinburgh notary might have a booth near the market place or use his own house or some public place such as church or churchyard. Booths were shared. James Nicolson shared a writing office with John Johnstone, scribe, from which his protocol book and precious instrument of creation were stolen in 1548.[29] In Edinburgh, a notary-scribe might be employed to write business letters and leave the humbler role of copyist to his underlings, and of course business was attracted to the capital from other parts of the country.[30] Rural notaries often used someone else's dwelling house as they travelled around from village to village. It was unusual for a notary to be beneficed and thus he was entitled to a salary; in Lanark in 1503 the fee was fourpence per instrument, but of course instruments varied in difficulty.[31] If payment for the writing up was not forthcoming, the act lost its force in law.[32] The value of the protocol books for exact sociological analysis is enfeebled insofar as the same categories of people, property-owners or benefice-holders, tend to recur, and the poor man's purse could not afford such services. However, the rich man could then as now fall on evil days, like the one who in 1471 claimed in Dumbarton tolbooth that he was living in destitution, and through his procurator, the local priest, warned his heirs to provide for his bodily needs as in his utter necessity he wished to sell all for food and sustenance.[33]

That it was sometimes possible for a youth to get some elementary training near home can be illustrated from the career of Patrick Maule, born in 1548 at Pitcur in Angus, 'broucht upe at the schole of Ketins,' sent from that parish to the school of Dundee 'quhair wes maister ane Mr Thomas Macgie (*sic* for Macgibbon)' and thence to Montrose till at 14 he married a daughter of Erskine of Dun.[34] For an apprentice notary some acquaintance with Latin grammar would be as much a desideratum as some training in a legible hand to be perfected and extended to other feats of penmanship in the service of another notary whose heavy duties are often referred to in the docquets (by some such phrase as that of Simon de Lendores in 1400, *aliis curis implicitus per alium scribi feci*).[35] The senior notary might himself be attached to a cathedral chapter or official's court, with possibly uniform models of composition ('styles') and handwriting patterns. There was no iron curtain between

[28] J. Durkan and A. Ross, *Early Scottish Libraries* (Glasgow, 1961), 185; Prot. Book Sir John Craufurd, fo. 10v; *Prot. Book James Young*, xi; John Craufurd's book opens with styles; William Douglas NP1/18, fos 241–312.

[29] Prot. Book James Nicolson, fo. 1v.

[30] *Edinburgh Records: The Burgh Accounts*, ed R. Adam (Edinburgh, 1899), i, 133.

[31] *Extracts from the Records of the Royal Burgh of Lanark* (Glasgow, 1893), 13.

[32] *Dunfermline Burgh Records*, no. 327.

[33] Prot. Book John Kerd, fo. 7.

[34] *Panmure Reg.*, i, xxxvii. True, Maule was a laird's son, but the Kettins school seems an institution.

[35] *Miscellany of the Scottish History Society*, iv (Edinburgh, 1926), 323.

spiritual and secular and lines are often crossed by, for instance, Thomas Kene and Edward Dickson, two sixteenth-century notaries involved in court and church matters. Some deal almost exclusively in sasines for the town's bailie as William Litstar who had a near monopoly, it would appear, in Stirling around 1528.[36] Others are travelling freelancers.

At first admission to the profession was strictly rationed and apostolic notaries or 'first' notaries, protonotaries, created at the papal court were rare birds and the privilege of creation jealously guarded. One of the complaints against Graham, archbishop of St Andrews, was his practice of making protonotaries on his own authority. A future successor of his, Andrew Forman, some years before appointment to St Andrews was made count palatine of the Lateran palace with powers to make simple notaries; the Lateran palace had come to mean the Roman curia, in this instance, as the popes accepted the fact of the donation of Constantine, which is confusing, as the emperors also made such counts palatine of the Lateran to create imperial notaries.[37] Moreover, notaries created at the Curia holding benefices were subject to having their vacated benefices reserved to Roman provision.[38] Bishops had authority after 1469 to appoint royal notaries or delegate others, such as their officials, to do so at will, though with a purely local validity in Scotland. Such a delegation is observable in 1523 when the see of Glasgow was vacant, and the vicar general, Adam Colquhoun, issued a commission to Mr John Doby, prebendary of Ancrum, making him official and dean in Teviotdale, with power to create and swear notaries and scribes.[39] It is likely that, with the advent of legates *a latere*, this situation was further eased to the point where, for a time, royal notaries almost disappeared. Another factor was the increased numbers of native counts palatine and their delegates, the viscounts palatine; but yet another must have been increased general literacy. Such indeed was the pullulation of notaries that it called for stricter controls from Church and parliament.

The preamble to the creation was generally in the form 'Sagax humane nature discretio' or 'Ne contractuum memoria' recalling the necessity of documentation to save acts from oblivion.[40] Each phrase could be the subject of a long commentary, but suffice to say that the supplicant for the office had to be suitable, not a serf, a soldier or advocate, for instance, and have the moral attributes necessary as well as an adequate standard of education in Latinity, penmanship and the law: the latter might mean familiarity with a compendium like Passaggeri's or books of styles and some practical experience in exercising the craft. Obviously age was another consideration. Presumably graduates in law might find the examination perfunctory, and

---

[36] *Extracts from the Records of the Burgh of Stirling 1519–1666* (Glasgow, 1887), 32.

[37] *CPL*, xiv, 59; *Vet Mon.*, no. 862.

[38] *CPL*, ix, 209–10.

[39] *APS*, ii, 95, 1469 c. 6.

[40] *Ne contractuum* is most frequent in *CPL* entries; for that and *Sagax*, Cheney, *English Notaries*, 44, 156; for the latter also, *St Andrews Formulare 1514–1546*, ed G. Donaldson (Stair Society, 1944), ii, no. 491.

Latinity need not mean too profound an acquaintance with the classics, though some notaries used Latin tags in their pen trials or cited verses of their own or another's composition. A layman created by David Gund, bachelor in theology, viscount palatine, in 1551 is said to have undergone lengthy examination.[41] The supplicant then took the oath, if an apostolic notary, to be loyal to St Peter, the Church and the pope; to carry out his duties faithfully; not to add or subtract anything that changed the instrument substantially; not to be involved in guile or fraud and to edit the minuted contract into a protocol. Investiture followed with inkhorn or penner and pen and delivery of parchment and possibly some additional solemnity like the kiss of peace. His work would include drawing up, publication, writing, dictation and exemplification, involving contracts, testaments, latter wills, decrees and other unspecified duties. Imperial notaries had procedures almost identical. The creation of the imperial notary, Dugall Cosour, priest, in 1482, wherein Cosour swore fidelity to the emperors or kings of Rome, and this despite the act of 1469 abolishing their services in civil cases, may be cited in this respect;[42] later still, a viscount by imperial authority, Patrick Lowis, was responsible for an Edinburgh creation, while royal notaries were appointed by letters under the royal signet, an instance of which occurs in 1506 when the candidate presented his letters of appointment to the Lyon King of Arms in whose hands he took the oath.[43] The visiting papal legate, Marco Grimani, patriarch of Aquileia, created Peter Spens a count palatine, who in turn created Thomas Murray, bachelor in theology, in 1553, one of the few theologians on record. The whole procedure of reception to notarial office followed a recognised formula which is almost invariable, as in the creation of Patrick Dodds in the same year with oath of loyalty to Julius III, the creator being a viscount palatine, John Greenlaw, himself made in Rome by a papal scribe.[44] After the break with Rome in northern Europe, James Nicolson could still appeal to legal tradition in his account of notarial duties: 'The duties of *tabelliones* are understood by law canon and civil to be laid down principally that the deeds performed by the unlearned commoner and the expert in letters may be drawn up in writing for future remembrance, lest truth being consigned to oblivion loss should occur to contracting parties and nobody should doubt that laws brought in for good reasons are being kept inviolably everywhere.' With the Reformation apostolic notaries quickly disappeared in Scotland, though one, Andrew Thomson, professor of arts, Aberdeen diocese survived as late as 1582.[45] The notary's instrument of creation was a cherished

[41] Verses, e.g. in *Protocol Book of Alexander Gaw* (Scottish Record Society, 1910), pp. iii–iv; the lay notary was created in St Andrews in a private house, SRO St James Hospital Perth, GD 79/6/87.

[42] J. M. Thomson, *The Public Records of Scotland* (Glasgow, 1922), 98, but Maitland Thomson could trace no instrument of Cosour's. There is at least one sample in SRO GD198/55, Haldane of Gleneagles muniments.

[43] *Prot. Book James Young*, pt. ii, no. 459; pt. vi, no. 1605.

[44] *Prot. Book Thomas Kene*, SRO NP1/2A, fo. 112 (re Peter Spens); SRO NP1/12. Prot. Book James Harlaw, fos. 67–8 (Dodds and Murray).

[45] Prot. Book James Nicolson, fo. 17v; for Thomson, *Ill. A.B.*, iii, 440.

document and a copy was sometimes attached to his protocol book and endorsed on his admission under post-Reformation regulations by the Lords of the Council.[46]

On creation, much of the notary's business might consist of fairly routine sasines symbolised by delivery, if landed property, of earth and stone or hasp and staple or both, if a paper mill by hopper and clapper, if fishing rights by 'cobil and net,' and so on. The breaking of sasine was symbolised by casting the objects away. If there was a disputed claim, resort could be had to casting lots, as with two relatives in 1516: 'we haif castyn cawills for soun and schadok' in both arable land and 'unland.'[47] Lands could be bought back by redemption at an altar, though in one of James Young's unprinted protocols the parties agreed that redemption in Walter Chepman's booth was just as good. On one occasion at the altar of St Ninian in Clackmannan kirk, redemption money was refused as silver had been specified whereas cash was offered in 'bawbies.'[48] Eviction was forced on tenants by an initial exposure of goods, tokens in Kirkcudbrightshire in 1541 being a widow's 'stuill', 'trest' and tub. Acceptance of a benefice was symbolised in different ways, as when Andrew Hay, appointed parson, took possession of the kirk of Rathven at the hands of the vicar pensioner, his namesake, 'by entering the great door or portal of the said church.'[49] Of these acts, redemption had to take place on a fixed day, and in consequence it is known that the date of Kirkintilloch's medieval fair was 'callit sanct dyneis daye' (9 October).[50] Some notaries were less totally involved in land transfers (some of which were short-term banking operations) and had a more personal, countrywide clientele. From the earliest days notaries were involved in such matters as appeals to the Roman Rota, the inquest on the Templars, investiture of churchmen in office, procuratories (in which expansion may have resulted from notarial activity), compromise arrangements within kin groups and between lairds and their tenants, extracting items from protocol and other registers and compilation of archival material.[51]

[46] William Douglas was created by Duncan Chalmer, chancellor of Ross, SRO NP1/18 Prot. Book William Douglas, fo. 2r; Henry Young by Peter Spens, count palatine, and admitted in February, 1564 by the Lords of the Council, Prot. Book Henry Young, flyleaf.
[47] National Register of Archives, Scotland, Johnston of Sands 0126. On sasine procedure, G. Donaldson, The Sources of Scottish History (Edinburgh, 1978), 20-2.
[48] SRO B22/22/17 James Young MS Prot. Book fo. 6v (recently transferred from NLS); SRO NP1/12, Prot. Book James Harlaw, fo. 42v.
[49] 'Protocol Book of Herbert Anderson (1541-1550), Notary in Dumfries,' ed Sir P. J. Hamilton-Grierson, Dumfriesshire and Galloway Natural History and Antiquarian Society Transactions, series 3, ii (1914), 176-224; SRO B58/1/5, Prot. Book of John Scott, Peebles, fo. 50.
[50] SRO NP1/199, Unidentified Paisley Notary, fo. 116 – this date not known to Sir J. D. Marwick, List of Markets and Fairs now and formerly held in Scotland prepared for the Royal Commission on Market Rights, 1890, appendix 635.
[51] At the inquest on the Templars, 1309, William de Spottiswood, imperial notary is unique in employing the Roman 'calends' style of dating, Spottiswoode Miscellany, ii, 7-16. In procuratories, sometimes one of the procurators initiates the request for

The role of notaries in the preservation of evidence is noteworthy. They were responsible for extracts from the lost Great Register of St Andrews, one by Mr Walter Bannatyne in 1602 of an alleged Malcolm III donation to Monymusk, where the extractor was presumably a notary; another by John Motto, notary, made in the mid-sixteenth century about the *Cursus Apri* in St Andrews. The old register of the dean and chapter of Glasgow likewise was still extant in post-Reformation times, as it must have been about 1566 that the chapter scribe and a fellow notary extracted the grant by William I to Kirkintilloch of burgh status.[52] Early charters from the lost register of Whithorn priory were copied and signed with the sign manual of Andrew Meligan, apostolic notary and Premonstratensian canon, a secular notary certifying that he had collated with the original.[53] Risk of wars and the continual mortality of men (a reference to the Black Death?) are among reasons adduced for John Rollo, common clerk of Edinburgh, copying charters into a register that became the Register of St Giles, others being the new generation's unawareness of the facts which were in danger of smothering; this was in 1368 and he can be identified with a notary from Moray diocese.[54] The first entry in a protocol book of Mr Alexander Mackenzie of Ross diocese was said to be a 'register of dispensations by . . . Robert, bishop of Orkney, commissary subdelegate.' A related matter is the record by a Stirling notary that the chaplain of Mr Patrick Leche, clerk register, had received from Matthew Forester twenty rolls, a book and a quire of the king's exchequer account.[55] Again certain charters concerning the Cistercian nunnery of Coldstream were entered up by John Laurencius, licentiate in decreets and apostolic notary.[56]

The process of handling, scrutinising, reading off to a less literate clientele, was also necessary in making exemplifications and transumpts: the practised eye looked out for forgeries, transactions cancelled or tampered with, before transcripts were made. Copies of a sentence involving a bishop

notarial instruments, as with Hector Boece, principal regent of Aberdeen university, at Edinburgh on 15 July, 1527, on behalf of Archibald Rede 'Scotus,' *fratruus* (nephew through a brother) of Alexander Rede, late burgess of Aberdeen, a transaction involving selling up the inheritance prior to going abroad, hence the 'Scotus,' SRO B30/1/1, Prot. Book James Meldrum, fo. 100.

[52] G. W. S. Barrow, *The Acts of Malcolm IV* (Edinburgh, 1960), 162 (it is not clear whether the register was merely in Bannatyne's keeping, as one version has 'apud' rather than 'per' Mr W. B., the former cited in *Historical Manuscripts Commission, 9th Report*, pt. 2, 238); *St A Lib.*, xxxi; G. S. Pryde, 'Two Burgh Charters: Kirkintilloch 1211–1214, and Rothesay, 1401', *SHR* xxix, 64–9.

[53] T. Talbot, *The Priory of Whithern and its lands and churches in Mann.* (Douglas, 1900), appendix iv–vi.

[54] *Registrum Cartarum Ecclesie Sancti Egidii de Edinburgh* (Bannatyne Club, 1–2,275. Rollo's handwriting and sign manual are illustrated in a fine document in *National MSS of Scotland*, ii, no. xliiia, but the elaborate floriated initial in the invocation is not his.

[55] SRO NP2/1 Register of Admissions of Notaries, i, fo. 161; Prot. Book James Darow, fo. 315.

[56] *Chartulary of the Cistercian Abbey of Coldstream* (Grampian Club, 1879), 43–4.

of St Andrews and a Florentine canon are mentioned in Lyons in 1248, one of
the witnesses, among other Scots listed, being an early Scots notary, John
Bell.[57] Copies were for the convenience of one or both parties, sometimes of
other instruments or protocol book extracts of vanished notaries. The
so-called 'black register' of Arbroath has a 'word-for-word' transumpt of a
precept from the royal chamberlain, by one who as late as 1333 failed to give
his diocese of origin, Alexander de Keth, apostolic and imperial notary.
Sometimes it was necessary to record that witnesses could recognise the sign,
handwriting and signature of the dead notary.[58]

Something has been said already about categories of men in notarial
employment. Because of its semi-secular nature, generally members of
religious orders were excluded and a notary entering religion disappears from
view as a notary, as did Alexander Lawson in Aberdeen on becoming a
Dominican friar, while Ralph Hudson, monk of Melrose, 'notary of the
Cistercian order,' only acted in the absence of a secular clerk and John
Westwater, monk of Culross, created by Archbishop Hamilton in the
immediate post-Reformation time, appeared in an emergency situation.[59] It
is not clear that simply through marriage a man lost his clerical privilege; the
law seems increasingly supple on these issues, and when a notary declared he
was too hard-worked to copy an act himself, it may be his business was with
wife and children. It is evident that notarial work was often a useful
supplement to a chaplain's meagre funds, and, though theoretically beneficed
men ought not to have engaged in it, some openly did.[60] Employment as
confidential clerks might lead to taking an oath additional to his notarial oath,
hence the epithet *iuratus*. Generally notaries acted as scribes to all sorts of
courts from the parliamentary to the burgh and one designated himself
university bedellus, William de Boyis.[61] Quite early notaries were found as
clerks to barons, as Henry de Wedale to James, earl of Douglas, in 1388.[62]

A notary could be called to act as co-notary to an important deed
requiring multiple notarial docqueting. The theft of his protocol book or of

[57] *CPL*, i, 245.

[58] NLS Adv MS 34.4.3, fo. 20, abbreviated in *Liber S. Thome de Aberbrothoc*
(Bannatyne Club, 1856), ii, 13.

[59] *Registrum Episcopatus Aberdonensis*, ii, 178 (Lawson); *Selections from the Records of
the Regality of Melrose* (Scottish History Society, 1917), iii, 162, 224; Admissions, i, 209r
and v.

[60] R. Passaggeri, *Corpus totius artis notarie perfectum* (Venice, 1528), pt. iii, fo. cxxx
col. b; J. J. Canis, *Tabellionum opus* is also included in this edition; useful also is D.
Murray, *Legal Practice in Ayr and the West of Scotland in the 15th and 16th Centuries*
(Glasgow, 1910). An example of a beneficed notary is Walter de Lownane, canon of
Dunkeld, *Ill., A.B.*, iii, 317.

[61] Some instances may suffice. In 1504, Mr John Murray, notary, was scribe to the
court of parliament, *APS*, ii, 373. From the 14th century, notaries are found at justice
ayres, for instance, John Symonis at Foulis in 1391, *Liber Insule Missarum* (Bannatyne
Club, 1847), 1. William de Boyis does not describe himself as cleric, but as bedellus,
not to be confused with another of the same name, monk of Dunfermline, who also
acted as notary, *Copiale Prioratus Sanctiandree*, ed J. H. Baxter (Oxford, 1930), 117, 419.

[62] W. Fraser, *The Douglas Book* (Edinburgh, 1885), ii, 73.

relevant leaves from it could be disastrous for the local laird as John Galloway's chief client, the laird of Bamff, found in 1534, denouncing the guilty parties as limbs of Satan. For more security the laird might extract entries concerning his kin or forbears as did an anonymous Carnegie from four protocol books, quarto and folio, of Andrew Greif. A personal note was struck in one minute, when on 11 December 1579, Mr Robert Carnegie, in whose gift was the marriage of his kinswoman, lined up three grooms for this independent lady, all of whom young Elizabeth refused, feeling no obligation to marry any but her sweetheart and unwilling to refuse John Inglis even to 'marie vith the king of France nor nane uther that is in Scotland.'[63] Because of the ease with which seals were forged, from 1525 parliament insisted on unlettered clients subscribing their names as guided by notaries; indeed it is paradoxical to find holders of public office like a chamberlain of Lesmahagow priory and a sheriff of Bute with their hands at the pen.[64] Despite being mentally a cut above their clients, there is little sign of notaries taking advantage of their position to become social climbers. Elsewhere the tale is told of the advancement of Thomas Bishop, notary, in Scotland and later in England, by the technique of wooing his mistress, of whom the rhyme went,

> 'First she was Lady Cawder
> Syne she was Lady Keir.
> And syne she was Tam Bishop's wife
> Wha clippit wi' the shear.'[65]

There was also an inherent conflict in being a confidant of a friendly client while still a public official whose acts were open to public inspection, as James Young found in 1541, when the king's advocate complained of him that he had turned down his request 'alluterlie and contempnandlie' for an authentic copy of a sasine regarding Aberdour lands, Aberdeenshire, in favour of a declared heretic, Captain John Borthwick. The Lords of Council ordered the notary's compliance.[66]

As notaries multiplied, governmental controls multiplied. Occasionally the collaboration of churchmen was invoked or volunteered, as in 1503 when

---

[63] *Bamff Chrs*, 62; extracts from protocols concerning Carnegies only, fos. 3v and 6 in the possession of the earl of Southesk, by whose permission the material is used here (through the kind offices of Mrs J. Auld, University archivist, Dundee).

[64] *APS*, ii, 295 1525 c. 3; *Hist. MSS Commission Report, Duke of Hamilton's Manuscripts*, 24; *Liber S. Marie de Calchou* (Bannatyne Club, 1846), ii, 485.

[65] J. Riddell, *Comments in refutation of Pretensions advanced for the first time and statements in a recent work 'The Stirlings of Keir and their Family Papers'* (Edinburgh, 1860), 234–48; W. Fraser, *The Stirlings of Keir and their Family Papers* (Edinburgh, 1858), 38–9. A notary admitted in 1565 was some years later keeper of the royal munitions in France, but his position was unusual, Reg. Admissions, i, fo. 224 and *Calendar of State Papers*, Rome (London, 1926), 221, 230. Prospects of advancement in the more tightly organised Italian notariate are discussed in J. Larner, *The Lords of Romagna* (London, 1965), 151.

[66] *ADCP*, 504.

bishops, who continued to employ imperial notaries after the declaration of 1469 that the Scots king had 'fre impire within his realme,' were urged to deprive unfit notaries and have the others enrolled as royal notaries; and again in 1540 when the bishop of Aberdeen called in his notaries for renewal of authorisation, this must be related to the extensive legislation in the parliament of that year: one, Thomas Daloquhy, described as layman, regularly appears as clerk of the diocese.[67] The 1549 provincial council merely spelled out this requirement, assigning supervision to the officials and their commissaries who had to keep records of signs manual in their custody, ensure for delivery to their archives of the protocols of dead notaries and see that they were foliated. Previously the protocols of a Dumbarton notary descended to his chaplain relative or to the local sheriff as in Inverness in 1542.[68] What the Church regarded as Church records, the State might very well consider to be State records.

Before considering crime and punishment, allowance has to be made for the likelihood that many men were repledged to church courts and, on the other hand, the notary himself could be pressurised into wrongdoing. The poet-notary, Patrick Johnston, asserted that he was compelled to fabricate an instrument of resignation of Plean lands never having been present, and despite legislation falsification increased, though it was not enough to declare a notary 'infamous', proof had to be adduced.[69] Possibly at first no more than renunciation of office was exacted. The trials of a notary awaiting judgment in Edinburgh, in his absence his goods 'wasted and sperpalit', his body in 'hevy infirmitie' and his expenses failing, are vividly delineated in 1537 by Patrick Duncanson, who seems to have antedated one instrument, though claiming local credit as 'ane trew and autentice manne.' Banishment and escheat was the fate of another in 1555 accused of counterfeiting the signature of an Italian, Francis Casar, on an acquittance; another lost his right hand for abusing his power of guiding the pen of unlettered clients. Another, John Sowtare, hanged in 1580, was a creation of 1526 who exercised his profession in Dundee and had been threatened with arrest in 1566 for keeping an illicit school there.[70] A less definitive instance was an alleged falsified will of James V excluding James Hamilton, earl of Arran, from his nominees to the governorship after his death. The notary was described on the dorso as Sir Henry Balfour 'that was never notar,' an endorsement, it may be presumed,

---

[67] APS, ii, 95 1469 c. 6 and 359, 1540 c. 11 to 16; Registrum Episcopatus Aberdonensis, ii, 323-4; for Daloquhy as clerk, Browne, Echt-Forbes Family Chrs., 255.

[68] Glasgow University, Scottish History Dept., Argyll Transcripts, iii, 195; iv, 121.

[69] HMC, 9th Rept., pt. ii, 188; The Acts of the Lords Auditors of Causes and Complaints, ed. T. Thomson (Edinburgh, 1839), 201-2.

[70] Thomas Quodquen renounced office in 1491, Acts of the Lords of the Council in Civil Causes, ed T. Thomas (Edinburgh, 1839), 189 col. a; Pitcairn, Trials, i, pt. 1, *211, *375, 402*, 432*; pt. 2, 85 (Sowtare) and for Sowtare's creation, Reg. of Admissions, i, 180v. For the automatic acceptance of the probatory force of instruments, Acta Dominorum Concilii et Sessionis 1532–1533 (Stair Society, 1951, 124, 125, 127 and the council's notary being sent to examine sick witnesses and refer to the Lords, ibid, 67); A. Maxwell, Old Dundee (Edinburgh, 1884), 89.

added after it came into Arran's hands. This is not accurate, and Buchanan's report that Cardinal Beaton got Balfour to forge it may have been current in circles close to Arran.[71] Vincent Strathauchin noted in his book, 'Speculator (i.e. Durandus) does not call for a penalty on a notary if he omits anything from the instrument through negligence, unless by guile or fraud to the benefit of one and the detriment of another, and to conclude thus proof is necessary.'[72]

The post-Reformation Registers of Admissions, imperfect anyway, do not account for every notary in the land or for every diocese either. The notaries presenting themselves range in age from seventy-six to quite young, one, John Muttou of St Andrews, appearing by proxy because of his advanced years. Many are unmarried, not a few married and in most cases they record their native village. None seems to be a law graduate, but there are several arts graduates, one bachelor of twenty-one, clerk of the Arbroath regality, and five professors of arts, all but one from Aberdeen diocese, the other, John Dunnat, called after his birthplace in Caithness.[73] Their apprenticeship is sometimes cited, the longest being Robert Wishart's seven years under the common clerk of Aberdeen. Each was to produce his instrument of creation, his protocol books with any inherited from previous notaries, and account for failure to do so. The age at creation varied, but limitations on age were clearly being neglected. The creators were generally protonotaries or counts or viscounts palatine, most of the last Scotsmen; a notary witnessed the instrument. Jean Damyte, of Evreux diocese, clerk to the queen, claimed to be made notary 'be the college of the writtaris of the archivy of the Court of Rome.' Other creators given include an Edinburgh bailie, Ross Herald, Archbishop Hamilton as legate and Roderick Maclean, bishop of the Isles (the witnessing notary in this last being Robert Pont).[74] The present occupation was sometimes entered, such as servitors to other notaries, writers to the signet or court clerks. One only schoolmaster appeared, John Henrison, of the grammar school at Dunfermline and a few were readers in the kirk.[75] Their personal residence was often indicated, some with lairds, some with lawyers like John Leslie or Edward Henryson. Mr Thomas Cranston, of Bold, near Traquair, lived with Lord Borthwick and the aged priest, John Castlelaw, dwelt at Samuelston with the lady thereof, the place probably once occupied by John Knox. Another, Mr Andrew Eldar, born at Benholm, lived with Erskine of Dun.[76]

[71] HMC, 11th Report, pt. 6, Duke of Hamilton (London, 1887), 205.

[72] SRO B22/1/5 Prot. Book Vincent Strathauchin, i, at end.

[73] Reg. of Admissions, i, fos 105 (John Muttou), 228v (David Lyel, BA), 166v (John Dunnat), professors of arts, 152, 236 (David Brody, Alexander Barroun) and ii, 30, 32 (Robert Leslie, Arthur Forbes).

[74] Reg. of Admissions, i, fos. 220 (Damyte), 224 (Wishart); fos. 5 (Ross herald), 8 (Bailie), 16 (Roderick Maclean), 93 (Archbishop Hamilton).

[75] Reg. of Admissions, ii, fo. 28 (Henrison); i, fo. 55 (Mr John Leslie, reader and exhorter at Carriden).

[76] Reg. of Admissions, i, fos. 84 (Castlelaw), 103 (Lord Borthwick), 113 (Erskine of Dun)', 147 (Edward Henryson), 215 (John Leslie).

Quite a few had lost their instruments of creation and protocol books. One Cupar notary claimed despoliation by men from Cunningham; another in Montrose lost his when the friars there were attacked in January 1544. William Seton of Balmerino lost his in 1559 from his chalmer at the kirk of Culsalmond and Thomas Irland had two destroyed and one stolen in his manse at Lundie the year before. George Cook's chalmer in Edinburgh was broken up in 1559, while Mr John Guthrie claimed that other writs were lost at the burning of Edinburgh and despoiling of Garden by 'the Inglismen the tyme thai war in brouchty be reason this notar usit to be noter to na materis bot to his master quhen he requirit him and specialy in besynes concernynge the curt of Rome.' Walter Mure, who lived at Torphichen, lost his protocol book and 'culd never sensyn upten nor get the samyn for no deligens, no lawboris, he culd do.'[77]

It remains to illustrate the diversity of information to be wrung from notaries' protocols, used in conjunction with other records where feasible, information confined here, apart from a few miscellaneous items, to those illuminating the contemporary economic and religious background.

Business men kept their own books, so there is astonishingly little about trade, internal or external, in the protocols. Something of the risk business is revealed, however. In 1552 Thomas Mair, from Leith, sold twelve lasts of salmon to a Dysart inhabitant for delivery to the latter's agents in Wick. The salmon was to be good value for the money, 'rede and sweitt;' in the event of non-delivery the cost was to be refunded and that is said to be 'the common sales practice in the town of Leith.'[78] Mining in gold in the Leadhills has been accredited to Joachim Hochstetter, but the royal grant was made originally to Guinterus de Langtz on 25 January 1526, and the king also wrote to foreign princes making Guinterus first master of his gold, silver and other mines and authorised him to import refiners. Langtz showed this authorisation in Antwerp to merchants Hochstetter and Gerard Sterek, who immediately bought half of the mineral rights. From them Anthonius Niketts got an eighth part, and, coming to Edinburgh to claim it, was to be given in all twenty-eight 'conckis,' which was said to be the German expression.[79] Cornelius de Vos who was also associated with mining in Scotland, was first employed in the introduction of new salt processes, necessitated by the scarcity of pure Bay salt from the Loire area. Here again the inventor of the process was not Angelo Manelio (or Mannuello), Florentine, but Caspar

---

[77] Reg. of Admissions, i, fos. 32 (Cupar notary), 104 (Montrose), 122 (William Seton), 118 (Irland), 169 (Guthrie), 189 (Cook), 192 (Mure).

[78] SRO B21/1/1 Prot. Book David Alexander, fo. 164v.

[79] P. B. James Meldrum, fo. 98; in 1531, Meldrum was paid for writing the 'Duchemenis contract anentis the myndis,' *Accounts of the Lord High Treasurer of Scotland* (Edinburgh, 1877–), v, 437. Additional material on mining is in *Acts of the Lords of the Council in Public Affairs*, 237, 247–9, 266–9 (1527 contract) and *James V Letters*, 136, 146, 160 and arrangements for their spiritual ministrations in *St Andrews Formulare*, i, 178 (for 24 persons in their chapel of St Anne, Wanlockhead). S. G. E. Lythe, *The Economy of Scotland in its European Setting* (Edinburgh/London, 1960), 52–3, shows mining continuing into the 1540s.

Sellar of Augsburg, to whom Queen Mary gave a licence in June, 1563. In the following November Sellar contracted with Francis Bartie, Florentine, who took on the responsibility of arranging monopoly rights. Knox wrote to Randolph in 1564, 'I fear thare trafique shalbe to macke salt upon salt,' by which he means engaging in undercover activities, though making salt upon salt was merely dissolving bay salt in salt water and boiling it into white salt. Manelio's activities failed, but meantime Sellar and Vos were teaming up with merchants in England and on behalf of Bartie, as authorised by his contract with Sellar and Berthold Holtzshuker of Nuremberg, his procurator George Rustici, Florentine, came to hurry the Englishmen led by de Vos to proceed with the work, security to be provided by Bartie in Antwerp or London.[80]

Much more abundant is the harvest to be gleaned concerning church affairs. It is useful to have accurate background information on monks and friars. A Franciscan friar, we know, was not expected to have personal property, so it is not surprising to find Adam Ireland resigning in favour of his burgess brother a backland in the Edinburgh Cowgate, Ireland being a novice with the Observant Franciscans in March 1530. Dominicans were less restricted and appear oftener in protocols in property transactions, one, John Letham, in a family of religious, received his father's property in 1528 from his brother, William, a monk in Paisley and son of an Edinburgh citizen.[81] The search for maximum security drove men to the notary. Friar Alan of Wedale, former warden (*custos*) of the Dominican house of St Mary in St Andrews, had bought some land there from a St Andrews citizen, Patrick Fendure. In Edinburgh tolbooth in May, 1451, in the presence of the new *custos*, John Graham, a notary was produced to record the fact, since Fendure's oral testimony would no longer suffice as he was leaving Scotland to visit the holy places. Nervous likewise of the perils of voyaging was William Mure of Edinburgh in 1555, confiding in the notary that he 'wes passand to the saill to Orkney and that he mycht perchance be vesyit be god in the meintym before his hamecuming,' therefore he desired a record that, in case of accidents, he was leaving twelve score merks to his natural daughter.[82] Litigation was omnipresent, and clerics at law are a study in themselves. Andrew Birkmyre, later himself as dean of Christianity responsible for clerical discipline, was not too overawed by the lawyers. In the official's court in Glasgow in 1510, when reminded of the official's power to bind and to loose, Mr Andrew retorted, 'Ye dow nocht to fessyn a scheip hede,' adding 'I sett nocht by zou a fert of zour ers.' In September 1471, John Lauder, archdeacon of Argyll, approached Mr John Moffat demanding his answer to the accusation that he was traitor to his king and bishop and a murderer.

---

[80] Ibid., 49–50. Prot. Book James Harlaw, fo. 18v (A. Niketts arrangements); *Calendar of State Papers Scotland 1547–1603* (Edinburgh, 1898–), ii, 61 (Knox comment); *RSS*, v, pt. 1, 1426. C. de Vos, Sellar and Bartie were all soon naturalised in England, *Calendar of Patent Rolls, Elizabeth* (London, 1960), iii, 486–7, 1223.

[81] Prot. Book John Foular, iv, 24 (Letham), 67 (novice).

[82] SRO Calendar of St Andrews Charters, no. 34: Prot. Book James Harlaw, fo. 95.

Moffat refused to answer except to his own ordinary, persisting in this attitude with 'What I've said, I've said,' when asked if he would accept the decision of a judge selected from the bishop of Glasgow, his official, the dean of the chapel royal, the conservator of Scotland or the provost of Kilmun. Originally of Glasgow diocese, he was perhaps then of Dunkeld.[83]

The information to be derived from testaments and other legal documents is legion. Nevertheless the law the lawyers principally knew about was that concerning property and land, and much of the notary's work was routine sasines, but just because of his everyday availability, the notary's protocols provide access to many private areas of life excluded generally from public record, though they are most fruitful when used in conjunction with them. Some things they relate are of marginal interest, but they seldom fail to throw light on the complexities of human relationships, within kin groups, between masters and servants, churchmen and laymen and even between a vicar and his God.

[83] *Prot. Book Cuthbert Simson*, 345–6; Prot. Book John Kerd, fo. 6. The stand of Moffat seems related to his having recently acquired a new patron, for in 1452 he was notary, Glasgow diocese and by 1468 of Dunkeld diocese, Glasgow University Archives 1245 and Adv MS 24.3.7, fo. 51.

JOHN DURKAN

3

Financing the Royal Household:
James V and his Comptrollers
1513–43

Most of the Stewarts succeeded to the throne as minors, but James V is the first whose minority is well documented by official records. From 1513 the 'Acta dominorum concilii', hitherto almost entirely confined to judicial matters, contain a large admixture of administrative business. The explanation for this may be that the governor, John Stewart, duke of Albany, who held the regency, was normally resident in France. In his absence the council may have thought it advisable to keep a record of administrative decisions. The practice continued after the nominal end of the minority, lapsing gradually as James gathered effective power into his own hands.[1]

Much of the business concerned the crown's finances, particularly those of the royal household, which was the largest branch of expenditure. This was the responsibility of the comptroller, who also paid fees and pensions, mainly those connected with offices in the household. He was also responsible for collecting the revenue appropriated to the household, which was known as the 'property', comprising the rents and produce of crown lands, customs duties on exports, and minor payments by sheriffs and royal burghs. Even in normal times this revenue was often inadequate; the comptroller's 'discharge' (expenditure or allowances) exceeded his 'charge' (gross receipts), leaving him 'superexpended'.[2] Sometimes he received assistance out of the 'casualty', the branch of revenue collected and managed by the treasurer. The comptroller supervised the 'ballivi ad extra' (chamberlains and receivers on crown lands) and the custumars at the various ports. When they accounted in exchequer their payments to him were charged in his account 'in rotulis' (according to the exchequer rolls), but he also received sums 'extra rotulos' (not previously accounted for in exchequer), including the grassums and entries of tenants of crown lands and the proceeds of sale or commutation of rents in kind. Though provisions for the household

[1] Entries relating to administrative and political business (and some judicial matters) are printed in *ADCP*.

[2] The origins and functions of the office of comptroller are discussed in A. L. Murray, 'The Comptroller, 1425–1488', *SHR* lii (1973), 1–29.

were purchased or acquired by subordinate officials, the comptroller was personally responsible for all expenditure, including debts incurred to suppliers. A detailed daily record of supplies and expenditure was kept in two volumes, the 'liber domicilii' and 'liber emptorum', which also contained separate accounts for wine, spices and chandlery, avery (provisions for the stable), and 'oncosts' (miscellaneous items). Many of James V's household books are missing, including all those prior to 1525, but final totals of each category of expenditure can be found in the comptrollers' accounts, most of which are extant.[3]

The minority affected both expenditure and revenue. Expenditure fell initially because an infant king did not need a large, costly household and an absent governor did not have to be maintained in suitable state. Revenue, especially that from the crown lands, was greatly curtailed. On James IV's death his widow took possession of approximately one-third of his lands in terms of her marriage settlement, retaining some until her death in 1541. The governor granted away lands and money to reward or buy support. Furthermore a weak administration was unable to assert the crown's rights in outlying areas, so that revenue which James IV had drawn from Kintyre and the Isles was lost for about twenty years.[4] Even less remote areas were affected; in 1522 and 1525 allowances had to be given to the chamberlain of Strathearn following depredations by malefactors from Argyll and other Highlanders ('silvestres manentes in alpibus').[5] The crown remained weak and impoverished until James V could re-establish its authority.

On 15 October 1513 Queen Margaret appointed Andrew Stewart, bishop of Caithness, to the offices of treasurer and comptroller, which he had previously held in 1511–12. He had returned from Flodden unscathed, apart from the loss of a box containing some of his official papers. His tenure of office was brief, ending sometime after 16 January 1514.[6] The comptrollership was then given to James Redheuch of Tullichedill, who had held it twice before, 1505–8 and 1512–13. He appears to have died before the end of 1514, when he was replaced by Sir Patrick Hamilton of Kincavil and James Kincragy, dean of Aberdeen, whose title of 'receivers-general of the property' may indicate greater powers than those normally given to a comptroller. In May 1515 Albany at last arrived in Scotland and in four months, July–October 1515, his household expenses swallowed up their entire receipts, leaving a deficit of £412, even before allowing for the more modest provision for the king and his brother and for payment of fees and

---

[3] The form of the household books and their relationship to the comptroller's account are discussed in 'The Comptroller', 17–20. Selections from James V's household books are printed in Excerpta e libris domicilii domini Jacobi Quinti Regis Scotorum (Bannatyne Club, 1836).

[4] ER xiv, 419, xv, 165–6, xvi, 104–5, 344, 480.

[5] ER xiv, 392, xv, 142.

[6] ADCP, 74–5; SRO MS Acta dominorum concilii CS.5/28 f.24; ER xiv, 29. Dates of appointment of treasurers and comptrollers are given in Handbook of British Chronology, ed. F. M. Powicke and E. B. Fryde (Royal Historical Society, 2nd edn., 1961), 180–5.

pensions. The treasurer, James Hepburn, could not assist them, as he had to pay for putting the palace of Holyrood into a fit state to receive the governor.[7] Kincragy ceased to hold office about November 1515 but Hamilton remained, as comptroller, until the following February, when he was succeeded by Sir Alexander Jardine of Applegarth. Between 1 March and 31 August 1516 Jardine's receipts of £4494 were only £135 less than his expenditure. The governor's household cost £3350, to which his argentar (pursebearer) made a small contribution of £277; the king's household a mere £400.[8] Jardine's removal from office soon after 26 September 1516 may have been connected with his acquisition of a long lease of the custom of English goods, which was said to have defrauded the king.[9] At the end of the year the treasury was so empty that the governor had to dispatch someone in haste to the sheriff of Forfar to get money 'to pay the Ducheman'.[10] By then, however, the comptrollership was in the capable hands of Robert Barton of Over Barnton, who had taken office on 12 October 1516. In January 1517 James Campbell of Thornton became treasurer, thus establishing a partnership which would last through the crises of the next eight years.

Barton belonged to a family which was prominent in Scottish commerce and shipping.[11] Gavin Douglas described him as 'ane very pyrett and sey-revare'[12] and, indeed, his previous mercantile background may have contributed to his success as comptroller. Realising that the Edinburgh customs formed his most important source of revenue he brought them under his direct control by himself taking the post of custumar.[13] In his first year of office he drew £1108 from this source, almost enough to cover the cost of the king's household, which was increasing as James got older. But the governor's household swallowed up over half his total receipts, not counting £1000 which Albany took for his personal use.[14] The treasurer provided some

---

[7] ER xiv, 116–23; TA v, 10–16. Throughout this paper amounts are normally given to the nearest £ Scots. During James V's reign £1 sterling was approximately equivalent to £4 Scots; see John M. Gilbert, 'The usual money of Scotland and exchange rates against foreign coin', in Coinage in Medieval Scotland (1100-1600), ed. D. M. Metcalfe (British Archaeological Reports xlv, Oxford, 1977), 131–53.

[8] ER xiv, 214–25. Throughout this paper the comptroller's charge and discharge have been taken as approximating to actual revenue and expenditure, which are impossible to establish from the evidence available. The comptroller's 'revenue' includes the additional charge at the end of his account arising from sales of surplus rents in kind. No attempt has been made to put a monetary value on provisions drawn from the crown lands and actually consumed in the royal household.

[9] ER xiv, 353.

[10] TA v, 95.

[11] There is a biography of Barton by W. Stanford Reid, Skipper from Leith (Philadelphia, 1962).

[12] Douglas also described Campbell (later Sir John Campbell of Lundy) as a 'bastard bribor quhilk had not 5s worth of good of his aun' (British Library, Cott. Calig. B iii fo. 311; summarised in Letters and Papers, Foreign and Domestic of Henry VIII, ed. J. S. Brewer, iii no. 1898). 'Hob a Barton', the pirate was already a familiar figure to the English (ibid, ii no. 261, iii, app. no. 33).

[13] ER xiv, 268.

[14] ER xiv, 270, 281, 284–6.

assistance in clearing off Albany's debts[15] and the latter's departure for France allowed expenditure to be cut. By August 1518 Barton could record a nominal surplus of income over expenditure of £1816.[16] In 1518–19 the Edinburgh customs produced £2653 gross and in 1519–20 £2701, more than enough to cover the cost of provisions for the king's household, which came to £1415 in the first year and £1881 in the second.[17]

The financial position began to deteriorate in 1519, when Barton was faced with unforeseen expenditure. A scheme for assisting the king of Denmark involved him in expenditure of nearly £1900.[18] Then in October 1519 the council ordered him to provide for Queen Margaret, who had complained that she could not collect the revenue of her lands, 'quhar throw sche may nocht leif efferand to hir estait and honour'. This assistance, limited at first to the short period up to Christmas 1519 but later extended indefinitely, reached an eventual total of £6408.[19] The internal peace of the country was disturbed, necessitating considerable expenditure for keeping and provisioning castles.[20] No exchequer was held in 1519 and very few accounts rendered in 1520, which meant that revenue was slow to come in. Worst of all the proceeds of the Edinburgh customs dropped from £2041 gross in the year ending July 1521 to £363 between then and the following May. Barton himself was unable to render an account between August 1518 and May 1522, yet it is remarkable that his net receipts from the Edinburgh customs (£7093) more than covered the entire cost of the royal household (£6978) during this period.[21] There were, of course, other expenses, for instance £2200 to the three lords (Borthwick, Ruthven and Erskine) who had custody of the king, and £1453 to the gunners in Edinburgh Castle. Despite everything Barton might have managed to balance his account, but for Albany's arrival back in Scotland. In the six months up to 31 May 1522 his household cost over £4000, leaving Barton with a final deficit of £3177. Over the next four months it cost a further £2300, but this expenditure ceased with Albany's return to France early in October 1522.[22]

Renewed hostilities with England helped to depress Barton's receipts from the customs. Between May 1522 and March 1524 these amounted to less than £1700, of which Edinburgh's contribution was only £946.[23] At Cupar, admittedly small and unimportant, 'throw weir and truble' within the realm 'the course of merchandice cessis'. Even at Aberdeen 'on account of the wars . . . between the realms neither the ships nor the merchants of the burgh could

[15] *TA* v, 129.
[16] *ER* xiv, 359.
[17] *ER* xiv, 442, 456–7.
[18] *ADCP*, 144–5; *ER* xiv, 459–60.
[19] *ADCP*, 148–9; *ER* xiv, 459. In October 1520 Margaret wrote that but for Barton, who had laid out £500 from his own purse, she would have been compelled to live like a poor gentlewoman; *L.P., Henry VIII* iii no. 1024, see also nos. 381, 396, 1919.
[20] *ER* xiv, 458–60.
[21] *ER* xiv, 444, 453, 457.
[22] *ER* xiv, 458, 473–4, xv, 89–90.
[23] *ER* xv, 85–6.

sail' and the custumar had to be given allowance of half the tack duty of the salmon customs.[24] When Albany made his final visit to Scotland, from October 1523 to May 1524, Barton had to defray his household expenditure and other costs arising from his abortive expedition across the Border to Wark, amounting to £1300.[25] Though the crown lands produced £7700 net in the two years 1522–4, Barton still had difficulty in getting payment from chamberlains and tenants. By March 1524 his deficit had risen to £4708.[26]

On 26 July 1524 James V, barely twelve years old, was declared capable of ruling, though in fact real power rested with the queen and Arran. The queen, however, was well disposed towards Barton, who had assisted her in the past.[27] In February 1525 parliament annulled gifts of the property because the king and his household could not be 'furnist according to his estate' unless his property 'cum in hale to the furnissing of the samin'.[28] This measure helped to boost Barton's revenue in the year 1524–5 to over £13000 and his deficit was reduced to £1036, despite the burden of renewed financial assistance to the queen, amounting to £812.[29] Since the cost of the household had risen to £6810, Barton warned the lords of the articles, on 30 July 1525, that the property could not bear this burden, which daily 'apperis to rise gretare'. Unless they provided some 'gud ordour and reule' the king could not be sustained 'to his honour as efferis'. Therefore, since he had 'oft and mony times advertist the lordis heirof, prayand their lordschips to avise and conclude ane gud and honourable way heirintill for the kingis honour', he protested that whatever might happen in future should not be laid to his charge, since 'he has done his exact diligence, spendit his awn geire and may sustene na forrare'. Later he agreed to be responsible for supplying the household for a few days longer, until his successor was ready to take office and to lend some wheat and bear which he had imported from England.[30]

His successor was James Colville of Ochiltree, one of the auditors of exchequer. Unlike Barton, Colville's background lay in the royal administration; he had succeeded his father as director of chancery. Though inexperienced in financial matters he was prudent enough to insist on certain conditions before taking on an office which nobody else wanted. His commitment was limited to the short period up to St Andrews Day (30 November 1525), 'traistand that your lordschips suld in that meyne tyme haif providit how that the kingis propirtee mycht have bene brocht in and ordour to have bene putt to the kingis hows efferand to his rentale'.[31] He also insisted

---

[24] *ER* xv, 38n, 67.

[25] *ER* xv, 90.

[26] *ER* xv, 86–7, 102; *ADCP*, 206–7; CS.5/34 ff.157, 199.

[27] *L.P., Henry VIII* iv no. 797.

[28] *APS* ii, 290.

[29] *ADCP*, 200; *ER* xv, 197, 199, 211. Barton's superexpenses were reduced to £774 by further payments after he left office.

[30] *ER* xv, 198; *APS* ii, 296; *ADCP*, 227.

[31] *ADCP*, 234. The notice of Colville (Sir James Colville of East Wemyss from *c.* 1532) in *Scots Peerage* ii, 546–7, is fuller and more accurate than the article in *Dictionary of National Biography*, but both misdate his appointment as comptroller.

on the right to appoint custumars, as well as the officers in the household for whom he was responsible. Furthermore the king and secret council should 'clois thar hands to the away giffing of ony of the kingis propirte', except for furnishing the household and paying ordinary fees. This last condition led to a dispute even before he took up his duties, for he treated an order to the custumar of Edinburgh to pay Robert Borthwick, the king's gunner, and some other persons as a breach of the agreement. On 14 August he told the auditors of exchequer that he would not serve, but they replied, somewhat evasively, that, as they did not have power to make a comptroller, they had no power to discharge him, and referred him to the king and secret council. A compromise was arranged, Colville agreeing to sign new precepts for payment of smaller sums to Borthwick, his two servants and the king's carpenter.[32] On 17 August he finally took over from Barton.

Colville's first year of office coincides with the earliest of the surviving household books, which shows expenditure on provisions rising from £559 in October 1525 to £645 in November and £667 in December, excluding spices, wine, the stables and 'oncosts'.[33] On 2 January 1526 Colville complained to the council that the daily expense was now greater than at any time since Flodden 'or laitlie befor the said feild'. He asked to be relieved of his duties from the following Monday or Tuesday and to be reimbursed for his excess expenditure, before he was utterly ruined.[34] Not wishing to find another comptroller, the council hit on a scheme for raising money out of the negotiations for settling the location of the Scottish staple in the Netherlands.[35] On 15 January the treasurer was instructed to arrange for it to be fixed at Campvere (Veere). Out of any payment received from Campvere £2000 was to be paid to the comptroller, £500 before Candlemas, the remainder once the negotiations were completed.[36] As no money had arrived by 1 March, they fell back on an alternative scheme, that of striking gold and silver coinage, the profits going to the comptroller. The treasurer, John Campbell, consented to this reluctantly, protesting that it should not prejudice himself or his office, to which the profits rightfully belonged as part of the casualty. He, too, was in difficulties and the secret council agreed that he should retain office until the sums owing to him were repaid.[37] On 24 June 1526, however, he was replaced by the master of Glencairn.

Campbell had advanced £321 to Colville against the profits of the coinage, which, in the event, amounted to only £210. By 21 June 1526 the latter was again threatening resignation. If, within the following week, the lords of the articles and the secret council provided 'ane sure way' for all the property,

[32] ADCP, 227; ER xv, 271-2.
[33] Excerpta e libris domicilii, app. 5-7.
[34] ADCP, 234-5.
[35] The full story of these negotiations appears in R. K. Hannay, 'Shipping and the Staple, 1515-1531', Book of the Old Edinburgh Club ix (1916), 49-77; see ibid 70-6 for the events of 1526.
[36] ADCP, 236.
[37] ADCP, 239-41. Campbell's superexpenses amounted to £4500 by June 1526 (TA v, 269).

with 'uther help of casualitie' amounting to £3000, to be paid to him, he would retain office until Lammas 1527; if not, he 'sall nocht be haldin to furniss the kingis hous ony ferrare'.[38] Meanwhile an envoy had arrived from Middelburg, raising hopes that £3000 might be realised by fixing the staple there. Accordingly Glencairn agreed to help Colville out until 14 July, when a decision on the staple was expected, and pay him the balance of the £3000 thereafter. On 14 July there was a further postponement, bringing yet another threat of resignation from Colville. Three days later the treasurer again agreed to support 'thame that beis comptrollar' in furnishing the king's expenses until 1 October.[39] This agreement, which perhaps contemplated replacing Colville, was soon superseded by another which committed him to holding office for another year. Under a contract, dated 2 August 1526, Colville agreed to furnish the household until Lammas 1527 and Glencairn to pay him £3000 'in supportatioun of his office', each finding six burgesses of Edinburgh as cautioners for fulfilling the bargain.[40]

Certain measures had been taken to ensure that the best use was made of existing revenue. Parliament revoked all gifts, fees, donations and pensions granted by the king since his father's death, 'sa that his hale propirte sall be inbrocht to our said soverane lordis comptrollare for the honourable furnessing of his houss as accordis for the estait royale'. On 31 July 1526 Colville protested that, if the auditors of exchequer disregarded this act, it would not be his fault and 'supos the king wantit thar suld na reproche be input to him tharthrow'.[41] The audit of his own account on 8 August showed that, while ordinary revenue had risen to £8556, expenditure on the household had also risen to £8329. The small balance, together with some miscellaneous receipts, including the profits of the coinage, was insufficient to cover the fees and pensions of household officers and servants, leaving Colville some £520 out of pocket.[42] But the king had directed the clerk of expense to look at James IV's household books and the auditors were to make sure that officials received no more than they had had 'in our derrest fadiris tyme and eftir the tenour of his saidis bukis'.[43]

Though Colville's agreement with the treasurer had provided that neither should be removed from office 'without ane notour and manifest fault', in October 1526 Glencairn was superseded by Archibald Douglas of Kilspindie, who was also appointed custumar-general of Scotland, being already custumar of Edinburgh.[44] Colville was left with the comptrollership, which was probably insufficiently attractive to any member of the ruling Douglas

---

[38] APS ii, 305.
[39] ADCP, 243-4, 246-7. Hannay, 'Shipping and Staple', 67-9, suggests that Middelburg had already made a payment to Albany at an earlier stage of the negotiations.
[40] ADCP, 251-2.
[41] APS ii, 306; ADCP, 250.
[42] ER xv, 285-6, 295-6.
[43] ADCP, 251.
[44] TA v, 280; ER xv, pp. xlviii, 270.

faction. Soon afterwards Middelburg paid 2000 merks for ratification of the staple,[45] of which Colville received £1000 and Douglas 500 merks. Hardly had the money been paid, when parliament rejected the whole scheme at the instigation of the burghs, who offered a special tax in return for freedom to pass with their ships and goods 'to quhat portis or partis thai think mast expedient for thair wele, utilite and proffet'. Their offer was accepted and letters were to be directed 'in the scharpest forme that the comptrollar can devis' to bring in the money 'for the furnessing of sic thingis as the king has ado with the samin'.[46] Colville collected some £2000 from the burghs, who were cheated in their turn. For early in December another envoy arrived, from the lord of Veere, bearing 'ane copburd of silver' for the king and 1000 merks in cash, which the treasurer passed on to Colville. So the staple was finally settled at Campvere and Middelburg did not even get their money back until 1531.[47]

Despite this profitable double-dealing the king's finances remained in a precarious state. Though five Germans had contracted to mine for precious and base metals,[48] this was no answer to a shortage of ready money. Justice ayres, a well-tried source, were held at Cupar, Perth and Forfar in January and February 1527, bringing in £1400 for the treasurer, who also got £385 from the mint. Despite this Archibald Douglas was overspent by £3654 at the end of August 1527.[49] Colville's own deficit of £1245 would have been much greater without the £3615 realised from the staple negotiations.[50] On 11 July 1527 he warned the king and council that the king's expenses were so great 'that he mycht nocht beir the chargis tharof'. He would carry on until twelve days after Lammas provided that, if no solution had been found, 'he may without displesour of the kingis grace and his lordis depart with the said office and nocht be haldin to furnis ony ferrar'. Accordingly the king instructed the auditors to admit no new gifts of pensions or fees and exemptions from customs and they ordered a proclamation at the mercat cross of Edinburgh for production of all such gifts on pain of nullity.[51] The treasurer himself renounced a customs exemption, a pension out of the Edinburgh customs was withdrawn at the king's direction and the auditors refused to enrol another. They also instructed Colville to economise by removing a yeoman and a groom from the kitchen and two yeomen from the stable.[52] Perhaps reassured, Colville remained in office after the expiry of his contract, 'quhilk has bene to him rycht hevy and chargeand'.[53] Further economies followed in April 1528. The comptroller and treasurer were ordered to pay no pensions before the next exchequer, when the auditors would consider 'quham to

[45] ER xv, 377; TA v, 294. The merk (mark) was equivalent to 13s 4d.
[46] APS ii, 314–15.
[47] ER xv, 377; TA v, 307.
[48] ADCP, 247–9.
[49] TA v, 294, 332.
[50] ER xv, 377, 390.
[51] ADCP, 260, 264.
[52] ADCP, 264; CS.5/37 f.221; ER xv, 365, 382–3.
[53] ADCP, 262.

pensionis suld be gevin or nocht', and unnecessary pensions out of the property were to be identified and annulled. Payment of sums by the king's precepts was stopped until the property and casualty could be brought in to supply his needs. Even the recalcitrant earl of Argyll was threatened with the loss of his feus, chamberlainries and other offices if he failed to account in the next exchequer.[54]

By the time the exchequer began in July 1528 James V had otherthrown the Douglases and taken full control of affairs. Archibald Douglas, the former treasurer, was charged with treason, but Colville, who had been closely associated with him, retained the comptrollership and was appointed custumar of Edinburgh.[55] James seemed to be determined to put his finances in proper order, instructing the auditors of exchequer to ignore discharges of casualties unless they were signed both by himself and by the new treasurer, Robert Cairncross. Later they were given a firm direction that pensions and gifts out of the casualty and property, which had been granted in the king's minority and 'be inoportune sollistatioun', were not to be admitted, 'nor nane uthir small tecatis of ouris that ar incontrar our profyte', except for pensions attached to certain offices and other gifts for which there was 'resonable caus'. These instructions were to be followed, notwithstanding 'ony tecatis of ouris', unless the treasurer or comptroller had consented to them.[56] The prohibition of 'tickets' was very necessary, as Scottish monarchs seem to have been easily prevailed upon to sign these informal warrants.

James' attitude may have encouraged Colville to enter into a new agreement with the treasurer on 10 August 1528. He was to supply the household for the following year, for which purpose he was to have the whole revenue from the property, together with a loan of £2000 from Cairncross. Part of this sum was raised by selling the ward and marriage of Glamis to the earl of Rothes, despite the fact that the former treasurer, Sir John Campbell, was entitled to it under an earlier assignment. Campbell had to be content with 500 merks and a promise of the remaining 1000 merks from another source.[57] The audit of Colville's account for 1527–8 showed that his superexpenses had risen by £849 to £2094, consequent upon revenue falling to £9766, but this last sum included £892 exacted from the higher clergy, a source which the king was to exploit successfully in the future. Furthermore the cost of the household had been cut to £8857, from £10883 the year before,[58] and there was some prospect of further reduction. Because the king had been 'gretlie scaithit' by 'browstaris, baxtaris, flescharis, catouris and uthiris byaris of furnissing' for the household charging him higher prices than they had paid in the market, fish, flesh, wheat, malt and other provisions were

[54] ADCP, 274.
[55] Diurnal of occurrents 11; ADCP, 277–9; ER xv, 514.
[56] ADCP, 281–2.
[57] ADCP, 281–2, 284.
[58] ER xv, 379, 455–7, 467–8.

henceforward to be purchased by the comptroller or his agents and servants.[59]

Events soon showed that Colville had been too optimistic, mainly because the Douglases were still capable of causing trouble. Preparations for besieging their stronghold of Tantallon revealed that the king's artillery was not 'providit, cartit nor ordourit'.[60] The money which had to be spent on repairs and supplies, together with other costs of military operations, made it impossible for the treasurer to keep his agreement with Colville, so that the promised £2000 was cut by a third to 2000 merks.[61] The king hoped to make 1000 merks by holding a justice ayre at Edinburgh, but this had to be postponed. Meanwhile the cost of the household was inflated 'throw occasioun of truble that hapnit' in the realm and 'throw the greit dertht that it raisit apoun flesche, fische, and all uthir thingis'.[62] The household book shows the cost of provisions fluctuating from £521 in September to £778 in October, £448 in November and no less than £951 in December, though that included £151 for Christmas Day.[63] Expenditure did fall back to £495 in January 1529, but Colville complained that by then he had spent altogether 5000 merks (£3333 6s 8d) more than he had received. Accordingly he asked the king to release him from office at the end of February unless this sum was repaid, together with the balance of the treasurer's £2000 and the 1000 merks from the justice ayre. James agreed and gave him a letter which instructed the council to find 'sum uthir sufficient man' to accept the comptrollership, 'swa that we be nocht destitute tharof'.[64]

Having offered his resignation unsuccessfully five times, Colville was evidently perturbed by its acceptance on the sixth, greeting the news of Barton's re-appointment with a protest that he himself 'was reddy to serve in the said office'. He made sure, however, that his own interests were protected, for the king prevailed on Barton to give high priority to repaying Colville. After the latter had accounted in the next exchequer, Barton was to refund one third of his superexpenses immediately and the rest 'as it may eselie be gottin in' out of the property or casualty, subject only to payment of the king's expenses and 'furnising'. Barton was to remain in office until Colville had been paid, but if he was removed or died the king was to be Colville's debtor for any balance outstanding. Colville, who remained director of chancery, was admitted as a full member of the council.[65]

On 6 March 1529 Barton was appointed treasurer, comptroller, great custumar, master of the artillery and conservator of the mines of Scotland, to which offices he added those of custumar of Edinburgh and chamberlain-depute of Galloway. No gift of property or casualty might pass the seals

[59] *ADCP*, 281.
[60] *ADCP*, 284-5.
[61] *ADCP*, 289, 299-300, 304; *ER* xv, 542.
[62] *ADCP*, 304.
[63] *Excerpta e libris domicilii*, 131-3, app. 14-17.
[64] *Excerpta e libris domicilii*, app. 17; *ADCP*, 304.
[65] *ADCP*, 306-7.

without his signature.[66] In all he wielded more extensive powers than any financial officer since James I curbed those of the great chamberlain in the 1420s. Yet neither these powers, nor Barton's proved ability, could make up for sheer lack of money. The greater part of the revenue for 1528–9 had already passed through Colville's hands, including £1710 from the customs and £3101 from the crown lands. In the next five months Barton could raise no more than £641 from the former and £1568 from the latter. In all, his receipts from the property fell short of his expenditure on the household alone by about £2000. A final deficit of £3537 in the comptrollery account was only partially alleviated by a surplus of £1102 in the treasury.[67] For the promised repayments to Colville he had produced no more than £400, leaving a balance of £2184, £1000 of which Barton paid off during 1529–30.[68] Furthermore Campbell was pressing for the sums still owing to him from the treasury.[69] Barton did what he could to economise, saving £600 a year by cancelling the assignment of the feu duties of Garioch and Kintore to the king's Italian minstrels. Some measures were taken to ensure that full accounts were rendered of the customs.[70] It was doubtless shortage of cash which made Barton ignore precepts for paying the keeper of Inchgarvie, who protested that he would not be responsible if the fort were taken, destroyed or damaged.[71]

By March 1530 matters were so desperate that James had to give a personal obligation to the earl of Huntly for 2000 merks to defray the expenses of an ambassador.[72] The responsibility for this lay not with Barton but with the king. The cost of household showed no sign of diminishing and he had embarked on an extensive programme of building and repairs at his palaces. This had begun before August 1529, when the master of works' account was sent for audit, but no record of expenditure has survived. In 1529–30, however, the treasury had to finance work amounting to £1569 at Holyroodhouse, as well as smaller sums at Stirling and Falkland.[73] During the year the treasury brought in nearly £13000, thanks to various windfalls, including the temporalities of vacant abbeys and the bishopric of Moray, but less than £800 of this was available for transfer to the comptrollery account.[74] The audit of this on 29 August 1530 showed that during the previous year £6723 had been expended on provisions for the household, together with £917 for spices, £646 for wine and £1050 for avery. Since the last audit Barton's superexpenses had risen by some £5000 to £7467, the equivalent of a year's net

[66] *Diurnal of occurrents*, 13; *RSS*, i nos. 4104, 4109; *ER* xv, 485–6, 515.

[67] *ER* xv, 530–2, 538, 540–1 (sums quoted include receipts *extra rotulos*). Barton's treasury account for 1529 is lost.

[68] *ER* xv, 542, 553–4.

[69] *ADCP*, 311, 315.

[70] *ER* xv, 494–5, 681–2; CS.5/40 ff. 93–4.

[71] *ADCP*, 314.

[72] *ADCP*, 325; *RSS* ii no. 601.

[73] *Accounts of the Masters of Works*, ed. H. M. Paton (Edinburgh, 1957) i, 1; *TA* v, 389.

[74] *TA* v, 354, 356, 391; *ER* xvi, 142.

revenue from the property.[75] Barton had failed, and on 9 September 1530 he was replaced by Colville. Shortly afterwards the treasurership was given to William Stewart, provost of Lincluden.

By December 1530 Barton was in serious difficulties with his creditors, especially various royal officers and servants who 'with gret inoportunite craifis him, and nocht alanerly craifis bot als purchessis lettres to compell him' and to distrain his lands and goods for payment of their fees and other sums, which had been allowed in his accounts. Because these debts were really the king's the council suspended further diligence against him until his superexpenses were repaid.[76] Following the belated audit of his treasury account James gave Barton a bond under the privy seal, on 12 February 1531, for repayment of £6779 15s 8d in annual instalments of £1000. The first followed promptly and Barton's final account, dated 7 September 1531, showed that only £5485 was still due.[77] Further repayments came intermittently. In 1533 the treasurer paid another £1000 and also assigned £330 due by the prior of Coldingham as arrears of taxes.[78] But from August 1531 Barton had been left to face his creditors with little protection from the king and council and several decrees had been given against him.[79] In 1534 Duncan Dawson, who had been master collier since James III's reign, followed up a decree by sending Ross herald to apprise Barton's goods for the £80 due to him. The herald had already taken some claret and silver at Barton's tavern in Edinburgh, when Barton snatched the silver back 'and said planly that nane sic as he nor nane uthiris suld have ony thing pertening to him'. The king intervened to protect Barton, who was 'of gret age, febill and vaik in persoun', but eventually, in June 1538, he was found guilty of deforcement, though the sentence of escheat and imprisonment was not carried out.[80] At least £4000 must still have been owing to Barton when he died, but in 1541 his widow and eldest son renounced their claims in return for a pension of £80 a year to two younger sons.[81] Thus was faithful service to the king rewarded.

Colville fared somewhat better during his second term of office (1530-8). Because administrative business figures less frequently in the council's records after 1530, the main source of information is his accounts, which show a gradual improvement in the household finances. Thanks to the arrangements which had been made for repaying his superexpenses, including assignments of specific sums, only £934 was still outstanding when Colville returned to office in September 1530.[82] This balance was carried

---

[75] The comptrollery account for 1529-30 is lost but the date and amount of superexpenses are known from ER xvi, 145. Household expenditure is taken from Excerpta e libris domicilii, app. 32-4.

[76] ADCP, 344.

[77] TA v, 333 (dated by ER xvi, 142); RSS ii no. 823; ER xvi, 142-5.

[78] TA vi, 231, ADCP, 412.

[79] ADCP, 361-2, 474, 476-7; Selected cases from Acta Dominorum Concilii et Sessionis, ed. I. H. Shearer (Stair Society, 1951), 3-6.

[80] ADCP, 419-20, 455-6, 470-1.

[81] ADCP, 509; RSS ii no. 3993.

[82] ER xv, 533-4; RSS ii no. 307.

forward into his new accounts, where it tends to obscure the true position. Thus revenue for the year 1530–1 actually exceeded expenditure by a small margin, though Colville's account shows final superexpenses of £907. Of this sum £722 was repaid by the treasurer immediately, but the repayment appears as part of the comptroller's charge for 1531–2. By August 1532 his superexpenses had increased to £975, again offset by the treasurer paying him £496.[83] Further hostilities with England affected revenue, and so in March 1533 the king, considering the expenses incurred by the treasurer in resisting English invasion and the comptroller's need for assistance 'now quhen our custumes failyeis', authorised the coining of 120 stones of alloyed money.[84] The profit from this, however, had only brought in £441 by the time Colville accounted on 1 October 1533 and the treasurer refunded £944 of his superexpenses of £1435 from another source, the taxation levied on the Church.[85] This was the last occasion on which Colville received direct assistance from the treasurer.

Revenue (excluding the subventions from the treasurer) had fallen from £9508 in 1531–2 to £8165 in 1532–3, increasing slightly in the following year to £8760.[86] Meanwhile the cost of the household had dropped from £8188 in 1531–2 to £7227 in 1532–3 and £6643 in 1533–4.[87] Colville's expenditure for 1533–4 was only £34 more than his receipts and his superexpenses of £514 were covered by a loan of that amount from the receivers of taxation, repayable at Lammas 1535. A big rise in the revenue for 1534–5 to £10313 enabled him to repay the loan, meet increased costs in the household (£8209) and still have a small surplus of £37 15s 9d, the first in any comptroller's account since 1518.[88] In 1535–6, however, revenue fell to £9385, which did not even cover the greatly increased cost of the household (£10623). After allowing for fees, pensions and other outgoings, Colville's superexpenses were no less than £2780.[89]

On 1 September 1536 James V sailed for France in search of a wife. His expenses there were defrayed by a special tax and his absence over the whole winter allowed a drastic reduction in the comptroller's expenditure on the household. The total cost of provisions for the eight months September 1536–April 1537 was no more than £960, the monthly figure falling as low as £53 in February. By contrast £106 was spent on 20 May 1537, the day on which James returned with his short-lived bride, Madeleine of France. Though expenditure over the next four months amounted to some £3000, thanks to the earlier savings the cost of provisions for the whole year was only £4133.[90]

[83] ER xvi, 133, 141, 170, 180, 290; TA vi, 37, 151.
[84] RSS ii, no. 1514; ADCP, 398–9.
[85] TA vi, 72, 231; ER xvi, 301, 345.
[86] ER xvi, 171, 180, 291, 301, 345, 354–5. These sums are calculated by deducting the treasurer's payments from the total charge and adding the additional charge at the end of the account.
[87] ER xvi, 172, 292, 346. See also Excerpta e libris domicilii, app. 35–45.
[88] ADCP, 428; ER xvi, 355, 391–2, 401.
[89] ER xvi, 480c–d, 481.
[90] SRO Liber emptorum E.32/6 ff.43, 63, 124.

'Oncosts' came to £972, but owing to the loss of the '*liber domicilii*' and of Colville's own account it is impossible to give figures for total expenditure and revenue; Colville's superexpenses were, however, reduced by £1677 to £1103.[91] Between October 1537 and May 1538 the average monthly expenditure on provisions was £500. This increased again with the arrival of James' second wife, Mary of Guise-Lorraine, on 16 June 1538. The total for June was £1140, for July £608 and for August £1005. The whole cost of the household in the year to 18 September 1538 was £13133[92] and Colville was faced with increases in other branches of expenditure. Under a new '*ordinatio domicilii*' the fees of all members of the royal household had been raised; even the humble 'turnbrochis' (turnspits) got 40s a year instead of 1 merk. These fees totalled £2132 and, although revenue for the year had risen to a record figure of £16258, expenditure exceeded it by £1554, bringing Colville's superexpenses to £2667.[93]

Colville was to have received £2780 out the proceeds of the tax for the king's expenses in France[94] to cover his deficit, but instead he was abruptly dismissed from office. An action heard in exchequer on 3 September 1538 revealed that he had assisted Archibald Douglas after the latter had been charged with treason in 1528. Himself charged with treason, Colville fled to England. In July 1539 he returned to submit to the king's will, paying £1000 to secure a remission.[95] His superexpenses were not repaid and, like Barton, he was left to face lawsuits by his creditors, including one for £879 in respect of wax, spices and other goods furnished to the household.[96] Threatened with imprisonment in August 1540, Colville again escaped to England, where he died before the end of the year. Meanwhile the treason charges against him had been revived. His goods were seized as escheat and on 14 March 1541 sentence of forfeiture was pronounced against him and his heirs, his barony of East Wemyss and other lands being thereafter annexed to the crown.[97] The king and treasurer did, however, assume responsibility for paying off his creditors.[98]

Colville's forfeiture was only one of those which James used to enlarge the crown estates: the Douglas lordships, including Tantallon, Crawford, Kirriemuir and Jedburgh Forest, Glamis and Avondale, as well as Liddesdale, which was taken from the earl of Bothwell. Moreover his general revocation, effected whilst he was in France, enabled him to annul all the alienations of crown lands and revenues made prior to 1537.[99] With the death of his mother late in 1541, her jointure lands reverted into the crown estates bringing these

[91] E. 32/6 f.143; *ER* xvii, 163.

[92] E. 32/7 ff.108, 116, 131, 148; *ER* xvii, 162–3.

[93] *ER* xvii, 162, 164–7, 177–8. The new fees are listed in SRO Household papers E.34/5.

[94] *ER* xvii, 162.

[95] SRO Acta dominorum concilii et sessionis CS.6/10 ff.177, 180; *APS* ii, 353–4; *TA* vii, 248, 375.

[96] *ADCP*, 477, 491.

[97] *Scots Peerage* ii, 547; *TA* vii, 385, viii, 13; *APS* ii, 368–9, 376.

[98] *TA* viii, 59, 92, 96, 109.

to their greatest extent ever, with a gross money rental of £16300.[100] This figure excludes some rents which were paid to the comptroller *extra rotulos*, as well as his receipts from the grassums and entries of tenants and the sale or commutation of rents in kind. With the growth of the king's power greater control could be exercised over the *ballivi ad extra* to ensure that more revenue actually reached the comptroller. As early as 1531 the earl of Argyll was induced to surrender his heritable chamberlainry of Kintyre and to offer to account for and pay of the rents of the lands 'quhethir the samyn happynnis to plenist or waist and nochtwithstanding pece or weir'.[101] The real increase did not come, however, until after the revocation. The comptroller's receipts *in rotulis* from *ballivi ad extra* were £5902 in 1531–2, £5316 in 1534–5 and only £3511 in 1535–6 (with £1225 *extra rotulos*), rising to £8132 in 1539–40 and £14947 in 1541–2.[102] The customs also yielded more net revenue; in 1531–2 £2603 was paid to the comptroller, in 1534–5 £3559 and in 1537–8 £5384,[103] partly owing to the refusal of the auditors of exchequer to allow exemptions granted to individuals, on the grounds that the king 'cannot owe his free custom to any person'.[104] General exemptions or preferential rates claimed by certain burghs proved more troublesome, as they were founded upon royal charters.[105] Nothing was done, however, to increase the rates charged on exports or to levy duties on imports, other than those from England.[106] As a result the comptroller's net receipts fluctuated according to the volume of trade, falling to £4488 in 1539–40 and rising slightly to £4660 in 1541–2.[107] The latter figure represented almost 90 per cent of the gross customs levied, though this very high ratio had been partly achieved by taking certain payments out of the custumars' accounts and putting them into the comptroller's. Similar book-keeping transactions had taken place between the accounts of the *ballivi ad extra* and the comptroller's account, presumably to subject such payments to closer scrutiny by the comptroller and auditors.[108] Despite the measures taken to improve his ordinary revenues the comptroller remained dependent on subventions from other sources, some of which were under the king's direct control. Thus in 1538 James ordered payment to Colville of 1000 merks

---

[99] APS ii, 357–8, 360. For the extension of crown lands under James V see ER xvii, pp. xli–xliv, and *An Historical Atlas of Scotland*, ed. P. McNeill and R. Nicholson (St Andrews, 1975), 72–3.

[100] ER xvii, p. xlix. Rental calculated from ER xvii, 473–607.

[101] ADCP, 356–7.

[102] ER xvi, 168, 389, 480a, xvii, 273. Figure for 1541–2 calculated from payments listed in ER xvii, 473–607. There was also an increase in the volume of rents in kind, including those consumed in the household.

[103] ER xvi, 167, 389, xvii, 157, 161 (including £1035 *extra rotulos*).

[104] ER xvi, 66.

[105] ER xv, 651, 682, xvi, 526–7, xvii, 769; ADCP, 507–8.

[106] ER xvii, 58, 60, 463–4; ADCP, 437, 493, 509.

[107] ER xvii, 271. Figures for 1541–2 are calculated from ER xvii, 457–64. See also *Historical Atlas of Scotland*, 74–5.

[108] ER xvi, 551–2, 567, 584–5, xvii, 168.

out of the temporalities of the bishopric of Moray, then in his hands.[109] Colville also intromitted with the fruits of the kirk of Forest (Yarrow) 'to our soverane lordis uys'.[110]

David Wood of Craig, who had been master of the king's larder since 1529, succeeded Colville as comptroller on 14 September 1538. His first account, for 1538–9, is missing, though the '*liber domicilii*' shows that household expenditure for the year amounted to £7483 for provisions, £1615 for spices and chandlery, £3000 for wine, £2166 for avery and £1772 for 'oncosts', in all £16036.[111] There are no figures for revenue, which exceeded expenditure by £1866, while the treasurer, James Kirkcaldy of Grange, was also left with an unexpended balance of £1019.[112] This unusual state of affairs enabled them to deal with a long-standing problem. Because of shortage of funds their predecessors had had to take allowances in their accounts for sums which they had not actually paid. It followed, therefore, that they could not use the entries in their accounts as proof of payment, though their creditors could use them as evidence that the sums were due and payable. Although the sums concerned were mainly annual fees and pensions, the same applied to other types of payments, including those for goods entered in the household books. Wood and Kirkcaldy complained that, in the absence of written receipts, their creditors, 'gif thair conscience wald serve thame', could claim payment more than once. Accordingly they obtained letters, proclaimed at the mercat cross of Edinburgh on 19 September 1539, charging all those having claims to bring their 'outdrauchtis' (extracts of entries) and receive payment before the next exchequer. On 7 September 1540, after a further proclamation, the auditors pronounced a decree extinguishing any outstanding claims, so that 'the saidis creditouris sall never be hard heireftir to craif the saidis sowmes nor the saidis thesaurar nor comptrollar sall nocht be haldin to pay the samin in tyme tocum'.[113]

In February 1540 the annual fees payable to Kirkcaldy and Wood were increased, by the king's direction, to 500 merks, partly to compensate them for the loss of their former entitlement to have six servants entered as 'houshald men' in the royal household.[114] It is doubtful whether this produced any actual financial benefit to them, as the great increase in the king's expenditure during the year 1539–40 totally wiped out their earlier surpluses and left them with huge superexpenses, £4267 for Kirkcaldy, and £2665 for Wood.[115] In Wood's case this meant that his expenditure and allowances had exceeded revenue by over £4500. This was partly attributable

[109] *ER* xvii, 161. See also A. L. Múrray, 'The revenues of the bishopric of Moray in 1538', *Innes Review* xix (1968), 40–56,

[110] *TA* viii, 72.

[111] SRO Liber domicilii 1538–9, E.31/8 ff. 107, 131, 154, 165. This volume is described by H. Ellis, 'Observations upon a household book of King James V of Scotland', *Archaeologia* xxii (1829).

[112] *ER* xvii, 270; *TA* vii, 231.

[113] *ADCP*, 494–5.

[114] *TA* vii, 362–3.

[115] *TA* vii, 361; *ER* xvii, 297.

to a massive increase in the cost of the household to £19229, including expenditure in connection with James' voyage to the northern and western Isles,[116] but other branches of Wood's discharge had expanded and diversified. Some allowances represented adjustments to bring his gross charge in line with his net receipts, for instance a deduction of £160 for the feu-farm of Kilmarnock, unpaid by Sir James Hamilton of Finnart at the time of his execution.[117] Others reflected the extension of royal power: payments to gunners and soldiers at Dunbar Castle and to the keepers of two castles in Islay. £167 was paid for the maintenance and clothing of Lord Glamis and his brother as state prisoners in Edinburgh Castle after the forfeiture of his estates.[118] Other expenditure related to assets which had been brought under the comptroller's direct management: the salmon fishings of Conan in Ross, a coal-pit near Linlithgow and saltpans at Preston in East Lothian.[119] There were numerous payments in connection with the king's flocks of sheep, which had been built up by purchase and confiscation, earning Henry VIII's reproof that James should 'establish his estate in such wise as he should be able to live like a king and yet meddle not with sheep, and those mean things, which be matters whereupon to occupy the meanest of his people'.[120]

As yet the comptroller's new sources of revenue did not make much contribution towards his total income. The bulk of the £8257 charged on Wood *extra rotulos* arose from funds under the king's own control: £1000 from the bishop of Moray in respect of a tack of the kirk of Haddington, £3781 out of the rents of the county of Gien in France granted to James on his marriage, and £2000 towards the cost of his voyage to the Isles.[121] No source is specified for this last payment, which may have come out of the 'boxes' in which James laid up his treasure.[122] By the end of the reign Wood claimed to be making 2000 merks annually from the profits of the king's sheep and cattle and 1100 merks from the coal-pits of Wallyford and Preston, but he seems to have become even more dependent on outside assistance, including £4000 from the rents of Gien. The Church, however, had to make the greatest contribution to the finances of the royal household, with £10000 a year assigned out of clerical taxation and unspecified sums from the revenues of the priory of St Andrews and the abbey of Holyrood, held by the king's sons.[123] In return the comptroller defrayed the household expenses of the

---

[116] *ER* xvii, 273, 276–7. The high cost of provisions led to an act of 14 March 1541 giving the king and his officers the right of pre-emption of imported wine, salt and timber (*APS* ii, 373).

[117] *ER* xvii, 286.

[118] *ER* xvii, 278–9, 285.

[119] *ER* xvii, 275, 284, 287, 291, 295, 346.

[120] *ER* xvii, pp. lii–lv, 287, 289–90, 296, 741; *The state papers and letters of Sir Ralph Sadler*, ed. A. Clifford (London, 1809) i, 8, 30.

[121] *ER* xvii, 273–5.

[122] See 'Accounts of the king's pursemaster 1539–40', in *SHS Miscellany* x (1965), 24–5.

[123] *APS* ii, 424. For James V's use of church revenues see Murray, 'Revenues of bishopric of Moray', 42–3.

Lord James, prior of St Andrews, which were entered in the king's household books.[124]

Wood's account for 1539–40 is the only one now extant. Apart from an incomplete series of accounts of Mary of Guise's expenditure, evidently financed from her personal income,[125] there are no surviving household records between September 1539 and August 1542. From then the '*liber emptorum*' for 1542–3 covers the closing months of James V's reign. It shows that provisions for the household cost £590 in September 1542, £1345 in October and £662 in November, indicating an annual rate of expenditure in excess of the £9773 spent in 1539–40.[126] The October total included £517 for the week ending 1 November, when the king led his army south to repel an English force, who '*pre timore nostri exercitus sine ictu terga dederunt*'.[127] Scarcely had these boastful words been written when the Scots suffered defeat at Solway Moss. Later entries in the '*liber emptorum*' show the movements of the household after James' return from Lochmaben until his death at Falkland on 14 December 1542. The dead king's household remained there until 7 January 1543, when his body was brought by way of Kinghorn for burial at Holyrood. From the following day the '*liber emptorum*' became the record of the household of the new governor, the earl of Arran.[128]

Wood remained comptroller long enough to witness the collapse of the financial structure which James V had built up. Once again the sovereign was a child, her governor lacking the power or the will to defend her rights. The king's sheep were rapidly dispersed. Within days of his death the laird of Buccleuch had seized some to compensate for those which had been confiscated from him; others were later handed back more formally by the governor's warrant.[129] The Douglases, Colvilles and others who had suffered forfeiture started proceedings for recovery of their lands.[130] Mary of Guise entered into legal possession of the property assigned to her on her marriage, estimated by Wood to be worth £10000 a year. On 14 March 1543 Wood drew parliament's attention to his lost revenues, complaining that the governor 'haldis ane greit houss and is at mair sumpteous expens' than the late king. Arran, who probably resented this implied criticism of his extravagance, removed Wood from office three days later. So it was his successor, the Aberdonian Thomas Menzies of Pitfoddels, who actually benefited from parliament's decision that the surplus fruits of the abbeys and priories held by the king's sons should be delivered to the comptroller for the 'honourable sustentatioun' of the queen and governor.[131] Thus the only part of James V's

---

[124] E. 32/8 f. 16.
[125] SRO Despences de la maison royale E.33/1–2.
[126] E.32/8 ff. 18, 25, 34 (less sums paid as arrears of fees); *ER* xvii, 276.
[127] E.32/8 f. 25.
[128] E.32/8 ff. 32–45.
[129] *Letters and papers, Henry VIII* xvii no. 1225; SRO Crown Office writs AD. 1/99.
[130] *ADCP*, 522; *APS* ii, 414–24.
[131] *APS* ii, 424.

fiscal policy to outlast him was the use of the wealth of the Church to satisfy the needs of the Crown, and this was to play a significant part in weakening and discrediting the Church in the final years before the Reformation.

ATHOL L. MURRAY

4

The Earl of Rothes in Denmark

The age of the Renaissance seems to have been a peak period for Scottish wanderings to Denmark. A tradition had developed of friendly attitudes between the two governments, and gradually the Scots were becoming aware of the ample possibilities in the Baltic countries – especially for traders and mercenaries. Norway might be the Scandinavian country with which the Scots became first acquainted, and Sweden might be the one where the Scottish influx left its most profound marks; but on its way from Norway to Sweden the Scottish attention focussed on Denmark.[1]

As seen from the Scottish scene of events Denmark could be viewed as a fringe area – a country near enough to be taken into account when circumstances dictated untraditional measures, and near enough to allow Scottish visitors or settlers to keep an eye on developments at home; but not so near that Danish authorities could be expected to take a very keen interest in Scottish home affairs. In consequence there was little risk of conflict between the governments with subsequent repercussions for Scots in Denmark. In this respect Denmark would be an obvious place of refuge for people who had had to leave Scotland because of internal political or religious upheavals. If there is anything unique in the earl of Bothwell's flight in 1567, it is not that it took him to Denmark. In 1469 a fugitive earl of Arran had preceded him. In 1489 several Scottish refugees could be met with in Aalborg.[2] The Dominican prior John MacAlpin, who left Scotland in 1534 because of his religious opinions, ended his days as professor of divinity at Copenhagen. In 1550 Christian III interceded with the Scottish government for the Protestant chaplain James Ska or Skea from Orkney.[3] And in 1546 and 1551 such notable Scots as George Leslie, 4th earl of Rothes, and his even better known son Norman made their appearance as political refugees in Denmark.

The immediate background of Rothes's flight to Denmark should be sought in the exploits of Norman Leslie. Nevertheless his own political

[1] For further elucidation of this see my article in the *SHR* xlix (1970), 125–45.
[2] *SHR* xlviii (1969), 104.
[3] William Dunn Macray, 'Second report on the royal archives of Denmark . . .', *46th Report of the Deputy Keeper of the Public Records* (London, 1886), app. II, no. 1, p. 63. Cf. *ADCP*, 549, *CSP Scot.*, no. 206, *Acts of the Privy Council of England*, ed. John Roche Dasent, ii (London, 1890), 114, 289.

career is not without significance in this respect. In so far as it is possible to ascertain Rothes's attitudes in the years following the death of James V he seems originally to have been an Anglophile. When in July 1543 cardinal Beaton's party made their attempt to secure control over the two queens at Linlithgow, Rothes was one of the five commissioners selected by the governor, the earl of Arran, to go there and ask for an explanation.[4] Next October, when the earl had already reversed his policy and sided with the cardinal, Rothes was still counted among the friends of Angus – and of Henry VIII.[5] In November governor and cardinal advanced in force against him and his friends,[6] and on 25 November Crichton of Brunstane could report that they had captured Rothes, Lord Gray and Henry Balnaves,[7] after which Rothes was warded in Craignethan castle.[8] Brunstane stated expressly that the captives had wanted to serve the cause of Henry. It is not clear whether Rothes entered into a bond of manrent with the cardinal for his release,[9] but at any rate his captivity was short, for on 26 December it was reported that an English messenger had read his message to a group of Scottish councillors which included the governor, the cardinal, and Rothes.[10] Under the impact of the English devastations some sort of understanding between the parties seems to have been established in November 1544, and at Ancrum Moor Norman Leslie fought against the English together with both Arran and Angus. Rothes was present at the meetings of the privy council at Stirling on 24–29 June 1545 and signed unanimous resolutions to prepare for war against the English together with the French. Besides, he was elected to standing committees for warfare and foreign policy.[11]

The most fateful event of these years was, however, the murder of cardinal Beaton on 29 May 1546. Norman Leslie was the leader of the action, while his uncle John Leslie took a very active part in it, and at least one more brother and two more sons of Rothes were or became involved.[12] No wonder that Rothes himself was suspected. On 28 June he complained for the second time to the council of 'sic murmiratioun' and claimed an exoneration, either by trial or by instruments.[13] His complaint was fruitless, and on

[4] The Hamilton Papers, ed. Joseph Bain, i (Edinburgh, 1890), 584-5, 590, 592; L. P. Henry VIII, xviii, i, nos. 938, 944, 951.

[5] Hamilton Papers, ii, 92; L. P. Henry VIII, xviii, ii, no. 255.

[6] Hamilton Papers, ii, 162; L. P. Henry VIII, xviii, ii, no. 378.

[7] Hamilton Papers, ii, 187–9; L. P. Henry VIII, xviii, ii, nos. 425, 428, 433; The Scottish Correspondence of Mary of Lorraine, ed. Annie I. Cameron (SHS 1927), 49 and n.

[8] Knox says all three of them were sent to Blackness, John Knox, Works, ed. David Laing, i (Edinburgh, 1895), 116, John Knox's History of the Reformation in Scotland, ed. William Croft Dickinson (Edinburgh, 1949), i, 55.

[9] 18 Oct. 1544 George Douglas believes that Rothes 'well be the cardenellis', Mary of Lorraine Corresp., 113.

[10] Hamilton Papers, ii, 244; L. P. Henry VIII, xiii, ii, no. 522.

[11] APS, ii, 594-7; RPC, i, 5-8; L. P. Henry VIII, xx, i, nos. 1027, 1039, 1049, 1054, 1059.

[12] Scots Peerage, vii, 286-7; L. P. Henry VIII, xxi, ii, nos. 611 (p. 311), 695 (p. 364).

[13] ADCP, 551.

20 September it was already known in Scotland that he was a fugitive in Denmark.

The relationship between these two kingdoms was governed by a triple entente between France, Denmark, and Scotland, which existed with varying degrees of effectiveness and formal validity, until the middle of the 1540s.[14] As late as 1541 the Franco-Danish alliance had been renewed.[15] In consequence Denmark had become involved in a war between France and the emperor in 1543, but within a year the complicated relationship between Denmark and the emperor was stabilised. A dispute had arisen following the deposition of Christian II and the elections of Frederik I and Christian III in 1523 and 1534 respectively. The emperor had recognised neither of these kings. To him the captive Christian II was still the rightful king of Denmark, while Frederik I and Christian III were only disloyal dukes of Holstein.[16] Understandably the Danish government seized the opportunity of a permanent peace, and for many years thereafter the Speyer treaty of 23 May 1544 became the cornerstone of Danish foreign policy.[17] In accordance with its terms, Denmark was to break off all alliances with and withhold any help to the emperor's enemies, and as this especially applied to France and Scotland, while England was made a party to the treaty, a period of hostility between Denmark and her former allies might have been expected. In support of this view the Danish chronicler Niels Krag quotes a letter from Christian III to François I, in which he actually repudiates him as an ally.[18] The preserved correspondence with France gives, however, no impression of strained relations. In fact the former alliance is sometimes hinted at as still existing, and it seems that François never received the letter from Christian.[19] The Scottish material supports this view. At the very time when the Speyer treaty was being concluded, John Hay happened to be in Denmark as an ambassador to ask for a renewal of the alliance and military aid against the English. The answers given in June were dilatory, but definitely not hostile, and no mention was made of the treaty.[20] Judging from Arran's letter of 1 January 1544-5, Hay had even received a definite promise of a fleet with 2000

[14] Cf. W. Stanford Reid, 'The place of Denmark in Scottish foreign policy, 1470-1540', *Juridical Review*, lviii (1946), 183-200.

[15] *Danmark-Norges Traktater*, ed. L. Laursen, i (Copenhagen, 1907), 404-15.

[16] Presumably it is a late reflection of the imperial view when such an excellent work as *Mary of Lorraine Corresp.*, 354 n., mentions Christian III as 'a successful usurper'.

[17] *Danmark-Norges Traktater*, i, 450-73.

[18] *Nicolai Cragii Annalium Libri VI . . . His Additi Stephani Jo. Stephanii Historiæ Danicæ Libri Duo* (Copenhagen, 1737), 267; Niels Krag & Stephan Stephanius, *Den Stormægtigste Konge Kong Christian den Tredie . . . Hans Historie*, i (Copenhagen, 1776), 274. – Of Krag and his work see *SHR* xlviii, 83-5, 87.

[19] *Aarsberetninger fra det Kongelige Geheimearchiv*, ed. C. F. Wegener, iv (Copenhagen, 1866-70), 265-6 n.

[20] Concerning Hay's mission see Wegener, *Aarsberetninger*, iv, 259; Thomas Ruddiman, *Epistolæ Jacobi IV, Jacobi V et Mariæ*, ii (Edinburgh, 1724), 201-11, 213-17; *The Warrender Papers*, ed. Annie I. Cameron, i (Scottish History Society, 1931), 10-14; L. P. *Henry VIII*, xix, i, nos. 418, 437, 751. Cf. BM Sloane 3199, fos. 238v-241v.

men.[21] This must be an over-interpretation, but it is a fact that rumour was busy with expected help from Denmark even later in the 1540s [22] – which does not tally with any sense of hostility. The Speyer treaty was concluded because both the emperor and the Danes wanted peace. The European system of alliances necessitated certain corollaries to this, as for instance the formal estrangement of Denmark from France and Scotland.[23] But the Danes went to Speyer to make friends, not to make new enemies,[24] and everything indicates that if the emperor could feel safe from Danish interference in Germany, he would be perfectly contented with a factual Danish neutrality in Western European affairs. And so, although officially invalid, the old alliances could still be the natural basis of the direct relations between the countries.

However, in the autumn of 1546 Arran suddenly saw both political and personal reasons to cultivate friendly relations. As the mutual trust between him and the cardinal had had its limits, Arran's son had been sent to live in St Andrews castle – officially to be educated. When the castle was seized, the boy suddenly became a hostage, not of his father's ally, but of his enemies. And as these were in communication with Henry VIII, there was a real risk that he should be taken to England.[25] Arran was undoubtedly troubled by this prospect, and so, on 20 September he wrote a remarkable letter to Christian. After having informed him of the murder of Beaton and the captivity of his son, he told him that Rothes was in Denmark and asked Christian to detain him there until further counsel could be taken. He represented it as a fact that Rothes was accessory to the murder, but it is quite clear that his real reason for wanting him detained was that he considered him – Norman's father – a suitable hostage for the delivery of his own son.[26]

To Christian this unexpected opportunity to meddle with Scottish affairs could hardly have been welcome, and throughout the affair he maintained a very guarded attitude. Still he did comply with Arran's wishes in so far that Rothes was detained – under circumstances referred to by Arran as '*libera custodia*'. Christian reported this to Arran, at the same time emphasising that a judicial inquiry into Rothes's affairs must be instituted. In this and in his references to decency is the clear hint that there would be no extradition if Rothes's guilt was not quite clearly proven. Finally he took the opportunity to complain of Scottish acts of violence committed in Danish ports.

[21] The Danish National Archives ('*Rigsarkivet*', henceforth RA), German Chancery, Foreign Department (henceforth TKUA), Skotland, 1; Macray, 'Second report', 60. Concerning the Danish manuscript material and the 'reports' of William Dunn Macray see Thelma Jexlev, 'Scottish history in the light of records in the Danish National Archives', SHR xlviii, 98–106.

[22] For instance CSP, Foreign, Edward VI and Mary, ed. W. B. Turnbull, i (London, 1861), 21, 23; CSP, Domestic, edd. Robert Lemon and Mary Anne Everett Green, vi (London, 1870), 378, 390; CSP Scot., i, nos. 313, 357 (10).

[23] L. P. Henry VIII, xix, i, no. 279.

[24] Ibid, no. 536.

[25] L. P. Henry VIII, xxi, ii, nos. 122–3; CSP Scot., i, 1.

[26] RA, TKUA Skotland, 1; Macray, 'Second report', 60-1.

The contents of Christian's letter can be inferred from the references made to it in subsequent letters from Scotland. On 26 February 1546-7 Arran wrote a letter in the name of the infant queen, and 4 April another one in his own name. The queen dowager wrote no less than three letters dated 22 February, 29 March and 10 May.[27] For some reason the tone had changed completely. In the letter from queen Mary, Arran thanked Christian for both his message and his admonition, and observing that Christian obviously meant no harm to Rothes, asked him to restore him to his former liberty and fortunes.[28] In his personal letter of 4 April he came close to making an apology for the temper in which, under the impact of the murder and the seizure of his son and the castle, he wrote his first letter. Now, when public opinion and his own passion had calmed down, he asked Christian to release Rothes and even let him leave Denmark, provided that he did not communicate with enemies. Besides, he stated that, in spite of the encumbrance of the administration caused by the war, the inquiry requested by Christian would now be instituted. In a similar vein the queen dowager asked for a favourable treatment of Rothes and liberty for him to return to Scotland. In two of her letters she declared that the divisions at home which had caused his departure and the harsh treatment of him in Denmark had all been settled – a statement which could be no more than partially true as long as the castle was still in Norman's hands; not to be surrendered until 30 July.

The queen dowager's participation in the correspondence should possibly be seen in light of the resolution made at Stirling on 29 June 1545 – that the queen mother's advice should be had in all matters between realm and realm.[29] It is certainly tempting to see her competent hand behind the sudden change of policy and the turn of the vacillating Arran. After all, it was very doubtful whether Christian could be persuaded to co-operate in the scheme intimated by him. There might be more effective ways of dealing with the problem of Rothes. It was quite possible that the events of May 1546 were intended to be the starting point of a general insurrection which, supported by the English, was to crush the Francophile party completely and initiate a new period of understanding with England. There may have been good reasons for the desperate undertone of Arran's first letter. But somehow the English assistance was too small and too slow and, when Henry VIII died on 28 January 1547, there were hopes of further delay. It might still be possible to keep the Scots loyal to the 'auld alliance' and isolate the 'castilians' as an unrepresentative group of desperadoes until aid could arrive from France. But in that case it might be important to get Rothes home – as the friend of the government. After all, St Andrews was situated in his own county of Fife. If not even he would side with the conspirators headed by his own son, why should the rest of the country?

[27] RA, TKUA Skotland, 1; Macray, 'Second report', 61–2 – where the letter of 26 Feb. 1546–47 is erroneously attributed to the queen dowager.

[28] The last words seem to corroborate the statement of the *Diurnal of Occurrents*, 43, that 'The erle of Rothes sta quietlie to Denmark, and tuik greit ritches with him'.

[29] *APS*, ii, 596; *L. P. Henry VIII*, xx, i, no. 1063.

But at any rate friendly contacts had been established with Rothes already while he was in Denmark. In a letter to the king of 1 May he thanked him for having forwarded a letter from Arran, at the same time mentioning that Arran had written favourably of him to the king. As the governor wanted Rothes home as soon as possible, and as the king was now, as he hoped, convinced of the falsity of the accusations made against him, he asked for his liberty, so that he could go home and serve his native country and the queen according to his rank and office. In view of the troublous times his help and advice could not very well be dispensed with.[30]

Christian was already considering the matter. On 3 May his trusted chancellor Johan Friis, at the request of the king, wrote his opinion as to what should be done with the Scottish earl.[31] He advised an honourable treatment. Rothes ought to be taken to the king's residence at Kolding, he ought to have dinner with the king, and the king ought to present him with a beautiful horse or a gold chain, so that they might part as friends. Johan Friis had got the impression that Rothes had quite a great following in Scotland, so that it might be useful to have him as a friend. He might be of service in the matter of duke Magnus[32] or in other affairs, 'which may well be worth a gold chain', as the industrious Friis quite candidly remarked.[33] Incidentally, Friis mentioned that he had been told that Rothes 'had returned to this country'[34] – maybe from Norway? At any rate his confinement cannot have been very close.

The new attitude of the Scottish government was thus making itself felt in Denmark, and within two months Rothes was back in Scotland. The castle had not yet been surrendered, still it was quite clear that Rothes backed the government. In July he participated in an expedition which, starting from Peebles, made a counter-attack against the English in the West and recaptured the castle of Langholm. Apparently there was too much opposition to the idea that a man under such suspicion as Rothes should be one of the leaders of

[30] RA, TKUA Skotland, 3; Macray, 'Second report', 62. – Macray says the signature does not look like an autograph. In fact it is written in the same chancery hand as the rest of the letter. Presumably it was written by some chancery scribe on instructions from Rothes, possibly transmitted to him by Machabæus. Rothes hardly knew German.

[31] RA, TKUA Skotland, 1; Macray 'Second report', 62. Macray gives the letter the same date as that of Rothes, but it is quite clear that Rothes's letter is dated the day of St Philip and St James, while Friis's letter is dated the Tuesday after.

[32] It has been known for a long time that in 1546 François I favoured a plan of a marriage between Mary queen of Scots and a son of Christian, through which the triple alliance could be restored and, if necessary, Orkney recovered by Christian. See Guillaume Ribier, *Lettres et memoires d'estat*, i (Paris, 1666), 606–7; *Historisk Tidsskrift*, 4th series, ii (1870–2), 901. *EHR*, xxii (1907), 43; *L. P. Henry VIII*, xxi, ii, nos. 360, 409, 600. It has, however, always been assumed that the son in question was the eldest son Frederik (II), and that the Danes were not very interested. Friis's letter seems to show that the younger son Magnus was the candidate, and that there was some interest on the Danish side.

[33] 'som vell kand vere en guld kede verdth'.

[34] 'Doctor Machabeus er uti dag kommet hiid tiil mig oc giver tiil kende at samme greffve er kommen hiidth tiilbage tiil landhet eghen'.

a national army, so on 12 July two justiciaries were commissioned to call and accuse him of being art and part of the murder of the cardinal and the seizure of the castle. On 15 July, when the army was already on its way, an assize was formed 'in the fields near the Water of Yarrow' before which Rothes was formally indicted. But as he categorically denied all the charges, he was fully acquitted by the court.[35]

Several peculiar circumstances are connected with these proceedings. Not only do the reports differ as to when and where these events are said to have taken place,[36] but the commission of the justiciaries also state that Rothes had returned from Hungary. Theoretically this could be construed to mean that Rothes had visited Hungary before returning to Scotland, but this appears highly improbable.[37] A question of greater interest is whether Rothes was acquitted by a fair trial. It appears unlikely that a very thorough inquiry could be carried through under such circumstances. And it looks suspicious that he could be unanimously acquitted after such short and presumably very imperfect proceedings. On the other hand, if the assize really consisted of the men enumerated it can hardly be said that it was packed in favour of Rothes. In the circumstances it appears most likely that the government, in return for the loyalty of Rothes, of which it was now convinced, was willing to stage a summary procedure in order to procure the formal exoneration he had always asked for, and that the majority of the nobility agreed in the political wisdom of doing so.[38]

In August and September Rothes was again made use of in the military defence,[39] and on 6 September his full resumption of his place in Scottish society was sealed by his redemption of the family estates which Norman had

[35] HMC 3, 4th Report, i, 504; Robert Lindesay of Pitscottie, The Historie and Cronicles of Scotland, ed. Æ. J. G. Mackay, ii (Scottish Text Society, 1899), 88; John Lesley, The History of Scotland, ed. Thomas Thomson (Bannatyne Club, 1830), 194, cf. Jhone Leslie, The Historie of Scotland, edd. E. G. Cody and William Murison, ii (Scottish Text Society, 1895), 294; George Buchanan, The History of Scotland, ed. James Aikman, ii (Glasgow, 1827), 363; Lord Herries, Historical Memoirs (Abbotsford Club, 1836), 17–18; Scots Peerage, vii, 282.

[36] The HMC 3, 4th Report states that the proceedings took place 15 July at seven o'clock in the morning at the water of Yarrow. Pitscottie says the army was to assemble at Peebles on 20 July, and that the proceedings took place at 'ane pairt callit Guddieiscleuch' in 'Meggat land' at ten o'clock – presumably the next morning is meant. Buchanan says it happened at Meggat river.

[37] John Leslie says Rothes was lately returned from Denmark. Colonel (Charles) Leslie, Historical Records of the Family of Leslie, ii (Edinburgh, 1869), 51, gives no authority for his assertion that Rothes had been in France.

[38] George Brunton and David Haig, An Historical Account of the Senators of the College of Justice (Edinburgh, 1832), 38, understand Buchanan's statement that 'both the time and the place was unfavourable' as if they were unfavourable to Rothes. It is a question whether it would not be defensible to understand it of the circumstances of an army progressing through difficult country with a heavy train and artillery (cf. TA, ix, pp. xvii–xix). Calderwood, History, i, 238–9, says that 'time and place were not convenient'.

[39] TA, ix, 107–8; Mary of Lorraine Corresp., 204 and n.

forfeited by being declared guilty of treason.[40] In November he was present together with Arran at the siege of Broughty Craig,[41] and in December it was reported to protector Somerset that he had taken over the defence of the coasts of Fife against the English.[42] His task was not an easy one,[43] however, and in February 1548 Somerset was told that Rothes had endeavoured by all means to collect men, but as this had been very difficult, he had protested with great rage that he would forsake them all and flee to Denmark.[44] In a letter to Christian of 26 March he used 'the most profuse expressions of gratitude for his treatment of him when in Denmark, and of devotion to his service'.[45] In florid language he described how persistently he had extolled Christian's humanity and generosity in Scotland, and how much his fame had spread all over the country. He apologised for not having written before, but explained that Scotland was flooded by the waves of war, by which he was in daily peril of his life. If he survived the war, he declared he would visit Denmark again.

Rothes actually was to return to Denmark, although not as a carefree visitor. In those unquiet times, with a weak government in Scotland and a permanent state of war with England and the Netherlands, a sharp distinction could scarcely be made between privateering and sheer piracy. Danish complaints were not infrequent, and in the autumn of 1548 the situation had grown complicated. For two years a suit had been dragging on at Edinburgh against some Scots who had robbed merchandise, belonging to citizens of Königsberg, from a ship of Danzig. Presumably it was the same case which had earlier been mentioned by Christian and referred to by Arran in his letter of 26 February 1546–7. If so, the robbery had been committed in a Danish port, which may explain the appearance of Christian in a case between Scots and citizens of Königsberg.[46] Later there had been another affair where the Danish councillor Claus Bille had been robbed of some guns while on his way to the Netherlands. Christian had protested forcibly, and possibly even with hints of taking justice in his own hands, but still with due respect for the friendly relations. But as the Scottish government later saw its own reasons for contacting the Danes, it picked out the Lyon king of arms, Sir David Lindsay, to go to Denmark as an ambassador to clear up the different matters.

---

[40] *RMS*, iv, nos. 149–50; *RSS*, iii, no. 2424. Cf. ibid, ii, no. 3139, *APS*, ii, 476, 477–80, *RMS*, iv, nos. 213, 215, *RSS*, iii, nos. 2807–9, *HMC 3, 4th Report*, i, 498–9, Colonel Leslie, *Historical Records*, ii, 51, 57–9, 68–71, 225.

[41] *CSP Scot.* i, no. 94.

[42] Ibid, no. 103.

[43] Pitscottie, *Historie*, ii, 104. See also *TA*, ix, 169.

[44] *CSP Scot.* i, no. 176.

[45] RA, TKUA Skotland, 3; Macray, 'Second report', 62–3.

[46] Other extant letters which possibly or certainly belong to the same case are: Arran to Christian, dated 'Dymburgii', 1 Sept. 1546; queen mother to Christian, dated Stirling, 7 July 1547; Arran to Christian, dated Stirling, 15 July 1547; the Senate of the College of Justice to Christian, dated Edinburgh, 23 July 1547. All in RA, TKUA Skotland, 1; Macray, 'Second report', 60, 62.

Lindsay went to Denmark at the end of the year 1548.[47] Credentials were issued by Arran in the name of Queen Mary on 22 November, and by the queen mother on 20 December.[48] Lindsay also brought an undated letter from Arran in the queen's name, which he delivered at Kolding in February 1549.[49] But the negotiations must have started before, for a Latin draft of the Danish answer is dated 20 January.[50] At any rate, January and February must have been the decisive months.

The several tasks of Sir David appear from his instructions.[51] In the first place, he was to justify the Scottish government in the cases of the Königsbergers and of Claus Bille. Next he was to give an account of the unhappy state of Scotland, of the devastations of the English, and of the French readiness to help. Furthermore he was to ask for naval aid from Denmark for the protection of the Scottish coasts – a help, it was said, which would be very useful indeed, not only because of the bravery of the Danes, but also because of the memory of the disasters they had inflicted upon the English in ancient times! Finally he was to ask permission for the Scots to provision, to trade, and especially to buy guns and powder in Denmark, and besides, if possible, to enlist Christian's help in obtaining similar permissions from his allies.

The very rumour of that embassy called forth an English counter-move by Protector Somerset, who sent an embassy to secure the friendship and understanding of Denmark.[52] In this case special reference was made to the religious question, as Denmark and England were at that time both protestant countries, while Scotland was still catholic. As a special effect Somerset selected as his ambassador the exiled Scottish protestant John Borthwick, who could be assured to tell Christian that he would act in the real interest of the Scots if he supported England against the catholic Scottish government. But Borthwick's case was less convincing than that of Lindsay. For instance, Christian suggested that Somerset should give up some of the occupied Scottish strongholds in order to pave the way for peace negotiations.[53]

In answer to Lindsay[54] Christian refused to send a fleet to Scotland to keep away the English; but references to the prohibitive effect of the Speyer treaty are conspicuously absent. Contrariwise, it is stated that the Scots will still be

[47] Cragius, *Annales*, 313; Krag, *Historie*, i, 321.

[48] RA, TKUA Skotland, 3; Macray, 'Second report', 62. The queen mother's letter is not calendared by Macray. Cf. *TA*, ix, 259.

[49] RA, TKUA Skotland, 1; Macray, 'Second report', 62.

[50] RA, TKUA Skotland, 3; Macray, 'Second report', 62.

[51] RA, TKUA Skotland, 3; Macray, 'Second report', 62. Cf. SRO, RH 2/7/6, fo. 142.

[52] Cragius, *Annales*, 314; Krag, *Historie*, i, 322.

[53] Cf. my article 'John Borthwick og hans plan om et samlet protestantisk Nordeuropa', *Kirkehistoriske Samlinger* (1976), 44–66.

[54] RA, TKUA Skotland, 3; Macray, 'Second report', 62; Cragius, *Annales*, 313–14; Krag, *Historie*, i, 321–2.

allowed to trade in Denmark, provided that equivalent rights were upheld for Danes in Scotland, and no injustices committed; and no exception was taken concerning guns and powder. As to the piracies, the answer also seems to have been reasonably conciliatory, so Lindsay's mission might not have proved unsuccessful[55] if his return to Scotland had not been delayed by rough wintry weather and ice in the Danish waters. In February he set out, but was ship-wrecked and barely saved his life. Not until spring did he get away, and by then he was accompanied by a Danish messenger, who was to tell the Scottish government that Christian was anxious to redeem the pawned islands of Orkney. Such a promise had been included in the election charter (håndfæstning) of each of the subsequent Dano-Norwegian kings and there can be no doubt that Christian III was serious in his intent.[56] A special tax to this end was levied in 1549 in order to procure the sum required for the redemption.[57]

But however weak a governor Arran might be, he would not give up the islands if it could be avoided. At first he simply ignored Christian's démarche. But on 30 September Christian wrote again, and the firmness of his purpose appears from the fact that on 1 and 3 October he also wrote to Henri II of France and the French connétable Anne de Montmorency.[58] He also appears to have written to the cardinal of Lorraine and duke Claude of Guise.[59] To Montmorency he characterised the matter as 'res gravissima atque ad fidem dignitatemque nostram pertinens'. In the letter to Arran he politely suggested that the lack of an answer to his first approach was due to the upheavals in Scotland and not to any purpose of violating his evident rights. Although he felt sure that the relevant documents must be in Scotland, he made assurance doubly sure by sending copies of those in Denmark to both Scotland and France. Asserting his readiness to pay, he requested the appointment of some day in the following May and some place in Orkney where the payment

[55] In October Lindsay was awarded 100 crowns of the sun in consideration of his service in Denmark (TA, ix, 347).

[56] In Hans's håndfæstning it is not expressly mentioned, but must be comprehended by the general obligation of § 8 to regain all the lands Norway had lost during the reign of Christian I (Wegener, Aarsberetninger, ii (1856–60), 48, cf. Diplomatarium Norvegicum, edd. C. R. Unger and H. J. Huitfeldt, ix, ii (Christiania, 1878), 431, 433). In Christian II's håndfæstning it is § 64, in the Norwegian håndfæstning of Frederik I § 35, and in Christian III's håndfæstning § 25 (Wegener, Aarsberetninger, ii, 64, 86, Diplom. Norv., vii, ii (1869), 606).

[57] Danske Magazin, series 4, iv (1878), 363–4, Cragius, Annales, 327; Krag, Historie, i, 335. And cf. n. 32.

[58] These and other letters relating to these negotiations are copied in a volume containing 28 official transcripts of diplomatic papers between Denmark and Scotland, mainly concerning the Orkney question, confirmed and sealed by the university of Copenhagen (RA, TKUA Skotland, 7; Macray, 'Third report on the royal archives of Denmark', 47th Report of the Deputy Keeper of the Public Records (1887), app., no. 5, p. 42). Several of them have been used by Thormodus Torfæus, Orcades seu Rerum Orcadensium Historiæ Libri Tres (Copenhagen, 1697), 207–15, whose accounts of the letters are often virtually verbatim transcripts. On Torfæus see SHR xlviii, 88.

[59] Cragius, Annales, 314; Krag, Historie, i, 322.

could take place, and the islands be taken over by his representatives. He expected no damage or depreciation to be done to them until that could happen.

Henri was the first to answer. In letters of 14 December 1549 and 3 January 1549–50 he referred Christian to Charles de Danzay, who had been his resident ambassador in Denmark since December 1548,[60] and early in 1550 Danzay made his personal appearance in order to explain the French attitude. Accounts of his representations agree that Henri without any reservation acknowledged the legitimacy and reasonableness of Christian's claim. Although they differ as to the reasons adduced, they also agree that he wanted a postponement of the matter for two years, until Mary Stewart, who had been transferred to France as his prospective daughter-in-law, would come of age.[61]

On 5 January Arran answered in the name of Mary 'ex oppugnatione Brochticrag'. He explained the lack of an earlier answer by war events which, as he said, had also made it impossible for him to search the archives or to keep a council, so that an opinion could be formed in the matter. After having appealed to Christian's understanding of the difficult situation during Mary's minority he promised, however, to send a fully instructed ambassador in March.[62] And thus an unexpected opportunity arose for Rothes to realise his intentions and revisit Denmark.

During the past three years he had maintained his position as a trusted friend of the government. On the other hand he had not completely forgotten his English sympathies, which might still be revived in straitened circumstances. On one occasion he even seems to have asked assurance from the English.[63] But this happened in March 1548, after the battle of Pinkie, but before the arrival of the French expeditionary forces. At that time Arran himself seems to have been wavering, and he even contemplated using Rothes to get into contact with the English.[64] At the end of May a French army landed, and on 7 July, during the siege of Haddington, a parliament was held, in which the conveyance to France of Queen Mary was unanimously agreed. Rothes was present and participated in the solemn reception of the sieur d'Essé, who was the representative of the French king and commander of the French forces.[65] Nevertheless, in August he was still considered susceptible to English bribery,[66] although in November he was ordered to prepare for resistance against an English fleet approaching Dundee.[67]

---

[60] RA, TKUA Frankrig, A6.

[61] Cragius, Annales, 327, 333; Krag, Historie, i, 335–6, 342–3.

[62] RA, TKUA Skotland, 1 and 7 (cf. n. 58) Arran still styles himself in the same way, although he had been created duke of Chatelherault already in Feb. 1549.

[63] CSP Scot., i, no. 183.

[64] Ibid., no. 180.

[65] APS, ii, 481–2; Hamilton Papers, ii, 604.

[66] CSP Scot., i, no. 323.

[67] TA, ix, 252.

Being of a suitably high rank and already known to Danish government circles, Rothes was ideally placed to represent his country in this delicate matter of Orkney. On 26 February 1549–50 he was appointed ambassador to Denmark – for renewing the old treaties of peace and alliance. Careful preparations were made, letters were written by Arran to the Scottish customs officer at Elsinore, Alexander Lyell or Sander Leiel; and 1 March Rothes received his credentials from Arran.[68] On 3 March Henri II issued new credentials for Danzay, and on 28 February the queen dowager signed a joint letter of credence for Rothes and Danzay – not specifically mentioning Orkney, only the problem of piracy.[69]

Rothes delivered his instructions at Itzehoe in Holstein on 15 April.[70] After a description of the disasters of more than seven years' warfare with England he stated that James V had given Orkney to his queen as a wedding present, and in consequence it could not be handed over to Denmark at this juncture. Furthermore, after Mary's conveyance to France, no decision could be made without Henri's approval. During the present state of war it would, however, be impossible to carry through the complicated procedure of a Franco-Scottish resolution within the month of May. Besides, it was doubtful if Arran and the parliament had the authority to alienate parts of the country while Mary was still under age. Referring to the bonds of consanguinity, the tradition of alliance, and Christian's general benevolence, an appeal was made to his understanding.

Concerning the permanent problem of piracy Rothes emphasised the Scots' willingness to see the injured righted. Attention was drawn to the fact that the English had sometimes sent out ships manned with Scottish renegades to commit piracies in order to spoil the reputation of Scotland. Much importance was attached to a possible renewal of the alliance, especially if it could be made to comprehend the liberty of commerce and reciprocal rights of customs-free exports.[71] Finally Rothes asked Christian to make approaches to the emperor concerning the conclusion of a peace.

Whatever the reason, the Danish government delayed its reply. On 1 June Rothes wrote a pathetic letter to Christian, in which he asked him to do something in the matter.[72] To please him, he had stayed such a long time in Denmark to the great detriment of his own fortunes. He had received letters from Scotland in which he was accused of negligence and

---

[68] Original of the letter patent in RA, the parchment collection (oak chests), no. 49, Skotland, no. 38 c; copy in TKUA Skotland, 7 (cf. n. 58); Macray, 'Second report', 63. Credentials in TKUA Skotland, 3 and 7 (cf. n. 58); Macray, 'Second report', 63. TA, ix, 377, 385–7. Concerning Sander Leiel see SHR xlviii, 104–5, xlix, 136.

[69] RA, TKUA Frankrig, A 1; Skotland, 3 and 7 (cf. n. 58).

[70] Instructions and German translation in RA, TKUA Skotland, 3; copy in TKUA Skotland 7 (cf. n. 58).

[71] The main interest was building materials, which were needed so badly that Archbishop Hamilton 1 March 1549–50 made a private approach to Christian in order to secure the right to import timber, probably from Norway, for the reconstruction of St Andrews (RA, TKUA Skotland, 1).

[72] RA, TKUA Skotland, 3 and 7 (cf. n. 58).

indifference to his duties, since he had not yet brought back an answer. According to his own account, dangerous suspicions were already being held against him. Most urgently he asked for an answer.

On 13 June Rothes had at length an interview with some of the Danish councillors, and on 14 June he wrote an elaborate answer to their representations.[73] In this he maintained that both legal and moral considerations must necessitate a postponement of the Orkney question until Mary came of age, which, he said, would happen in three years and four months. After that Christian could of course have all his wishes fulfilled. Concerning the piracy he must ask the Danes to send specially instructed representatives with written indictments to Scotland, so that those guilty could be found. As for the renewal, or rather the continuation of the alliance, it is quite clear that he was speaking of a practical entente, which might be more or less formally instituted. His suggestion of a renewal was in fact just as much a complaint that the Danes had broken the existing practical entente, among other things by collecting new and heavy customs from the Scots. He pressed very hard for special permission for the Scots to import just a few cargoes of oak timber, and expressed his gratitude for the promises of Danish approaches to the emperor.

The Danish answer is dated 21 June. It is preserved in two versions, of which one is long and polite, while the other is shorter and less curcum-locutional.[74] Essentially they say the same.[75] Although Christian's right was considered incontestable, the postponement was granted on the following conditions: the Scottish authorities should within a year send either solid legal reasons for doubting their validity or authoritative guarantees that no further respite would be required than the one mentioned by Rothes. If neither of these conditions was fulfilled within a year, the islands should be delivered at once. Of this part of the answer a special copy was made, on which Rothes had to testify in his own handwriting that he had received it.[76] A formal renewal of the alliance was not considered advisable as long as the Orkney question was not settled, especially if the reason was to be unjustly alleged Danish breaches of the old alliance. Nothing like that had happened – apart from possible individual infringements, which would be prosecuted if proper charges were made. The customs mentioned were a royal prerogative, and Christian did not remember that special liberties had ever been given to the Scots in that respect. But if it could be proved, they would be respected. The oak timber was badly needed by Christian's own countries, and the Scots were asked to content themselves for a short time with other kinds of wood. And finally it was confirmed that the Danish

[73] RA, TKUA Skotland, 3 and 7 (cf. n. 58).

[74] 'Responsum Georgio a Rothes' occupies well over 15 pages and 'Alia brevis . . . declaratio' $6\frac{1}{2}$, both in the copy-book mentioned n. 58. Another copy of the short version in RA, TKUA Almindelig del, i, 16. Excerpts in TKUA England, A 1.

[75] Apparently it is a copy of the copies which were despatched and has been preserved in BM Add. MS. 14854, fos. 7r–21v.

[76] RA, TKUA Skotland, 3. Copy in 7 (cf. n. 58).

government would gladly be instrumental in bringing about peace negotiations between Scotland and the emperor.

The tactics of delay had thus proved successful, simply because the islands were too remote from Denmark to justify a war.[77] Rothes probably left Denmark in July, carrying a letter from Christian to Arran of 29 June, in which flattering remarks about Rothes were made, while apologies and explanations were given for the late answer, and appeals were made to Arran's sense of equity and justice.[78] But together with Rothes went a Scot in Danish service, who called himself Jacobus Deidonanus – James of Dundee. In a letter received at Kolding in February 1551 this acute observer could already tell Christian that the Scots would probably never give any other answer.[79] And next June when Arran informed Christian that he had been included in the peace between Scotland and the emperor, he also told him that he would certainly not give any guarantees during Mary's minority.[80] Ahead lay more than a century of fruitless Danish démarches.

Rothes had thus discharged his task in a way which could not possibly be unsatisfactory to his employers. As for his Danish contacts, it cannot be ascertained whether they blamed him personally for the indisputable dissimulation embodied in his whole mission, or whether they distinguished between his office and his person. In all probability he never saw Denmark again.

One single piece of evidence may indicate a certain Danish disappointment in Rothes. Spottiswoode relates that Norman Leslie in 1550 on his release from imprisonment in France went home to Scotland, 'but fearing the governor, he went into Denmark, where not finding that kind reception which he expected, he betook himself to England'.[81] In the Danish chancery

[77] It is hardly conceivable that the Danish government ever really contemplated a military action. It is true that Krag has some dubious sentences (Cragius, *Annales.* 327; Krag, *Historie*, i, 335), but considering their lack of clarity and the context of the whole diplomatic situation, they cannot warrant H. F. Rørdam's understanding that Christian was planning an expedition in order to repossess the islands with force (*Historiske Samlinger og Studier*, iii (Copenhagen, 1898), 262, retold by Alfred Richard, *Un diplomate poitevin du XVI siecle* (Poitiers, 1910), 38). According to Stephanius a Danish fleet actually did go out in 1554, which consequently gave rise to some rumours, also concerning Scotland. His own account is, however, quite clear. The fleet was directed against French and Scottish privateers. Orkney is not even mentioned, and, incidentally, nothing was achieved (Cragius, *Annales,* 368; Krag, *Historie*, i, 375).

[78] RA, TKUA Skotland, 7 (cf. n. 58); cf. *TA*, ix, 428.

[79] RA, TKUA Skotland, 3; identifiable from the hand-writing of his reports to Anders Bille of 19 April 1552 (Erik Kroman, *Privatarkiver før 1660 i Rigsarkivet* (Copenhagen, 1948), 11; Macray, 'Second report', 68) and to the king of 1 June and 10 July 1552 (RA, TKUA England, 38; Macray, 'Third report', 43). Cf. *Acts Privy Council*, iii (1891), 370, 377, 467; iv (1892), 34, 47, 58, 81; *CSP Foreign, Edw. VI and Mary*, i, 217.

[80] RA, TKUA Skotland, 3 and 7 (cf. n. 58); Cragius, *Annales*, 351–2; Krag, *Historie*, i, 359–60.

[81] John Spottiswoode, *History of the Church of Scotland*, i (Bannatyne Club, 1847), 177–8; cf. Leslie, *Historie*, ii, 352.

books there is actually a note of 21 June 1551, saying that 'Normand Leslige af Skotlandt' has been given a safe conduct, so that he may freely come to Denmark, stay there, and leave the country when the king will not allow him to stay there any more.[82] Spottiswoode's remark may reflect a certain Danish animosity towards a son of the man who had done his work so well.

In conclusion a comparison may be drawn between the attitudes of the Danish governments in the two cases of fugitive Scottish earls, separated by only twenty years – Rothes and Bothwell. In both cases the governments seem to have practised as far as possible that time-honoured principle of non-interference. However, as the two fugitives were of such high rank and so deeply embroiled in internal political upheavals an absolute neutrality could not be maintained. In each case the fugitive was detained. Regarding Bothwell, there was no relaxation of the Scottish government's attitude. Indeed, it asked the Danish government to let its representatives behead him in Copenhagen and bring his head to Scotland. The most neutral attitude the Danish government could take in that situation was not to grant the request, but to keep him detained. And so Bothwell ended his days as a madman in a Danish prison. In Rothes's case the enmity of the Scottish government was somehow replaced by an agreement of close co-operation. As long as there could be doubts of the sincerity of that shift, the Danes hesitated. As soon as they were convinced, they allowed him to return to Scotland. And this is exactly the reason why his stay in Denmark, unlike that of Bothwell, has for more than four centuries been consigned to near oblivion.[83]

[82] *Kancelliets Brevbøger*, i, ed. C. F. Bricka (Copenhagen, 1885–6), 49.
[83] Editorial revision has necessitated some changes in the author's presentation of this article, intended both to compress it and to bring it into line with the general approach of this volume. In addition, it has unfortunately also been necessary to leave out some specific points of interest to Scandinavian readers. A fuller version of the same article will shortly appear in English in Denmark, and will be available, as long as it is in stock, on application to Institut for Kirkehistorie, Hovedbygningen, Aarhus Universitet, DK-8000 Århus, Denmark.

THORKILD LYBY CHRISTENSEN

5

Patronage, Provision and Reservation, Pre-Reformation Appointments to Scottish Benefices

The Indult of 1487 provides the key to a study of ecclesiastical patronage in the sixteenth century. This concession accorded to James III by Pope Innocent VIII stipulated that on the occurrence of vacancies in benefices worth more than two hundred gold florins of the camera in cathedral churches and monasteries, the pope would postpone provision for eight months and during that period await supplications from the king and his successors so that 'on receiving intimation, we may the better be able to proceed to the provisions, as we should think expedient'.[1]

This undertaking arising directly from a conflict following papal provisions in 1483 to the bishoprics of Dunkeld and Glasgow which had not been in accord with royal wishes, was not perpetual, but Innocent urged his successors 'that in such provisions they take equal care to observe our practice'.[2] More often than not this advice was followed, but in the confused situation which followed the battle of Flodden, Pope Leo X, though eventually confirming the Indult in January 1518/19, seized the initiative and provided to several consistorial benefices without awaiting intercession.[3] In taking this step, however, Leo was assisted by internal political rivalries in Scotland between supporters and opponents of the queen mother, Margaret Tudor. Such squabbles were not infrequent during the troubled royal minorities of the first half of the sixteenth century and provided the opportunity for successive popes, even within the terms of the Indult, to support a rival candidate, or on occasions to provide a nominee of their own choosing.[4] English intervention likewise allowed the papacy a certain

[1] J. Herkless and R. K. Hannay, *Archbishops of St. Andrews* (Edinburgh, 1907-15), i, 157-8.
[2] J. Dowden, *The Bishops of Scotland*, (Glasgow, 1912), 78-80, 329-31; Herkless and Hannay, *Archbishops of St. Andrews*, i, 158.
[3] C. Eubel, *Hierarchia Catholica Medii Aevi*, 2nd edn. (Munster, 1913-23), iii, 108; *The Letters of James V*, edd. R. K. Hannay and D. Hay (Edinburgh, 1954), 31, 36-7, 41, 71-2.
[4] D. E. R. Watt, *Fasti Ecclesiae Scoticanae Medii Aevi* (Scottish Record Society, 1969), 296-8; *James V Letters*, 12-19, 23-4.

manœuvrability and it appears to have been the rejection, at the instance of Henry VIII, of presentations made by the governor, the Duke of Albany, to the abbacy of Melrose and bishopric of Moray which led to an act of November 1526 in which the Scottish parliament claimed that 'quhen prelacyis sic as bischeprykis or abbacys hapnis to vaik the nominacioun thairof pertens to our soverane lord and the provision of the sammyı. ‑o our haly fader the paip'.[5] The royal right of nomination was expressly admitted by Pope Paul III who at the same time extended the period of delay in awaiting supplication to twelve months.[6] Nonetheless, while this further concession may have compromised further independent action by the papacy, provisions contrary to royal will brought about by political uncertainty in Scotland remained a feature of the system.

Irrespective of the nature of the concessions made to the crown, papal claims to provision were always safeguarded and with them the right to the common services which continued to be rendered to the papal camera without opposition until the Reformation.[7] Delay in nomination for eight or latterly twelve months did mean, however, less speedy payments of these taxes and to this extent placed the papacy at an evident disadvantage. On the other hand, maximum delay should have proved financially advantageous to the crown as during a vacancy the crown not only enjoyed the temporalities of such benefices, but also, in the case of bishoprics, rights of presentation *sede vacante*.[8] Despite these apparent advantages, benefices were seldom kept vacant for the full term allowed, even under the eight month rule. There was no doubt a risk of an unwelcome provision if a benefice was unfilled for too long, while on grounds of expediency a benefice filled by a member of the royal family or granted under heavy pensions might be more lucrative in the long run as both spiritual and temporal revenues were available to an occupant.[9]

As far as bishoprics were concerned, no set pattern is discernible. Kinship certainly helped to minimise delays in appointment and although the nominations of both Stewart archbishops of St Andrews were withheld for some four to five months, William Stewart, son of Sir Thomas Stewart of Minto, was nominated to the see of Aberdeen only twelve days after the death of his predecessor.[10] If the provision of Andrew Stewart to Caithness was delayed for some eight months after the death of John Sinclair in 1501, two subsequent Stewart holders of this bishopric were appointed with only a month's delay at each vacancy.[11] Speedy appointments frequently arose from resignation in favour or from the appointment of a coadjutor, both effected

[5] Ibid., 127; *APS*, ii 309-10.

[6] R. Keith, *History of Affairs of Church and State* (Spottiswoode Society, 1844-50), i, 461-4.

[7] Obligationes et Solutiones (Vatican Archives), 91, fo. 121.

[8] See G. Donaldson, 'The Rights of the Scottish Crown in Episcopal Vacancies' in *SHR*, xlv (1966), 27-35.

[9] Ibid., 33.

[10] Watt, *Fasti*, 4, 296; Dowden, *Bishops*, 35-8, 139-41.

[11] Watt, *Fasti*, 60-1; Dowden, *Bishops*, 247-50.

during the previous bishop's lifetime. The succession of Chisholms at Dunblane, without any apparent intervention from the crown, between 1487 and 1569, owed its success to these devices.[12] The appointment of coadjutors, in this instance by the crown, seems to have ensured continuity in the bishopric of Orkney between 1498 and 1526 and royal nominations thereafter appear to have been made with the minimum of delay.[13] This was also the case in the Isles before 1514, and although the complexities of the succession after that date render the situation obscure, crown presentations were not unduly delayed if two or three months is taken as the norm.[14] This was also true in most other dioceses. The pattern of nomination in the bishopric of Ross reveals a situation in which little over a month separates one bishop from his predecessor, and in Galloway too, the succession was equally stable until the eve of the Reformation.[15] At Aberdeen likewise a two-month interval which arose between the death of William Elphinstone and the nomination of George Learmonth appears to have been the longest hiatus.[16]

These three sees were also remarkably free from succession disputes, but this may have been a matter of chance as none of these bishoprics fell vacant during the political power struggles which were most the frequent cause of delays in appointment. In Moray, which despite apparent difficulties in the appointment of Robert Shaw in 1525, had hitherto experienced vacancies of less than two months, a crisis arose following upon Shaw's death in 1527. The nomination of Archibald Douglas by the earl of Angus seems to have been postponed for several months and further delay was occasioned by the earl's fall from power.[17] In consequence the provision of Robert Stewart, following upon crown nomination, did not take place until some two years after the death of his predecessor.[18] Thereafter, the normal pattern was resumed, Stewart's successor being nominated some two months after his death.[19]

At Glasgow and St Andrews, the situation was equally complicated by disputes. In the early sixteenth century Glasgow presented few problems, for with the exception of a delay of three months in nominating Blackadder's successor, which can be attributed to the circumstances of his death en route for the Holy Land, vacancies were of unexceptional length.[20] With the rejection of the nomination of James Hamilton in 1548, ostensibly because of his illegitimacy, but in practice as part of the power struggle between the earl of Arran and Mary of Guise, uncertainty prevailed and some eighteen months elapsed before the nomination of James Beaton paved the way for his ultimate success.[21] Short delays in nominating are also apparent at St

[12] Watt, Fasti, 77–8; Dowden, Bishops, 207–8.
[13] Watt, Fasti, 253–4; Dowden, Bishops, 263–8.
[14] Watt, Fasti, 204–5; Dowden, Bishops, 290–3.
[15] Watt, Fasti, 132, 269–70; Dowden, Bishops, 222–30, 370–5.
[16] Watt, Fasti, 3–4; Dowden, Bishops, 129–43.
[17] Watt, Fasti, 216–7; Dowden, Bishops, 163–71.
[18] Watt, Fasti, 217; Dowden, Bishops, 170.
[19] Watt, Fasti, 217; Dowden, Bishops, 171–2.
[20] Watt, Fasti, 49–50; Dowden, Bishops, 331–52.
[21] Watt, Fasti, 149–50; Dowden, Bishops, 349–52.

Andrews where the choice of James and Alexander Stewart was followed by
a many-sided contest in 1513/14 initiated by Leo X's provision of his nephew
Innocenzo Cibo as administrator of the see on 13 October 1513 and then by
the nomination of other contestants supported on the one hand by Margaret
Tudor and on the other by the magnates who favoured Albany as governor.[22]
The ultimate triumph of Andrew Forman brought this contest to an end, but
on his death in 1521 a further eight months was to elapse before the
nomination of James Beaton as his successor.[23] The appointment of his
nephew David as coadjutor avoided a similar problem on his uncle's death in
1539, and following upon Beaton's own assassination in 1546, the almost
immediate grant of the temporalities to John Hamilton heralded a return to
normality even though his actual appointment was not fully effective until
June 1549.[24]

In both 1521 and 1549 the prolongation of the vacancy may have been
deliberate as no other circumstances seem to have intervened. This was also
the case in the dioceses of Argyll and Brechin in both of which long vacancies
became commonplace. In the former, vacancies apparently uncomplicated
by the presence of other contestants occurred in 1496, 1523 and 1538 and
resulted in gaps of thirteen, twenty and five months respectively, an
exchange of benefices breaking this pattern in 1553.[25] The Brechin vacancies
were of a less extreme nature, but in 1516 a vacancy of seven months
occurred, followed by another of six months before the nomination in 1557 of
Donald Campbell, who in the event never effectively held the bishopric.[26]

In the case of monasteries, the length of vacancies is more difficult to
determine. Long vacancies were certainly not unknown and the wealthy
abbey of Arbroath was kept vacant between the death of George Hepburn at
Flodden on 9 September 1513 and the provision of James Beaton, archbishop
of Glasgow as commendator on 2 December 1517. Beaton paid part of the
common services on 17 January 1518 but was not admitted to the
temporalities until 18 March.[27] Such a long vacancy, without the pressure of
other competitors, does appear to have been unusual, and nomination usually
followed quickly upon a vacancy. A variety of causes may have contributed
to this end. Laymen could be nominated *in commendam* to monastic benefices
which were thus available to the crown as a means of providing for its own
illegitimate offspring or rewarding other faithful servants.[28] In such circumstances pensions could be more readily imposed upon those who held
monastic benefices. Finally, and perhaps not least important, the possibility

[22] Watt, *Fasti*, 296–8, Dowden, *Bishops*, 38–9.

[23] Watt, *Fasti*, 298; Dowden, *Bishops*, 39–41.

[24] Watt, *Fasti*, 298; Dowden, *Bishops*, 41–4.

[25] Watt, *Fasti*, 27; Dowden, *Bishops*, 387–91.

[26] Watt, *Fasti*, 41; Dowden, *Bishops*, 189–91.

[27] Acta Vicecancellarii in Vatican Archives, 2, fo. 39v; Introitus et Exitus in
Vatican Archives, 557, fo. 108v; *RSS*, i no. 2975.

[28] *Vetera Monumenta Hibernorum et Scotorum Historiam Illustrantia*, ed. A. Theiner
(Rome, 1864), no. mxxx.

of intrusion by other candidates appears to have been greater in the case of monastic benefices than bishoprics.

This fear had certainly not been allayed by the Indult, and even before disaster at Flodden gave Leo X an opportunity to reassert papal authority, controversies were raging over the headship of several religious houses. The *cause célèbre* was a dispute over Melrose between David Brown and Bernard Bell which raged for twenty years and more after the Indult. The former had been provided shortly before the Indult on 1 September 1486, but the convent relying apparently on a privy seal writ of 5 November 1463 affirming their right to elect the abbot had successively elected three monks, the last of whom was Bell and to whom James III apparently gave his support. In consequence, Bell also obtained provision and retained possession of the abbacy despite litigation in Rome by Brown, who continued to pursue his case against William Turnbull in whose favour Bell had resigned at the turn of the century.[29] In order to resolve the difficulty James IV on 1 October 1506 nominated Robert Beaton, abbot of Glenluce as abbot and asked for the claims of Turnbull and Brown to be extinguished.[30] This was not easily achieved; Turnbull was placated by translation to Coupar-Angus, but Brown did not resign his claims until the grant of a pension in 1510.[31]

Similar disputes abounded in the period after Flodden. At Glenluce, the pope ignored a crown request to confer the commendatorship of the abbey upon David Hamilton, bishop of Lismore and provided instead the Cardinal of St Eusebius.[32] The cardinal in turn resigned but decided in so doing to back the claims of Alexander Cunningham who had been elected by the monks and confirmed in his appointment by the father abbot of the Cistercian order.[33] The ensuing controversy was long and litigious and was resolved only by the seizure and imprisonment of Cunningham who was eventually prevailed upon to surrender his rights on 7 June 1516, although litigation continued thereafter.[34] In this case local interests obviously played a major part in the dispute, for Cunningham was a cousin of the earl of Glencairn who actively supported his cause.[35] Further controversies between 1544 and 1547 characterise the history of this house and other monasteries in Ayrshire and the south-west such as Crossraguel, Kilwinning and Soulseat.[36] At Tongland

---

[29] *The Letters of James IV 1505–13* edd. R. K. Hannay and R. L. Mackie (SHS, 1953), nos. 48–50; Registra Supplicationum in Vatican Archives, 917, fo. 169v; 929, fo. 13v; 931, fo. 286; 953, fo. 222v; 958 fos. 299 r–v.

[30] *James IV Letters*, nos. 48–51.

[31] *James IV Letters*, nos. 91–2, 311, 335.

[32] *James V Letters*, 3, 13, 31, 71–2.

[33] Ibid., 31.

[34] ADCP, 10, 22, 34, 67–8; *Statuta Capitulorum Generalium Ordinis Cisterciensis* 1116 – ed. J. M. Canivez (1933) 1518, no. 84.

[35] For fuller details, see *Wigtownshire Charters* ed. R. C. Reid (SHS, 1960), 44–6.

[36] *Archaeological and Historical Collections relating to Ayrshire and Galloway* (1878–99), i, 180–3; *Charters of the Abbey of Crosraguel* (AHCAG, 1886), i, no. 41; *Wigtownshire Charters*, 95–8.

likewise, various proposals were made in 1529 for the disposition of the abbey until annexation to the bishopric of Galloway was adopted as a solution to the problem.[37] At Whithorn too, difficulties had arisen at an earlier date owing to the provision by Leo X of Silvio, cardinal of Cortona in opposition to the crown's nominee, Alexander Stewart, Albany's natural brother.[38] Although the governor took a strong line and informed the pope that Scottish interests would not let him have the priory even if he won his case in Rome, Silvio maintained his right which he eventually ceded to Ninian Fleming, then a boy of fifteen on 19 May 1525.[39] In the event some compromise seems to have been reached as on 8 July 1525, Gavin Dunbar was provided following the resignation of Silvio, but on Dunbar's provision to the see of Glasgow in 1533, Ninian Fleming was then nominated as commendator in July or August of that year. By this stage, however, another contender had appeared in the person of Abraham Vaus, provided on 26 July 1532.[40] His efforts to obtain the priory brought bitter complaints from James V, and Fleming's claims to the priory were eventually recognised.[41]

Such disputes appear to have punctuated the history of most Scottish abbeys during the first half of the sixteenth century. Political rivalries continued to foment discontent as at Paisley in 1548/9 when the Angus faction attempted to prevent Claud Hamilton succeeding his uncle as commendator, but on other occasions sheer opportunism on the part of petitioners seems to have been the motivating force.[42] The suit of David Douglas, who was provided to Holyrood on 15 July 1530, was clearly of this nature but he sustained litigation against Robert Cairncross, whom he claimed was the intruder, for at least a year, if without any apparent success.[43] Papal intervention seems to have diminished thereafter although Pope Paul III made a determined effort to obtain the wealthy abbey of Dryburgh for the blind archbishop of Armagh and distinguished theologian, Robert Wauchope. He was provided by the pope on 8 November 1539, one day after James V nominated Thomas Erskine, but protests by the king on 22 February and 4 May 1540 led to provision for the royal candidate on 6 May 1541. Nevertheless, Wauchope continued the struggle until at least 1544.[44] Such challenges to royal authority ensured that the maintenance of the Indult depended upon the continual vigilance of the crown.

If disputes over the headship of major monastic foundations were not

[37] James V Letters, 153–4, 161–2; Reg. Supp., 1980, fo. 203v; Registra Vaticana in Vatican Archives, 1403, fos. 137–40.

[38] James V Letters, 36–7, 41, 48–9.

[39] Ibid., 64–6, 70–1, 73–5, 80, 84; Reg. Supp., 1820, fos. 202 and v; 1850, fos. 235 and v.

[40] Watt, Fasti, 149, James V Letters, 246–7.

[41] Reg. Supp., 2086, fos. 244 and v.

[42] James V Letters, 246–7; Reg. Supp., 2157, fos. 73 and v.

[43] Ibid., 2029, fos. 137v–138; 2049, fos. 244 and v.

[44] Ibid., 2354, fos. 212 and v; Reg. Vat., 1694, fos. 244 and v; James V Letters, 380, 392–3, 398; Reg. Lat., 1730, fos. 16–21v

entirely eliminated in terms of the Indult, the situation at lesser religious houses, and especially priories, remained even more uncertain. The problem appears to have been two-fold, whether the benefice was worth more than two hundred gold florins of the camera, and whether the headship was elective or not. The abbey of Saddell and priory of Beauly appear to have been treated in the fifteenth century as though falling below this value, and in this respect paid annates rather than common services.[45] By 1507, however, Saddell was united to the bishopric of Argyll, and though Beauly was the object of multiple disputes and evidently free of royal interference in the early sixteenth century, the intervention of James V in 1529 seems to have been decisive and the royal will prevailed thereafter.[46] The relationship of priories to their mother house caused equal difficulties. In some cases such as Canonbie and Lesmahagow control by Jedburgh and Kelso respectively seems to have ruled out claims by all but the most intrepid of benefice seekers.[47] This was not so in other dependent priories and Coldingham, Inchmahome, Loch Leven, Monymusk, Pittenweem, Restennet and St Mary's Isle were bedevilled by successive disputes throughout the fifteenth century, the papacy apparently treating them as reserved benefices from which annates were leviable rather than benefices provided in consistory from which common services would have been payable.[48] On the papal side this distinction appears to have been maintained in the sixteenth century, but the crown for its part apparently regarded Coldingham and St Mary's Isle as consistorial benefices.[49] On the other hand Loch Leven, Monymusk, Pittenweem and Restennet for one reason or another seem to have been deemed as lying outside the terms of the Indult.[50] In the long run the distinction may have been academic, for all these priories were racked with internal disputes during the sixteenth century. A controversy was raging at Monymusk in 1524 and no fewer than three rival candidates were seeking Restennet in the early 1530s.[51] In the same period Pittenweem was in dispute between Adam Blackadder and John Roull who had attempted to exchange their priories of Coldingham and Pittenweem only to be thwarted by James

[45] Reg. Supp., 2524, fo. 188v; Beauly was still paying annates rather than common services in 1529; Libri Annatarum in Vatican Archives, 66, fo. 4.

[46] *The Apostolic Camera and Scottish Benefices, 1418–88* ed. A. I. Cameron (Oxford, 1934), 104, 113, 170.

[47] A petition for Lesmahagow by Alexander Alani on 6 and 10 March 1502 (Reg. Supp. 1139, fos. 126, 183–4) is the only petition noted for either of these priories.

[48] For payments or annates by the priories the index to Cameron, *Apostolic Camera* should be consulted; fifteenth-century disputes are analysed in Huisdean Duff, 'An aspect of Scottish Monasticsm: The Houses of the Order of St. Augustine, 1418–1488' (unpublished Glasgow M.Litt. thesis, 1977), 158–223.

[49] *James V Letters*, 315, 317, 334–5; cf. Libri Annatarum, 39, fo. 48; 64, fos. 34v, 67.

[50] Neither James IV or James V appeared to have interfered in succession disputes relating to Loch Leven, Monymusk or Restennet; James V did, however, seek Pittenweem for John Roull in 1534 (Reg. Supp. 2132, fos. 94 and v).

[51] Reg. Supp., 1815, fos. 219 and v; 2079, fos. 30–1; 2013, fo. 94; 2054. fo. 50; 2065, fos. 253 and v; 2078, fos. 101 and v.

V's refusal to accept Roull as prior of Coldingham.[52] The extent to which such disputes continued in the years preceding the Reformation must await a full analysis of the Vatican records, but rival petitions for the priories of Monymusk and St Mary's Isle in 1558 appear to suggest that controversy over these lesser religious houses continued unabated.[53]

If the terms of the Indult did not extend to all religious houses, they were equally inapplicable in respect of all non-elective benefices which were subject to the general rules of reservation. These rights established in the course of the fourteenth century, not only extended the papal rights of disposing of such benefices, but also established a call on the payment of annates, or first fruits, of each benefice so reserved.[54] Of the actual rules those most likely to be invoked related to the death of a benefice holder at, or in the neighbourhood of, the Curia and to the death of a papal chaplain at any time or place, or in Scotland at least through death in one of eight designated months; March, July, September and December being the only four months in which the benefice was still at the patron's free disposal.[55]

These papal rights remained unregulated after 1487. Yet it was perhaps these claims, rather than those of provision which had lain behind James I's acts against barratry for it was the rules of reservation, which might apply to all non-elective benefices, which had led clerks to Rome in the hope that they would gain by litigation either the benefice, or a substantial pension from its fruits. It was this practice which parliament in 1424 had attempted to curb by forbidding clerks to 'purches any pensione out of benefice secular or religious'.[56] Only by special permission of the king, or in 1428 by leave of the diocesan bishop, or royal chancellor, was an overseas journey to be undertaken on pain of various penalties for the crime of 'barratry' or unauthorised dealings at Rome.[57] The provisions of this act were repeated in 1482 and 1484, but no mention of this particular grievance was found in the Indult.[58] The practice continued unabated and legislation of 1496 not only indicates that elective benefices were still the object of unofficial petitions, but also refers to pleas for 'diverse utheris that mycht be gavin and providit within the realme'.[59] On occasions licences were sought and obtained to 'pas to the courte of Rome' or 'to impetrat a pensioun', but these were the exception, rather than the rule; the tide of petitions could not be stemmed and

[52] Ibid., 2035, fos. 289 and v; 2047, fos. 281 and v; 2130, fos. 94 and v, *James V Letters*, 334–5.

[53] Reg. Supp., 2940, fo. 105; 2941, fos. 59 and v; 2963, fos. 290–1.

[54] G. Mollat, *The Popes at Avignon, 1305–78*, translated by Janet Love (London, 1963), 335–42; G. Mollat, Introduction to *Lettres Communes de Jean XXII, 1316–33* (Paris, 1921), 9–17.

[55] *Copiale Prioratus Sanctiandree* ed. J. H. Baxter (Oxford, 1930), 89, 435; *St Andrews Formulare 1514–46*, ed. G. Donaldson and C. Macrae (Stair Society, 1942–4), i, no. 193.

[56] APS, ii, 5.

[57] Ibid., ii, 16.

[58] Ibid., ii, 144, 166.

[59] Ibid., ii, 237–8.

supplications to the pope continued in undiminished numbers until the Reformation.[60]

Such petitions normally sought to establish that the benefice in question was reserved for the pope's disposal and in this respect the determination of the date of death of the previous incumbent might be of vital importance. Thus, James Lauder in seeking the vicarage of Kilmany which lay in the patronage of Dryburgh abbey claimed that the previous possessor died in April or May 1525, while John Thornton in seeking the prebend of Advie and Cromdale in Elgin cathedral established his predecessor's death in November 1526.[61] Similar petitions abound as do the number of consequent provisions.[62] In some instances the suppliants already possessed the benefice in virtue of presentation by the patron and episcopal collation and in such an event petitions were designed to make tenure double sure by the addition of papal provision to already existing rights. Such was the case with Thomas Dickson who petitioned the pope on 1 April 1503; he had been presented to the vicarage of Markinch by the prior and convent of the priory of St Andrews and had received episcopal collation, but doubting the validity of the process, petitioned the pope for provision.[63]

The majority of petitions, however, were not of this confirmatory character, but rather stemmed from benefice seekers who hoped to oust the patron's nominee in favour of themselves. Patrons, both lay and clerical, suffered in this manner, and not always directly at the hands of the pope, for the papacy could on occasions delegate its rights to others. In this way, James Hay, bishop of Ross was permitted on 8 March 1527 to present to benefices in his diocese in all months, while William Stewart, bishop of Aberdeen was allowed on 30 January 1534 to provide to benefices in the church of Aberdeen in the months of February, April, June, August, October and December.[64] The practical results of such concessions are illustrated in a dispute between the archbishop of Glasgow and abbot of Paisley on 12 May 1507 in which it is related that the archbishop had refused presentations by the abbey to the vicarages of Cathcart, Eastwood and Kilmacolm and in each instance had provided candidates of his own choice by virtue of an indult granted to him by Pope Innocent VIII.[65]

The setting aside of patronage rights in this fashion was, nevertheless, more frequently the result of direct papal provision and a cross sample of such cases clearly illustrates the uncertainty which faced patrons in this respect. At Aberchirder, the parsonage revenues of the parish church were appropriated to the abbey of Arbroath which on 1 December 1525 presented David

[60] *RSS*, i nos. 999, 2273, 4087; A number of supplications post-date the Reformation, the latest so far noted being a petition on 13 July 1565 for the parish church of Benholm (Reg. Supp., 3154, fo. 297; cf. *RSS*, v, no. 2036).

[61] Reg. Supp., 1872, fo. 141v; 1921, fo. 69.

[62] Ibid., 1947, fos. 88 and v; 1952, fo. 118 and v.

[63] Ibid., 1162, fos. 9 and v.

[64] Ibid., 1920, fo. 270; 2130, fo. 82.

[65] *Prot. Book Cuthbert Simson*, i, nos. 229-32.

Cristesoun to the vicarage vacant by the death of Alexander Symson.[66] This was quickly countered in Rome by the provision of James Brown on 8 January 1526 to be followed a day later by the provision of Robert Gray.[67] The abbey in the face of this challenge compounded the problem by presenting two further candidates – James Scrimgeour, canon of Lismore on 18 March 1526 and Thomas Coutts, official of Lothian on 21 December of the same year.[68] Shortly before the last of these presentations, yet another contestant John Thornton had ceded a right which he had acquired in the benefice to John Innes, clerk in Moray diocese.[69] The process by which the competing claims were resolved is not clear, but Innes evidently prevailed and appears as deceased vicar on 2 June 1547.[70] In consequence the crown presented Robert Hamilton, *sede vacante*, but in the background lurked John Thornton, junior, to whom John Thornton, senior, had ceded on 9 October 1546 rights which he had apparently still retained.[71] On this occasion Thornton was the victor, although the appearance of yet another John Innes as his vicar pensioner adds another dimension to this tangled web of presentations.[72] What is clear is that Arbroath's wishes in this matter seem to have played little part in the outcome of these disputes. This too was the situation at Banchory-Ternan, also vacant by the death of Alexander Symson and to which the abbot and convent of Arbroath presented James Symson on 1 December 1525.[73] Rival candidates appeared in the shape of Alexander Spittal provided on 23 December and James Lindesayage or Knokis provided on 9 January 1526.[74] John Innes also appeared as a competitor and was litigating in the Curia with Symson on 10 January 1527 when he was re-provided to the benefice.[75] In the event Spittal appears to have been successful as on 1 February 1530, he resigned on exchange with Thomas Currar, prebendary of Auchendoir in Aberdeen cathedral, who was thereupon presented to the vicarage by the abbot and convent of Arbroath.[76] Not all cases were so complex and on occasions the abbey's wishes were apparently respected and unopposed, as in successive presentations to the vicarage of Tarves.[77] Whether this was because the rules of reservations did not apply is uncertain and more specific information about the previous incumbents and their date of death or resignation would be required before this could be ascertained.

Other abbeys had equal difficulties. In 1531 the abbot and convent of

[66] I. B. Cowan, *The Parishes of Medieval Scotland* (SRS, 1967), 1; *Liber S. Thome de Aberbrothoc* (Bannatyne Club, 1848–56), ii, no. 611.

[67] Reg. Supp., 1879, fo. 34v, 100v–101.

[68] *Arbroath Liber*, ii, nos. 615, 635.

[69] Reg. Supp., 1904, fos. 157 and v.

[70] *RSS*, iii, no. 2301.

[71] Resignationes: series A in Vatican Archives, 107, fos. 167v–8.

[72] *RMS*, iv, nos. 1208, 1963.

[73] *Arbroath Liber*, ii no. 610.

[74] Reg. Supp., 1879; fos. 100v, 182.

[75] Ibid., 1916, fos. 245v–246.

[76] *Arbroath Liber*, ii, no. 739.

[77] Ibid., ii, nos. 589, 789, 798.

Dunfermline presented David Young to the vicarage of Cleish, lying within their patronage, and he subsequently received episcopal collation.[78] Nevertheless, an adversary appeared in the person of Thomas Horne who obtained papal provision.[79] Despite royal intervention on Young's behalf on 21 March 1531, Horne was re-provided on 19 October.[80] Young in turn was re-presented by Dunfermline in March 1533, but litigation between the contenders was only halted by Horne's death in August or September.[81] Far from settling the issue, however, this brought forth further claimants in the shape of John Duncanson, Thomas Brown and Alexander Duncan, all of whom had obtained provision on Horne's death.[82] Brown disappears from the case thereafter, but the other two litigants harried Young in Rome for many years and as late as 11 September 1538 the king complained on Young's behalf that Alexander Duncan, relying on financial support from John Duncanson, had reduced Young to extreme poverty by their malicious persecution.[83] It would seem that Young had possession, but his tenure was far from peaceful.

Canons regular who served vicarages of churches appropriated to their religious houses were not immune from such intrusion. The vicarage of the parish church of St Cuthbert, Edinburgh, was normally served by the Augustinian canons of Holyrood to which the church was appropriated.[84] Yet the decease shortly before 3 July 1534 of the vicar George Donan, who had intruded against the rule, was followed by further conflict in which another secular priest, Richard Bothwell sought the vicarage.[85] The outcome on this occasion is uncertain but on the death of the incumbent before 28 July 1538, the abbot and convent in virtue of a papal indult that cures in the presentation of canons should only be conferred upon canons of the order, chose Nicol Wilkinson, one of their number, as vicar.[86] Nevertheless, James Salmond obtained provision to the benefice at Rome and instigated litigation against Wilkinson.[87] On this occasion James V's plea that the pope 'restrain this litigious person and give no opening to infringe papal privileges and royal statutes' appears to have prevailed.[88] Nevertheless, on Wilkinson's death in 1547, the crown *sede vacante* presented two rival secular priests to this

[78] Reg. Supp., 2010, fos. 266v–267. This is a new provision dated 21 May 1530; the presentation and original provision took place in 1528/9 (*James V Letters*, 191, 332, cf. 351).

[79] Reg. Supp., 1992, fo. 261; 2010, fos. 267 and v.

[80] *James V Letters*, 191; Reg. Supp., 2061, fos. 282v–3.

[81] *Registrum de Dunfermelyn* (Bannatyne Club, 1842), no. 518; Reg. Supp., 2108, fo. 211; 2130, fo. 94v.

[82] Ibid., 2120, fos. 169 and v; 2123, fos. 339 and v; 2127, fos. 284 and v, 2130, fo. 94v.

[83] *James V Letters*, 351.

[84] Cowan, *Parishes*, 177.

[85] Reg. Supp., 2143, fo. 118.

[86] *James V Letters*, 348.

[87] Ibid., 349.

[88] Ibid., 349.

benefice, one of whom Robert Hamiltown, son of James Hamiltown of Stanehows eventually obtained the living.[89]

Not only monasteries faced this problem; other ecclesiastical patrons were equally in danger. At Tealing, the perpetual vicarage was in the presentation of the archdeacon of Dunkeld, but his presentee William Lyell had not only to seek a new provision on 6 March 1534, but face rival claimants in the shape of James Brown and John Gardyn both provided by the pope on 1 June of that year.[90] Lay patrons were equally at risk and on 14 February 1533 litigation was taking place between James Melvill and Alexander Howe over the parsonage of Kirkgunzeon in the patronage of the Lord of Terregles.[91] Cathedral prebends were equally vulnerable and a dispute between Robert Erskyn and Henry White over the canonry and prebend of Glenbervie in the cathedral of Brechin and which lay in the patronage of the Douglases of Glenbervie was only finally resolved on 6 July 1525 by the grant of a pension of fourteen pounds to White.[92] Settlements in this form were commonplace and no doubt resulted in much bargaining, as exemplified in the case of Patrick Forrest, a litigant over the parish church of Tannadice who on 12 April 1532 ceded his rights to John Campbell for a pension of eighty marks Scots payable in the parish church of Haddington, but three days later again ceded his rights for a similar sum to another of the contestants, James Salmond.[93]

Much of this litigation took place in Rome before the auditors of the sacred Roman Rota, the records of which reveal a stream of litigants and witnesses testifying to the cases before the court.[94] Many of the disputes were, however, heard in Scotland. Thus, John Sanquhar, vicar of Walston, obtained a papal rescript ordering three judges delegate to hear a case between himself and Andrew White who also claimed to be vicar.[95] In another dispute over the vicarage of Bathgate, the litigant James Livingstone sought a copy of apostolic letters directed to judges delegate in 'a case moved against him'.[96] An instance of such procedures in action is seen in the case of Alexander Romannos, chaplain, who had been provided in Rome to the parsonage of Lyne and had attempted to claim possession on his return to Scotland.[97] At the instance of Thomas Muirhead, parson of Lyne he was cited to appear in the chapter house of the cathedral by one of the vicars-general of the Archbishop of Glasgow, but having compeared, he had failed to produce 'the principal provision or collation' without which the vicar-general refused to admit Romannos as parson.[98]

[89] *RSS*, iii, nos. 2487-8.
[90] Reg. Supp., 2133, fo. 186v; 2142 fos. 122, 123v.
[91] Ibid., 2101, fos. 274v-275.
[92] Cowan, *Parishes* 74; Reg. Supp., 1858, fo. 140v.
[93] Ibid., 2077, fos. 12v-13.
[94] J. J. Robertson, 'The Development of the Law' in *Scottish Society in the Fifteenth Century* ed. Jennifer M. Brown (London, 1977), 151-2.
[95] *Protocol Book Cuthbert Simson*, i, 331, 336.
[96] Ibid., i, 353-4.
[97] Ibid., i, 314-9.   [98] Ibid., ii, 315.

Such litigation was usually terminated by a resignation in favour of the successful party to the action; this was at times unconditional, at other times with a right of regress attached and frequently after some form of pension arrangement. In this respect the device of 'resignation in favour' has frequently been misrepresented, for in many cases the resignation was not by an incumbent, but only by a litigant who if his claims or ultimate chance of success were slight might be only too happy to settle for monetary compensation, while on the part of the actual possessors, a pension on the fruits of their benefice might prove infinitely cheaper than the cost of litigation.[99]

If possible, litigation was to be avoided; it was costly, time-consuming, and the outcome frequently uncertain. Devices to ensure the smooth transition of benefices from one incumbent to the next were thus highly favoured. Resignation or exchange of benefices was one way in which this might be achieved, but unless the consent of both patrons involved in such a transaction had been obtained in advance, this in turn might only lead to further litigation. Such exchanges may indeed have been equally planned as a means of thwarting native patronage rights. This appears to have been the case after an exchange in 1507 involving the parish church of Kirkpatrick, for when an alleged presentee of the abbot and convent of Paisley to whom the patronage belonged requested collation from the archbishop of Glasgow, this was refused because 'the said vicarage . . . was in his hands by reason of exchange and not otherwise resigned and demitted'. In consequence he had conferred and provided it to another suitable person, and 'so his pastoral hands with respect to conferring such a vicarage anew were closed'. If the presentee, George Blair, wished to bring the possessor of the vicarage before him, or his officials, or his commissaries, he was, however, willing to hear the allegations of both parties.[100]

In yet another case in 1546 John Thornton senior, without recourse to the patrons Arbroath abbey, resigned his rights in the vicarage of Aberchirder in favour of John Thornton, junior, for a pension of forty marks Scots with privilege of free regress, access or ingress to the vicarage if the incumbent died, resigned or stopped paying the pension.[101] The latter was an important stipulation, for the temptation to cancel such a payment must have been strong. Examples occur from time to time and may be demonstrated by the case of the canonry and prebend of Tarbolton in Glasgow cathedral, the patronage of which lay with the earl of Lennox, and from which a pension of seventy marks had been assigned to James Lennox. The holder of the prebend Robert Crethtown had, however, failed to meet his obligation and Lennox sought his deposition under right of regress on 9 May 1526.[102]

[99] Scottish entries from the Vatican Archives series of *Resignationes et Consensus*, on a study of which these observations are based, are held on microfilm in the Department of Scottish History, University of Glasgow.

[100] *Protocol Book Cuthbert Simson*, i, 392.

[101] Resignationes, series A, 107, fos. 167v–8.

[102] Reg. Supp., 1893, fos. 103v–104.

In this instance the agreement would appear to have stemmed from a resignation in favour designed to avoid a vacancy open to impetrations at Rome and subsequent papal provision. Many such resignations were certainly designed towards this end and the arrangements many and varied, although resignation of the title with reservation of the fruits was possibly the most frequent and certainly the most simple of such agreements. The procedure is seen in practice at Kirkbean in 1512 when the vicar John Hucheson died. Prior to this event, John had resigned his title to the benefice in favour of Richard Hucheson who in turn had resigned the fruits in favour of John, but with right of regress in the event of the death or demission of John who in the meantime was to retain the benefice. On John's death, however, Richard was expected to succeed without opposition, 'no need of new provision being made thereupon'.[103]

Such arrangements may have loosened the incidence of competition stimulated by papal reservations, although in so far as papal approval was sought for such resignations, it is improbable that the interests of the papal camera was adversely effected.[104] The interests of patrons may not have been similarly safeguarded and in consequence not only papal rights of reservation were being bypassed but rights of patronage were also at risk. In this respect the threat to patrons arose not only from papal claims, but also through the legal ingenuity of unscrupulous clerks. A threat from another quarter was to prove equally dangerous as the crown's power over the disposition of benefices slowly but surely increased.

Quite apart from privileges accorded to the crown by the papacy, the ecclesiastical patronage enjoyed by Scottish monarchs in parish churches and prebends in both cathedrals and collegiate churches, including Lincluden, Restalrig, St Mary on the Rock and the Chapel Royal at Stirling, was extensive.[105] In addition patronage might frequently fall to the crown by reason of wardship or forfeiture.[106] In this respect the greatest windfall had occurred in 1493 when the forfeiture of Lord of the Isles brought to the crown not only the patronage of a large number of parish churches in the diocese of the Isles but also the patronage of most, if not all, the churches in the deaneries of Kintyre and Morvern in the diocese of Argyll.[107] If some of this patronage was being re-granted in the course of the early sixteenth century, much of it still remained in crown hands.[108] The retention of patronage in this manner

---

[103] *Protocol Book Cuthbert Simson*, i, 529–30.

[104] Annates were payable to the camera following upon the actual resignation of a benefice; pensions received in virtue of the resignation of a right claimed in a benefice were also subject to annates (Cameron, *Apostolic Camera*, 223–4).

[105] For royal presentations to the headship and prebends and these collegiate churches and cathedral prebends within crown patronage (e.g. Ayr, Crieff, Kincardine O'Neil, Crimond), see indices to *RSS* i–v.

[106] *RSS* i, nos. 245, 474, 507, iii, no. 185.

[107] *Origines Parochiales Scotiae* (Bannatyne Club, 1851–5), II, i, 1–42, 170–209, 210–44, 260–75, 343–62, 370–2, 376–84; *RSS*, i, no. 911.

[108] *RSS*, iii, no. 2963; *Origines Parochiales Scotiae*, II, i, 37.

was perfectly legitimate, but on other occasions the crown arrogated patronage to itself which rightfully belonged to others. On one occasion royal and archiepiscopal interests appear to have clashed following rival presentations to the parsonage of Kirktown in Teviotdale. Initially the presentation by the crown of Archibald Heriot on 23 August 1509 was rejected by the archbishop of Glasgow on 4 September on the grounds that he 'firmly believing that the said rectory was at his collation and disposition, as belonging to him and his successors in full right, and to no one else' had conferred ordinary collation upon another suitable clerk as soon as the vacancy was made known to him, but clearly discretion prevailed and the archbishop citing the actual possessor annulled his previous collation and instead collated Heriot.[109] Somewhat earlier in 1501, the parsonage Cranshaws which lay within the patronage of the Swynton family during the fifteenth century had been annexed, apparently without the patron's consent, to the Chapel Royal at Stirling. Thereafter, the patronage of the church was omitted from confirmations of the barony to the Swyntons until in 1598 it was restored to Robert Swynton of that ilk 'although in divers retours . . . the same was negligently omitted'.[110]

Such opportunities if symptomatic of the crown's interest in utilising the patronage rights of others to its own advantage were necessarily few and far between. A more sustained opportunity of utilising such rights arose through the crown's privileges *sede vacante*. Claims to this end had been made for several centuries and both Alexander II and David II had presented to the common church of Fordyce during episcopal vacancies at Aberdeen.[111] Capitular protests are recorded on both occasions, but the concern expressed seems less with the action itself and more with the fear that the next bishop might in consequence claim the church as pertaining to his *mensa*. If this in itself lends some credence to the idea that *sede vacante* presentations should only extend to churches within the bishop's actual patronage, it is clear that the crown was already extending this definition. A further extension of such rights may be discerned in 1440 when the pope attacked as 'pretended custom', the claim of the king to the 'collations of canonries and prebends and dignities' of the church of Dunkeld during the vacancy of the see.[112] Whether this claim extended to prebends within lay patronage is uncertain, and possibly unlikely, but was undoubtedly far-reaching. Such demands were at first unrecognised but on 24 January 1459/50 in return for the acceptance by James II of a bishop's right to dispose of his moveable goods by testament, the prelates in turn acknowledged the crown's right to the temporalities during the vacancy of a see along with the right to present to benefices in episcopal collation during the same period.[113]

[109] Ibid., I, 337–8; *Protocol Book Simson*, i, 449–50.
[110] Cowan, *Parishes*, 37–8; *RSS*, i, no. 373.
[111] *Registrum Episcopatus Aberdonensis* (Spalding Club, 1845), i, 29–30, 74–5.
[112] *CPL*, ix, 146.
[113] *APS*, ii, 37–8, 61–2, *RSS*, ii, no. 307.

If taken literally the extent of the concession appears remarkably wide since a bishop gave 'collation' to nearly every benefice in his diocese. In consequence, it has been suggested that only benefices already in episcopal patronage were covered by this clause.[114] Whatever the position in the mid-fifteenth century, the evidence for the following century does not support this conclusion. As far as cathedral dignities were concerned, deanships which were elective appear to have been treated as falling within the terms of the Indult and so subject to royal presentations at all times.[115] Other dignities, however, including archdeaconries, were only on the rarest of occasions subject to royal nomination in circumstances other than episcopal vacancies.[116] Bishops were zealous in protecting their own rights of patronage as exemplified at Aberdeen in 1508 when an attempt by the crown to present Thomas Halkerston to the vacant archdeaconry was successfully resisted by the bishop.[117] The crown for its part was equally anxious to preserve its rights *sede vacante* against papal claims to reserve such benefices. This also materialises in the crown's defence of a presentation to the chancellorship of Aberdeen in 1534 and in the forfeiture and deprivation of John Duncanson from the chantership of Glasgow for his 'pretendit purchessing and fleying of the archidenry of Murray in the court of Rome, in hurt and prejudice of his grace's privilege and patronage of the said archidenry *sede Moraviensi vacante*'.[118] Cathedral prebends were treated in a similar fashion, although as far as can be ascertained only prebends in the ecclesiastical patronage of either the bishop, chapter or of religious houses appears to have been claimed.[119] The number of prebends in lay patronage constituted but a small minority of the total, and they do not seem to have been filled by royal presentations except when the patronage lay in royal hands for some other reason, such as wardship.[120]

The position of lay patrons also seems to have been safeguarded in relation to presentations made to parish churches *sede vacante*, for although a few crown presentations to churches in lay or unidentified patronage remain unexplained, none of the remaining eighty-odd parish churches with known lay patrons were effected by such presentations.[121] This was also the case with the holders of prebends whose rights of patronage over the vicarages of the parish churches which constituted their prebends appears, with the exception of unexplained crown presentations to the vicarage pensionaries of Sanquhar on 26 November 1508 and Ashkirk on 23 March 1550, to have remained

---

[114] G. Donaldson, 'Crown Rights in Episcopal Vacancies' in *SHR*, xlv (1966), 34.

[115] Watt, *Fasti*, 8–9, 44–5, 82, 105, 155–6, 220–1, 274–5.

[116] See Watt, *Fasti, passim.*

[117] Watt, *Fasti*, 20.

[118] *James V Letters*, 276–7; *RSS*, ii, no. 2368.

[119] *RSS*, ii, no. 2412; iii, nos. 739, 1126, 2272, 2294.

[120] Ibid., iii, no. 739; presentation belonged to the earls of Atholl (*James V Letters*, 6), but the earl in 1544 appears to have been a minor (*Scots Peerage*, i, 443–4).

[121] A comparative study of these parishes (for which *see* Cowan, *Parishes*, 226 and *passim*), and presentations made under the privy seal supports this conclusion.

unchallenged.[122] Indeed on the granting of collation to the vicarage of Govan on 2 December 1508 the president and chapter specifically recorded that presentation pertained to the prebendary of Govan.[123] If in such cases the crown made no attempt to exercise patronage *sede vacante*, this was equally clearly not the case with parish churches or their vicarages which lay within the patronage of religious houses. An examination of the privy seal register between 1487 and the Reformation reveals over fifty crown presentations to parish churches in the patronage of over twenty monastic houses.[124] The attitude of the religious houses to this erosion of their privileges is not ascertainable and only one counter-presentation has been located. This relates to the vicarage of Newtyle to which on the death of Andrew Howesone, the abbot and convent of Arbroath presented John Androssone to the prior of St Andrews on 22 March 1496/7, the see of St Andrews being vacant.[125] Three months later on 20 June 1497 the crown *sede vacante* presented Sir Henry Kingorne.[126] The outcome is unclear, but as Androssone was later presented by the abbot and convent to the vicarage of Dunbog, it does not appear that his quest for Newtyle was successful.[127] Such presentations may also have been subject to papal reservation, but an examination of this aspect of the problem must await a full analysis of Scottish supplications to Rome. The extent to which royal claims in this respect were constantly followed must also await further examination; a presentation by the abbey of Arbroath to the vicarage of Fyvie *sede vacante* on 17 March 1531/2, for example, has no corresponding presentation under the privy seal.[128] What is clear, however, is that royal claims in this respect had grown considerably and if not as yet threatening the rights of lay patrons had successfully undermined those of ecclesiastical patrons in this particular sector.

Royal claims taken in conjunction with those of the papacy clearly illustrate that patronage rights were in jeopardy during the first half of the sixteenth century. Papal claims to reserve benefices in both lay and ecclesiastical patronage were as strong as ever, and even the Indult had not totally deprived the papacy of its ability to provide to consistorial benefices which had been recognised by successive popes to pertain to royal nomination. If the crown's position in this respect was not as strong as it might have been it had, nevertheless, significantly increased its range of presentations in other directions. In consequence it possessed a far greater degree of patronage in the sixteenth century than it had ever previously commanded. The maintenance of papal rights constituted a perpetual threat

[122] *RSS*, i, no. 1764; iv, no. 612; cf. *Protocol Book Cuthbert Simson*, i, 414.

[123] Ibid., i, no. 414; but on 2 October 1551 presentation to this vicarage is made by the crown *sede vacante* (*RSS*, iv, no. 1367).

[124] *RSS*, i, no. 1034, ii, no. 922, iii, no. 2356, iv, no. 456; v, no. 781 provide a random selection over the period.

[125] *Arbroath Liber*, ii, no. 372.

[126] *RSS*, i, no. 89.

[127] *Arbroath Liber*, ii, no. 406.

[128] Ibid., ii, no. 763; no information is given in the actual presentation that this is made *sede vacante*; the rubric alone adds this detail (ibid., ii, xxxvii).

to that dominance and the Reformation alone ensured absolute rights over the disposal of all major Scottish benefices to the crown. For a time thereafter its right to dispose of other benefices may have been equally strengthened, but in the long run the ultimate effect of the Reformation was to promote the untrammelled exercise of a far greater degree of individual lay patronage than had ever been possible in pre-Reformation Scotland.

IAN B. COWAN

6

The Exercise of Ecclesiastical Patronage
by the Crown, 1560–1572

The success of the Reformation raised the entire issue of the fate of ecclesiastical property. The trend from the Indult of 1487 had been towards the secularisation of this extensive patrimony.[1] After 1560, the protestant reformers sought to arrest such a process with plans for a reorganisation of ecclesiastical finances.[2] Yet the sixteenth-century descendants of pious ancestors were more intent on recouping what had been lost to the 'dead hand'[3] of the church.

During the sixteenth century, the crown and nobility, the lairds and some tenants on ecclesiastical estates had all gained access to the patrimony of the church. This was achieved through taxation of the clergy and through the feuing of church lands, the leasing of the teinds, the reservation to laymen of pensions from parochial and episcopal revenues, and the appointment to abbacies of an *oeconomus*, as steward, or of a commendator, as titular head of a religious house. The church's wealth, estimated to have yielded £400,000 in annual revenues (ten times that of the crown),[4] had been subject to systematic exploitation; and it proved far from easy to stem the drain of ecclesiastical resources.

As the largest owner of property in the kingdom, the pre-reformation church also possessed an extensive patronage of ecclesiastical appointments. During the middle ages, the appropriation of parish churches to higher ecclesiastical institutions meant that the rights of patronage, were usually transferred to the appropriating institution which, on acquiring the

---

[1] G. Donaldson, *The Scottish Reformation* (Cambridge, 1960), 37–43.

[2] *The First Book of Discipline*, ed. J. K. Cameron (Edinburgh, 1972), 108–13, 156–64; *The Booke of the Universall Kirk: Acts and Proceedings of the General Assemblies* [*BUK*], ed. T. Thomson, 3 vols. and appendix vol. (Maitland Club, Edinburgh, 1839–45), i, 5, 7, 21–3, 59–60, 70, 82–4, 107–8, 127–8.

[3] *APS*, i, 612, 614, 725; *The Practicks of Sir James Balfour of Pittendreich*, ed. P. G. B. McNeill, 2 vols. (Stair Society, Edinburgh, 1962–3), i, 142–3. In 1391, parliament had confirmed an act of mortmain prohibiting grants of property to the church without the crown's express consent (*APS*, i, 577).

[4] G. Donaldson, *James V to James VII* (Edinburgh, 1965), 133; cf., *Accounts of the Collectors of Thirds of Benefices, 1561–1572*, ed. G. Donaldson (Scottish History Society, Edinburgh, 1949), xv, 170–1.

patronage of a parish church, became responsible for the presentation of a vicar. Very few parish churches[5] remained unappropriated by the time of the Reformation; and it is safe to conclude that the late medieval church engrossed the patronage of the vast majority of the country's parishes. Only at the higher levels did the crown successfully challenge the church's near monopoly of making ecclesiastical appointments.

Apart from the prelacies where the crown had established its rights of nomination, and with the exception of chaplainries, altarages and certain prebends where laymen retained their rights of patronage, the bulk of ecclesiastical patronage on the eve of the Reformation still remained in the control of ecclesiastical institutions. The extent to which patronage had become concentrated in ecclesiastical hands can be gauged when it is recalled that among the parsonages and vicarages appropriated by 1560 more than 470 benefices pertained to religious houses, over 460 were united to cathedrals, two dozen were assigned to university colleges, some 90 parochial benefices belonged to collegiate kirks and three permanent unions had been made to independent hospitals.[6] In most instances, the patronage of the benefices was likewise annexed, though by the fifteenth century it had become not uncommon for laymen to reserve to themselves the patronage of parochial benefices erected into prebends of cathedral and collegiate kirks; and where monasteries were held *in commendam*, the titular might make presentations to the appropriated churches.[7]

It nonetheless remains curious that, at a time when laymen were gaining control of church lands and revenues, there was little indication of any widespread surrendering to laymen by clergy of the patronage of ecclesiastical benefices. Before the Reformation, it was unusual for feuars of ecclesiastical estates to acquire the patronage of parish churches which, instead, continued to reside with the ecclesiastical superior. Laymen, therefore, were still denied a larger say in the selection of parish priests – indeed their participation in appointments may even have diminished – for in only a small minority of parishes in 1559 was the patron still a layman. Not many laymen were likely to be offended by the reformers' contention in 1560 that 'it appertaineth to the people and to every severall Congregation to elect their Minister'. Indeed, the reformers' aim of abolishing ecclesiastical patronage had obvious attractions for laymen who wished to eliminate the clerical stranglehold of appointments.[8]

Although, as a legal entity, the financial system of benefices survived the Reformation and continued to exist alongside the structure of the reformed church, there was little indication that the two structures might merge through the appointment to benefices of ministers serving in the reformed church. Even though parliament in August 1560 had abolished papal jurisdiction and the celebration of mass, existing benefice holders remained in

---

[5] Cowan, *Parishes*, v.
[6] These calculations are made on the basis of the lists provided in Cowan, *Parishes*.
[7] *Calendar of the Laing Charters*, ed. J. Anderson (Edinburgh, 1899), no. 727.
[8] *First Book of Discipline*, 96 ff.

possession of their livings and continued to enjoy the fruits, apart from a portion assigned to the reformed ministry.[9] Similarly, the intention of the reformers was not to gain access to the benefices but to dismantle the old financial system, abolish patronage, and to reallocate the church's patrimony by separating the spirituality from the temporality. The prospect that the two structures might coalesce remained remote; and reformers in the Book of Discipline disregarded the appeal by the Catholic primate to maintain for their use 'the old policy, which had been the work of many ages'.[10]

It is true that clergy who conformed and accepted service in the reformed church used their benefices in the interests of the new faith, but the majority of clergy, declining to conform, continued to draw their revenues without undertaking service of any kind. The immediate beneficiary of the survival of the ancient financial structure was not the reformed church but the crown which fell heir to a great deal of patronage formerly administered by churchmen. Since continued countenance of papal provision was hard to reconcile with protestant ascendancy, it was easy for the crown to extend its rights of nomination to the prelacies into something more comprehensive. Before the Reformation, most monasteries were held *in commendam*. Not even the Book of Discipline advanced claims for the reformed church to inherit monastic temporalities, and after 1560 the crown assumed full power to appoint commendators and *oeconomi*.[11]

This development was the culmination of a tendency which had emerged in the years immediately before the Reformation; hence the crown's contention in 1557 that, with the death of the commendator, Kelso abbey was 'becuming in oure soverane ladies handis', thereby enabling the crown to appoint an *oeconomus* to administer the spirituality and temporality.[12] Such powers extended well beyond the crown's customary right to dispose of the temporality of abbacies during vacancies. It is true that in the disposal of the property of Pluscarden shortly after the Reformation, Queen Mary reverted to immemorial usage and claimed merely that the temporality of the monastery was at the disposal of the crown, 'sen the deceis of umquhile Maister Alexander Dunbar, last prioure thairof', thus allowing the whole temporality to be assigned to lord Seton, in April 1561, as 'commissar and iconymus of the said prioure'. Yet it is equally true, a mere four months later, that Mary granted Balmerino to John Hay with power to uplift all its revenues. In the former grant, admittedly Seton was to enjoy the revenues only until the vacancy was filled, whereas in the second, Hay was entitled to possess the fruits for life, though his status was evidently considered to be

[9] *APS*, ii, 526-35; *Thirds of Benefices*, ix ff.; *RPC*, i, 201-2.
[10] *First Book of Discipline*, 94, 96 ff., 108 ff., 115 ff., 156 ff., 174 ff.; J. Spottiswoode, *The History of the Church of Scotland*, ed. M. Russell, 3 vols (Spottiswoode Society, Edinburgh, 1851), i, 372.
[11] *RSS*, v. no. 845.
[12] *RSS*, iii, no. 2823; v, nos. 227, 276; Reg. Supp., 2673, fo. 125v.; 2661, fo. 4v.; *Essays on the Scottish Reformation*, ed. D. McRoberts (Glasgow, 1962), 45.

that of *oeconomus,* and not that of commendator, 'albeit he be nocht specialie providit thairof in the . . . courte of Rome, or uthirwayis namit yconomos thairto'.[13] All this became a pattern for some future grants.

In March 1561/2, William Cranstoun, provost of Seton, received a gift of the priory of Pluscarden 'pertening to oure soverane ladeis nominatioun and dispositioun be the privilege of hir croun'. In the week preceding the crown's gift, Cranstoun had also obtained provision at Rome, which was scarcely surprising since he was understood to be 'a great favorer of papystes'. Indeed, in his supplication to the pope he described himself as principal of St Salvator's college, 'ac vere religionis et orthodoxe fidei necnon sedis apostolicae in regno Scotie protector'. In the end, however, he owed his title to the queen's grant.[14] John Hay obtained a similar gift of Monymusk in March 1561/2 though his title was expressly that of 'yconomus'. There was, however, no mention of the spirituality being conveyed in a grant of January 1562/3 to the earl of Argyll of two thirds of the revenues of Coupar abbey (the remaining third being reserved to the crown) which the earl was to enjoy 'als frelie as the said umquhile Donald, last abbot, or ony utheris provydit thairto of befoir mycht have done in tymes bygane'.[15]

The device of appointing *oeconomi* was repeated in December 1563 when Sir Richard Maitland of Lethington and his son, John, were jointly made 'yconomusis, factouris and chalmerlanis of hir hienes abbacie of Hading-toun', with power to 'dispone and apply' the revenues and teinds for 'thair awne use at thair plesour', and, again, in January 1563/4 when John Spens of Condy was chosen *oeconomus* of Coldingham.[16] Nor was it easy to distinguish the office of an *oeconomus* appointed, sometimes for life, to act as an administrator of a vacant abbacy from that of a titular abbot or commendator; and although the forms of appointment differed in the styles adopted, it is evident after 1560 that the offices, in practice, were apt to be confused.

Other vacant abbacies were also at the crown's disposal. In May 1565, the queen granted to Gilbert Brown, 'sumtyme professit bruthir of the abbacy', the abbacy of Sweetheart, whose revenues Brown 'as abbot' was to enjoy, subject to the reservation of certain fruits to the former abbot. Again, in July 1565, the earl of Athol received a gift of the fruits of the abbey of Coupar Angus, 'as the abbot thairof mycht have done' until such time as the vacancy was filled and 'ane abbote be lauchfullie provydit thairto'; and he was further accorded the right of choosing an *oeconomus* to uplift the fruits.[17] Further

[13] *RSS,* v, nos. 819, 845.

[14] Ibid., v, no. 1008; *The Works of John Knox,* ed. D. Laing, 6 vols. (Wodrow Society, Edinburgh, 1846–64), vi, 144; *Register of the Minister, Elders and Deacons of the Christian Congregation of St Andrews,* ed. D. H. Fleming, 2 vols. (Scottish History Society, Edinburgh, 1889–90), i, 169–70; *The Calendar of State Papers relating to Scotland and Mary, Queen of Scots* [*CSP Scot.*], ed. J. Bain et al., 13 vols. (Edinburgh, 1898–1969), i, nos. 1031, 1139; Reg. Supp., 3022, fo. 167r–v; 3032, fo. 36v; 3040, fo. 88r; 3044, fo. 8r.

[15] *RSS,* v, nos. 1009, 1198.

[16] Ibid., v, nos. 1510, 1524.

[17] Ibid., v, nos. 2072, 2229.

dispositions of abbatial property followed. With the death of abbot Quintin Kennedy, Allan Stewart obtained a gift in July 1565 of Crossraguel; in the same month, James Drummond received 'the abbay and benefice' of Inchaffray; in September 1565, Alexander Seton was promoted to Pluscarden; William Rutherford acquired St Mary's Isle in September 1566; Alexander Colville obtained Culross in February 1566/7; and Marion McLean was promoted to the nunnery of Iona in the same month.[18] Similarly, the nunneries of St Bothans, Coldstream, North Berwick and Eccles were bestowed by the crown to titular prioresses.[19] Yet when it came to disposing of the dependent priory of Lesmahagow, a cell of Kelso, the crown simply granted the priory in October 1561 as 'ane pension' to James Cunningham, the earl of Glencairn's son, with 'jurisdictioun spirituall and temporall' over the lands, teinds, parsonages and vicarages, as if he had been provided at Rome, though the matter of a pension of £190 from the mother house had earlier been the subject of a supplication to the Vatican in January 1559/60 on behalf of Cunningham.[20] Pensions were also assigned to individuals from the fruits of vacant houses, notably from the Charterhouse of Perth in November 1561.[21] The property of friaries was similarly understood to be at the crown's disposal. In February 1561/2, the privy council had assigned the buildings and revenues of the friaries to the town councils of certain burghs for the maintenance of 'hospitaliteis, scolis and utheris godlie usis'. Yet, as late as October 1566, the crown made a grant of the friary of Peebles to Thomas Hay, the brother of lord Yester.[22]

Although no legislation survives to illuminate the process whereby the crown assumed greater power after 1560 to dispose of ecclesiastical property, the crown's comprehensive rights over certain prelacies are nonetheless apparent as early as 1562 when Queen Mary claimed that 'the haill patronage of the kirk landis and benefices pertening to the abbacie of Haliruidhous pertenit and pertenis to hir hienes as patrimonye of hir croune' despite the fact that her half brother, Robert Stewart, was already commendator.[23] It may emerge that the consolidation of such powers was no more than the culmination of a trend, already evident before 1560, whereby the crown was assuming control over monastic patronage by making presentations to appropriated churches.[24]

Since the holders of benefices continued in their livings, vacancies occurred only through the process of demission, death, or, occasionally, escheat. Most benefices annexed to religious houses continued, therefore, to

[18] Ibid., v, nos. 2187, 2211, 2315, 3078, 3201, 3255.

[19] RMS, iv, no. 1716; RSS, v, nos. 2682, 2912, 2917, 3041.

[20] RSS, v, no. 871; Reg. Supp., 2978, fos. 272v–273r; J. Durkan and J. Kirk, *The University of Glasgow, 1451–1577* (Glasgow, 1977), 233 and n. 63.

[21] RSS, v, no. 915.

[22] RPC, i, 202; RSS, v, no. 3097. For further examples of the disposition of the property of friaries, see RSS, v, nos. 1218, 1275, 1956, 1980, 2009, 2109.

[23] RSS, v, no. 965.

[24] This is based on an examination of the relevant entries, from 1549, in RSS, iv and v; see Cowan, 'Patronage, Provision and Reservation', above, p. 91.

be occupied. Nor is there evidence in the register of the privy seal for the 1560s (other than a gift of the vicarage of Kinghorn Easter in October 1566)[25] of any grants by Mary of parochial benefices pertaining to Holyrood, whose patronage the crown now claimed. Even so, the queen considered the patronage of Inverkip, appropriated to Paisley abbey, and that of Bourtie, annexed to St Andrews priory, to belong at that point to the crown, for she bestowed both vicarages by simple gift in April 1565 and April 1566 respectively.[26] Again, the vicarage of Dunning, which belonged to Inchaffray, was understood in April 1566 to be 'now pertening to oure soveranis and being at thair hienes gift and dispositioun' through the death of the holder. Yet the candidate to whom the crown granted the benefice was unsuccessful in securing his title, for eight months later in December the queen confirmed the rights to the benefice of another candidate by virtue of 'the donatioun, provisioun and collatioun ordinar' by the chancellor and vicar general of Dunblane in May 1566. During the vacancy, the vicar general evidently considered that the vicarage was at his disposal since the newly appointed commendator of Inchaffray had still to receive institution.[27]

When the crown appointed commendators and titular prioresses after 1560, there appears to have been no specific recognition of the inclusion in such grants of the 'advocation' of appropriated churches, until a grant of 1565 expressly acknowledged one commendator's right 'to dispoun all benefices pertening thairto to qualifeit personis sa oft as thai sall vaik',[28] phraseology which Mary does not seem to have repeated in other grants. In some titles, the right of presentation may have been assumed to be incidental to the conveying of 'all and sindrie beneficies'[29] with the rest of the abbatial property, but in other titles any mention of benefices is omitted;[30] and *oeconomi* were apparently not accorded the right of exercising the patronage of appropriated churches.[31] Not only this, but in succeeding decades, the crown acted as if the patronage of practically every benefice annexed to the religious houses had come into the patrimony of the crown.

Even so, royal control over the religious houses was nonetheless exercised in a manner which did not entirely disregard the interests of other parties. Queen Mary recognised her mother's gift to lord Erskine of Cambuskenneth with the right to nominate an abbot or commendator and, in his favour, provided Adam Erskine as commendator in 1562. In the same year, Mary granted Dundrennan anew to John Maxwell of Terregles, with 'sufficient title thairto', and 'in his name' promoted Edward Maxwell to the

---

[25] *RSS*, v, no. 3093.

[26] Ibid., v, nos. 2029, 2761.

[27] Ibid., v, nos. 2743, 3155; *Charters, Bulls and other documents relating to the Abbey of Inchaffray*, ed. W. A. Lindsay (Scottish History Society, Edinburgh, 1908), 160–165, 246–248.

[28] *RSS*, v, no. 2182.

[29] Ibid., v, no. 1008; cf., nos. 1066, 1656, 2072, 2187, 2211, 2912, 2917, 3041, 3078, 3201, 3212; *RMS*, iv, nos. 1716, 1765.

[30] *RSS*, v, nos. 1101, 2315, 3255.

[31] Ibid., v, nos. 845, 1009, 1510, 1524.

abbacy; and in 1565 Francis Stewart received the commendatorship of Coldingham, with power 'to nominat and elect ane prioure or priouris of the said abbacy als oft as he sall think expedient', though by February 1567/7 the priory had once more come into the hands of the crown and was granted for life to John Maitland.[32] Indeed, in order to safeguard the customary rights enjoyed by some noble houses to nominate their own candidates, the crown was even disposed in March 1565/6 to annul its earlier grant of the nunnery of Haddington to William Maitland, younger of Lethington, and 'to certane personis nominat be him, yconomusis of the same, quhill the lauchfull provisioun of ane priores to the said abbay', and to accede to the earl of Bothwell's petition recalling that the nunnery was 'his maist native rowme and kyndlie possessioun', and had been 'a lang tyme broukit be his freindis, promovit frome tyme to tyme at the nominatioun of his predecessouris'; all of which led Mary to appoint to Haddington, Bothwell's kinswoman, dame Isobel Hepburn.[33] Even papal claims were not completely ignored. Not only did Thomas Hay's successful supplication to the papacy in April 1560 for provision to Glenluce go uncontested by the crown, but the queen herself considered petitioning the pope in 1565 that the commend of Inchaffray be granted to James Drummond, in the belief that 'good men, devoted to learning' should be appointed to ecclesiastical dignities at a time when the Catholic church was 'so grievously afflicted'. Yet her claim that the pope should admit free of charge the resignation of Alexander Gordon, as commendator, on account of the 'heavy losses' which Gordon had incurred 'in the defence of the Catholic religion' is hard to reconcile with Gordon's active ministry in the reformed church. Mary proved to be a disappointment to the papacy, and, indeed, proceeded to 'provide' Drummond to the abbacy in July 1565 'in the accustomed form' under the privy seal, which was recognised to be as valid as if provision had been made at Rome.[34]

Occasionally, too, the crown confirmed presentations by commendators to the benefices of annexed churches. In February 1564/5, Queen Mary confirmed a presentation, dated March 1555, to the vicarage of Earlston, which had been made by her brother, John Stewart, the commendator and by the convent of Coldingham, 'undoutit patronis', to which the archbishop of St Andrews had refused to give collation, thus necessitating appeal to Rome.[35] Similarly, the commendator of Lindores sought confirmation from the crown in January 1565/6 of his presentation of a candidate to the vicarage of Inverurie and Monkegie. In March 1565/6, a presentation to the vicarage of Kirkcaldy, annexed to Dunfermline abbey, was held to have the same force as if it had been made by the queen's 'awin provisioun'; in February 1566/7 the crown also confirmed a presentation of 1566 by the commendator of Whithorn to the vicarage of Whithorn; and in the same month, Mary ratified another presentation to the same benefice, which, it was stated, pertained to

[32] *RSS*, v, nos. 1066, 1101, 2182; *RMS*, iv, no. 1765.
[33] *RSS*, v, no. 2686.
[34] Reg. Supp., 2984, fos. 224v–225r; *Inchaffray Charters*, 160–165, 246–248.
[35] *RSS*, v, no. 1922.

the 'collatioun, provisioun and dispositioun' of Alexander Gordon, bishop of Galloway, 'be ressoun of the inhabilitie of Malcolme, commendator of Quiterne, patrone thairof, to present and nominat ane qualifit persoun thairto throw his being denuncit rebell'.[36] The continued recognition of the rights of other patrons clearly placed limitations on the crown's ability to control presentations to churches appropriated to religious houses. It is harder, however, to appreciate the circumstances which permitted the earl Marischal to present his own candidate on 10 June 1565 to the vicarage of the united churches of Longley and Fetterangus, appropriated by Arbroath abbey, and, then, to have his 'gift and presentatioun' confirmed by the queen on 30 June 1565.[37]

The proprietary attitude displayed by the crown in its bestowal of monastic property is also apparent in the crown's policy towards the bishoprics. At the Reformation, the only vacancy among the bishoprics was the see of Brechin, though several occupants of the remaining bishoprics had not been consecrated.[38] Five bishops conformed to the Reformation, and three of them – Orkney, Caithness and Galloway[39] – undertook an active ministry, but there was no indication that bishops who declined to conform would be dismissed. The survival of the bishoprics – in contradiction to the reformers' aims of dissolving them – clearly enabled the crown to gain further access to the bishoprics as financial entities, and to ignore the demands of the reformed church that the spirituality of the bishoprics should be devoted to the ministry and that the temporality should be assigned to support the universities and to pay superintendents.[40]

In accordance with traditional practice,[41] during an episcopal vacancy Mary was entitled to the temporality of the see and at least the patronage of benefices in the bishop's gift. In November 1561, the crown gifted to David Murray a yearly pension, confirmed in December 1564, to be paid for the duration of his life, and not merely for the duration of the vacancy, from the revenues of the bishopric of Brechin. In Galloway, too, where Gordon was only bishop elect, Steven Wilson received a pension, again for life, from the crown in July 1561 and, in January 1562/3, a further pension for life was granted from the bishopric of Galloway to Thomas Stewart.[42] Similarly,

    [36] Ibid., v, nos. 2563, 2607, 3249, 3269.
    [37] Ibid., v, no. 2148. In May 1566, the Earl Marischal and Master of Marischal were recognised as patrons of the parish church of Longley (RSS, v, no. 2822). In September 1592, the current Earl Marischal and his eldest son received a grant, in life rent and fee respectively, of the barony of Straloch with the advowson of the parsonage and vicarage of Fetterangus and of the vicarage of Longley (RMS, v, no. 2176).
    [38] Watt, Fasti, 132, 205; 61.
    [39] See G. Donaldson, 'Bishop Adam Bothwell and the Reformation in Orkney', in RSCHS, xiii. (1959), 85–100; G. Donaldson, 'Alexander Gordon, Bishop of Galloway (1559–1575) and his work in the Reformed Church', in TDGAS, 3rd ser., xxiv (1945–6), 111–28; G. Donaldson, The Scottish Reformation, 58–60.
    [40] First Book of Discipline, 150, 161–2.
    [41] G. Donaldson, 'The rights of the Scottish crown in episcopal vacancies', SHR, xlv. (1966), 26–35.
    [42] RSS, v, nos. 893, 1865; 824; 1198.

when Ross fell vacant in January 1564/5, Mary rewarded Johannes Franciscus de Busso, as master of the royal household, with the grant in February 1564/5 of a yearly pension for life from the vacant bishopric of Ross.[43] Again, with the death of Bishop William Chisholm of Dunblane, Mary lost little time in granting in March 1564/5 a yearly pension for life to 'Eme de Saunctjean, furrour to oure soverane ladyis body', even though Chisholm's nephew had been appointed coadjutor by the pope in June 1561, and by the end of March 1565 was present in Scotland as bishop.[44] All in all, there was no incentive for the crown to fill vacant sees without delay.

Although, on the eve of the Reformation, the crown's nominee, Henry Sinclair, had still to receive papal provision to the bishopric of Ross (forthcoming on 2 June 1561), the crown had felt entitled, nonetheless, to place him in possession of the temporality in November 1558 and had granted him, as 'elect of Ross', full power in March 1559/60 to present to all benefices, in the bishop's patronage.[45] Thereafter, in January 1564/5, Patrick McLean, bishop elect of the Isles, agreed to transfer his rights to John Carswell, superintendent of Argyll, supposedly on the grounds of the 'impotence of his awne bodie'; but the decision to demit was evidently the product of a dispute between the McLeans and Campbells and the decision in favour of Carswell marked a victory for the earl of Argyll. As the new bishop elect, Carswell was obliged, however, to pay the stipends of the ministers of the diocese; and in the royal confirmation of March 1566/7 his right to dispose of vacant benefices was expressly recognised.[46]

The precedent of gifting a bishopric to a superintendent was not repeated, and any prospect that the kirk might benefit from the appointment of superintendents to bishoprics quickly disappeared. Instead, resort was had to the expedient of granting vacant bishoprics to lay titulars. Total secularisation now seemed the fate of the bishoprics. Thus, with Sinclair's death in January 1565, Mary made a gift of the bishopric of Ross in May 1565 to the earl of Ross for life, as lay titular, with the patronage of all benefices in the bishop's gift, and with power to bestow the whole bishopric or any portion of it on whomsoever he might choose.[47]

Such a policy was interrupted in September 1565 when Mary freed herself from the policies of her protestant advisers and obtained papal provision to Brechin for her nominee, John Sinclair.[48] The practice of seeking provision proved, however, to be erratic. By May 1566, the policy of bestowing bishoprics in favour of laymen was resumed, with the grant to Alexander Campbell, who was still a minor, of the bishopric of Brechin. Experimental styles were also devised during 1566 and 1567 for disposing of the bishoprics

[43] Watt, *Fasti*, 270; *RSS*, v, no. 1918; cf., no. 3268.
[44] Watt, *Fasti*, 78; *RSS*, v, no. 1937; Vatican Archives, Acta Miscellanea, 17, fo. 690.
[45] Vatican Archives, Acta Misc., 17, fos. 690-1v.; *RSS*, v. nos. 507, 768.
[46] *RSS*, v, nos. 1885, 3373; D. E. Meek and J. Kirk, 'John Carswell, Superintendent of Argyll: a reassessment', *RSCHS*, xix. (1975), 1-22, at 10-14.
[47] *RSS*, v, no. 2066.
[48] Watt, *Fasti*, 41; Vatican Archives, Acta Misc., 17, fo. 759r-v (7 Sept. 1565).

of Moray and Dunkeld, in anticipation of a vacancy arising, to nominees of
the crown.[49] Such a policy was consistent with Mary's efforts at conciliating
protestant opinion for reasons of political expediency; and it was only
towards the end of the reign, that John Leslie was appointed to Ross,
apparently after papal provision and with royal approval in January 1566/7.[50]

Mary's device of appointing titulars to bishoprics with power to dispose
of vacant benefices in the bishop's gift meant that the crown deprived itself of
powers of patronage over certain parochial benefices *sede vacante*. And in
cases where the bishop was merely elect, the normal procedure of episcopal
provision followed by institution could not take place, and so candidates
were required to be presented by the bishop elect to the vicar general of the
see for collation before institution could take place.[51] Yet what the crown was
prepared to relinquish was offset by gains elsewhere. For a start, the
patronage of parochial benefices in the gift of laymen devolved on the crown,
from time to time, through wardship, through nonentry, and through the
forfeiture of the property of a patron.[52] Besides, by an act of the privy council
in 1562, the crown was permitted to dispose of benefices whose rentals had
not been produced for assessment by the crown.[53]

With the appointment of collectors of the thirds,[54] the crown was able to
utilise at least a portion of this newly found source of finance by making gifts
or remissions of the thirds.[55] In addition to its share of the thirds, the crown
also assumed control of the property of the 'common churches' belonging to
the canons and chaplains of cathedrals, whose revenues, along with those of
certain collegiate churches, had been uplifted by the crown from 1561
onwards.[56] The numerous grants of these properties by the crown took the
form either of a lease or of a simple gift. Thus, in July 1565, Mary leased to
Robert Douglas, provost of Lincluden, and his heirs for nineteen years the
parsonage and vicarage of Glencairn, a common church of Glasgow
cathedral.[57] Again, in January 1566/7, James Hering received a gift of the
canonry of Forgandenny, a common church of Dunkeld;[58] and in the same
month, John Leslie, bishop of Ross, received from Mary a lease for nineteen

[49] *RSS*, v, nos. 2806, 3099, 3100, 3553.

[50] Watt, *Fasti*, 270.

[51] *RSS*, v, no. 768.

[52] Ibid., v, nos. 237, 238, 365, 515, 610, 929, 1196, 1222, 1723; vi, no. 972; vii, no. 613;
(forfeiture:) *RSS*, vi, nos. 123, 1433, 2815; vii, no. 1767.

[53] *RPC*, i, 199-202, 204-6; *RSS*, v, nos. 2659, 3279; vi, no. 2250.

[54] *RSS*, v, no. 998; *Thirds of Benefices*, xi, xv-xvi.

[55] *RSS*, v, nos. 1127, 1179, 1327, 2283, 2340, 2401, 2548, 2659, 2791, 2811, 3013, 3245,
3279, 3316, 3323; *Thirds of Benefices*, 83-91, 147-9, 155-6, 221, 230, 241, 249, 260, 274, 283,
289. A general revocation of such grants, with certain exceptions, was issued in
September 1566 (*RPC*, i, 477-9).

[56] *RSS*, v, nos. 1709, 1751, 1998, 2092, 2192, 3173, 3286; *Thirds of Benefices*, 2, 4, 6, 8, 16,
21, 24-6, 28.

[57] *RSS*, v, 2192.

[58] Ibid., v, no. 3178; Reg. Supp., 3032, fo. 168r-v. (A subsequent supplication to
Rome in 1560 by John Leslie, priest of Moray diocese, was evidently ineffective: Reg.
Supp. 3033, fos. 53v-54r.)

years of the whole common kirks of Ross.[59] Even after Mary's reign, the crown continued to claim in 1570 that the benefices formerly held in common by the chantry priests of Dunkeld, 'now vakand be ressoun the singing of the saidis preistis ceassis', still pertained to the king's presentation, 'becaus of the lait ordinance of the kirk anent the gift and dispositioun of sic small thingis', an apparent allusion to the general assembly's decision by 1569 that chaplainries should be assigned to the support of the colleges and the poor.[60]

Laymen – other than the crown and the crown's nominees to the prelacies – may have had little opportunity to exercise ecclesiastical patronage, but at almost every level they had gained as recipients of patronage. The prospect of the complete secularisation of the church's patrimony, however, was drastically modified and ultimately reversed by the inheritance, in effect, from 1567 of the lesser benefices, as they fell vacant, by the reformed church. As early as 1562, the assumption of the thirds suggested that the church's legitimate claims might be met not by dissolving the structure of benefices, to which the crown was opposed, but by adopting the old financial system. As it was, some conforming ministers were already in possession of benefices, and others, by obtaining a portion of the thirds, were also receiving some financial support from the existing structure. At a time when the crown's increased demands upon the thirds actually had led to a corresponding reduction in stipends, any scheme designed to provide more satisfactory stipends was likely to prove attractive to ministers, and the queen's proposal in October 1566 that ministers should finally succeed to the lesser benefices provided sufficient financial inducement to secure the church's further co-operation in the existing structure of parochial benefices.

The origins of this scheme are to be traced to the assembly's novel claim first advanced in June 1565 that the parochial 'benefices now vaikand or hes vaike be disponed to qualified and learned persones'. The queen's initial and discouraging reply in December 1565 was that 'her Majestie thinkis it no wayes reasonable that scho sould defraude her selfe of sa great a pairt of the patrimonie of her crowne as to put the patronage of benefices furth of her awin handis'. In reply, the assembly reassured Mary that its intention was not to deprive patrons of their rights but merely to gain recognition of the church's right to grant collation to benefices.

The assembly's contention that the system of patronage should survive intact and that the kirk should not only inherit the parochial benefices but also operate the machinery for admission was in contravention of the programme of the first Book of Discipline; and if the intention now was to secure agreement through compromise, the assembly's claim was still not conceded by the crown until political necessity finally dictated the adoption by Mary of a policy designed to win support from the kirk. But even with the crown's recognition by October 1566 that ministers should succeed to the lesser benefices, there was no wholesale capitulation to the assembly's claims of 1565, for Mary continued to favour the disposition of benefices by simple

[59] *RSS*, v, no. 3173.
[60] Ibid., vi, no. 955; *BUK*, i, 155; cf., 127-9.

gift, instead of by presentation, and, partly as a consequence, she avoided transferring the machinery for granting collation and admission to the reformed church, machinery ultimately forthcoming only after the accession of a 'godly' prince in 1567.[61]

The plans announced in October 1566 to finance ministers from the revenues of parochial benefices was, however, markedly at variance with Mary's earlier policy. Indeed, immediately after the Reformation crown presentations to the lesser benefices – though on a noticeably reduced scale – continued to be made in traditional form, for not only did the old financial structure remain intact but the titles of benefice-holders were still secure. This being so, presentations continued to be directed to the existing bishops regardless of their religious persuasion.[62] That the old system of episcopal administration persisted and continued to operate, well after 1560, is also evident in the crown's confirmation of presentations, specifying episcopal collation, which had been made by other patrons.[63]

Increasingly, however, Queen Mary resorted to bestowing lesser benefices in royal patronage by means of a simple gift without having recourse to episcopal collation. Earlier presentations to vicarages, prebends and even to chaplainries were quickly followed by gifts of archdeaconries,[64] deaneries and subdeaneries,[65] chancellories,[66] provostries,[67] chantories and subchantories,[68] canonries and prebends,[69] of certain parsonages and vicarages[70] unattached as prebends of cathedrals and collegiate kirks, and of a number of chaplainries[71] at the crown's disposal. Any dubiety about the propriety of resorting to gifts instead of presentations was overcome by the crown's recognition that such gifts were as valid as any other form of grant. The gift of the vicarage of Balmaclellan in November 1563 was understood to be as sound in law as if the candidate had been 'providit thairto be waye of presentatioun and collatioun ordinare eftir the auld maner of provisioun to benefices'; and the candidate who received a gift of the vicarage of Linton in March 1563/4 was held to have as sufficient a title 'as onye utheris vicaris within this realme hes of thair vicaraiges'.[72] Again, in December 1565 a gift of the parsonage and vicarage of Duns was said to be as lawful as if provision had

[61] RPC, i, 487–8; BUK, i, 59, 68–70; APS, iii, 23.

[62] RSS, v, nos. 827, 869, 876, 965, 1884, 2475, 2786, 3070.

[63] Ibid., v, nos. 2721, 2722, 2828, 2836, 2840, 2846, 2852, 3031, 3246, 3249, 3269, 3270, 3308, 3042, 3091, 3112, 3120, 3155, 3174, 3433, 3469, 3533.

[64] Ibid., v, nos. 1445, 1894, 2025, 2121.

[65] Ibid., v, nos. 1416, 1733, 2036, 2217, 2466, 2478, 2757, 3156.

[66] Ibid., v, no. 1469.

[67] Ibid., v, nos. 3123, 3146.

[68] Ibid., v, nos. 1551, 1785, 2036, 2039, 2978.

[69] Ibid., v, nos. 1321, 1368, 1513, 1660, 1917, 1941, 2314, 2369, 2445, 2446, 2456, 2675, 2691, 2743, 2908, 2973, 3029, 3045, 3049, 3060, 3089, 3144, 3158, 3399.

[70] Ibid., v, nos. 1490, 1657, 1899, 2029, 3044.

[71] Ibid., v, nos. 2313, 2370, 2426, 2676, 2761, 2853, 2918, 3028, 3282, 3283, 3061, 3076, 3355.

[72] Ibid., v, nos. 1490, 1657.

been made at Rome.[73] Occasionally, too, a gift might be forthcoming in the expectation of a 'presentatioun to be maid under the prive seile'.[74]

By 1 October 1566, however, in anticipation of an enactment of 3 October, Mary bestowed the vicarage of Inchcadin on William Ramsay, minister of that parish; and this gift was followed in March 1566/7 with the appointment of David Wemyss, minister of Glasgow, to the vicarage of Glasgow, then 'pertening to oure soverane ladyis gift and dispositioun be the ordour laitlie tane and proclamatioun set furth thairon anent the dispositioun of sic small benefices to ministeris for thair sustentatioun'.[75] A further gift to a minister was made in April 1567, when Patrick Creich, minister at Ratho, received a prebend of Corstorphine, which he was to possess as freely as if provision 'had bene maid at Rome'.[76]

The access of ministers to the lesser benefices on such a modest scale was, however, transformed with the accession, in July 1567, of James VI, for not only was the way then open for the statutory recognition of the reformed church, but parliament also transferred to the reformed church the right to receive presentations to benefices from patrons and to grant collation and institution. The traditional machinery for conveying title to a benefice was finally to be operated by the reformed church and in favour of candidates willing to serve in the kirk. By a statute of December 1567, it was recognised that, within six months of a vacancy arising, patrons should direct presentations to the superintendent or the commissioner of the province. On a patron's failure to present, the right to fill the vacancy fell to the superintendent or commissioner. Where a dispute arose, the patron might appeal to the superintendent and ministers of the province, and finally to the general assembly. Not only was recognition thus accorded to the higher courts of the church, but it looked as if parliament had conceded that ecclesiastical courts were the appropriate courts of appeal. It is noticeable, too, that statutory recognition was withheld from the conforming bishops.[77] Such a restriction, however, accorded with the general assembly's policy of regarding the bishops who conformed at the Reformation as acting merely as 'commissioners' of the assembly. The occasional crown presentation directed to a bishop in the late 1560s presumably rested on this assumption, for it would have been hard on any other ground to reconcile such a development with the express terms of statute law.[78]

In the years between December 1567 and January 1572/3, when a further statute required benefice-holders to subscribe the Confession of Faith (though they still need not serve as ministers) and to acknowledge the king's authority or to suffer dispossession,[79] more than 150 crown presentations were directed to superintendents and commissioners in favour of ministers;

---

[73] Ibid., v, no. 2511.   [74] Ibid., v, no. 2313.
[75] Ibid., v, nos. 3080, 3347; 3213.
[76] Ibid., v, no. 3399.
[77] APS, iii, 23.
[78] BUK, i, 15, 26–32, 34–5, 39–40, 44, 51–2; RSS, vi, no. 200.
[79] APS, iii, 72.

Mary's earlier device of granting simple gifts was all but eliminated;[80] and thereafter, with the enforcement of the act depriving nonconformists,[81] the prospect was that all benefices would be assigned to those willing to undertake service in the kirk. The first grant of a benefice in the new reign to a candidate serving in the reformed church – the bestowal of the vicarage of Walston to an exhorter in September 1567 – had taken the form of a simple gift, but the special circumstances were twofold: the gift was made three months before the act of parliament setting down the procedures to be observed in presentations; secondly, the gift was designed to clarify the anomaly arising from an earlier presentation of the same candidate by the earl of Bothwell, as patron, in May 1567 which had been directed to the vicar general of the old regime who gave collation 'as use was in tyme of papistrie'. Yet before institution had taken place, Bothwell had been denounced rebel; the vicarage, which was held still to be vacant, then came into the hands of the king, who by means of a simple gift made good the exhorter's title to the benefice.[82] The first presentation, as such, in James' reign on 25 December 1567 – of an exhorter to the vicarage of Saline – followed the procedure of 1566 'according to the act maid and set furth be our soverane lordis derrest moder and lordis of secreit counsale thairanent', but thereafter some subsequent presentations explicitly acknowledged the authority of the new, and more comprehensive, parliamentary legislation of late December 1567.[83] Occasionally, too, presentations recognised the general assembly's supervisory rôle; and it is evident that the ecclesiastical authorities displayed a readiness to take advantage of the new act to make presentations *iure devoluto*. In one instance in 1568, the crown decided to present a minister to the vicarage of Bothwell, 'na uthir persoun being presentit be the patroun within the tyme appointit be the law'. In another case, however, it was the superintendent of Fife and Strathearn who presented an exhorter to the parsonage of Dupplin in 1569, since 'Lord Oliphant, patrone of the said parsonage nowthir presentit or nominat ony qualifiit persoun thairto be the space of sex monethis . . . be ressoun quhairof the said nobill lord tint his rycht of the presentatioun thairof as for this tyme, and the rycht thairof pertenit to the superintendent *jure devoluto*. . . .'[84]

The disposition of ecclesiastical property in favour of ministers extended beyond the strictly parochial benefices to include canonries, prebends, the common kirks attached to cathedrals, and even to chaplainries. At the same time, the crown extended its newly acquired, additional rights of patronage considerably beyond the common kirks, to whose disposition Mary had laid claim, to encompass the benefices in the patronage of prelates. The transference of the bulk of ecclesiastical patronage from the control of churchmen, or at least men who were nominally ecclesiastics, into the hands

[80] *RSS*, vi, nos. 10, 123.
[81] Ibid., vi, nos. 2030, 2034, 2125, 2130, 2170, 2171, 2198, 2224, 2240, 2241, 2286, 2292, 2419, 2437, 2468, 2532, 2608.
[82] Ibid., vi, no. 10.   [83] Ibid., vi, nos. 68, 82, 87.
[84] Ibid., vi, nos. 95, 214, 582; cf., vii, no. 2689.

of the crown was finally effected in the early decades of the new reign. This silent revolution was achieved with little dislocation.

The assumption of such comprehensive rights by the crown, however, is not attributable to any surviving act of parliament or council. Nonetheless, from as early as 1569, the crown felt confident to make presentations to benefices in ecclesiastical patronage, and it was later recognised, in July 1578, that 'be the Lawes custome and ordour ressavit within our realme all benefices of befoir at the donatioun and presentatioun of prelatis ar now cum in use and ordinit be Parliament to be at our patronage in tyme cuming'. The existence, therefore, of 'ony actis of parliament or lawes of our realme quhairby the richt of presentatioun of ecclesiasticall benefices may appear to cum in our handis sen the reformatioun of religioun and to appertene to us allanerlie' was considered to provide justification for the crown's action of invading the traditional rights of patronage exercised by the bishops, abbots and priors.[85]

Thus in the years between 1569 and 1592 the crown made some 41 presentations to 23 churches annexed to Arbroath abbey, despite a succession of commendators there. Five presentations were made between 1570 and 1583 to the parish of Dun, annexed to Elcho priory; and at Holyrood, whose patronage Mary had claimed, around 38 presentations by the crown were made to 21 annexed churches belonging to the abbey between 1568 and 1589, regardless of the existence of a commendator. A similar pattern is evident, too, in the case of other religious houses such as Kelso, Kilwinning, Lindores, Paisley, St Andrews and Whithorn.[86]

The plenary powers exercised by the crown[87] over ecclesiastical property were applicable also to bishoprics where the crown assumed a right to present candidates to churches annexed as prebends (as well as to the common churches) not merely during episcopal vacancies but also where the bishop was lawfully provided to the see. From 1569, the crown began to assert its claims to present to prebends annexed to cathedral churches.[88] What is more, from the 1570s the crown proceeded to make presentations even to independent benefices where the bishop happened to be patron. Presentations were accordingly made to the churches of Carrington, Collace, Edzell, Fettercairn, Logy Montrose, Muckhart and Nevay which, hitherto, were recognised to lie within the patronage of the archbishop of St Andrews.[89] Similarly, the unappropriated churches of

[85] *APS*, iii, 106.

[86] This calculation is based on relevant entries in *RSS*, vi–vii, and SRO, CH4/1/2, Register of Presentations to Benefices; and PS1/59–63, Register of the Privy Seal.

[87] Cf. J. Mirehouse, *A Practical Treatise on the Law of Advowsons* (London, 1824), 130.

[88] This information is based upon a study of the sources listed in note 86 above; it does not include prebends in lay patronage.

[89] *RSS*, vii, no. 156 (Carrington); vi, no. 2084; SRO, CH4/1/2, Register of Presentations to Benefices, fo. 81r. (Collace); *RSS*, vi, nos. 1152, 2053 (Edzell); vii, nos. 631, 2458 (Fettercairn); vi, no. 2311 (Logy Montrose); vii, nos. 1229, 2027, 2051; SRO, CH4/1/2, Reg. Pres. Ben., fos. 134v., 145r. (Muckhart); *RSS*, vi, no. 1674 (Nevay).

Castlemilk, Kirkpatrick-Fleming, Kirkton, Lochmaben and Redkirk, formerly pertaining to the patronage of the archbishop of Glasgow, were understood to be at the crown's presentation.[90] It is noticeable, too, that at the Convention of Leith in 1572, which provided the machinery for future episcopal and abbatial appointments, the crown's rights over 'benefices of cure under prelaciis' were once more affirmed; and while the rights of lay patrons were expressly confirmed, those of churchmen looked like being eclipsed.[91]

All along, the survival of the ancient financial structure after the Reformation had suggested at least three possibilities. One solution – the complete secularisation of the property of the old church – had been averted. Another possibility was that the continued existence of the old structure might have invited a papalist reaction. The third solution – which looked like being achieved in the years after 1567 – was that the financial system of the old church should become wholly identified with the work of the reformed ministry, the needs of schools and universities, and of the poor. There was even a fourth possibility that by first utilising this financial structure the reformed church might succeed in its original intention of reorganising the chaotic state of ecclesiastical finances along the lines suggested in the Book of Discipline.[92]

So far, the accession of a 'godly' prince had brought full statutory recognition of the assembly's claim in 1565 that the supervision of admissions should belong to the kirk; but no solution was forthcoming on the fate of the bishoprics and abbacies. It is, no doubt, attractive to regard the access of ministers to the bishoprics, achieved in 1572, as the logical sequel to the statutory inheritance of the lesser benefices by ministers from 1567. Yet this was scarcely the attitude of the assembly which proceeded from petitioning for the adoption of the lesser benefices in 1565 to the demand that:[93]

'no bishoprik, abbacie, pryorie, deanrie, provestrie, or any uther benefices havand many kirks annexit therto, be disponit altogither in any time comeing to any one man, bot at the least the kirks therof be severallie disponit and to severall persons, swa that every man having charge may serve at his awin kirk according to his vocatioun. . . .'

Such language is a clear expression of the assembly's attitude toward the prelacies, for whose dissolution it continued to campaign.

Although the assembly's petition to parliament in December 1567 for a dissolution of the abbacies met with little response, the matter was not allowed to rest; and in the aftermath of the parliament of August 1568, the Regent Moray reported to the assembly in July 1569 that 'ye know at the

[90] *RSS*, vii, no. 358; SRO, PS1/60, Register of the Privy Seal, fo. 84r; PS1/63, fo. 112r (Castlemilk); *RSS*, vii, no. 1442 (Kirkpatrick Fleming); SRO, CH4/1/2, Reg. Pres. Ben., fo. 143v (Kirkton); SRO, PS1/63, Register of the Privy Seal, fo. 263r (Lochmaben); *RSS*, vii, nos. 315, 1964 (Redkirk).

[91] *BUK*, i, 211.

[92] Ibid., i, 107.

[93] Ibid., i, 59-60.

Parliament . . . we exped in our travell, and inlaikit only a consent to the dissolution of the prelacies; qherunto althogh we were earnestly bent, yet the estates delayit and wold not aggrie therunto'. That the church continued to contend for a dissolution of the bishoprics, as well as of the abbacies, was understood as late as November 1571, when the government's earlier announcement of appointments to the vacant archbishoprics provoked superintendent Erskine of Dun to defend the assembly's programme in favour of 'the dismembring (as they call it) of great benefices', and to remind the government that 'the kirk hath continuallie suted (of old als weill as now) . . . when ever anie of the great benefices vaiked, having manie kirks joyned thereto, that all the kirks sould be divided, and severallie dispouned to severall men, to serve everie one at his owne kirk: of which minde all that beare office in the kirk continue'. But if this ideal could not be granted until at least the king attained his majority, Erskine expressed the hope that 'in respect of this confused troublous time', the church might compromise 'whill further order may be tane in these maters'; and the Regent Mar responded by recognising the need 'to procure the reforming of things disordered in all sorts, als farre as may be, reteaning the priviledge of the king, crown and patronage'.[94]

The background to Erskine's intervention had been the government's decision to fill several bishoprics without consulting the church. The problem of the bishoprics had not been unforeseen. Indeed, the crisis was precipitated by the government's action of instituting proceedings from 1567 against the leading Marian bishops. By December 1567, William Chisholm, the Catholic bishop of Dunblane, had been forfeited. Somewhat later John Leslie, the bishop of Ross, was dispossessed in August 1568. At the same point, 'the process and dome of forfaltour ordourlie led aganis Johnne, sumtym Archbischop of Sanctandrois', and his execution in April 1571, resulted in the primatial see falling vacant. The lords of council, in September 1570, declared the archbishopric of Glasgow to be vacant through the forfeiture for treason of James Beaton. Thereafter similar sentences of forfeiture for treason were passed against four other bishops who had supported Mary: William Gordon, bishop of Aberdeen; Alexander Gordon, bishop of Galloway; Robert Crichton, bishop of Dunkeld, and Patrick Hepburn, bishop of Moray, though both Gordons were soon pardoned and restored in February 1572/3.[95] All in all, the government's action in dispossessing Marian supporters had created vacancies in half the bishoprics which were thus declared to have come into the hands of the crown.

Nor was it a foregone conclusion that successors would be chosen to fill the vacant sees; there were obstacles to be overcome before appointments might be forthcoming. For a start, no procedure existed for making appointments. The traditional method of episcopal appointment by crown nomination and capitular election could scarcely operate since the chapters,

[94] APS, iii, 37; BUK, i, 151; Calderwood, History, iii, 159–60.

[95] RSS, vi, nos. 56, 590, 729; 501; APS, iii, 54; RSS, vi, nos. 518, 2142; 1265; 1262; 1254, 1255; RPC, ii, 196.

where not extinct, still consisted of the unreformed variety. There was always the option of disposing of episcopal temporalities by simple gift; and to a government short of finance, there were attractions in permitting episcopal vacancies to continue, thereby enabling the crown to enjoy the fruits *sede vacante*. A further obstacle to filling the sees with protestant successors was, of course, the general assembly's aversion to any policy at variance with its objective of dissolving the bishoprics as administrative and financial entities.

As administrative entities, the thirteen bishoprics, with their antiquated diocesan boundaries, were no adequate substitute for the rationalised provinces assigned to the superintendents. Moreover, the continued existence of the bishoprics, as financial entities, impeded the assembly's efforts to disentangle the revenues of the appropriated churches for reallocation to the parishes, and to subvert the remaining episcopal resources so that the finances would be released for the maintenance of the universities and superintendents.

The decision taken at Leith in January 1571/2 to identify the bishoprics with the work of the reformed church arose unexpectedly. It was not the outcome of any predetermined plan to complete the process begun in 1567 of identifying the pre-reformation structure of benefices with the work of the new church. It came about rather as the accidental by-product of an episode which ultimately had the effect of reconciling the government and church in the aftermath of the impasse created by the government's unilateral action in making promotions to the bishoprics without consulting the church.[96]

Hitherto, the government had been predisposed to use the finances of vacant bishoprics to reward loyal supporters and to win over those who wavered in their allegiance. As the queen's party disintegrated in the summer of 1571, Argyll transferred his allegiance to the Regent Lennox and was rewarded by the succeeding Regent Mar, first with a gift in September 1571 of the fruits of the vacant bishopric of Dunkeld, and then, in January 1571/2, with a further gift of the temporalities of the bishopric; and a year later he rose to become chancellor of the kingdom. The staunchly protestant earl of Morton, who, as Regent, resigned the chancellorship in favour of Argyll in January 1572/3, had earlier received an escheat of the fruits of the bishopric of Dunkeld in December 1570; Morton also acquired an escheat of the fruits of the archbishopric of St Andrews in September 1571, presumably in recompense for his loss to Argyll of the fruits of Dunkeld; provision was made to one of Morton's natural sons of an annual pension from the bishopric of Aberdeen; and the same individual later acquired the fruits of the bishopric of Galloway.[97] In a similar way, the Master of Graham acquired an interest in the bishopric of Dunblane: in April 1569 he had obtained the escheat of the revenues of the bishopric and in August received a grant of the temporality and spirituality of the bishopric.[98] In September 1571, the brother of lord

[96] *BUK*, i, 207.
[97] *RSS*, vi, nos. 1276, 1421, 1820; 1052, 1272, 2448; *RSS*, vii, no. 730.
[98] Ibid., vi, nos. 590, 729.

Ruthven received a yearly pension for life of 300 merks from the bishopric of Moray.[99] Another adherent of the king's party, lord Methven, obtained in the same month a gift of the bishopric of Ross and goods escheated from the former bishop, and in November secured the temporalities of the bishopric.[100] The Regent Mar enabled a member of a cadet branch of his family to enjoy a yearly pension for life from the bishopric of the Isles, in September 1572; an indentical pension was assigned to a Stewart; while from the archbishopric of Glasgow, the Boyds received pensions before their kinsman was finally promoted to the see.[101]

In the north, Donald Gormson of Skye received, in February 1571/2, a gift of a pension from the bishopric of Aberdeen for his service in advancing the king's authority; in the same month Lachlan MacIntosh of Dunachton, obtained a similar pension from the bishopric of Moray; and, at the same point, lord Lovat, the king's lieutenant in the north, was made chamberlain of the vacant bishopric of Moray.[102] In addition, lesser men were recompensed for their service in the civil war through the bestowal of pensions from vacant bishoprics.[103]

As early as January 1570/1, a style had been devised for the provision of an archbishop to Glasgow, but no appointment was immediately forthcoming.[104] Nonetheless, the government's decision by the summer to fill the two bishoprics of St Andrews and Glasgow was made without any apparent awareness – at this stage at least – that the candidates promoted as bishops should exercise an active ministry. On the other hand, making appointments to the archbishoprics did at least provide the government with an additional source of patronage. This was accomplished through the device of bestowing the bishopric on a nominee who, as kinsman of a particular family, was well placed to divert episcopal property not only by grants of pensions but also of feus and tacks, which only a bishop, titular or otherwise, with the consent of his chapter could legally do. By August 1571, the government proceeded to make a gift of the archbishopric of St Andrews to Morton's kinsman, John Douglas, the elderly principal of St Mary's college; and John Porterfield, a minister apparently sponsored by the earl of Glencairn, was named as the candidate for Glasgow.[105] The government made no pretence of its purpose in filling the sees. The reason for the unilateral appointments was not to secure the service of bishops in the reformed church nor even to provide the church with a new source of finance, but merely to permit leading members of the king's party access to episcopal revenues as an extension of the crown's system of political patronage.

[99] Ibid., vi, no. 1255.
[100] Ibid., vi, nos. 1277, 1358, 1515.
[101] Ibid., vi, nos. 1736; 1722; 1791, 1874.
[102] Ibid., vi, nos. 1491, 1495; RPC, i, 654; RSS, vi, no. 1494.
[103] Ibid., vi, nos. 892, 1004, 1051, 1185, 1186, 1265, 1399, 1459, 1680, 1769, 1785, 1792, 1841, 1843, 2003, 2184, 2446, 2700, 2701.
[104] Ibid., vi, no. 1107.
[105] Calderwood, History, iii, 54–59; RSS, vi, no. 1228; cf., no. 2810.

With parliament's rejection, in August 1571, of the assembly's petition that benefices should be bestowed upon qualified persons, the barons, rallying to the kirk's defence, complained to the Regent Lennox of the 'corruption begunne' whereby 'the kirk sall be compelled to admitt dumbe dogges to the office, dignitie, and rents appointed for sustentatioun of preaching pastors', and they proceeded to condemn the milking of the prelacies.[106]

Faced with mounting criticism, the Regent Mar sought to placate the opposition by agreeing to appoint two superintendents, two of the assembly's commissioners and two laymen to examine the qualifications of the new archbishops; and in September 1571 the government belatedly acknowledged that candidates promoted to sees 'ar to have the charge and owersicht of the inferior ministeris' so that 'na avowit inyme to the trewth of God, nor ignorantis be sufferit to enjoy the patrimony of the kirk'. The government was anxious to make concessions, but no consideration seems to have been given to working out an agreed formula for admissions. This was illustrated, on the very day when the government announced its intention to examine the archbishops, with the gift by the crown of the bishopric of Dunkeld to James Paton, who had at least served as a minister.[107] The apparent continued disregard by the government of the church's right to examine such candidates drew a sharp response from Erskine of Dun, the superintendent of Angus, who admonished the Regent, in November 1571, for 'that great misorder' in intruding false bishops in defiance of the kirk; but he was realistic enough to see the need for compromise 'in respect of this confused troublous time'. He acknowledged the need to safeguard 'the king or others in their patronages' and to assign surplus finances from the prelacies, beyond the church's immediate needs, for the king's support 'whill further order may be tane in these maters', provided that 'the examinatioun and admissioun perteane onlie to the kirk, of all benefices having cure of soules'.[108]

The outcome was the Convention of Leith where a financial settlement was negotiated in January 1571/2. It was to offer a practical and practicable solution to the vexed question of the church's endowment, and at its inception appeared to reconcile the needs of the church with the interests of the crown and the nobility. Nevertheless, it was clearly conceived only as a temporary expedient by both the Regent Mar and the church. The search for a permanent solution was protracted; and, in the process, the rights of presentation to the parochial benefices increasingly fell into the possession of laymen other than the crown. Changing patterns in the ownership of former ecclesiastical properties in the decades after 1572 made it increasingly difficult

[106] Calderwood, *History*, iii, 137, 144–6; R. Lindsay of Pitscottie, *The Historie and Cronicles of Scotland* (Scottish Text Society, 1889), ii, 260; R. Bannatyne, *Journal of the Transactions in Scotland* (Edinburgh, 1806), 246, 250–3, 255.

[107] *RSS*, vi, nos. 2810–12; *Fasti Ecclesiae Scoticanae*, ed. H. Scott, 9 vols. (Edinburgh, 1915–61), v, 67.

[108] Calderwood, *History*, iii, 156–62; cf., the Regent's reply, ibid., 164.

for either crown or church to recover what had been lost; and by the end of the century, the continued acquisition by laymen of ecclesiastical patronage (linked as it was to the ownership of teinds) made it increasingly improbable that these rights would be readily surrendered to either crown or parliament for the benefit of any churchman be he archbishop or presbyter.[109]

[109] Lack of space has precluded further discussion of the topic, for which see J. Kirk, 'Royal and Lay·Patronage in the Jacobean Kirk, 1572–1600' *Church and Society, 1450–1929*, ed. N. A. T. Macdougall (forthcoming).

JAMES KIRK

7

Scotland and the Italian Renaissance

The Italian Renaissance may conveniently be summarised under three or four heads: a new style in painting, sculpture and architecture: a new educational pattern based on the ancient, and especially the Latin, classics and which stressed, as medieval literature had done to a minor degree only, the moral content of the authors studied; a conviction that education was just as important for the laity who were in positions of importance as it had earlier been for clerks; and – perhaps this is implied in the last point – a reverence for eloquence and the power of effective communication, whether in Latin (the model) or in the vernaculars of Europe. The latter, so far as Scotland was concerned, was by the sixteenth century rapidly becoming English, however it might differ in vocabulary, orthography and pronunciation.

If these matters are considered in turn the influence of Italy at first seems fairly remote in the Scotland of the century which ended in 1603.[1] Certainly in the fine arts it seems hard to trace more than very marginal Italian effects, whether arrived at directly by imported craftsmen or indirectly through travellers and books. As in England, the period sees the slow, slower than south of the Border, admiration of decorative details – the finish of a mantelpiece, the turn of a door-post or the decoration of a ceiling.[2] There is seldom anything large, dramatic, or unquestionably in the new manner. When James VI had the Half-Moon battery erected in Edinburgh Castle in 1573 there is no evidence (as there is for the even more impressive ramparts of Berwick) of Italian workmen or workmanship. Perhaps the most impressive innovation of this nature is the remarkable north range at Crichton Castle, built by the earl of Bothwell after his return from Italy in 1581. The architect who designed the diamond rustication and other details which seem unquestionably of direct Italian inspiration is not apparently known and the innovations introduced by Bothwell had no immediate influence.[3]

[1] I am much indebted to the advice of Dr John Durkan as well as to his paper 'The beginnings of humanism in Scotland', *Innes Review* iv (1953), 5-24. Among many people who have tried to plug gaps in my knowledge I must first of all thank Professor William Beattie, who was good enough to read an early draft of this essay.

[2] On the *Painted Ceilings of Scotland* see the book of that title by M. R. Apted (Edinburgh 1966).

[3] Colin McWilliam, *Lothian except Edinburgh* (The Buildings of Scotland, Harmondsworth 1978), 146.

What prompted this extravaganza in a building which in other respects had all four feet on the ground is far from obvious and remains mysterious insofar as the older style of fortified nobleman's house covered the country. Even less can be said for painting. It is true that the Trinity College altar-piece brought something of the new manner into Scotland. The four beautiful panels, perhaps by Hugo van der Goes and to be dated to the 1470s and 1480s, are nevertheless unquestionably northern in manner, however much Italians at the time admired such work. Again the work seems to have had no native emulators.[4] Native Scottish painters of a sort there were soon in plenty, 'but none of their surviving work suggests any first-hand knowledge of the continental traditions of painting'. The great wall of (imaginary) portraits of Scottish kings in Holyrood palace is late seventeenth century, but clearly by the end of the previous century there were a good number of uninspired likenesses being made of famous men, mainly reformers.[5]

As for sculpture, no evidence is to be found in the authorities of any sixteenth-century work carrying an Italian or even an Italianate flavour before the tomb of George Home, who was Chancellor of the (English) Exchequer when he died in 1611. His tomb in Dunbar parish church is perhaps better described as Jacobean than Renaissance as such; it is certainly not in the least medieval and was probably made in London, where Home died.[6]

If the Italian arts had to wait for their full-scale reception in Scotland, this is much less true of educational and moral attitudes. There is no doubt that confessional controversies seriously interrupted the peaceable introduction of the new methods of teaching and learning, but in Scotland, as elsewhere in Europe, the worst violences of the Reformation did not prevent fundamental if episodic changes in schools and universities.

There was much educational activity in sixteenth-century Scotland. There was certainly much need for it. The three universities of St Andrews, Glasgow and Aberdeen were at a low ebb;[7] this in turn affected the provision

---

[4] Stanley Cursiter in Roy. Comm. on the Ancient Monuments of Scotland, *Inventory of the . . . Monuments of the City of Edinburgh* (Edinburgh 1951), 38–40.

[5] Duncan Thomson, *Painting in Scotland 1550–1650* (Scottish National Portrait Gallery, 1975), 10; cf. the same author's *Life and Art of George Jamesone* (Oxford 1974), 44–50.

[6] McWilliam, *Lothian except Edinburgh*, 161–2.

[7] Hastings Rashdall, *Universities of Europe in the Middle Ages* second ed., revised by F. M. Powicke and A. B. Emden, ii (Oxford 1936), 301–24 are virtually unrevised), see also G. D. Henderson, *Founding of Marischal College, Aberdeen* (Aberdeen 1946) and the attractive *mise au point* by Leslie Macfarlane in *Aberdeen University Review* xlviii (1979), 2–17. John Durkan and James Kirk, *The University of Glasgow 1451–1577* (Glasgow 1977) has a wide-ranging bibliography. James K. Cameron's work on the early history of St Mary's College, St Andrews, is awaited with interest and Edinburgh University is planning a celebratory volume in the near future. For George Buchanan's influence on later sixteenth-century changes, see *Buchanan* (London, 1981) by I. D. MacFarlane and also the interesting early biography by David Irving, *Memoirs of the Life and Writings of George Buchanan* (Edinburgh 1807) and the biography by P. Hume Brown (Edinburgh 1890).

of schoolmasters and (at a later stage) ministers for the reformed kirk as well as lawyers to staff the courts at Edinburgh, although the need for the latter was felt more by the judges than the advocates. Lack of endowment accounts for some of the troubles at St Andrews and Glasgow but the three older Scottish universities had, in fact, little occasion to influence Scottish education along Italian lines. The Italian universities, while not as hostile to the new learning as were some northern institutions like Oxford, Paris and Louvain, had been successful and significant partly because they were involved in the training of the many men who became notaries,[8] but mainly because of their training of professional men of higher legal status, especially civil and canon lawyers. It is significant that this need for legal instruction was especially emphasised by Bishop Elphinstone at Aberdeen, who had studied law at Paris and taught it at Orleans. The French background was to be typical of early Scottish universities, together with an admixture of German academic influence. Nevertheless, it is advisable not to depreciate the value of the Aristotelianism prevalent in the older European universities, where original ideas were not necessarily inhibited, whatever critics like Erasmus might say.[9] And we may perhaps interpolate here Elphinstone's supposed connection with the act of the Scottish Parliament of 1496 'which required all barons and freeholders to have their eldest sons instructed in "Arts and Jure"'. This sentiment expressed the essence of Renaissance educational principles as stated by writers in Italy like Vittorino, or elsewhere by, for instance, Elyot in the *Governor* (1531).[10]

Nonetheless, the future of the humanities owed little to the Italian or northern universities, despite a few with 'trilingual colleges' such as Busleyden's foundation at Louvain, or Corpus Christi College, Oxford, despite the accommodation which some of the old practitioners were prepared to afford to Latin and Greek and the moral imperatives of Cicero.[11] The real roots of what was novel lay outside the old centres of scholarship, where a doctorate in divinity was as good as a doctorate in canon and civil law

---

[8] For notaries public in Scotland see above, 22–40.

[9] See *Studies in the Renaissance* (1974–80) in which Charles H. Lohr surveys *seriatim* Renaissance Aristotelian commentaries, the latest instalment reaching authors whose names begin with Sm; cf. also James McConica, 'Aristotle and Humanism in Tudor Oxford', *EHR* xcv (1979), 291–317, in which he argues for the compatibility of Aristotelian teaching with concepts which can be termed 'Christian humanism'. Euan Cameron's lecture, 'Archibald Hay and the Paduan Aristotelians at Paris, 1530–45', delivered at the Fourth Neo-Latin Conference at Bologna (1979), shows Euhemerism surprisingly making an appearance in this context; it was Archibald Hay who urged the teaching of classical languages at St Mary's College, St Andrews. For the background see many works of P. O. Kristeller, e.g. 'Platonism and Aristotelianism' in *Renaissance Thought* II (New York 1965), 89–118.

[10] W. H. Woodward, *Vittorino da Feltre and other Humanist Educators* (Cambridge 1897; Stanford E. Lehmberg, *Sir Thomas Elyot: Tudor Humanist* (Austin 1960), chaps. 3–5.

[11] Not the totality of intellectual activity between, say, 1450 and 1650, but the concept as defined by Kristeller.

for purposes of promotion in church or state. It is to the extra-university establishments that we should look, to the 'Academies' of which the earliest and for a time the most influential was that associated with Ficino at Florence. In sixteenth-century Europe such bodies both multiplied and became formalised. It is in this intellectual climate that Edinburgh steps upon the Renaissance scene.

The new university had, to begin with, a chequered career. Dogged by the meanness of the burgesses and the crown, the actual foundation is doubtless to be dated to 1583, but it is of the greatest interest that a generation earlier the Regent Mary of Guise had established Alexander Sym in the name of the infant Queen Mary 'lector and reader in the laws or any other sciences at our burgh of Edinburgh or where he shall be required by our said dearest mother thereto; and also to give all other young men of fresh and quick ingynis occasion to apply their whole minds to study for like reward to be had of us in time coming'. In 1556, a similar appointment was made of Edward Henderson, LLD. In both cases a pension of £100 p.a. was to be involved. These steps have reasonably been compared with the establishment by Francis I of 'lecteurs royaux' in the 1530s (a development which Mary of Guise must have known about) which was ultimately to develop into the Collège de France, the present highest French academic institution.[12] Francis I was bypassing the Sorbonne and its generally sullen resistance to the new humanities. This was not paralleled in Edinburgh, where there was as yet no university to offer resistance, although Robert Reid, bishop of Orkney, had already in mind the endowment of legal, literary and philosophical studies. The bishop's main aim was to encourage the study of law, but it was to be long before any of Reid's money was to be applied to academic purposes. Likewise the Regent's appointments of two scholars who could fairly be termed 'lecteurs royaux' did not last long nor lead to the evolution of a new centre of higher education similar to the Collège de France. But there does seem every reason to believe that Reid, in an old-fashioned way, and Mary of Guise in a much more adventurous and up-to-date way, were aiming to redress the odd position which left the premier city without any centre of higher learning.[13] After all, it was not to be long before the *First Book of Discipline* (1560) was to lay down, in a protestant milieu this time, the need for parish schools, grammar schools in towns, and universities.[14] The aim of the reformers was, of course, to establish the means for producing a godly laity and a learned ministry. But then this had been the aim of John Colet in re-establishing St Paul's school in London, which almost at once became one of the focal points of the new learning south of the Border. An even more

[12] The Collegium Trilingue at Louvain was not part of the (fairly recent) university; see the study in English by Henry de Vocht, 4 vols. (Louvain 1951-55).

[13] The best account of these developments and of the establishment of the university is D. B. Horn, 'The Origins of the University of Edinburgh', *University of Edinburgh Journal*, spring and autumn 1966, 213-25, 297-312.

[14] *First Book of Discipline*, ed. J. K. Cameron (Edinburgh 1972), 128-55; in the section regarding schools there are curious reminiscences of *Utopia*.

important reflection of the Collège de France is probably to be seen in the *nova erectio* of Glasgow University in 1577. Here the influence was Andrew Melville's, who had studied in the new French institution and who was successful in introducing a system of scholarly instruction, abrogating the old regent arrangement and making provision in the Arts for three professional experts respectively in Greek and rhetoric; dialectic and logic together with moral philosophy and arithmetic and geometry; and natural philosophy and astronomy 'and likewise general chronology and history'. The principal, Melville himself, was in charge of theology and biblical languages.[15]

The most impressive display of innovation along humanist lines, or at least on Italian precedents, in sixteenth-century Scotland was, however, in the field of legal reform. There was something very like a 'reception' of Roman law, in marked contrast to what, in the end of the day, was to happen in England. The outward symbol of the process, which was to be a long one, was the establishment, with papal connivance, of the erection from church income, of the College of Justice. The term covered the institutionalisation of the court known earlier as the 'session' and it seems likely that the expression 'college of justice' was derived from the name used in Pavia.[16]

Education was also to the fore; provision for teaching at parish and burgh level was laid down in the *First Book of Discipline*. In theory there was to be an elementary school in every parish and a grammar school in every town. If this fell short of the mark, it was not altogether without effect.[17]

The extent to which new principles were put into effect in any European country may be partly measured by the attention paid to the education of the Prince. Here James V's education seems to mark the beginning of a serious effort to produce learning and morality. Certainly his tutors – Dunbar, Bellenden, Lindsay and Inglis – were intellectually superior to the men who had taught James IV and his predecessors. But a really great man was the chief instructor of James VI – the historian and poet George Buchanan, not the only scholarly tutor allotted to the child but potentially far and away the most influential, if only because his pupil was to rule England as well as Scotland.[18]

James V, despite his familiars including literary figures, was not himself a man of learning or aptitude in letters and doubts have been expressed about the degree of his Latin literacy. But there seems certainty that Gavin Dunbar was mainly responsible for such competence as he had and there is no doubt that James V's reign witnessed the most remarkable collection of

[15] See the very complete survey in Durkan and Kirk, *University of Glasgow*. I leave aside the question of Ramist humanism, as it is now often termed. The influence of Ramus on Scottish scholars is certainly important, not least on Buchanan. This remarkable scheme was to last until 1640, and, if it then petered out at Glasgow in favour of regenting, by then its innovatory effects were being experienced elsewhere in Scotland.

[16] The standard work remains R. K. Hannay, *The College of Justice* (Edinburgh and Glasgow 1933); 49–50 on the putative Pavian model.

[17] Cameron, *Book of Discipline*.

[18] For the tutors of James VI and I see the biography by D. H. Willson (London 1956), chaps. 1 and 2.

writers. They owed little to Renaissance Italy, though Gavin Douglas's translation of the Aeneid has been described as one of the high points in 'British' literature. 'To read the Latin again with Douglas's version fresh in our minds is like seeing a favourite picture after it has been cleaned . . . the fine flower of medieval Vergilianism.'[19] Douglas and Dunbar should not be labelled 'Scottish Chaucerians'; they write in a strong native tradition on which Vergil impinges, so to say, as a traditional heroic poet.

Earlier there seems little doubt that Henryson at the end of the fifteenth century came under the influence of Italian vernacular poets, as did later Gavin Douglas. Italian (as opposed to Latin humanist writings) from time to time continued to have direct influence on Scottish writers, though the main route by which new styles and techniques reached Scotland was normally France or England.[20] In consequence much more would have emerged on the literary front in a theme not confined to 'Renaissance' unqualified by 'Italian' and not limited in range to the sixteenth century. From the mid-sixteenth century onwards the Italian poets and novelists, direct or via France, exercise a fascination for many Scots including writers as famous as Sir David Lyndsay (though hardly in his masterpiece, Ane Satyre of the Thrie Estaits). Some of this cultural contact was to produce very impressive results: the sonnet was acclimatised and there were major adaptions of Italian works, most notably perhaps the Roland Furious of John Stewart of Baldynneis; it has been noted that Stewart derived some of his inspiration from the 'wider Scottish literacy tradition he inherited.[21] On the other hand, it must be remembered that much of this writing was not published and that it was therefore influential if at all at a remove. The same remark applies to William Fowler's partial translation of Machiavelli's Prince.[22]

With Machiavelli the influence of the humanities on Scottish literature is manifest. Argument there may be over the degree to which the Prince reflects ancient models, but it certainly was in the Florentine tradition, stemming from Leonardo Bruni and the republican period; after all there is no doubt that by predilection Machiavelli was a republican. Fowler's version is, it seems, the first in English so that, even if his translation circulated only

[19] Oxford History of English Literature (1954), 66–119; quotations 86–7.

[20] Aside from Durkan's essay, above n. 1, see the full treatment of the second half of the sixteenth century by R. D. S. Jack, The Italian Influence on Scottish Literature (Edinburgh 1972), especially 29–143. On Henryson cf. the more cautious approach of John MacQueen (Oxford 1967), who nevertheless sees Italian influences at work.

[21] Introduction to A Choice of Scottish Verse, 1560-1660 (London 1978), 15. Dr Jack discusses Stewart's use of Ariosto (with some French intermediaries present) and of Petrarch in Italian Influence, 57–74. There is little doubt of the Italian competence of William Fowler, living at the turn of the century; on him see Jack, Italian Influence, 74–86 and next n.

[22] On Machiavelli see the lecture by Mario Praz (British Academy 1928), reprinted in Machiavelli in Inghilterra (Florence 1962), 97–151, especially at 100, quoting the Introduction by John Purves to the Scottish Text Society's edition of Fowler's Works, iii (Edinburgh 1940); see also Jack, Italian Influence, 87–8 and the essay by Nicolai Rubinstein in Il Rinascimento: interpretazioni e problemi (Laterza, Rome-Bari 1979), especially 227–35 and references.

among a restricted court circle, it is perhaps the most telling evidence of Italian vernacular influence in Stuart Scotland. The rest (save a letter derived from the *Decameron*) was from the Italian poets. Poetry is easier to emulate, if not to excel in, than prose. And it is easier, in a sense, to cheat at this time by the use of aureate English, the equivalent of the style of the *grands rhétoriqueurs*. It should, incidentally, be remembered that 'aureation', making three long words do the work of one, is also found in the Latin of the period.

In the Machiavellian era prose with both an Italianate and Renaissance tinge was found in Scotland. In this respect a change had overtaken the prose writers of medieval Scotland, where no strong native tradition existed to sustain them in an independent course, and brought them in the sixteenth-century into a much more renaissance-dominated world. It was, after all, a world of books and if few English or Scottish publishers ventured into publishing works in Latin, they (hardly as yet to be regularly distinguished from booksellers) sold those imported from continental centres such as Venice, Lyons, Basle and Paris. In consequence there was a good deal of intellectual traffic between Scotland and the continent. But the greatest bridge which joined both halves of Britain to their neighbours was built of printed books.

Our initial guide here are the surviving books from Scottish libraries down to about 1560, when the Reformation did so much damage to the older collections.[23] These supply a very impressive picture of what the Scottish scholar acquired: virtually all of the main classical authors are represented, with Latin and Greek, and, equally important as transmitters of the ideas of classical antiquity, the patristic and early Christian writers.[24] The extant volumes are necessarily selective; there is no clue to what is missing, nor of course what was actually read and regarded as important. But something of this is revealed in the prose writers of Jacobean Scotland, and especially the historians, traditionally the purveyors of moral precepts, 'teaching by example' as men had said in antiquity and as they went on saying all through the Middle Ages and repeated with a new urgency during the Renaissance in Italy and, as it spread, everywhere in Europe.

Scotland, unlike England and France, did not import her humanist historians: 'from the start it was in the hands of natives'.[25] They are a

---

[23] John Durkan and Anthony Ross O.P., *Early Scottish Libraries* (Glasgow 1961), in effect reprinted from the *Innes Review*. See also Sears Jayne, *Library Catalogues of the English Renaissance* (Berkeley 1956), 23 and notes. Although it deals with a collection later than 1603 attention must also be drawn to the catalogue of books of Drummond of Hawthornden compiled by R. H. Macdonald (Edinburgh 1971). See also C. P. Finlayson, 'Clement Littill and his Library: The origins of Edinburgh University Library' in *Edinburgh Bibliographical Society and Friends of Edinburgh University Library*, Edinburgh 1980.

[24] Durkan and Ross, *Early Scottish Libraries*, Introduction, 12–13. This is reminiscent of the books recorded in the *Library Catalogue of Syon College*, ed. Mary Bateson (Cambridge 1898).

[25] E. Furter, *Geschichte der neueren Historiographie* (1911), best read in the only revised edition, the French translation (Paris 1914), used here; for quotation see 209.

remarkable lot, even if John Major's *Historia majoris Britanniae tam Angliae quam Scotiae* (Paris 1521), with its punning title, may be regarded as the product of an old-fashioned Parisian schoolman. His aim, as one might have expected, was to provide his patron James V with lessons of a practical sort and to do this with all the freedom of a scholastic disputant.[26] Hector Boece, another theologian, may be characterised as a humanist on the strength of his *Scotorum historiae a prima gentis origine libri XIX*. This came out, incomplete, at Paris in 1526, although it is hard to see why it was not finished. His book was completed by Ferrerio and is chiefly remarkable for its invention of the myth of the 'jus primae noctis' and the lists of mythical kings of early Scotland.[27] So far the clouds of religious discussion had not crossed the horizon. The subsequent historians reflect the religious storm. John Lesley's *De origine, moribus et rebus gestis Scotorum* was explicitly defending the old church; the first edition of his history came out in Rome in 1578.[28]

Much the greatest and most influential of the Jacobean historians was in the end a protestant and his works were among the most influential in the whole field of European neo-Latin scholarship. George Buchanan's career was not unlike that of Major's at the beginning, but he was primarily a writer and in the new manner. His experience as a professor at Bordeaux and Coimbra took him for a time away from letters and instruction; later he was tutor to James VI, which led directly into his involvement in politics.[29] He was unquestionably the most influential Scottish writer of the sixteenth century in Europe at large. As a historian his version of the events of the Reformation period was taken over by De Thou (Thuanus); his *Rerum Scoticarum historia*, published in Edinburgh in 1582, took the story down to

[26] Most accessible now as *A History of Greater Britain as well England as Scotland. . .*, trans. Archibald Constable with a life by Aeneas J. G. Mackay (Scottish History Society, Edinburgh 1982); cf. Fueter *loc. cit.*

[27] Boece's book ends with the accession of James III; it was reprinted by the Bannatyne Club in 1825 and by the New Spalding Club in 1894. On the nonsense about the 'jus Primae noctis' see Fueter; not only were contemporaries gulled (e.g. Polydore Vergil, *Anglica Historia*, Basel 1534, 167–8) but it continues to lead a shady journalistic life, as on p. 1 of the *Guardian* for 15 September 1979: 'Ancient right to a profitable gift shop'.

[28] A vernacular version written in Mary's reign and covering the period 1436–1561 was reprinted by the Bannatyne Club in 1830. It is hard (as Fueter acknowledges, 319–20) to regard John Knox's *History of the Reformation in Scotland* as history in the same sense as the others mentioned here; it is polemics, with an historical preface added later as book i; but see ed. W. Croft Dickinson, 2 vols (Edinburgh 1949), intro. lxxx–lxxxi.

[29] For the older studies of Irving and Hume Brown and the recent work by I. D. McFarlane, see above n. 7. An admirable paper on the composition of his dramatic verse was read at Bologna (above n. 9) by Dr Peter Sharratt. A recent study of the *History* and the *De jure regni* was published by H. R. Trevor-Roper, *George Buchanan and the Ancient Scottish Constitution*, third supplement to the EHR (London 1966), which is entertainingly cut down to size by G. W. S. Barrow in a review in *Annali della Fondazione per la storia amministrativa* 4 (1967), 635–5. And see now Quentin Skinner, *The Foundations of Modern Political Thought*, 2 vols (Cambridge 1978), ii 340–5 with references.

1571 and had enormous authority not least because of the author's deserved reputation as a Latinist.[30] He was, of all the persons mentioned here, the most 'humanist' and, though the inspiration of his interpretation of events was Calvinist and not in any sense Italian, the notion of the ex-statesman writing history in his latter days cannot fail to evoke Machiavelli and Guicciardini. His poetry, his grammar, even his variety of republican sentiment may convey more than is just an echo of a 'renaissance' element. But the influences which were most important to him were French, as with so many Scots referred to above, and of the historians he regrettably paid exaggerated attention to Boece.

If France bulks much larger than Italy in the cultural contacts of Scotland and Scots, there were steady and regular visitors from Scotland to the Peninsula and in the other direction. Of Scottish connections down to the Reformation the most productive occasions were due to membership of the Roman Church. The petitions flew from Scotland to Rome under James IV and James V, especially after 1517 when the king could threaten the pope that his country would desert orthodoxy until his insatiable demands were met.[31] For the most part the royal (and noble) demands were met and it was a financially denuded kirk which moved into the Reformation. Popes, of course, occasionally tried to see that their beneficence reached the right channels; such was a task performed for the last time by Pietro Lippomano, bishop of Verona, in 1548. These political and administrative contacts between the Scottish Crown, Scottish clergy and the curia have been much studied.[32] They had few detectable cultural consequences (or even for that matter spiritual ones). To this there is one exception in the activities of Giovanni Ferrerio, a Piedmontese who was indisputably an 'Italian humanist' and who taught for a few years at the abbey of Kinloss in the 1530s and 1540s. He also continued the history of Hector Boece, this work being published in Lausanne in 1574. He was involved in the diplomacy of Lippomano's nunciature and if his stature as a humanist is modest there is no doubt that he played an important role, more cultural than that of most Italians, among Scots in Paris.[33]

[30] Subsequent editions in the *Opera omnia*, ed. T. Ruddiman (Edinburgh 1715, repr. Leiden 1725). For some pertinent remarks on Scottish sixteenth-century historiography see Thomas I. Rae, 'The historical writing of Drummond of Hawthornden', SHR liv (1975), 22–62.

[31] Documented in R. K Hannay's two posthumous collections: *Letters of James IV*, ed. R. L. Mackie and Anne Spillman (Scottish History Society, Edinburgh 1953) and *Letters of James V*, ed. Denys Hay (Edinburgh 1954).

[32] For these diplomatic contacts see W. J. Anderson, 'Rome and Scotland' in *Essays on the Scottish Reformation*, ed. David McRoberts (Glasgow 1962), 463–83 with an important correction at 468 n. of Hannay ed. Hay (see previous n.). On Grimani and Lippomano see the recent study of John E. Law and John M. Manion, 'The nunciature to Scotland of Pietro Lippomano, bishop of Verona', *Atti e memorie della Accademia di Agricoltura, Scienze e Lettere di Verona*, ser. vi, xxii (1970–71), 403–48.

[33] John Durkan, 'Giovanni Ferrerio and religious humanism in sixteenth-century Scotland' in *Studies in Church History*, 17 (Oxford, 1981). I have to thank him for letting me read the text of this and also of his essay on 'Giovanni Ferrerio, Gesner and French Affairs'.

Ferrerio left no account of his experience as such, but only incidental allusions and impressions. Indeed the only Italian who did so was Pius II (as Aeneas Sylvius Piccolomini) whose contribution to Scottish cultural life was nil; true, an idealised picture of the future prelate figures among the paintings in the Piccolomini Library in Siena Cathedral. But Pinturicchio just painted an imaginary sylvan scene in which to place king and future pope.

Two other indices of Italian influence may be pointers to a change in the intellectual climate – the introduction of italic and roman in printing and of humanist script in writing. Roman and italic type penetrated into the few books published in Scotland during the mid-sixteenth century.[34] This is to some extent an unreal point, since Latin-reading scholars in both England and Scotland habitually bought their books from the great continental centres. Handwriting is complicated by another consideration; there is no fixed time when italic or roman scripts replaced the older native chancery or court hands. It was a gradual process but as and when humanist secretaries were employed by popes and Italian princes the practice of writing in the new manner (cancelleresca) began to spread. For long, however, a scholar, even a dyed-in-the-wool humanist, often used both hands – a stylish italic or the traditional book or court hand of his neighbourhood, or a mixture of the two. In general it was, once again, not till the seventeenth century that the new manner became an essential sign of learning, or at any rate a pretence to good breeding.[35] This transition remains unstudied, but examples of the new way

[34] H. G. Aldis, *List of Books published in Scotland before 1700* (rev. ed. Edinburgh 1970). The National Library of Scotland maintains a copy in which additions are recorded. Some 400 books were printed in Scotland before 1603. William Beattie, 'Some early Scottish books', in *The Scottish Tradition* ed. G. W. S. Barrow (Edinburgh 1974), 107–20, esp. at 116. Professor Beattie tells me that 'the first printer in Scotland to use Roman and italic' was Thomas Davidson, 1541; sparingly to begin with, e.g. for chapter headings.

[35] Above n. 23. The complications explain why the subject has not been definitively studied and perhaps cannot be. A perusal of the copies of James V's Letters in NLS MSS 35 5 9 A, B, C, D, shows that, although there are occasional words in italic even in the 1520s, the royal secretaries did their business in a good traditional hand; italic influences manifest themselves regularly only at a later date, in the 1560s and 1570s; cf. the last folios of MS 35 5 9 D. Mr J. F. Hudson of the British Library, who kindly consulted two similar volumes, Royal MSS 13 B II and 18 B VI, on my behalf reached a similar conclusion. For the other collections see Hannay's brief survey (ed. Hay, xi–xiii, above n. 31). These are of course copies kept for the record and not the originals as despatched, which Hannay did not chase up: it would have been an enormous task, though essential for a true answer to the problem posed. Two other points may be made. It seems almost certain that many men of learning and or of public importance *signed* their names in italic, while habitually employing an old-fashioned hand, a point to be remembered in considering the book inscriptions mentioned above and the author's observations in *The Italian Renaissance in its Historical Background* (rev. ed., Cambridge, 1977), 202 and plate XXIV. Finally it should be remembered that manuals of the new art (*cancelleresca*) began to be published in Italy in and after 1520s: *Three Classics of Italian Calligraphy*, ed. Oscar Ogg (New York, 1953). For *cancelleresca corsiva* and the books based on it, see James Wardrop, *The Script of Humanism* (Oxford 1963), chap. iii and references. Pertinent remarks on the Scottish scene appear in the very useful work of Grant Simpson, *Scottish Handwriting 1150–1650* (Edinburgh 1973), 19–31.

of writing in early sixteenth-century Scotland are represented by two beautiful italic signatures of Bishop Chisholm of Dunblane.[36] George Buchanan likewise seems to have written habitually a fine italic.[37]

In conclusion, the Italian Renaissance as such made a relatively delayed appearance in Scotland and it was in general transmitted by Scots and Italians based in France. The Reformation of 1560 unquestionably interrupted this process, but the influence of new ideas can be seen in the steady growth of libraries (containing for the most part books printed on the Continent) and in a strong historiographical tradition, notably represented by George Buchanan. He, too, may reflect some part of Renaissance Italian republican sentiment, though Calvinist theology had a more powerful influence on his thought. Nor were the Scottish historians, or other writers, affected much by the rhetorical temptations which are so marked a feature of much humanist historiography.[38]

[36] Durkan and Ross, *Early Scottish Libraries*, plates XXXA, XXXVI.

[37] Those examples of his undoubted hand which I have seen are all in impeccable italic: the Lisbon inquisition of 1550, to be found, aside from other reproductions, in plates II and III of D. A. Millar, ed., *George Buchanan: a Memorial 1506–1906* (St Andrews and London, n.d.) and NLS Adv. MS. 15.1.6, fos. 18, 49, the former in French, the latter a Latin Testimonial addressed to Beza, dated respectively 1574 and 1581). The only oddity is that in the same MS, fos. 3–11 there are Buchanan's proposals for university reform at St Andrews, written in a traditional court hand; on fo. 12[vo] someone (perhaps the clerk who copied the document?) has written the foregoing 'pages are in Buchanan's own hand'. Dr T. I. Rae of the National Library of Scotland was good enough to look at this piece and confirms what I have said.

[38] Cf. Dr Rae's remarks on Drummond in art. cited above n. 30, at 47–49.

DENYS HAY

8

The Darker Vision of the Scottish Renaissance: the Devil and Francis Stewart

On Hallowe'en 1589 a mysterious group of figures approached North Berwick kirk. Some had sailed down the Forth in sieves, others had used bundles of straw as their mode of conveyance. As they entered the kirkyard the company danced a reel singing,

> 'commer go ye before, commer goe ye,
> gif ye will not goe before, commer let me'.

They were led by Gellie Duncan from Tranent who provided hellish music on her jew's harp. Eventually the procession of 'abone a hundreth persounes, quhairof thair wes six men, and all the rest wemen' entered the church, each individual bowing towards the pulpit which was surrounded by 'muckle black candles'. When all were assembled the temperature within the building suddenly dropped as 'the Devill stert up himselff in the pulpett, lyke ane mekle blak man, and callit ewerie man be his name and everie ane answerit "Here maister"'. On his command they opened up graves 'twa within and ane withoot the kirk' and removed the joints of the toes, fingers and knees of the disinterred corpses to be distributed among the company. 'The Devill commandit thame to keip his commandmentis quhilkis war, to do all the ewill they could. Before they depairtit thay kist his erse. He had on him ane goun and ane hatt, quhilkis wer baith blak; his body was hard lyk yrn as they thoucht that handled him; his faice was terrible, his nose lyk the bek of an egle, gret bournin eyn, his hands and legs wes herry, with clawis upon his handis and feit lyke the griffon and he spak with a rough deep voice'.

If anyone dared to take their eyes off this daunting spectacle they were able to distinguish a few well known faces in the black congregation. There was Anny Sampson, the wise woman of Keith, John Cunningham or Fian, the schoolmaster from Prestonpans who stood on the deil's right hand, Euphemie MacKalzane, daughter of Lord Cliftonhall a senator of the College of Justice, Barbara Napier, wife of an Edinburgh burgess and Richie Graham, 'notoure and knawin nigromancer, ane commoun abusar of the peopill'. They were plotting a veritable deed without a name, nothing less than the destruction of King James. Venom of toads, the use of 'pictours' or wax images of his majesty, and charmed cats swung three times round the head widdershins before being launched into the sea to conjure storms, were all to no avail. When the deil asked how the king fared a more than usually gormless individual, 'an ald selly pure plowman callit Gray Meill', chanced to remark (forgetting the company he was in) ' "naething ails the king yet, God be thankit" ', whereupon the deil 'gaif him a gret blaw'. When the devil was asked why he bore such malice towards James, his answer would have been to that monarch most gratifying. 'By reason the king is the greatest enemy I have in the world'.[1]

The affair of the North Berwick witches is one of the most familiar episodes in Scottish history yet until comparatively recently it has received surprisingly little serious attention. It presents the historian with a classic dilemma – of how to cope with abundant testimony, much of it legal record, the content of which must be intellectually rejected? A possible approach is to investigate the political, social and intellectual origins of the Scottish witch craze and to use the experience of one man implicated in the witch trials – Francis Stewart, earl of Bothwell – as a lens through which to view some of the complex problems which beset Scotland in the last tortuous decade of the sixteenth century.[2]

For their alleged part in the sabbath at North Berwick, for being party to a demonic pact with the devil, many were to suffer appalling tortures from which judicial murder came as blessed release. Anny Sampson was condemned to be 'wirreit' or strangled and her body burned. John Cunningham was brutally tortured by the boot, knotted cords tied round his head and by the 'turkas', pincers used to extract his nails. He steadfastly maintained his innocence but was executed. Euphemie MacKalzane was one of the few to be burned alive, presumably because of her social status. It has been estimated that between three and four thousand persons were executed for witchcraft during the century 1590 to 1690.[3] Scots often pride themselves on the bloodlessness of the Scottish Reformation, on the relative absence of martyrs on either side;[4] these thousands were perhaps the true martyrs of the reformation era.

In this respect although there is much comedy in the accounts of the witch trials, witchcraft proves a sadly humourless subject. The tract, *News From Scotland*, on which Shakespeare possibly drew when writing *Macbeth*, can

[1] The foregoing composite is drawn from Pitcairn, *Criminal Trials* i, 239–40, 244; Sir James Melville, *Memoirs* 395; *News from Scotland* printed in Pitcairn 213–23.

[2] Two most useful recent studies are Christina Larner, 'James VI and I and Witchcraft' in Alan G. R. Smith (ed.) *The Reign of James VI and I* (London 1973) pp. 74–90, and Arthur H. Williamson, *Scottish National Consciousness in the age of James VI* (Edinburgh 1979). See also on this topic F. Legge 'Witchcraft in Scotland' *Scottish Review* xvii (1891), Helen Stafford, 'Notes on Scottish Witchcraft Cases 1590–91 in *Essays in honour of Conyers Read* (Chicago 1953) and Stuart Clark, 'King James's *Daemonologie*: Witchcraft and Kingship' in Sydney Anglo (ed.) *The Damned Art. Essays in the Literature of Witchcraft* (London 1977).

[3] George F. Black, *A Calendar of Cases of Witchcraft in Scotland 1510–1727* (New York 1938) 17–18.

[4] See e.g. Gordon Donaldson, *Scottish History and the Scottish Nation*, University of Edinburgh Inaugural Lecture (1964) 7–8.

only be described as sadistic pornography. Torture was freely employed to obtain confessions. Thumbscrews and the boot were the favoured implements but one expedient was simply to keep the victim awake, 'the choicest means they use in Scotland for discoverie of witches' according to an English commentator.[5] This was an inversion of the widely held belief that witches, since they were unnatural beings, could not sleep, just as they were supposedly incapable of shedding tears. It is noteworthy that Macbeth never sleeps after the murder of Duncan thus indicating that he is plainly a witch.

There had always been a belief in Scotland in black and white magic. John Major of Haddington related that witches were well known in East Lothian during his childhood but he considered them harmless, regarding them with the same dispassionate interest as he did the superstitions of the local country people who always put fire in the water after they washed their feet or spilled a little boiling water for the spirit of the hearth. Though such beliefs were vain and superstitious 'the good women to whom these customs were handed down by their ancestors are not to be condemned as sinners until they are told that such acts are wrong.'[6] There were isolated witch trials in the course of the sixteenth century[7] but it was only with the devil at North Berwick that the idea of the demonic pact first surfaced. The explanation is apparently to be sought in the Danish connection.[8]

James was described at the time of his marriage by proxy to the fourteen year old Anne of Denmark as a 'yong king, chast and continent as Hypolites, a lover distracte with a wourld of passionat cogitacioones'.[9] Three times Anne set sail for Scotland and three times her fleet was driven back by storms the like of which the Danish admiral, Peter Munk, could not recall but which he attributed to witchcraft.[10] When James learned of Anne's misfortune he ordered Francis Stewart, fifth earl of Bothwell, Admiral of Scotland to sail to Denmark to fetch his bride. When Bothwell who was nephew of Mary queen of Scots' third husband submitted estimates they were dismissed as exorbitant by Chancellor Maitland who suggested that James collect his bride himself. James therefore with totally uncharacteristic heroism committed himself and his hopes 'Leanderlike to the waves of the ocean and all for his beloved Eroes sake', departing on 21 October in a vessel packed with delicate victual, live cattle and poultry as well as other foodstuffs and large quantities of wine.[11] Maitland accompanied him while Bothwell remained at home with a fair share of responsibility for governing the country. James arrived safely in Norway 'efter mikle foull wather of a stormie wintar' whence he proceeded to Denmark where he 'drank stoutlie till the spring tyme'.[12]

---

[5] Black, *Calendar of Witchcraft* 15.
[6] Aeneas Mackay, *Memoir of John Major* (Edinburgh 1892).
[7] On these see Williamson, *National Consciousness* chapter two.
[8] Larner, 'Witchcraft' 81.
[9] *CSP Scot*, x, 164.
[10] Ethel C. Williams, *Anne of Denmark* (London 1970) 15–18.
[11] *CSP Scot*, x, 181.
[12] James Melville, *Diary* (Bannatyne Club, 1829), 186.

It has been suggested that the Danish connection may have helped to stimulate witch persecution in Scotland.[13] Against the background of the catholic scare in Scotland there is a particular reason why the Danish experience might be found appealing. The Danish reformers had early adopted the expedient of labelling all who opposed or attacked the reformed church as witches. In the 1540s Peter Palladius told all good christians that they must not remain silent if they knew of a witch. He related that witches were being hunted as wolves and recently fifty two had been burned at one time. 'One reveals the other and they pass out into the other world together'.[14] That the Danish precedent simply reinforced Scottish prejudices may be indicated by the case of Bessie Dunlop of Ayr in 1576 who was allegedly invited by the devil to become a catholic.[15] Like Bessie and so many of the accused throughout the period of the witch craze Gellie Duncan of Tranent was possessed of suspiciously abundant knowledge of herbal preparations and medical care. According to *News From Scotland* which, however unpleasant and sensational, seems to present a fairly reliable chronology, Gellie's employer questioned her expertise and put her to the torture. When the *stigmata sagarum*, the devil's mark, was found on her body, she confessed the names of her accomplices. There is little to specifically connect Gellie with the old faith save that her inquisitor, David Seton, was in the employ of his kinsmen, one of the most prominent recusant families in Scotland.

The connection is much more explicit in the case of Anny Sampson. She is attributed with two conjurations, or prayers, supposedly uttered in the name of the devil, yet clearly by their content, to be assigned to the pre-Reformation church. The same woman also used '*ave Maria*' in her spells.[16] The popular perception of recusancy in Scotland was almost identical in context and environment to that of witchcraft. One woman who wished the priest to baptise her child met a group of strangers beside a burn 'of whom one clad with a black plaid' performed the sacrament. Recusants attended ruined church buildings for private prayer. Funerals were conducted according to popish rites. Pilgrimages continued to take place at Beltane. Just as witches incriminated their associates, pilgrims who visited a shrine in Aberdeenshire were asked to give the names of their fellows.[17] If some sort of gathering really did take place, at some time, at North Berwick, it may have been a recusant service. The suggestion that Bothwell was actually present is

---

[13] Larner, 'Witchcraft' 81.

[14] H. F. Rørdam and T. S. Rørdam (eds.) *Ny Kirkehistoriske Samlinger Selskab for Danmarks Kirkehistorie.* 6 vols. (Copenhagen 1857–73) iv, 581–2. This reference is drawn from Frederik Bredahl Petersen, Dr Johannes Macchabaeus, John McAlpin. Scotland's Contribution to the Reformation in Denmark. Unpublished Ph.D. Thesis, New College 1937.

[15] Pitcairn, *Trials*, i, Pt. I, 49–58.

[16] Pitcairn, *Trials*, i, Pt. III, 237–8.

[17] These references are usefully collected in Margaret Sanderson, 'Catholic Recusancy in Scotland in the Sixteenth Century' *Innes Review*, xxi, (1970) 104.

purely fanciful but there were enough rumours of his catholic complicity to tie him in with the victims.[18]

Early in July 1590 a crazed woman from Lubeck arrived at Leith proclaiming that James was the 'prince in the north' of whom noble acts were prophesied. Later that month the news reached Edinburgh that five or six Danish witches had been arrested for conjuring the storms which had kept Anne in Scandinavia. That same day 'sindrie witches' were arraigned for manufacturing a 'pictour' of the laird of Wardie.[19] In November the first of the North Berwick congregation was examined. Although it was feared that 'some of good qualities are like to be blotted by the dealings of the wickett sorte',[20] it was not until April 1591 that Bothwell, who had fallen out of favour within a month of James's return, was specifically implicated. The chronology is highly significant.

The witch examinations and trials commenced in November and December 1590. Those compulsively curious peddlars of gossip, the English agents in Edinburgh, knew little of what transpired save that James had an audience with Anny Sampson 'to discover sundry things touching his own life'. If this was the same interview as that noted in *News From Scotland* when Anny recounted the exchanges between James and Anne on the night of their honeymoon it was an historic occasion for it transformed the royal sceptic into a believer in witchcraft.[21] The trial and conviction of John Cunningham or Fian took place on 26 December. His main weaknesses, to judge from the available evidence, included women and an inability to withstand the most hideous tortures that could be devised. Anny Sampson was tried a month later. Sir James Melville's memory must have been at fault when he recalled that Anny had testified to the devil holding up a 'pictour' of Scotland's Solomon with the words, 'this is King James the Sext ordorit to be consumed at the instance of a noble man Francis Erle Bodowell'.[22] Doubt is cast on his story because *News From Scotland*, published in 1591, while discussing the trials of Cunningham and Sampson, nowhere mentions Bothwell.

English agents were a little perplexed when some of the accused fled across the border. James sent David Seton after them, urging the English wardens to apprehend and return the refugees. Robert Bowes was decidedly sceptical about the whole business for the good reason that some of the testimony implicated himself, described unflatteringly as 'a litle black and fatt man with black haire'. Many things, besides the attempt to besmirch his own good character, were told by the witches 'to plaise the examiners'. Even Cunningham at his death confessed that he told his tales 'by fear of torture and to save his life'.[23] It was only when the fugitives were arrested and

[18] Margaret Murray, 'The Devil of North Berwick' SHR, xv (1918), 318–20.
[19] *CSP Scot*, x, 348, 365.
[20] *CSP Scot*, x, 425.
[21] *CSP Scot*, x, 430; Pitcairn, *Trials*, i, Pt. III, 218.
[22] Melville, *Memoirs*, 395.
[23] *CSP Scot*, x, 464–7.

returned north, early in April, that Bothwell was first implicated, accused in the testimony of Ritchie Graham.

Yet James had no intention of bringing Bothwell to trial. He simply applied further pressure to persuade Francis to fulfill his long expressed intention of going into exile. James told Maitland to instruct Bothwell to hold himself in readiness until a ship could convey him to Germany or Italy. 'Quhat lettir is milorde craving of recommendation to other princis, graunt thaim sa being thay be honorabill. As for the cullourid cause of his departure, adwyse upon sum honorabill excuse, for thair is na vant of maitter'. That same letter contained James's notorious advice with regard to one of the more celebrated witches. 'Trye by the medicinairis aithis gif Barbara Napier be with bairn or not. Tak na delaying ansour. Gif ye finde sho be not, to the fyre with her presentlie and cause bowell her publiclie'. He also offered counsel on the treatment of Euphemie MacKalzane. Lesser witches were also to be pursued with the significant exception of Richie Graham who was to be left until James could 'take further ordoure with him'.[24] Richard or Richie may have been a Graham of Netherby, the family of 'ould Rich' who, with his brothers, populated that part of Eskdale.[25] By April 15 his assertion that Bothwell had urged him to conjure the king's destruction was common knowledge. It later transpired that Bothwell was very well acquainted with Graham for the earl's manservant, Renian Chirnside, had acted as an intermediary between the two since at least 1588. Bothwell had sheltered Graham within his bounds and he had arranged for Graham to attend his dying brother-in-law, the earl of Angus.[26]

When Bothwell appeared in Edinburgh on April 16 to answer charges, he threatened the life of any that would affirm that he had conspired with Graham against the king, offering to undergo torture to prove his innocence.[27] He was warded in Edinburgh Castle, his supporters were forced to remove themselves from the city and an order was issued for the arrest of Chirnside and another servant. Examination of Bothwell having been set for 6 May, James was convinced that the evidence against him was so weak that the convention or assize of the nobility would never find him guilty. The Scottish peers agreed, hastily manufacturing excuses to stay away from Edinburgh, reluctant as they were to try one of their own.[28] Two weeks later, however, it is possible to detect a significant hardening of James's attitude as well as a more widespread realisation that Francis might actually be in real danger.[29]

James's change of mind is open to various explanations. One speculation is that when James interviewed Richie Graham he came to believe that his story was genuine, much as he had been convinced by Anny Sampson. It is

[24] *CSP Scot*, x, 510.
[25] *Border Papers*, ed. J. Bain, 2 vols. (Edinburgh, 1894–6), i, 124–5.
[26] *Border Papers*, i, 487.
[27] *CSP Scot*, x, 504.
[28] *CSP Scot*, x, 518.
[29] *HMC Salisbury*, iv, 178.

well attested that James was outraged when the court threw out the charges against Barbara Napier who was accused of plotting the deaths of Angus and the king. Barbara must have been a formidable lady for she ably defended herself in a terrifying situation yet still found time to send a message to Bothwell bidding him stand firm against the conspiracy to implicate him.[30] When her verdict was returned James was so incensed that he claimed assize of error, marshalling learned arguments to explain his personal intervention in the case. 'Witchcraft, which is a thing growen very common amongst us, I know it to be a most abhominable synne'. It is hardly surprising that some thought 'there shall be great probations deduced against (Bothwell) in time, and that there is some farther matter in it nor yet appears, and that his majesty would not have taken so deep a conceit upon so weak a ground except he had some more for him nor every man knows which he reserves to be opened in his own time'.[31] The trial of Euphemie MacKalzane in mid June seemed to reinforce the king's concept that the 'erle is fowle in practyse of the king's death'.[32] Francis had no wish to feed the fire. On 22 June he broke ward, challenging the chancellor to seize him and boasting that he would give 'ony man a croune'. Three days later he was forfeited.[33]

Francis Stewart was never in any doubt about who was behind the conspiracy to charge him with witchcraft. At almost every opportunity both he and his apologists identified the culprit as John Maitland of Thirlestane, who 'caused feade a process of witchcraft' against Bothwell.[34] There is little evidence in James's statements that he was consciously part of the conspiracy though he probably convinced himself of Francis's guilt. The question of whether Bothwell deserved such a reputation will be discussed below.

After his forfeiture Bothwell created his own legend. He flitted back and forth between Crichton and Edinburgh, riding beneath the city walls and dining openly and ostentatiously at Leith.[35] In a series of hairsbreadth escapes he eluded capture to return like the moth to the flame. His name was linked with that of Queen Anne who also loathed Maitland. His servants were tortured to reveal his whereabouts. In December he assailed the king and queen in their private chambers at Holyrood, a move which was construed as an attempt on James's life. Seven of his accomplices were subsequently hanged. A service of thanksgiving was held in St Giles for the king's delivery and a reward was offered for Bothwell's arrest.[36] In January James boldly galloped through East Lothian to take Bothwell by surprise, an expedition which ended ignominiously when the king's horse threw him into the chilly waters of the Tyne.[37]

[30] Pitcairn, *Trials*, i, Pt. III, 242–3; *CSP Scot*, x, 506.
[31] *HMC Salisbury*, iv, 110.
[32] *CSP Scot*, x, 531.
[33] Moysie, *Memoirs* (Bannatyne Club, 1830), 86; Pitcairn, *Trials*, i, 259–60.
[34] *CSP Scot*, xi, 61–4, *Warrender Papers*, ed. A. I. Cameron (*SHS*, 1931–2), ii, 162, *Border Papers*, i, 488, Calderwood, *History*, v, 138, 150–6.
[35] *CSP Scot*, x, 547–8, 550.
[36] Calderwood, *History*, v, 140, 144.
[37] *HMC Salisbury*, iv, 178, Calderwood, v, 144.

Throughout 1592 Bothwell's exploits and activities, real and imagined were the subject of constant speculation. One week he was reported in the Hebrides, another riding through the Merse and Lothian, on yet another he was in Caithness. James was so bent upon the earl's destruction 'that he says if he should seek revenge out of all the world he will give his life'.[38] The king fumed when the outlaw's supporters found refuge in England. Various abortive schemes were devised to capture Bothwell before he could seize the king's person. It required a mere whisper that Francis had been seen between Edinburgh and Leith for James to order the fortification of the city and to command all his subjects to be ready with weapons and armour to seize the earl. Bothwell became even more of a potential danger following the slaying of his uncle, the Bonnie Earl o' Moray in February 1592. James's failure to punish Huntly was contrasted with his obsessive persecution of Bothwell. 'The present state in this realm is tossed with dangerous storms', wrote Bowes, 'troubling the passage of religion and justice and greatly sounding to the peril of the king's honour, estate and person by the intention of sudden surprise of his court with violence to be enterprised by Bothwell and his accomplices'.[39] For once the rumours had considerable substance. Bothwell crossed the Forth with four hundred men and attacked the king at Falkland in what became known as the 'Falkland Raid'. The affair was botched; James pursued the earl to the West March. Some of Bothwell's correspondence was seized, revealing that he had been in communication with the catholic earls, Angus and Errol who had been party to the Falkland raid. Bothwell withdrew to the Highlands where a serious illness generated reports of his death. His recovery brought another attempt to surprise the king, a plan which the ever attentive Bowes discovered, warning James. The idea was to place thirty men in two small fishing boats behind Inchkeith in order to ambush James as he sailed from Leith to Kinghorn. Once again the scheme was foiled. Further attacks on Falkland were planned but nothing came of them.[40] Attempts to surprise Bothwell enjoyed no greater success. And so the comedy of the cousins continued. Bothwell made several appearances, sometimes in disguise, in Edinburgh, thumbed his nose at a royal expedition sent to arrest him in the Borders and he continued to negotiate with both Parma and Elizabeth. Another catholic scare was sparked off by the arrest of George Kerr in possession of the Spanish Blanks at the end of the year. It appeared that a number of Scottish nobles were prepared to rise for the pope.[41] Although there would later be an attempt to implicate Bothwell in the Kerr affair the earl for the moment had other matters on his mind. He celebrated Yuletide by launching another attack upon Holyrood and he brought in New Year in the North of England so creating a diplomatic incident since James threatened to 'break amity with any prince in the world

[38] *CSP Scot*, x, 653.

[39] *CSP Scot*, x, 697.

[40] *CSP Scot*, x, 730–1, 735–40.

[41] M. Lee, *John Maitland of Thirlestone* (Princeton, 1959), 256–9, Francis Shearman, 'The Spanish Blanks', *Innes Review*, iii, (1952), 81–103.

who should take the maintenance of Bothwell against him'.[42] For good measure Edinburgh was fortified against him in January.

King James's neurosis had created a monster whose adventures continued to astonish and amaze. English commentators were reminded of Robin Hood. When James heard that Bothwell intended to don a false beard to enter Edinburgh and throw himself at the king's feet on his way to parliament he ordered that he be shot with pistols while he was on his knees.[43] There was of course no evidence that Bothwell had any such intention. In a surprise move which captured the imagination of contemporaries, as it has that of posterity, Francis came face to face with his monarch at Holyrood on 24 July 1593. James had just risen from the privy when Francis appeared in his bedchamber, sword in hand. Elizabeth had been trying to persuade James for some months to accept Francis back into his peace. She deplored James's failure to prosecute Huntly for the Moray slaying and she feared a catholic assault through Scotland. Maitland was currently in disgrace but James was about to invite him back to court. In an attempt to block such a move the 'Stewart party' at court, headed by Lennox, smuggled Bothwell into Holyrood. There are several extant versions of the confrontation between the two cousins (and two different versions which Bothwell communicated to different individuals); some believed that the whole affair had been carefully rehearsed. James vowed that he would die rather than suffer the indignity of taking Bothwell into his peace but he relented when the earl presented his sword and invited James to strike off his head. Thereafter all embraced and remained in quietness at Holyrood.[44]

Francis immediately took it upon himself to inform James of the dangers threatening the commonwealth – the boldness of the papists, the murderous effusion of blood, the failure to punish Moray's murderers, the oppression of the poor, the danger of a breach with England and 'the bareness of his estate'. He also told James that he would never, for all the crowns in France, all the ducats in Spain, all the silver and gold in the Indies East and West, for all the kingdoms in Europe, Africa and Asia, utter one word in council, or bear arms in the field, 'against the amitie of the two realmes and and princes, and the religion nowe by them auctorised'.[45] In return for his fine words Francis received a royal protection and the promise of a trial on the old charge of having conspired with Richie Graham. Yet even as he basked in his monarch's uneasy affection Francis was in correspondence with Elizabeth's agents, pledging support for protestantism and England against the disciples of Anti-christ. He offered to raise a force for Elizabeth but counselled that this proceeding be kept secret from James 'lest our purpose being revealed to our adversaries and our designs impeached'.[46]

[42] *CSP Scot*, xi, 25.
[43] *CSP Scot*, xi, 82, 128.
[44] *CSP Scot*, xi, 130–5, *Border Papers*, i, 481–6, *CSPD*, 1591–4, 368, Calderwood, *History*, v, 256–7, Lee, *Maitland*, 261–2.
[45] *Border Papers*, i, 483, *CSP Scot*, xi, 143.
[46] *CSP Scot*, xi, 705–6.

The accommodation with the king was what Francis had sought all along. The attacks on Holyrood and Falkland as well as the Inchkeith escapade and the resort to disguises had all aimed at securing the king's presence and, hopefully, a royal pardon. Persistent reports that Bothwell intended to remove or imprison the king and reign in his place were quite without foundation. The threat was doubtless real enough to James who never forgot the precedent of his mother's deposition but the reports of violence and resistance to authority conceal the real issue in the Bothwell affair. The attack on Bothwell was perceived at the time as a great contest between the crown and the nobility, the great test of the policies of Chancellor Maitland.

It was believed that James had resolved, during his sojourn in Denmark, to establish a new form of government and that 'thereby the wholl nobilitie shalbe prejudiced in their auncient priveledges for their free accesse to the king's person and vote in counsell and matters of estate'.[47] There was no need to fear any kind of Danish model but it is a truism of history that what people believed to be the case is always as important, if not more so, than the reality. Back in 1586 Francis and James had exchanged harsh words when the king refused to allow Bothwell and another nobleman to accompany him as he rode to Falkland. They expected their noble birth to confer the privilege upon them but James would have none of it, he would be no-one's slave and would ride with whomsoever he wished.[48] In March 1592 a 'little pamphlet' was displayed in St Giles setting out Bothwell's career and intention to reform. That pamphlet may be identified with an anonymous tract among the Warrender papers, 'In Defence of Earl Bothwell: To the Nobility'.[49] The tract warns the Scottish nobility that their safety is endangered by the 'unjust' pursuit of Bothwell. 'When a fire bursts out, men cast aside their greatest affairs to quench the flame, but you nobles of Scotland who call yourselves sons of your country and brethern of her children are content to be gaping onlookers at the peril which threatens your country and order'. Bothwell, a nobleman, suffered an 'incredible and unnaturall accusation . . . by an infamous person moved by the disposition and humour of his devilish nature'. Bothwell had acquitted himself with great honour during the king's absence. The tempest which has engulfed him will overwhelm the rest of the nobility. 'The peril of one is the peril of all'.

The Master of Gray explained to Burghley that 'almost the whole body of the Scottish nobility' shared Bothwell's cause. They sought to secure reformation of the kirk, to honour and serve their 'natural king' who was subject to bad counsel and 'to see such settled dealing between these two realms that neither of them be the footstool of foreigners for the overthrow of both'.[50] Robert Bowes thought that the Scottish courtiers were unable to

---

[47] *CSP Scot*, x, 285.

[48] *Border Papers*, i, 224.

[49] *Warrender Papers*, ii, 154–64. I share Professor Lee's doubts about attributing the 'defence' to Robert Bruce. (*Maitland* 230n.). The style is reminiscent of that of John Colville.

[50] *CSP Scot*, xi, 723, 744–5.

sustain the burden of government without the assistance of more of the nobility and the advice of well affected persons from the baronage, the burghs and the church. Bothwell refused to leave Scotland because he believed he could sway the balance between the courtiers and their opponents. He directed many letters to his peers trying to win them over to his point of view.[51] In his 'Lamentation to the Ministers' which attempted to avoid the sentence of excommunication in 1592 he returned to the theme of unjust accusation, begging the clergy not to ban one who was 'conjoined in religion and heart'. In his conclusion he implicitly compared his own situation to that of a free nobleman – he was forbidden rest, his kinsmen and friends were suborned to betray him while others aimed to murder or poison him.[52]

Elizabeth was both displeased by, and suspicious of, James's sudden *volte face* on Bothwell. She lambasted James for accepting an outlaw into his peace without notice and she criticised Francis for his familiarity with the king. She need not have feared. Bothwell's restless spirit was not to be tamed. A convention was called to Stirling for 7 September when James intended to reconcile the catholic earls and their opponents. The Humes, driven out by the Stewart coup, returned to court. James had ordered them to return Coldingham to Bothwell who vowed to seize it by force if they refused. Hume taunted the earl by saying that all the Stewarts should not take 'one silly bee out of the moss of his bounds against his will'.[53] The old enmities and ugly suspicions resurfaced. James, possibly in response to Elizabeth's promptings, backtracked on his remission to Bothwell, leaving the decision to a November parliament, provided that the earl would find surety for the removal of himself into exile shortly thereafter. Bothwell failed to keep an appointment with the commissioners for restitution because he believed the Humes were waiting to ambush him. He was ordered to Crichton, and from there for his greater safety to Jedburgh, pending parliament's decision. He was still consulted by English agents who remained apprehensive about a catholic revival at the Scottish court. 'Hearken what Bothwell does and where he is', Burghley advised Bowes, 'and if you find him not divided in his courses from religion, and that the churches have a care of him, you shall then give him all convenient comfort'.[54]

Parliament's decision went against Francis Stewart. The king was discharged of all promises made to him and it decided against restitution. He was ordered to quit the country within fifteen days. Bothwell in consequence went down the wind, alternately wooed and reviled on all sides. No-one could fathom his motives or intentions during the remainder of his time in Scotland. Mar thought he might be restored after a decent period in exile. Others believed that, with the ministers he would attempt to kidnap the king. He and Hume stalked one another on Tweedside and skirmished on the outskirts of Edinburgh. In April 1594 the Stewart faction, Bothwell among

[51] *CSP Scot*, x, 774–5, 781.
[52] *CSP Scot*, x, 825–8; see also his answer to 'the calumniers' (*CSP Scot*, xi, 61).
[53] *CSP Scot*, xi, 170.
[54] *CSP Scot*, xi, 212.

them, took up arms to resist the 'Spaniard' but barely a month later he was condemned from the pulpit, the devasting instrument of the very cause he claimed to champion. He was approached by the catholic earls, banded with the borderers and skirmished with the Humes at Dean Mills.[55]

So desperate was Bothwell by August 1594 that he informed Sir Robert Cecil that he would reject twenty five thousand crowns offered him by the papist faction if Elizabeth would intervene on his behalf. All Scotland feared some initiative on his part at the baptism of Prince Henry. There were persistent rumours as the army gathered which was to defeat Argyll at Glenlivet that Huntly had made overtures to Bothwell. The demon in Francis Stewart was that same devil of chaos and confusion which haunted Scotland in the 1590s. To the last moment Francis clung to the illusion that he was the only man who might save Scotland while simultaneously saving himself. He neatly summed up his predicament in a letter addressed to the presbytery of Edinburgh in September 1594, in which he admitted that he was in contact with the catholic earls who wished him 'to put in practice the lovable custom of our progenitors at Lauder'.[56] In this effort to rescue James from pernicious counsels he remained in regular contact with the recusant earls and undoubtedly planned a descent upon Holyrood in September, with a gang of cut-throats and borderers, to seize the king. The lesson had been well learned that if bad councillors could not be removed from the king, the monarch could be parted from the counsel. The plot was discovered but Bothwell was no longer in the mood for denial. He had been abandoned by his natural ally, the kirk. 'I am constrained, for safety of my life and for revenge . . . to conjoin with whomsoever are in the like case'.[57]

Bothwell was thereafter almost completely isolated. Even the borderers deserted him. He was driven deeper and deeper into the arms of the papists. Early in 1595 his own brother, Hercules Stewart, betrayed it was said by Bothwell's sometime ally John Colville, became the latest in a long line of Bothwell adherents to go to the gibbet. That execution broke Francis Stewart. By April 1595 he had left the country never to return. He departed excommunicate, the church having cut him off, delivering him to 'Satan to the destruction of his flesh'.[58] The devil at last had received his own.

When Francis Stewart departed for France to join with 'Goddis enemies all honest men left him'. James urged John Colville to track Bothwell down, refusing to receive the ambassador of the kingdom which had granted his enemy asylum.[59] Bothwell petitioned Elizabeth to make him her pensioner in France, relating the by now familiar details of his plight and offering in return to communicate intelligence from Spain and the Low Countries as well as information about Huntly and Errol's dealings with the Jesuits at Rome. Elizabeth apparently tried once more to persuade James to pardon his cousin.

[55] *CSP Scot*, xi, 284–370 *passim*.
[56] *CSP Scot*, xi, 429.
[57] *CSP Scot*, xi, 454.
[58] *CSP Scot*, xi, 544-5.
[59] Colville, *Letters* (Bannatyne Club, 1858), 132, 159; *CSP Scot*, xii, 126.

There was to be no accommodation. By mid-summer of 1596 Bothwell was known to be making overtures to Spain while corresponding with the Scottish catholic earls.[60]

A contemporary French proverb observed that when the wicked were asleep the devil was uneasy. Francis seldom slept. Even in exile he had lost none of his ability to generate panic and rumour in his native country. He was said to have made a raid on Orkney, to have secretly returned to Scotland or to have received shelter at the English court so that he might be 'hounded out upon fit occasion and time to work the king's ruin'. There was also a most improbable report that the ministers sought his return to head a coup.[61]

By 1598 Bothwell was definitely in the pay of Spain, 'at Madrid in great estimation', planning an attack on England while simultaneously assuring Elizabeth of his loyalty. On a brief visit to France he narrowly avoided capture. For three years he was involved in a series of tortuous plots and plans to invade England or Scotland or both, with Spanish backing. '*Il est devenu un archecatholique*', wrote an anonymous reporter. Those who knew him well were equally baffled. Colville found him 'light as a feather', '*en son faite il ny a ny ryme ny raison*'.[62] There was an abortive scheme in 1599 to seize and occupy Kirkwall with a Spanish force. The earl intended to join with his half brother, the earl of Caithness and then sweep through the Hebrides to Ireland. He 'debauched sundry Scottishmen in Paris to go with him, promising them golden mountains' and he raised some troops in Flanders. James took the threat very seriously, ordering that castles on the west coast be victualled and fortified.[63] Bothwell's failure to mobilise led to his temporary disgrace in Spain for 'it was not the shadow that fed the Spaniard'.[64] He visited London briefly in 1600 when Sir Walter Raleigh advised that Elizabeth should 'hold him while she hath him. He will ever be the canker of her state and safety. Princes are lost by security and preserved by prevention. I have seen the last of her good days and all ours after his liberty'.[65]

Bothwell regained his credit with Spain and Portugal 'and all the young gallants' there. He recruited in France, Germany, the Netherlands and the Iberian peninsula for the force which met disaster at Kinsale, an expedition in which he was widely expected to take part. The last occasion on which he generated any real apprehension was in 1602 when he was said to be sailing for Dumbarton with ten thousand men in order to seize Prince Henry and carry him off to Ireland. Alternatively he would land at Montrose 'and with the sword seek his re-establishment and expel all such from about the king as are not lovers or will not adhere to the Spanish course of revenge against England'. Yet there were still those who believed that he might be won over

[60] *HMC Salisbury*, v, 225, vi, 447; *CSP Scot*, xii, 138, 219.
[61] *CSP Scot*, xii, 161, 197, 311, 422, 464.
[62] *HMC Salisbury*, viii, 331, 568.
[63] *CSP Scot*, xiii, 390, 419, 422, 447, 452, 465, 475; *HMC Salisbury*, viii, 568; ix, 33.
[64] *HMC Salisbury*, ix, 123; *CSP Scot*, xiii, 518–9.
[65] *HMC Salisbury*, x, 440; Colville, *Letters*, 290.

to Elizabeth, or who argued despite the ten thousand men, that Bothwell merely sought an accommodation with King James.[66]

The Bothwell threat, real or imaginary, evaporated when James succeeded to the English throne, though the earl continued with his endless schemes and fruitless negotiations. In 1609 Bothwell consulted William Chisholm, bishop of Vaison in France, while his associates solicited support at Rome and in Spain. But Francis's days of scheming were almost over. He spent the summer of 1611 'in the surgeon's hands at Naples, and is past doing any hurt, though he want not malice'. Two years later King James received the welcome tidings that Francis Stewart had died in Naples.[67]

There is some evidence that while in Italy Francis encountered the fashionable concern with neoplatonism. Scholars are divided on whether there is necessarily any connection between neoplatonism and the witch craze.[68] It was well known that Bothwell had consulted astrologers in Italy who predicted that he would kill two men 'but lastly be put to death for attempting somewhat against the person of his prince'. Richie Graham allegedly confessed that Bothwell had urged him to devise the king's death in order to avoid the destruction of the earl predicted by a necromancer in Italy. Robert Hepburn, who became the master of Bothwell's household, 'a very wyse and dyscrete man', had been told in Italy by the woman who washed the earl's shirts that their owner would be beheaded by his prince. In later years Francis often jested about the prophecy.[69]

Several Scots studied in Italy at this period including William Fowler, translator of Machiavelli and secretary to Queen Anne. The 'Admirable Crichton' was another as was his model, James Bonaventura Hepburn who allegedly mastered a knowledge of the Tower of Babel's seventy two languages. The earl of Gowrie acquired a knowledge of the cabbala during his sojourn on the peninsula. It is possible that while in Italy Bothwell became genuinely interested in magic. Indeed a mutual interest in magic may have brought Francis and Richie together since Bothwell admitted at his trial in August 1593, when he was finally acquitted of the charge of witchcraft, that he had known Graham since at least 1588. Graham had shown him a charmed ring which could predict the future as well as indicate the loyalty of Bothwell's servants. Francis undoubtedly believed that Richie had certain medical knowledge for he admitted that he sent him to attend the dying earl of Angus. On another occasion Graham had shown Bothwell and Maitland 'a sticke with nickes in yt all wrapped about with longe heire eyther of a man or a woman and said yt it was an enchanted stick'.[70] In 1595 the earl of Caithness

[66] CSP Scot, xiii, 901, 907–8, 927, 955–6; HMC Salisbury, xi, 373, 383.

[67] HMC De L'Isle and Dudley, iv, 193; HMC Digby, 533; HMC Mar and Kellie Supp., 48.

[68] H. R. Trevor Roper, The European Witch-craze of the 16th and 17th Centuries, (Harmondsworth 1969) 60 has doubted the connection. Julio Caro Baroja, The World of Witches (London 1964) 133 is more positive.

[69] CSPD, 1591–4, 48; CSP Scot, x, 501; Warrender Papers, ii, 161; Border Papers, i, 290, 293.

[70] Border Papers, i, 487.

delivered three witches to Edinburgh who had consulted with Bothwell in Caithness. Bothwell appeared at Brussels in 1598 with three Italians, 'les plus grands sorciers qui soient au monde'.[71] Two of them accompanied him to Paris, including Signor Cesare, 'grand magicien'. When George Sandys the English traveller visited Naples he was told that he must have 'insight in magicke for that Erl Bothel was my countryman, who lives in Naples, and is in these parts famous for suspected negromancie'.[72]

Some of the most convincing evidence for the reception of neoplatonism in Scotland came to light with the exciting discovery in 1962 of the mysterious ceiling in Prestongrange House, immediately labelled a 'witchcraft ceiling'.[73] Dated 1581 and covered with obscene figures and ambiguous symbolism, the ceiling was apparently covered up at a subsequent date. It has been demonstrated that the four grotesques on the ceiling derive from figures published in *Songes drolatiques de Pantagruel* (Paris 1565).[74] This volume was contained in the impressive library of Adam Bothwell, bishop of Orkney, who also possessed copies of such classics of witchcraft literature as the *Malleus maleficarum* and Bodin's *De la démonamanie des sorciers*.[75] Prestongrange House belonged to Mark Kerr, first earl of Lothian, about whom some interesting traditions of an involvement in diablerie are recorded. Mark Kerr was also educated in Italy, probably at Padua, where his son also received his education. Kerr also spent some time at Paris. Returning to Scotland by way of England he was accused of being involved in the Ridolphi plot.[76] His brother George, a doctor of laws, was at the centre of the Spanish Blanks affair. Mark married Margaret, daughter of John Maxwell, fourth lord Herries of Terregles; the latter's son, William fifth lord Herries married Mark's sister, Katherine. The Kerrs were thus closely allied (as was Bothwell through his wife) to one of the most prominent recusant families in Scotland.

Mark Kerr, as Master of Requests, was a familiar figure at the Scottish court and he was involved with Bothwell in government in 1589–90. There was one further link between the two men which, however tenuous, may be highly significant. A fairly prominent catholic agent in Scotland in the 1590s, who later carried letters to Bothwell on the continent, was Alexander Dickson who hailed from Errol, He was known as 'Dickson of art of memory', a member of the Sydney circle in London and an associate of Giordano Bruno. He published books on the complex subject of the art of memory; he was like Bruno, a magus who had absorbed and digested the

[71] *HMC Salisbury*, viii, 568; ix, 46.
[72] Quoted Murray, 'Devil of North Berwick', 321.
[73] G. Murray, M. R. Apted, I. Hodkinson, 'Prestongrange and its Painted Ceiling', *Trans. East Lothian Antiq. and Field Nat. Soc.*, 10 (1966), 92–132.
[74] M. R. Apted and W. N. Robertson, 'Four "drollities" from the painted ceiling formerly at Prestongrange, East Lothian'. *PSAS*, 106, (1974–5), 158–60.
[75] *Warrender Papers*, ii, 403.
[76] *CSP Scot*, iv, 404–5, 409, 672; *Scots Peerage*, v, 456, 458.

esoteric lore of Hermes Trismegistus.[77] The art involved the stimulation of memory through the use of striking (usually mental) images, 'beautiful or hideous, comic or obscene'.

Given the association of Dickson and the recusant Kerrs the suggestion may be permitted – it can be no more – that the Prestongrange ceiling was designed as a memory chart. Bothwell's splendid Renaissance piazza at Crichton may also be intended to symbolise harmony. Hermeticism by the late sixteenth century was considered the key to all knowledge. It has been described as 'that strange third world between dogmatic catholicism and dogmatic protestantism, the citizens of which were to be found in the Valois and Habsburg courts, in the London of Sir Philip Sidney and the Antwerp of the printer Christopher Plantin and the Spanish theologian Benito Arias Montano. It was a world whose secrets were locked away in the mysteries of neoplatonism and "Egyptian" magic; a world of affinities and harmonies which was controlled by the movements of the celestial bodies'.[78] This is the world to which Francis Stewart belonged. He was a very *minor magus*, far removed from Prospero conjuring the tempest, but his interests in magic link him less with the primitive past than with the scientific future. Those interests survived the politically motivated accusations of witchcraft. Nonetheless, in the final analysis, this one time champion of the kirk, the nobility, the monarch and of amity between Scotland and England found it impossible to reconcile the Scottish Renaissance and the Scottish Reformation.[79]

[77] Frances A. Yates, *The Art of Memory* (London 1966), 10. See also Yates, *Giordano Bruno and the Hermetic Tradition* (London 1964). On Dickson see Yates, *Memory*, 266–86, *HMC Salisbury*, vi, 427; *CSP Scot*, x, 271, 626, 686–7; ibid., xi, 98, 377, 609, 639, 674–6; Colville, *Letters*, 106–7, 204.

[78] J. H. Elliott, *Europe Divided 1559–1598* (Glasgow 1968), 392.

[79] Since this article was written, Christina Larner has published a comprehensive account of the witch-hunt in Scotland in *Enemies of God* (London, 1981).

EDWARD J. COWAN

9

Adam Bothwell: A Conserver of the Renaissance in Scotland

Accounts of the life and career of Adam Bothwell, bishop of Orkney, whose reformation of his diocese was obviously motivated by the best cultural and theological movements of his time and yet owed little or nothing to the life and work of reformers such as John Knox, have been few but succinct.[1] Indeed, the only significant record relating to him which has not been considered is the inventory of his library[2] which provides information concerning the wide and varied intellectual influences exerted upon him.

If the multiplicity of the motives and methods of those involved in the renewal of the sixteenth century Scottish Church is to be fully appreciated, then a wider perspective than that of the past has to be employed. Too many have looked back from within the limits of specific traditions. Thomas Carlyle claimed, 'This that Knox did for his Nation, I say, we may call a resurrection from the dead'[3] and the theologian James Walker maintained that 'the theology of Scotland begins with the Reformation, and the first of our great theological writers is John Knox himself.'[4] The question was recently put, 'Has there not been a certain tendency for post-medieval ecclesiastical history to become imprisoned within its own categories? – a certain shyness to seek appropriate illumination from the fact of the inevitable and organic connections of ecclesiastical bodies with the movements and forces of history in other spheres?'[5] One of the 'other spheres' is the impact which the renaissance made upon Scotland.

It is only in recent times that historians in Scotland have been significantly relating the life and letters of sixteenth century Scotland to European

---

[1] J. Spottiswoode, *History of the Church of Scotland* (Spottiswoode Society, 1851) ii. 71–80 and J. B. Craven, *History of the Church in Orkney. 1558–1662* (Kirkwall, 1893), 16–33; G. Donaldson, 'Bishop Adam Bothwell and the Reformation in Orkney', *RSCHS*, xiii (1959), 85–100; e.g. Knox only mentions Bothwell once in his *History* and this is merely a reference to his marrying Mary and Bothwell (*History*, ii, 207).

[2] *The Warrender Papers*, ed. A. I. Cameron, 2 vols. (SHS, 1931–2), 396–413.

[3] T. Carlyle, *Heroes and Hero Worship* (Edinburgh, 1904), 146.

[4] J. Walker, *The Theology and Theologians of Scotland* (Edinburgh, 1888). 2nd ed., 1.

[5] H. O. Evennett, *The Spirit of the Counter-Reformation* (Cambridge, 1968), 2.

renaissance thought,[6] although the results of such research has not always been incorporated into the work of some recent ecclesiastical historians.[7] There are, however, considerable difficulties in attempting 'to understand how *new* beliefs and intellectual fashions are introduced and diffused, . . . For the process can hardly be made intelligible until the natures of the separate ideas which enter as factors in·it are discriminated and separately observed in their general historical working.'[8] The renaissance in Scotland presents such a multifold problem. 'The various forms of intellectual activity which together make up the culture of the age, move for the most part from different starting points, and by unconnected roads . . . Art and poetry, philosophy and the religious life, and that other life of refined pleasure and action in the conspicuous places of the world, are each of them confined to its own circle of ideas, and those who prosecute either of them are generally little conscious of the thoughts of others. There come, however, from time to time, eras of more favourable conditions, in which the thoughts of men draw nearer together than is their wont, and the many interests of the intellectual world combine in one complete type of general culture.'[9] Adam Bothwell stood within such an intellectual and cultural convergence in Scotland and such currents of unitive thought played a great part in moulding his life and activities.

Furthermore, the status of Edinburgh as the capital city of an independent nation must not be overlooked when considering the intellectual ethos in which Bothwell developed. The diplomatic missions with their retinues, particularly from France,[10] the papal legates and nuncios with their lesser clergy,[11] the wandering Greeks, refugees from the Turks,[12] the Italian bankers,[13] and the Scottish and foreign churchmen, students, craftsmen and

[6] J. Macqueen, 'Some Aspects of the Early Renaissance in Scotland' in *Forum for Modern Language Studies* iii, (1967), 201–22: J. Durkan, 'The Beginnings of Humanism in Scotland' in *IR*, iv (1953), 1–24 and 'The Cultural Background in Sixteenth-Century Scotland' in ibid., x (1959), 382–439: J. D. Mackie, 'Scotland and the Renaissance' in *Proc. of the Royal Phil. Soc. of Glasgow* lxi, (1934), 74–89.

[7] E.g. J. H. S. Burleigh, *A Church History of Scotland* (London, 1960), gives no consideration to the renaissance in Scotland. Only in two occasions is a passing reference made to those influenced by European humanism (121, 145), while Ridley can maintain that Scotland, at that time was 'the most backward and lawless country of Western Europe'. (*John Knox* (Oxford, 1968), 102).

[8] A. O. Lovejoy, *The Great Chain of Being* (Harvard, 1936), 20.

[9] W. Pater, *The Renaissance: Studies in Art and Poetry* (London, 1912), xv.

[10] *Mission de Beccarie de Pavie, Baron de Fourquevaus, en Écosse, 1543: documents originaux du fonds Fourquevaux* ed. G. Dickinson (Oxford, 1948); *Two Missions of Jacques de la Brosse: an account of the affairs in the year 1543 and the journal of the siege of Leith, 1550* ed. G. Dickinson (SHS 1942).

[11] R. K. Hannay, 'Letters of the Papal Legate in Scotland' in *SHR*, xi (1911), 1–26: J. E. Law and J. M. Manion, 'The nunciature to Scotland in 1548 of Pietro Lippomano, Bishop of Verona' in *Attie Memoria della Academia di Agricoltura Scienze e Lettere de Verona* xxii, 403–48.

[12] D. McRoberts, 'The Greek bishop of Dromore' in *IR*, xxviii (1977), 22–38.

[13] E.g. Evangelist Passer, a Neapolitan banker and burgess of Edinburgh (*RMS*, iii, nos. 872, 1300).

traders, who travelled to and from many very different parts of Europe, brought with them books, ideas and personal experiences which added to the intellectual ferment in Scotland. It was in Edinburgh that the movements which led to the reformation of 1560 found much of their leadership and inspiration from the convictions of those within the royal household, the church, the court of session and the town council.[14]

All these influences were concentrated within Bothwell's family circle. His father, the son of a provost of Edinburgh, was one of the original senators of the college of justice[15] and his close kinsman, Richard Bothwell, rector of Ashkirk, was also a senator and significantly also Director of Chancery to James V[16] and is referred to as a professor of theology.[17] In addition, it is very likely that his predecessor in the see of Orkney, Robert Reid, previously abbot of Kinloss and a Lord President of the court of session, whose cultured renaissance influence and reforming intentions are well known,[18] was one of the leading personalities in the early life of Bothwell.

Unfortunately, the details of Bothwell's education cannot be ascertained but it is obvious from what is known of him that he must have studied at one or more continental universities.

The extent and quality of Bothwell's library, and the breadth of interests it reveals, is comparable with those of Mary, Queen of Scots,[19] and of her son.[20] It was far superior to the collection which Clement Litill bequeathed to the University of Edinburgh.[21] In this connection, a note of caution, sounded some years ago, cannot be overlooked. 'We have to be careful in ascribing particular interests to any individual on the evidence of his bookshelves, but at the very least these shelves will illustrate the interests of the class to which he belongs and others with whom he is associated.'[22] While this aspect is important in assessing the impact of the renaissance on Scotland in general, because of other sources of information, some marginalia, and his own career, it can be demonstrated that a considerable proportion of the library was effectively in use.

This paper is 'little more than the scaffolding of its subject'[23] and, in view

[14] W. S. Reid, 'The Coming of the Reformation to Edinburgh' in *Church History* xlii (1973), 27–44; M. Lynch, 'The Two Edinburgh town councils of 1559–60' in *SHR*, lvi (1975), 117–39 and 'The "Faithful Brethren" of Edinburgh: the Acceptable Face of Protestantism' in *Bulletin of the Institute of Historical Research* li (1978), 194–9 and his recent book *Edinburgh and the Reformation* (Edinburgh, 1981).

[15] G. Brunton and D. Haig, *An Historical Account of the Senators of the College of Justice* (Edinburgh, 1832), 28.

[16] Ibid., 10–11.

[17] *James V Letters*, 275.

[18] J. Dowden, *The Bishops of Scotland* (Glasgow, 1912), 265–7.

[19] J. Sharman, *The Library of Mary, Queen of Scots* (London, 1889).

[20] 'The Library of James VI. 1573–1583' ed. G. F. Warner in *Miscellany* (SHS, 1893), (later referred to as *Library of James VI*), i. xi–lxxv.

[21] C. P. Finlayson, *Clement Litill and his Library* (Edinburgh, 1980).

[22] J. Durkan and A. Ross, *Early Scottish Libraries* (Glasgow, 1961), (later referred to as *ESL*), 10; for further additions cf. *The Bibliotheck*, x (1980), 88.

[23] H. Waddell's description of *The Wandering Scholars* (London, 1927), v.

of the extent of the library and the specialist interests it displays, it is only possible to outline the manifold areas of reading and the width of knowledge which formed the background of this scholarly renaissance prelate. The fields of study most in evidence were the classics, contemporary literature and language, law, theology and biblical exegesis, the sciences, particularly medicine, mathematics and astronomy, and the skills associated with the life of a gentleman. There is considerable evidence of a catholicity of interest among students from the late fifteenth century onwards.[24] Bothwell's wide reading began during his student days for there are a number of books which were required reading for late medieval students: for example, Euclid's *Elementa*, and several books on algebra and arithmetic, Johannes de Sacrobosco's *Sphera* and Boethius' *de consolatione philosophiae*. The classical tradition which is strongly present is indicative of the silent influence which must have existed in comparatively wide circles within Scotland, similarly to Christian Europe generally[25] and, as in the Erasmian tradition,[26] it can be deduced that Bothwell conceived of a unity existing between the classical heritage and contemporary theological movements[27] in contradistinction to his alienation from scholasticism under the influence of renaissance humanism.[28]

The fruits of contemporary scholarship are seen in the stock of Greek as well as Latin authors. Among the Greeks books, there is a manuscript of Homer's *Iliad* with a printed edition of them edited by the famous humanist, Lorenzo Valla,[29] and works by Aristotle,[30] Diogenes Laertius,[31] Isocrates,[32] Lucian,[33] Pindar,[34] and Plotinus.[35] Greek texts can be positively identified of Isocrates, Lucian, Pindar and Plotinus. All ages of Latin literature are represented from the classical age onwards: those influenced by the Greeks, such as Terentius Publius,[36] the late republic with its rhetoric, history and

---

[24] E.g. a Paris student, Jean Bouchard, who died in 1522, had in his library a Bible, Virgil's works, several volumes of Cicero, a Valla, and Ovid's *Epistles* (R. Villoslada, *La Universidad de Paris durante los estudios de Francisco de Vitoria (1507–1522)* Analecta Gregorians xiv. (Rome, 1938), 445–6).

[25] R. F. Bolgar, *The Classical Heritage and its Beneficiaries* (Cambridge, 1954).

[26] R. Pfeiffer, 'Erasmus und die Einheit der klassichen und der christlichen Renaissance' in *Historisches Jahrbuch* lxxiv (1955), 186f.

[27] E.g. he had W. Budaeus, *De transitu hellenismi ad christianismum* Paris, 1535.

[28] Cf. e.g., P. O. Kristeller, 'Humanism and Scholasticism in the Italian Renaissance' in *Byzantion* xiii (1944–5), 345–74. His library contained little of the old theological tradition: he had Gabriel Biel, *In tertium librum sententiarum* which the young Luther used. (P. A. Vignaux, *Luther, Commentateur des Sentences* (Paris, 1935)).

[29] There are many editions.

[30] P. Melanchthon, *Moralis philosophiae epitome. Item in quintum ethicorum Arist: commentarius, . . .* 1539 and his, *Commentarius de anima*, (Wittemberg, 1540).

[31] *De vita et moribus philosophorum.*

[32] Ἰσοκρατους ἁπαντα, δια Ἱερωνυμου Βολφιου ἐπανορθωθεντο... *Isocratis scripta, quae nunc extant, omnia . . .* Basle, several editions from 1558.

[33] *Dialogi selectiores,* 1554.

[34] *Olympia, Pythia, . . .* Geneva, 1560 or 1566.

[35] *Opera philosophicorum omnium libri liv* (Basle, 1580).

[36] *Comoediae opera:* There are many editions.

poetry, as seen in Marcus Tullius Cicero,[37] Julius Caesar[38] and Lucretius,[39] the Augustans, Vergil,[40] Horace,[41] and Ovid,[42] the post-Augustans, Seneca the younger,[43] his nephew Lucian,[44] and the elder Pliny[45] and the later part of that period was recognised by the possession of Tacitus,[46] Marcus Valerius Martialis[47] and Apuleius[48] leading on to the Christian Latin writers, for example, Lactantius[49] reaching down to what many claim to be the tradition's culmination in Boethius.[50]

With such sensitivity for the contemporary significance of the classical tradition, he turned to the Greek and Latin Fathers, as carefully edited texts came off the printing presses: Ambrose,[51] Augustine,[52] Basil,[53] Chrysostom,[54] Cyprian,[55] Cyril,[56] Epiphanius,[57] Ignatius,[58] Jerome,[59] and Theodoretus.[60] He did not possess Irenaeus which was surprising in view of Irenaeus' views on the renewal of the church[61] which might well have been similar to his own.

The influence of the Fathers on the various streams of thought in the sixteenth century has been wide appreciated. There was a definite humanist interest in Christian antiquity[62] as well as the authority which the reformers

[37] Several of Cicero's works are in the library: *De officiis*, two copies of *Orationes*, and *Rhetorica ad Herennium* which is of uncertain authorship. There are a number of editions of each of these.

[38] *Commentarii:* There are several editions.

[39] *Poemata* (Paris, 1539).

[40] Three editions of his *Opera* are held including one with a commentary, probably by Badius Ascensius.

[41] *Opera:* One of several editions.

[42] *Metamorphoseos, Epistolae* and *De festis:* the latter bound up with other works.

[43] *Tragoediae:* There are a number of editions.

[44] *Opera:* One of several editions.

[45] *De Naturali Historia:* a few editions exist.

[46] *Historiae Augustae.*

[47] *Opera.*

[48] *L. Apulegio tradotto in volgare dal conte Matteo Maria Boiardo* Venice, 1544 onwards.

[49] *L. Coelii Lactantii Firmiani opera, . . .* (Basle, 1563).

[50] *De Consolatione philosophiae.*

[51] *Opera* (Paris, 1549).

[52] *De gratia et libero arbitrio* (Paris, 1542), *Diui Aurelii Augustini de doctrina Christiana* (Cologne, 1527), *Opera* (Paris, 1531-2), 6 vols. (10 vols. in 6).

[53] *Orationes in Hexaëmeron. Joachimo Periono interprete* (Paris, 1552).

[54] *Opera* (Paris, 1536), 5 vols. in 4.

[55] *Opera* (Paris, 1541).

[56] *Opera Latine* (Basle, 1542).

[57] *Opera Graece* (Basle, 1543).

[58] *Commentarius in Pauli Epistolas* (Florence, 1552 or 1557).

[59] *Opera omnia qua extant . . . cum indice novo et copiosissimo* (Paris, 1534 or Basle, 1537), 9 vols.

[60] *Commentarius in Pauli epistolas* (Florence, 1552 or 1557).

[61] K. Prüm, *Zur Terminologie und zum Wesen der christlichen Neuheit bei Irenaüs* (Leipzig, 1938).

[62] E. F. Rice, 'The Humanist Idea of Christian Antiquity: Lefèvre d' Etaples and his Circle' *Studies in Renaissance* ix (1962), 126-60.

acknowledged in the writings of the Fathers,[63] particularly Melanchthon,[64] Bullinger[65] and Calvin[66] who, in common with all the reformers, used the works of the Fathers to demonstrate to their opponents that the theology there expounded was identical with their own.[67] Thus the later patristic influence in Scotland was often mediated through such theologians. The result was an interest in early church history[68] and in polemical as well as dogmatic theology.[69]

It might be noted here that the theological books which interested him were no different from those which were being read by his contemporaries in England. For example, the list of books[70] owned by Edmund Grindal, archbishop of Canterbury,[71] bears witness to the same broad interest in the early Fathers and an awareness of the varied theological contributions of reformation theologians, e.g., Brenz, Bullinger, Peter Martyr and Musculus, while at the same time continuing to keep up his reading of Luther:[72] although Luther did not seem to interest Bothwell greatly.

The variety of protestant theological literature in Bothwell's library is a reminder that the confessional frontiers within protestantism, until the latter part of the sixteenth century, were very fluid and reflects the outlook expressed by John Jewel, bishop of Salisbury, when contradicting the charge of dissension between Lutherans and Zwinglians, 'In very deed they of both sides be Christians, good friends, and brethren. They vary not betwixt themselves upon the principles and foundations of our religion, nor as touching God, nor Christ, nor the Holy Ghost, nor of the means of justification, nor yet of everlasting life, but upon one only question which is neither weighty nor great; neither mistrust we, or make doubt at all, but they will shortly be agreed.'[73]

In spite of legislation which forbade the importation of Lutheran books,[74] there is little evidence that there were vast numbers of the works of

[63] A. Nygren, *Urkristendom och Reformation* (Lund, 1932).

[64] P. Frankel, *Testimonia Patrum: the function of the Patristic Argument in the Theology of Philip Melanchthon* (Geneva, 1961).

[65] J. M. Barkley, 'Bullinger's Appeal to the Fathers' in *Henry Bullinger, 1504–1575* ed. D. J. Keep. (Exeter, 1975), 1–17.

[66] This can be traced from his early *Psychopannychia* (T. F. Torrance), *Kingdom and Church: A Study in the Theology of the Reformation* (Edinburgh, 1956), 19n, to the final edition of the *Institutes* (*Institutes of the Christian Religion*) ed. J. T. McNeill. 2 vols (London, 1960), 18–22 and Source Index, 1592–1634): for a general introduction to such patristic influences cf. R. J. Moii, *Het kerk- en dogmahistorisch element in de werken van Johannes Calvijn* (Wageningen, 1965).

[67] J. Koopmans, *Das altkirchliche Dogma in der Reformation* (Munich, 1955).

[68] E.g. P. Simson, *Short compend of the . . . first ten presecvtions* (Edinburgh, 1613) and his *Short compend of the Arrian . . . persecvtions* (Edinburgh, 1615).

[69] E.g. P. Simson, *Short compend of the . . . Romane Antichrist* (Edinburgh, 1616).

[70] Queen's College, Oxford, MS. 556.

[71] P. Collinson, *Archbishop Grindal 1519–1583: The Struggle for a Reformed Church* (London, 1979).

[72] *The Zurich Letters, (Second Series)* ed. H. Robinson (Parker Society, 1815), 24.

[73] J. Jewel, *Works* ed. J. Ayre (Parker Society, 1848), iii, 69–70.

[74] *APS*, ii, 295 c.4.

Luther in Scottish hands during his lifetime.[75] The only book by Luther was *In Genesim Enarrationes*, Nurnberg, 1550 which was published six years after his death.[76] It is also the case that no single works of Zwingli were held by Bothwell, only his *Opera* edited by his son-in-law, Rudolf Gwalther, and published in two volumes in Zurich in 1545. The early Swiss reformers, Wolfgang Weissenberger[77] and Oecolampadius,[78] however, were considered important. This may have been accounted for because the latter's works were more widely known in Scotland than almost any other prior to the reformation in Scotland. This is seen, for example in the polemical works of Quintin Kennedy[79] which are dependent on reading undertaken before 1560, although it is possible that Kennedy may have used the comments of English Roman Catholic apologists[80] rather than consulted the original works of reformers such as Oecolampadius.

From his acquisitions, it can be seen that Bothwell continued to read the works of those representative of the Zwinglian school of theology such as Bullinger[81] and several other theologians in Zurich[82] and Bern.[83] He kept up his reading in this field until late in life. There are quite a number of works by Rudolph Gwalter,[84] who had a significant influence on England.[85] Another

---

[75] *ESL*, passim.

[76] P. Meinhold, *Die Genesisvorlesung Luthers und ihre Herausgeber* (Stuttgart, 1936).

[77] *Antilogio Papae* (Basle, 1555).

[78] *Annotationes piae ac doctae in euangelium Ioannis* (Basle, 1533), *Commentarii omnes in libros Prophetarum* (Geneva, 1558), *De Ritu Paschali* (Basle, 1518).

[79] *Quintin Kennedy (1520–1564): Two Eucharistic Tracts* ed. C. H. Kuipers (Nijmegen, 1964), 64–65.

[80] E.g. R. Smith, *The assertation and defence of the sacrament of the aulter* (London, 1546) and subsequent works: J. Fisher, *De veritate corporis et sanguinis Christi in Eucharistia adversus Joannem Oecolampadium* (Cologne, 1527): S. Gardiner, *Confutatio cavillationum quibus sacrosanctum Eucharistiae sacramentum ab impiis Capharnaitis impeti solet* (Paris, 1551): C. Tunstal, *De ueritate Corporis et Sangvinis Domini nostri Iesu Christi in Eucharistia* (Paris, 1554).

[81] *Aduersus omnia Catabaptistarum praua dogmata, Daniel sapientissimus propheta . . . expositus homiliis lxvi, De scripturae sacrae praestantia, dignitate . . . authoritate . . . disertatio, In Acta Apostolorum . . . commentariorum libri vi, In omnes Apostolicas Epistolas. Divi videlicet Pauli xiii et vii Canonicas, commentarii H.B. . . ., In Apocalypsim Jesu Christ revelatam quidem per angelum Domini . . ., Isaius excellentissimus Dei propheta expositus homilijs cxc, Sermonum decades quinque de potissimis Christianae religionis capitibus.*

[82] T. Bibliander, *Ad omnium ordinum reip. Christianae Principes . . .* (Basle, 1545), *De ratione temporum* (Basle, 1551). L. Lavater, *In Libros . . . Chronicorum commentarii* (Zurich, 1573).

[83] W. Musculus, *Ad Epistolas Apostoli Pauli, ad Galatas et Ephesios commentarii* (Basle, 1561), *In sacrosanctum Davidiis Psalterium commentarij* (Basle, 1551), *In Genesim plenissimi commentarii* (Basle, 1554), *Loci Communes theologiae* (final edition published Basle, 1560) and B. Aretius (cf. infra n. 86).

[84] Nine volumes in all: sermons on the Minor Prophets, each of the four evangelists, the Acts of the Apostles, Paul's epistles to the Galatians and Corinthians, and the Catholic epistles.

[85] H. Kressner, 'Die Auseinandersetzung zwischen Zürich und Genf und der Einfluss Rudolf Gualters auf England' in *Schweizer Ursprünge des anglikanischen Staatskirchentums* (Gütersloh, 1953), 73–98.

theologian of this period who propounded views which were similar to his own was Benedictus Aretius, professor of theology at the academy of Berne from 1563 to 1574. The ownership of his three volume work, *Problemata theologica*, Berne, 1573 is significant. This book influenced by the federal theology of Zwingli and Bullinger, incorporated a study of medicine and natural science and presented a comprehensive exposition of scientific knowledge.[86] Such an approach may have commended itself more to Bothwell than the more theoretical approach of Calvin.[87]

With the strong influence of the Genevan reformation in Scotland, particularly after 1560, it is not surprising to find six volumes of Calvin's comments or sermons on the Old Testament[88] and two on the New[89] as well as his *Opuscula* and *Defensio orthodoxae fidei de sacra trinitate*. The *Defensio* was written at the request of the German cities as an *apologia* for the incineration of Michael Servetus.[90] Bothwell did not have any of the works of Servetus, in spite of his significant role in medicine.[91] Notwithstanding the actions of Richard Bothwell,[92] it is highly unlikely that he would have adopted the inquisitorial methods used by Roman Catholic or Calvinist theologians to deal with heretical views on this matter. This might be indicated by his having Sebastien Castellion's *Psalterium et precationes* who had problems in Geneva on account of his theological opinions.[93] It is also noteworthy that three books by Bernardino Ochino[94] were in the library[95] including his *Prediche* which Calvin advised should not be translated into French when Ochino emigrated to Geneva: he later joined Castellion in Basle. However, the presence of three different editions of Calvin's *Institutes*[96] is clearly the result of Bothwell's intention to keep abreast with Calvin's systematic theological development[97] upon which the post-reformation Scottish church doctrine[98] and education of its ministry[99] was based. He seems to have kept up

[86] E. Blösch, 'Benedictus Aretius' in *Realencyclopedia für protestantische Theologie und Kirche* (1896–1913). 3rd ed., ii, 5f.
[87] E. Choisy, 'Calvin et la science' in *Recueil de la Faculté de Théologie protestante. Université de Genève* (Geneva, 1931), i, 3–19.
[88] *Commentarii in quinque libros Mosis, In librvm Iosve breuis commentarius, In librum psalmorum J. Caluini commentarius, Commentarius in Isaiam, Praelectiones in librum prophetiarum Danielis, Praelectiones in duodecim prophetas (quos vocant) minores.*
[89] *Commentaire . . . svr l'épistre aus Ebrieux, In omnes Pauli apostoli epistolas.*
[90] There is an immense bibliography, cf. W. Niesel, *Calvin Bibliographie 1901–1959* (Munich, 1961), 51–3.
[91] Cf. infra, 161f.
[92] He was one of those who passed sentence on James Hamilton of Kincavil. (*James V Letters*, 274–5).
[93] R. Buisson, *Sébastian Castellion* (Paris, 1892). 2 vols. and H. M. Stuckelberger, 'Calvin und Castellio' in *Zwingliana*, vii, (1939), 91–128.
[94] R. H. Bainton, *Bernardino Ochino Esule e Riformatore Senese del Cinquecento* (Florence, 1940), B. Nicolini, *Il Pensiero di Bernardino Ochino* (Naples, 1939).
[95] *Dialogi sette, Il catechismo, o vero Institutione Christiana. . .* (other works bound up with it), *Prediche.*
[96] *Institutiones . . .* (Geneva, 1536), *Institution de la religion chrestienne* (Geneva, 1541), *Institutiones . . . recentissime* (Geneva, 1559).

to date with Genevan theological thought until the end of his life as works of Theodore Beza were being acquired well into the 1580s.[100]

The two European theologians, whose personal participation in English ecclesiastical affairs was important, found a place in the library and, while Martin Bucer is only represented by his *Psalmorum libri quinque ad Hebraicam veritatem tradvcti et summa fide,* . . . and *commentarii in librum Judicum, & in Sophoniam prophetam,* seven volumes by Peter Martyr are there, including his *Defensio doctrinae veteris et Apostolicae de sacrosancto Evcharistiae . . . adversus Stephani Gardineri* (Zurich, 1559),[101] which was published some years after his challenge to Richard Smith at Oxford who fled to Scotland and was an inspiration to Quintin Kennedy.[102]

The influence of Philip Melanchthon on the bishop was more than humanistic[103] as the presence of his *Loci Communes* . . . and some New Testament commentaries show.[104] The interest in German protestant theology was always present as the variety of authors from that area illustrates.[105] In his theological reading, 'the example of Denmark[106] was not forgotten. Two volumes by Nils Hemmingsen were in the library.[107] They were probably acquired in view of the close intellectual relations between the two countries[108] and indicate that, with James VI having four volumes by this

---

[97] B. B. Warfield, *The literary History of the Institutes of the Christian Religion* (Philadelphia, 1909), J. Pannier, 'Comment Calvin a révisé les éditions successives de l'Institution' in *Bull. Soc. hist. prot. fran* lxxxix (1930), 79–81.

[98] J. Kirk, 'The Influence of Calvinism on the Scottish Reformation' in *RSCHS*, xviii, 157–79.

[99] S. Mechie, 'Education for the Ministry in Scotland since the Reformation' in *RSCHS*, xiv, 115–20.

[100] *Icones vivorum doctorum, In Canticum Canticorum Solomonis . . ., Epistolarum theologicarum . . ., Jesu Christi D. N. Nouum Testamentum . . . interprete, Opuscula.*

[101] *In duos libros Samuelis prophetae,* . . . *commentarii, In epistolam S. Pavli ad Romanos . . . commentarii, In selectissimam S. Pavli Priorem ad Corinthios Epistolam, Loci Communes . . ., Melachim id est, Regvm Libri dvo posteriores cum commentarijs . . ., Preces Sacrae ex Psalmis Davidis desumptae.*

[102] Cf. supra n n and J. C. McLelland, *The Visible Words of God: a study of the theology of Peter Martyr 1500–1562* (Edinburgh, 1957), 17–23.

[103] Cf. supra n. 30.

[104] *Commentarii in Epistolam Pauli ad Romanos,* . . .

[105] E.g. John Brenz, *In Evangelii quod inscribitur secundum Lucam duodecim priora capita, homiliae centum & decem,* Mattheus Flacius, *Catalogus testium veritatis, qui ante nostram aetatem reclamarunt,* Urbanus Rhegius, *Catechesis.*

[106] G. Donaldson, '"The Example of Denmark" in the Scottish Reformation' in *SHR*, xxvii (1948), 57–64.

[107] *Enchiridion theologicum* (Leipzig, 1568) and *Pastor, sive Pastoris optimus vivendi agendique modus . . . Accesserunt huc XXXVII, propositiones de legitima cultus Dei ratione.*

[108] E.g. it should not be forgotten that two Scots, Alexander Kinghorn, teaching medicine, and Thomas Scott, philosophy, were in the University of Copenhagen (E. D. Werlauff, *Kiøbenhavns Universitet fra dets Stiftelse indtil Reformationen* (Copenhagen, 1850), 27) long before John Macalpine (F. B. Petersen, *Dr Johannes Macchabaeus, John MacAlpin: Scotland's Contribution to the Reformation in Denmark.* Edinburgh Ph.D. Thesis, 1937) who was a colleague of Hemmingsen there.

author in 1575,[109] Hemmingsen's were being considered before the king and he met in 1590.[110]

His catholicity of concern in theological and religious-political matters was not confined to those which arose within the context of Scottish affairs: he took an interest in developments within the whole of Europe.

This is illustrated in the attention he paid to the influence of the Ottoman Turks which had been widely discussed in Scottish political and ecclesiastical circles since his youth.[111] In spite of the great fear of the Turks in Scotland,[112] England,[113] Germany,[114] and Europe generally, his attitude to them probably developed along lines similar to the views of Luther who considered war against the Turks as resistance to God's visitation.[115] This is seen in the presence of two significant volumes on this very serious contemporary problem. The first was the edition of the Koran published in Zurich in 1543.[116] It was a protestant production and indicated the Zwinglian reformers' desire to have the matter considered theologically as well as politically.[117] The second was Christopher Richter's *De rebus turcarum* which showed his attempt to understand Turkish history. Both were probably in his possession before 1560 and reflect the renaissance and Zwinglian liberal outlook[118] which may be paralleled in his mind with the attitude of Theodore Bibliander,

[109] Four volumes were bought in 1575, viz., the two mentioned in n. 107 above and *Catechismi quaestiones* (Wittenberg, 1564) and *De Methodis* ('The Library of James VI' xlviii).

[110] P. A. Munch, 'Samtidig Beretning om Prindseese Annas, Christian den 4des Systers, Giftermaal med Kong Jacob d. 6te af Skotland, og hendes paafölgende Kroning' in *Norske Samlinger, udgivne af et Historisk Samfund* (Christiania, 1852), i, 450–512.

[111] Cf. e.g., *James V Letters*, 22, 91, 133, 150n, 180–2, 188, 212, 219, 223–4, 271, 329, 353: for earlier fears, cf. R. Nicholson, *Scotland: The Later Middle Ages* (Edinburgh, 1974), 594 and nn 103–5.

[112] Ibid.

[113] S. S. Chew, *The Crescent and the Rose: Islam and England during the Renaissance* (Oxford, 1937).

[114] R. Ebermann, *Die Türkenfurcht: Ein Beitrag zur Geschichte der öffentlichen Meinung in Deutschland während der Reformationzeit* (Halle, 1904).

[115] H. Lamparter, *Luthers Stellung zum Türkenkrieg* (Munich, 1940); G. W. Forell, 'Luther and the War against the Turks' in *Church History*, xiv, (1945), 256–71 and H. Buchanan, 'Luther and the Turks 1519–1529' in *Archiv für Reformationsgeschichte*, (1956), 145–60; M. Kohler, *Melanchthon und der Islam*, (Leipzig, 1938).

[116] R. Pfister, 'Die Zürcher Koran Ausgabe von 1542/43' in *Evangelisches Missionsmagazin*, lxxxix, (1955), 37–43. There was a long tradition of editions of the Koran being produced as a first step towards the conversion of the infidel. Peter the Venerable, abbot of Cluny, organised a group of scholars to translate the Koran and other Arabic mahommedan writings from 1141 to 1143. (M.-T. d'Alverny, 'Deux traductions latin du Coran au moyen âge' in *Archives d'histoire doctrinale et littéraire du moyen âge*, xvi (1948), 69–131).

[117] R. Pfister, 'Reformation, Türken und Islam' in *Zwingliana*, x, (1956), 345–75.

[118] L. von Muralt, 'Italienischer Humanismus und Zwinglis Reformation' in Ibid., x, 398–408 and R. Pfister, *Die Seligkeit erwählter Heiden bei Zwingli* (Zurich, 1952), cp. Erasmus, *De Bello Turcico* in *Opera*, ed. J. LeClerc, (Leiden, 1703–6), v. 346–68.

whose books he possessed.[119] While he did not have his *Consultatio*, it is likely that he accepted Bibliander's opinion that the long term solution to the Turkish menace was an awareness of the failures of Christendom and the need for an evangelical missionary approach to the Turks.[120] He certainly would not have had the imperialistic outlook of John Major who considered the Turks to be inferior beings.[121] Bothwell knew too much about their contributions to science to think in that way.

Controversial and polemical theology, in spite of the large amount which was produced, did not feature strongly in his reading, although controversies, having constitutional or social implications, were studied, such as, the primacy of the Bishop of Rome[122] and the doctrines of the Anabaptists.[123]

His interest in the Bible, a widespread renaissance phenomenon, is apparent from the large number of biblical commentaries he had. Such an interest may have found its initial inspiration in the activities of such a man as Alexander Mylne, the first president of the Court of Session.[124] In 1515, the abbey of St Victor in Paris experienced the inauguration of a brief golden age[125] which came to an end in 1543.[126] In 1522, Mylne, then abbot of the Augustinian canons of Cambuskenneth, wrote to his fellow abbot at St Victor requesting that his novices, rather than being educated at universities, should be taught at the Parisian abbey so that 'they may acquire a complete knowledge of the sacred scriptures and may afterwards be instrumental in the propagation of learning and piety'.[127] It is against such a background that the presence of Nicolas de Lyra[128] has to be placed as he represented the culmination of a movement for the study of Hebrew and rabbinics in the

---

[119] Two of Bibliander's works were owned by Bothwell: *Ad omnium ordinum . . .* and *De ratione temporum. . . .*

[120] R. Pfister, 'Das Türkenbüchlein Theodor Bibliander' in *Theologische Zeitschrift*, iv, (1953), 438–54. Such views were inherited from Zwingli (*Sämtliche Werke*, i, 439f.) who had taken them over from Erasmus (*Ausgewählte Werke*, ed. H. Holborn, (Munich, 1933), i, 111).

[121] P. Leturia, *Maior y Vitoria ante la Conquista de América, Estudios Eclesiásticos* (Madrid, 1932), *passim*, especially the Appendix. Although Bothwell had two of Major's works, he did not have his *Quartum Sententiarum* which propounded these theories.

[122] He had, for example, R. Gualter, *Antichrist, id est, homiliae quinque, quibus Romanum pontificem verum et magnum ille Antichristum esse probatur,* yet he still retained, B. Platina, *De vitis pontificum romanorum.*

[123] E.g. H. Bullinger, *Aduersus omnia Catabaptistarum praua dogmata.*

[124] Brunton and Haig, *Senators* 5–10.

[125] P. Debongnie, *Jean Mombaer de Bruxelles* (Paris, 1927), 286.

[126] Ibid., 287. Robert Richardson was one of those who was sent as a novice by Mylne to Paris. (*Commentary on the Rule of St Augustine by Robertus Richardinus.* Ed. G. G. Coulton, (SHS, 1935), 3).

[127] *Epistolae Jacobi Quarti Jacobi Quinti, et Mariae Regum Scotorum,* (Edinburgh, 1722), i, 335–6.

[128] *Biblia cum glossis interlinearia et ordinaria.*

middle ages.[129] He was honoured by the famous Hebraist, Johannes Reuchlin,[130] as a teacher.[131]

The absence of commentaries by Thomas Aquinas in this humanist library is not surprising, as Erasmus' *Annotationes*[132] are there. Erasmus supported the views of Laurentius Valla[133] regarding the shortcomings of Aquinas' commentaries in view of his ignorance of Greek[134] and stated his preference for the work of Basil, Gregory of Nazianzus, Chrysostom and Ambrose, Jerome and Augustine.[135] While the criticism of de Lyra of the St Jerome version of the Bible was based on a comparison of the Hebrew text with the Vulgate, he considered that Valla's position was even stronger than de Lyra's.[136]

Furthermore, Bothwell's competence in the biblical languages was typical of the cultured scholars who took the bible and biblical exegesis seriously. He benefited from work done in Wittenberg.[137] He possessed Matthaeus Aurogallus' *Grammatica hebraeae*, printed there in 1525, and, Reuchlin's pupil, Johannes Campensis on the Psalms[138] which was used both by Sir Thomas Wyatt and Henry Howard, earl of Surrey. In addition to Santes Pagninus, O.P., *Institutiones Hebraicae*,[139] he had a further Latin, Greek and Hebrew grammar by Peter Becker,[140] and two unpointed Hebrew Bibles. It is interesting to find a word written in his hand in Hebrew in the margin of Frances Hotman's *Commentarius uerborum Iuris* (Basle, 1558)[141] while his annotations, including Hebrew and supplying pointing, were in his copy of Calvin's *Commentaria in Isaiam* (Geneva, 1551).[142]

In addition to Becker, he showed a continuing interest in Greek. He had a grammar of Nicolaus Clenardus,[143] who was involved in the foundation of

[129] B. Smalley, *The Study of the Bible in the Middle Ages* (Oxford, 1952), 355.

[130] L. Geiger, *Johannes Reuchlin* (Leipzig, 1871).

[131] *De Rudimentis Hebraicis* (Pforzheim, 1506), 549.

[132] *Annotationes in Novum Testamentum*. There are several editions.

[133] *Opus Epistolarum Des. Erasmi Roterodami*, edd. P. S. and H. M. Allen, and H. W. Garrod, (Oxford, 1906), i, No. 182.

[134] Laurentius Valla, *In Latinam Novi Testamenti Interpretationem ex Collatione Graecorum Exemplarium Adnotationes*, ed. Erasmus (Paris, 1505), f. xxxi.

[135] Ibid., (cf. The list given by Jacques Lefèvre, 'Cyprian, Hilary, Origen, Jerome, Augustine, Chrysostom, Athanasius, Nazianzus, John of Damascus . . .'. (*Politicorum libri octo* (Paris 1506), 124r.).

[136] Erasmus, op. cit.

[137] G. Bauch, 'Die Einführung des Hebräischen in Wittenberg' in *Monatsschrift für Geschichte und Wissenschaft des Judentums*, (1904) xlviii, (N.F.12), 22-32, 77-86, 145-60, 214-23, 283-99, 328-40, 461-90.

[138] *Psalmorum omnium iuxta Hebraicam Veritatem Davidis Paraphrastica Interpretatio* (Paris, 1534).

[139] There are several editions from 1525.

[140] *Latinae, Graecae et Hebraicae Linguae grammatica . . . Item Ionas Propheta & Psalmi xv. trium linguarum cum commentarijs P. Artopoei* (Basle, 1545).

[141] Folio c 8. In the possession of the writer.

[142] *The Scottish Antiquary*, vii, 133.

[143] *Institutiones ac Meditationes in graecam linguam . . . cum scholiis & praxi P. Antesignani.*

the College of France,[144] and Adolphe van Meetkercke's study of Greek pronunciation and accentuation.[145] Both of these were published in the 1560s and they may have been bought for the instruction of his own family and his nephew, John Napier. He had several copies of the New Testament, one, at least, almost certainly in Greek and, of course, a biblical concordance, most probably *Concordantiae Bibliorum*, (Basle, 1549). Among the New Testament commentaries, there are three on the Revelation of St John, which are very significant, by Theodore Bibliander, Martin Borrhaus and Henry Bullinger.[146] This is interesting in view of the ambivalent attitude of renaissance humanism to the Apocalypse, the doubts expressed by Zwingli regarding its canonicity,[147] and Calvin's neglect of it,[148] while Luther, in spite of his early difficulties and his continuing doubts regarding its apostolic authorship, considered that it demonstrated that 'neither force nor lies, neither wisdom nor holiness, neither tribulation nor suffering shall suppress Christendom, but it will gain the victory and conquer at last.'[149] His selection of these commentaries is important in face of the many other published during the century.[150] Bibliander's unusual approach which interpreted the book as describing the whole sweep of history since the creation was balanced by Bullinger's more conservative use of the book as being the key to events since the birth of Christ. The latter's preference for patristic commentators to the medieval would also have recommended the book to Bothwell. However, Bullinger's defence of the apostolicity and canonicity of Revelation which appeared in his *De omnibus sanctae scripturae libris expositio*, prefaced to the Zurich Latin Bible of 1539, was unlikely to be of real concern to him. It is much more likely that he paid more attention to the Apocalypse, in addition to its theology, in view of what he considered to be its help in understanding history[151] and the supernatural. Although his nephew, John Napier, in *A Plaine discouery of the whole Revelation of St John*, records that he

[144] A. Lefranc, 'Nicolas Clénard humaniste belge et les commencements du Collège de France' in *Humanisme et Renaissance* (1940) vii, 253–69.

[145] *De veteri et recta pronuntiatione linguae Graecae commentarius . . . Accessit appendix de Graecorum accentibus, cum scholiis.*

[146] T. Bibliander, *Ad omnium ordinum reipublicae christianae principes viros, populumque christianum, relatio fidelis* (Basle, 1545), 114–61. Martin Borrhaus, *In Jesaiae*, and J. Bullinger, *In apocalypsim Jesu Christi revelatam quidem per angelum Domini, visam . . . atque conscriptam a Joanne apostolo . . . conciones centum.*

[147] *H. Zwinglis Sämtliche Werke*, ed. E. Egli, et al. (Berlin, etc. 1905–), i, vi, 223, 395, 397, 401–2.

[148] T. H. L. Parker, *Calvin's New Testament Commentaries* (London, 1971), 75–8.

[149] *Luther's Works*, ed. J. Pelikan, xxxv, 409; cf. W. E. Peuchard *Die grosse Wende. Das apokaliptische Saeculum und Luther* (Hamburg, 1948). It should not be forgotten that the apocalyptic had an influence within the Lutheran churches through the publication of the sixteenth century edition of Joachim of Fiore. (R. H. Bainton, 'Eyn Wunderliche Weyssagung, Osiander-Sachs-Luther' in *Germanic Review*, xxi (1946), 3).

[150] R. H. Charles, *Studies in the Apocalypse* (London, 1915), 2nd ed.

[151] W. Kamlah, 'Apocalypse und Geschichtstheologie' in *Historische Studien*, cclxxxv (1935).

had heard Christopher Goodman of St Andrews[152] preach on the book,[153] it was undoubtedly the influence of his uncle, Adam Bothwell, who guided his thinking about the subject, although this influence has not been mentioned in the most recent study of Napier's apocalyptic thought.[154]

Bothwell's commentaries on Daniel were acquired also on account of his interest in the apocalyptic.[155] The chief role of apocalypticism in Scotland until its gradual disappearance at the end of the seventeenth century was to provide a key to an understanding of history rather than of theology[156] and such ideas were part of Bothwell's intellectual approach to an interpretation of historical movements as, in common with his contemporaries, he had a fascination for history. Almost all the popular historians were in his library. His interest would have arisen to a large extent from the generally accepted view that the events of history had a didactic value,[157] as maintained, for example, by John Major,[158] whose *History* was among his books, and by Gude Counsall in *The Three Estates*.[159] This doctrine is summarised by Francis Bacon: 'Histories make men wise; poets, witty; the mathematics, subtile; natural philosophy, deep; moral, grave; logic and rhetoric, able to contend.'[160]

His interests ranged from the earliest period with authors such as Julius Caesar and Justin to contemporary history e.g. Guillaume Paradin's *Histoire de notre temps* and Paolo Giovio's *Historiarum sui temporis*. It is doubtful if his dominant interest was in the theological interpretations of history as typified by the reformers,[161] even when they provided a comforting proof as to the inevitable bad end for the evil doer[162] or the total confidence that all was of

[152] J. E. A. Dawson, The early career of Christopher Goodman and his place in the development of English protestant thought. Durham Ph.D. thesis. 1978.

[153] 'To the Godly and Christian Reader.' f. Abr.

[154] K. R. Firth, *The Apocalyptic Tradition in Reformation Britain. 1530–1645* (Oxford, 1979), 132–49.

[155] H. Bullinger, *Daniel sapientissimus propheta . . . expositus homiliis LXVI* and J. Calvin, *Praelectiones in librum prophetiarum Danielis . . .*

[156] A. H. Williamson, *Scottish National Consciousness in the age of James VI* (Edinburgh, 1979), 20–38.

[157] M. Gilmore, 'The Renaissance Conception of the Lessons of History' in *Facets of the Renaissance*, ed. W. H. Werkmeister (New York, 1963).

[158] *A History of Greater Britain . . . by John Major*, ed. A. Constable, (SHS, 1892), cxxxiv–v.

[159] 'The Croniklis to knaw, I yow exhort,
      Thair sall ye finde baith gude and evill report:
      For everie Prince, efter his qualitie,
      Thoucht he be died, his deidis sall never die.
      Sir, gif ye please, for to use my counsall,
      Your fame and name sall be perpetuall.'
      (at the end of the first part of *The Three Estates*).

[160] *Essays*, 50, Of Studies.

[161] H. Bornkamm, *Gott und die Geschichte nach Luther* (Lüneburg, 1947): G. W. Locher, 'Das Geschichtsbild Huldrych Zwinglis' in *Huldrych Zwingli in neuer Sicht* (Zurich, 1969), 75–103; H. Berger, *Calvins Geschichtsauffassung* (Zurich, 1955).

[162] E.g. Luther, *Werke*, li, 207, 30f.

God in the Scottish reformation.[163] Even in these circumstances, however, it is somewhat surprising that he did not have *The Magdeburg Centuries*[164] in view of its great influence: there was a copy in the King's library.[165] The key to his attitude is more likely to be in accord with that of Jean Bodin's *Methodus ad facilem historiarum cognitionem* which he had.

With the widespread interest in John Carion's *Chronicle* throughout Europe and within Scottish circles, such as those around Sir David Lindsay[166] and the author of *The Complaint of Scotland*,[167] together with contemporary Scottish references to John (Philippson) Sleidan, [168] such an environment dictated the presence of both authors in the library. The use of sources by Sleidan was following in the tradition of the histories of Italian cities which were an important product of the renaissance.[169] It is therefore natural to find such works as, Peter Bembo, *Historiae Venetae*, Venice, 1551, and one of many editions of both Pandolfo Collenuccio, *Compendio del historie de regno de Napoli* and Niccolò Machiavelli, *Historie Fiorentine*. The last combines an interest in accurate historical method and political interpretation. Such interpretation would not be lost on Bothwell, with Gasparo Contarini's *La republica, e i magistrati de Vinegia* among his books. The contemporary emphasis in Machiavelli's work was closely related to that of Paradin and Giovio. In addition, the mediator of modern historiography to the English speaking world, Polydore Vergil's *De inventoribus* was present with a wide range of histories of nations including the Scots, Hector Boece and John Major.

While there were legal libraries owned by less significant lawyers[170] and there are indications of widespread interests in legal literature within the ranks of the pre-reformation Scottish clergy,[171] Bothwell's collection must have been one of the most comprehensive and compares most favourably with those of practising lawyers in Europe.[172] His library illustrates the continuity of influence as well as the effect of renaissance jurisprudence on the theory and practice of law in Scotland. Both civilists and canonists are well

[163] *John Knox's History of the Reformation in Scotland*, ed. W. C. Dickinson (Edinburgh, 1949), i, 6.

[164] For the importance of this work in Protestant historical writing, cf. J. W. Thompson, *A History of Historical Writing* (New York, 1942), i, 531.

[165] *Library of James VI*, xlii.

[166] A. Lange, *Lindsays Monarche und die Chronica Carionis* (Halle, 1904), and *The Works of Sir David Lindsay*, ed. H. Hamer (STS, 1934), iii, 238–42.

[167] R. Wedderburn, *The Complaynt of Scotland (c. 1550)* (STS, 1979), xxiv–v, lvii, n. 67.

[168] Knox, *Works*, v. 422, cf. the long quotation, 423–32.

[169] D. Waley, *The Italian city-republics* (London, 1969).

[170] E.g. Mr David Whitelaw of Cauldsyde who, in 1557, owned works by Joannes Andreae, Baldus, Bartolus de Saxoferrato, Paul de Castro, Cino da Pistoia, Durandus, Jason, Panormitanus, and Salicetus, *Protocol Books of Dominus Thomas Johnstoun, 1528–1578*, ed. J. Beveridge and J. Russell (SRS, 1920), 107.

[171] Durkan and Ross, passim.

[172] E.g. for the contents of Parisian lawyers' libraries, cf. R. Doucet, *Les Bibliothèques Parisiennes au XVIe Siècle* (Paris, 1956), passim.

represented. The holding of legal texts and commentaries is very impressive, but not unexpected, as most probably he inherited a number from his uncle Richard Bothwell[173] and from his father.[174] Some may also have come from his predecessor in Orkney, Lord President Robert Reid,[175] while others may have been bought in Edinburgh, just as James IV had purchased the *Decretum Magnum*, the *Decretals*, the *Sextus*, and *Clementines* from Androw Myller, his printer, in 1503,[176] in addition tò importing some, like the king directly from Paris[177] or elsewhere, and buying others during his travels abroad. However, many of the contemporary lawyers' works which had been greatly influenced by the renaissance are not in the library particularly those most influenced by Jacques Cujas who is, himself conspicuous by his absence – the only exception is Francis Douaren but it relates to canon not to civil law.[178]

Yet the general trends in the development of law which were being set in contemporary Scotland, in spite of the humanist criticism of Bartolus and Baldus,[179] were responsible for the considerable holding of the works of Bartolus[180] and neo-Bartolists such as Guido de la Pape.[181]

There are interesting names, such as Zabarella,[182] among his legal authorities, who were associated with the conciliar movement and whose influence continued into the sixteenth century.

The most significant of these was Niccolo de Tudeschi, archbishop of Palermo.[183] It is not surprising to find his *Commentarii Decretalium*[184] in view of his high standing as a canonist but there is also his other important work, *Concilia, tractatus quaestionis* which shows the continuing interest in the doctrines of the conciliarists within Scotland generally and by Bothwell in particular. Such works provided the medieval constitutional theories for the establishment of Scottish conciliar church government. The various questions which were being discussed regarding the place of the sovereign within the state made it imperative that Bothwell should be well informed. A few books on the subject were in his library and reflect some of the aspects of the

[173] Cf. supra, 143.

[174] Cf. supra, ibid.

[175] Cf. supra, ibid.

[176] *TA*, ii, 364. This co-incided with his initial attempts to improve the administration of justice. (R. K. Hannay, *The College of Justice* (Edinburgh, 1933), 18f.).

[177] *TA*, ii, 206.

[178] F. Douaren, *De sacris ecclesiae ministeriis ac beneficiis*.

[179] G. Dahm, 'On the Reception of Roman and Italian Law in Germany' in *Pre-Reformation Germany*, ed. G. Strauss (London, 1972), 282–315, especially 300–2.

[180] C. N. S. Wood, *Bartolus of Sassoferrato* (Cambridge, 1913).

[181] L. Chabrand, *Etude sur Gui Pape* (Paris, 1912). Pape was cited by Spottiswoode in *Practicks* (Edinburgh, 1706).

[182] G. Merzbacher, 'Die ekklesiologische Konzeption des Kardinals Francesco Zabarella' in *Festschrift Pivec*, edd. A. Haidacher and H. Mayer (Innsbruck, 1966), 279–87.

[183] J. Schweizer, *Nicolaus de Tudeschi, seine Tatikeit am Basler Konzil* (Strassburg, 1924), and K. Nörr, *Kirche und Konzil bei Nicolaus de Tudeschis (Panormitanus)* (Cologne, 1964).

[184] A. Black, 'Panormitanus on the Decretum' in *Traditio*, xxvi (1970), 440–4.

matter: the ways in which a king might be advised,[185] the place of the king within the kingdom,[186] and the king as the head of the state and the church.[187] While, in spite of parliamentary condemnation in May 1584,[188] George Buchanan's *De Jure Regni apud Scotos*[189] remained in his library until the end of his life, it should also be noted that he had a copy of Bodin, *Six livres de la République*[190] which was published at the same time as the volumes on kingship. His interest in this matter was not new as the presence of Gasparo Contarini's work shows.[191]

The constitutional reforms which he brought about in the diocese of Orkney within the pre-reformation ecclesiastical structure,[192] continuing the constitutional ecclesiastical restructuring of his predecessor Robert Reid,[193] shows his humanistic appreciation of the place of canon as well as civil law. It would seem that his position was neither that of Luther, who claimed that canon law had been 'written in an unchristian oppostion to Christ, by the inspiration of an evil spirit',[194] nor that of Calvin, who stated that such law was 'against the clear prohibition of God'.[195] His attitude to the canonists after the reformation, was probably nearer Zwingli's[196] although not always for the same reasons. He would have, of course, a continuing involvement in canon law in view of its place in consistorial cases after 1560. As far as Roman law was concerned, the role of Justinian within the thinking of those who sought to reform the Roman,[197] Lutheran,[198] or reformed

---

[185] B. Philipp, *The Counsellor. A Treatise of Counsels and Counsellers of Princes . . .* englished by I(ohn) T(orius) . . . (London, 1589).

[186] J. Viperanus, *de rege et regno.*

[187] J. Bridges, *Superemacie of Christian Princes, over all Persons throughout their Dominions, in all Causes so well ecclesiastical as temporall* (London, 1573).

[188] *APS*, iii, 296.

[189] First published in 1579. One of the best commentaries is still W. S. McKechnie, 'De Jure Regni apud Scotos' in *George Buchanan: Glasgow Quatercentenary Studies 1906* (Glasgow, 1907), 211–96.

[190] Paris, either 1576 or 1580.

[191] F. Gilbert, 'Religion and Politics in the Thought of Gasparo Contarini' in *Action and Conviction in Early Modern Europe: Essays in Memory of E. H. Harbison*, edd. T. K. Rabb and J. E. Seigel (Princeton, 1969).

[192] Cf. supra, 141.

[193] Cf. the constitution of the cathedral which was issued on 28th October, 1544 and gradually implemented. (A. Peterkin, *Rentals of . . . Orkney* (Edinburgh, 1820), app. v, 18–25 and *RMS*, iii, no. 3102).

[194] *WA*, vii, 168: cf., however, J. Pelikan, *Spirit versus Structure: Luther and the Institutions of the Church* (London, 1968), 98–111.

[195] *Institutes*, iv, x, 7: cf. J. Bohatec, *Calvin und das Recht* (Feudingen, 1934).

[196] F. Schmidt-Clauging, 'Das Corpus Juris canonici als reformatorisches Mittel Zwinglis' in *Zeitschrift für Kirchengeschichte*, lxxx (1969), 14–21.

[197] E.g. in Herman von Weid, archbishop of Cologne, in his plans for a school for clergy in Bonn, proposed one professor to expound the *Institutes* of Justinian, with no reference to canon law (Hermann von Wied, *A Simple and Religious Consultation* (London, 1548), ff. cclxvi–xix).

[198] At least from 1536, when the Justinian Code is appealed to in the *Gutakten* of 6th December, 1536 (*WABr.*, vii, 604f.).

churches[199] would have been appreciated by Bothwell. His interest in legal reformists such as Hotman,[200] reinforces the impression that the many intellectual movements within this discipline were not overlooked by him. In particular, he continued to acquire books on ecclesiastical legal matters into the 1580s.[201]

While a good deal is known about Bothwell's reorganisation of his diocese, little can be gleaned from the library concerning his practical involvement in the life of the Church. One aspect, agriculture and land management, occupied his thoughts even although most ecclesiastical lands were feued.[202] He had books by Petrus de Crescentiis,[203] Charles Estienne,[204] and Cassianus Bassus.[205] The possession of three copies of the last author's work may indicate the life-long use of a book which could not always be found.

Whether his architectural books[206] were bought with a view to the maintenance of buildings such as the cathedral and palace at Kirkwall[207] or later construction is uncertain but they at least show an informed awareness of a subject of great importance in the renaissance era.[208] There were no liturgical books of the pre-Reformation period nor a copy of the Book of Common Order. However, there was a Roman Missal still in the library when it was catalogued. It may be that he parted with some of the former books earlier but the reasons for his retention of the Missal, if consciously done, will never be known. As one would expect, in addition to the

[199] The Scottish reformers appealed to Justinian in 1558. (Knox, *History*, i, 151 and *Calendar of State Papers, Foreign. Elizabeth*, ed. J. Stevenson (London, 1863), i, 8). Bishop John Leslie wrote, in 1575, that what is thought necessary to pacify a controversy is 'citet out of the Roman Lawes.' (*The Historie of Scotland . . .*, ed. E. G. Cody (*STS*, 1888), i, 120). Justinian is also mentioned in the preface to the Second Helvetic Confession of 1566. (*Bekenntnisschriften und Kirchenordnungen der nach Gottes Wort reformierten* Kirche, ed. W. Niesel (Zurich, 1938), 221). The place given by Calvin to Justinian is illustrated in the *Institutes* and elsewhere (Bohatec, op. cit.).

[200] F. Hotman, *Commentarius uerborum Iuris*, . . . was in Bothwell's library: for a short account of Hotman, cf. D. B. Smith, 'François Hotman' in *SHR*, xiii, 328–65. This work followed Andrea Alciato's *De Verborum Significatione* which was an outstanding example of 'the methological innovations of humanist jurists of the sixteenth century. (R. Abbondanza, 'Jurisprudence: The Methodology of Andrea Alciato' in *The Late Italian renaissance 1525–1630*, ed. E. Cochrane (London, 1970), 90). It is not known if Bothwell actually had a copy of this work as the catalogue only lists *Omnia Emblemata 'cum aliis.'*

[201] F. du Jon, *Ecclesiastici sive de natura et administrationibus ecclesiae Dei*; F. Duaren, *De sacris ecclesiae ministeriis ac beneficiis*, etc.

[202] M. H. B. Sanderson, 'The Feuars of Kirklands' in *SHR*, lii, 117–36.

[203] P. de Crescentiis, *de omnibus agriculturae partibus, & de plantarum animaliumque . . .*

[204] C Estienne, *L'agriculture et Maison rustique . . .*

[205] C. Bassus, *Constantini Caesaris selectarum praeceptionum de agricultura.*

[206] P. Cataneo, Senese, *I quattro libri de Architecture*, S. Serlio, *Il libro tertio d'architectura.*

[207] W. D. Simpson, *The Castle of Bergen and the Bishop's Palace at Kirkwall* (Aberdeen, 1961).

[208] R. Wittkower, *Architectural Principles in the Age of Humanism* (London, 1952), 2nd ed.

university text books already mentioned,[209] the library contained more advanced literature on many such subjects in which the renaissance scholar would be interested and which have not yet been mentioned. One or two important areas should be noted.

There is the field concerned with the general approach to education and particularly with the upbringing of the young as considered by authors, such as, Erasmus,[210] Freigius[211] and Manuel.[212] The concepts elaborated by these thinkers formed the background against which, not only Bothwell but the next generation of the family developed. The life and work of John Napier shows this. The holding of mathematical and geometrical books[213] too was certainly of paramount importance to him. The great attention which was paid to the apocalyptic and the occult,[214] in addition to the scientific, is reflected in a similar dualistic renaissance approach to astronomy and astrology. Authors on both aspects and those which conflated the two are found among his books,[215] while the related subjects of cosmography[216] and geography[217] were not forgotten. The various departments of philosophy, while obviously not one of his major concerns, in view of the rather small number of books on the subject, are, nevertheless, represented by several significant volumes spanning thought from Aristotle[218] to the *Dialectics* of his contemporary Ramus.[219]

For a bishop, who by his very office was ipso facto a preacher, there is to

---

[209] Cf. p. 144 above.

[210] Erasmus, *Declamatio de pueris ad virtutem ac literas liberaliter instituendisinque protinus a nativitate.*

[211] Johannes T. Freigus, *Paedagogus; hoc est, libellus ostendens qua ratione prima artium initia pueris quam facillime tradi possint.*

[212] Manuel II (Palaeologus), *Imp. Caes. Manuelis Palaelogi Aug. praecepta educationis regiae, ad Ioannem filium. His adiecimus Belisarii Neritinorum Ducis, eiusdem argumenti librum: cum aliis ad principum studia pertinentibus, nec unquam hactenus editis.* For further information regarding Manuel cf. G. L. Schumberger, *Un Empereur de Byzance à Paris et à Londres* (Paris, 1916).

[213] E.g. N. Tartaglia, *La prima (-sexta) parte del general trattato di numeri et misure*; C. de Boissière, *Les très excellent et ancient jeu Pythagmrique, dict Rythmomachie*; Euclid, *Elementa*; O. Finé, *Quadratura circuli tandem inventa & clarissime demonstrata. De circuli mensura, & ratione circuferentiae ad diametrum, demonstrationes duae. . . .*; W. Fulke. Μεταμαχια, *sive Ludus geometricus.*

[214] Cf. p. 164 below.

[215] E.g. *Annuli astronomici, instrumenti cum certissimi, tum commodissimi, vsus, ex variis authoribus, Petro Beausardo, Gemma Frisio, Ioāne Dryandro, Boneto Hebraeo, Burchardo Mythobio, Orontio Finaeo, vna cum Meteoroscopio per Ioāne Regiomontanum, & Annulo non vniuersali M.T. authore:* C. Gemma, *de arte cyclognomica, tomi III. Doctrinam ordinum universam, . . .*; Marcellus Palingenius (Pietro Angelo Manzolli), *Zodiacus vite, hoc est de hominis vita, studio ac moribus optime instituendis libri xii, . . .* Interest in the related subjects of chronology and horology is also shown in his having, G. Mercator, *Chronologia, hoc est temporum demonstratio. . . .*: S. Muenster, *Compositio horologiorum.*

[216] E.g. P. Apian (or Bienewitz), *La Cosmographie.*

[217] E.g. the Geographies of A. Ortel and C. Ptolemy.

[218] E.g. P. Melanchthon, *Commentarius de Anima.*

[219] In this connection, cf. P. Sharratt, 'The Present State of Studies on Ramus' in *Studi Francesi*, xlvii–xlviii (1973), 201–13.

be found *Rhetorica* which is attributed to Cicero.[220] Yet, in view of the large
number of volumes of sermons by sixteenth century reformers,[221] it is much
more likely that the latter had a greater influence on his attitude to homiletics
than classical rhetorical rules, although it must not be forgotten that, even
among contemporary preachers of considerably less education than Bothwell, the teaching which they had received on the subject prior to the
reformation left a definite mark upon their preaching and writing.[222] It has
also to be remembered that some of these classical influences on the style of
the written and spoken word were also to continue through the secular
literature which was appearing throughout Europe and of which Bothwell
had a first hand knowledge. The reading of contemporary foreign literature
was typical of his class although the acquisition of a knowledge of foreign
languages was not new in the sixteenth century.[223] He seems to have been
competent in French and Italian but there is little evidence of any great
interest in the actual grammar of the languages. However, with the presence
of *Dialoghi della lingua* by Sperone Speroni degli Alvarotti,[224] which was one
of the sources of Joachim de Bellay's *Deffence et illustration de la langue francoise*, he obviously had a taste for language ás well as literature. The Italian
renaissance influences in England,[225] on education,[226] literature,[227] poetry[228]
and much more, have been studied in considerable detail. Such influences in
Scotland have also been investigated to quite an extent.[229] It is seen from the
library that Bothwell's interest in Italian literature was at first hand although
some of the authors are only present in French translations. Petrach could not
be absent[230] and, reflecting classical influences, an Italian translation of
pseudo-Apuleius by Boiardo.[231] The *Novellae* of Matteo Bandello, bishop of
Agen,[232] in the tradition of Boccaccio's *Il Decamerone*,[233] were both to be
found. There are also *Didone Tragedia* by Ludovico Dolce and the main
works of Cardinal Pietro Bembo: his *Prose*[234] and *Asolani*, the latter in

[220] Marcus Tullius Cicero, *Rhetorica ad Herennium*.

[221] Cf. above, 153f.

[222] D. D. Murison, 'Knox the Writer' in *John Knox: a Quatercentenary Reappraisal*,
ed. D. Shaw (Edinburgh, 1975), 33–50, esp. 35, 40–2.

[223] B. Bischoff, 'The study of foreign languages in the middle ages' in *Speculum*,
xxxvi (1961), 209–24.

[224] There were several editions published in Venice from 1544 to 1560.

[225] L. Einstein, *The Italian renaissance in England* (New York, 1902).

[226] F. A. Yates, 'Italian teachers in Elizabethan England' in *Journal of the Warburg and
Courtauld Institutes* (London), v, 103–17.

[227] M. A. Scott, *Elizabethan Translations from the Italian* (New York, 1916) and Q. P.
Rebora, *L'Italia nel dramma inglese (1558–1642)* (Milan, 1925).

[228] A. L. Sells, *The Italian Influence in English Poetry* (London, 1955).

[229] Cf. R. D. S. Jack, *The Italian Influence on Scottish Literature* (Edinburgh, 1972),
29–89.

[230] *Il Petrarche con l'Expositione*.

[231] *L. Apulegio tradotto in volgare dal conte Matteo Maria Boiardo*.

[232] *La Prima (secundo, terze) parte de le nouelle del Bandello*.

[233] There are many editions of this title from 1516.

[234] *Prose della volgar lingua*.

French.[235] There is also a French translation of Ludovico Ariosto's *Orlando furioso*,[236] while the poets Belizario's[237] and Sannazaro's[238] sonnets appear in the original language. As well as Aesop's *Fables* in Italian,[239] there was also Bidpai's *La Moral' filosophia* which was a translation of Johannes de Capua's Latin version and edited by Antonio Francesco Doni.[240]

In comparison with Italian authors, the French literary tradition was not strongly represented which is surprising in view of the considerable influence of French literature on Scotland.[241] Some of the more important are present: Clement Marot, whose metrical psalms had such a wide influence,[242] Rabelais,[243] who was also present in a number of other Scottish libraries, and Jean de Marconville.[244] He also had a few French translations of the Bible.

A few Spanish authors are there too: two editions of Garciá Ordeñes de Montalvo's *Amandis de Guala*,[245] both in French, and several works by the universally popular Antonio de Guevara,[246] either in Italian[247] or Latin.[248] The medical, surgical and pharmaceutical works which Bothwell used are considerable in number and include almost all the important contemporary literature in the field. While it was not unusual for men of standing to have some medical books in their own libraries for consultation by the physicians and surgeons who might be called to attend some member of the household in case of illness, his books indicate an intimate knowledge of the state of medical studies at that time and the extent of this section of the library compares very favourably with the known libraries of the sixteenth century.[249] His medical reading may have begun during his student days considering the presence of traditional authors yet his studies were obviously being directed to modern developments. Furthermore, the possession of many books which were published in the middle of the sixteenth century bears witness to his lifelong interest in all areas of contemporary medicine.

The three classical works, Dioscorides,[250] Galenus[251] and Theophrastus,[252]

[235] *Les Azolains de . . . Bembo. De la nature d'amour.* French trans. J. Martin.
[236] *Rolland Furieux . . . Traduict en prose Francoyse.*
[237] *Sonetto de Belizario.*
[238] *Sonetti et Canzoni.*
[239] *Las fabulas del . . . fabulador Ysopo . . . con su Vita.*
[240] *La Moral' filosophia del Doni, tratta da gli antichi scrittori.*
[241] J. M. Smith, *The French Background of Middle Scots Literature* (Edinburgh, 1934).
[242] *Les Oeuvres.*
[243] *Les Oeuvres* and *Les Songes Drolatiques de Pantagruel,* . . .
[244] Some of the works published from 1563–74.
[245] Difficult to identify.
[246] For influence in Scotland, cf. R. Wedderburn, *The Complaynt of Scotland (c. 1550)* by Mr Robert Wedderburn, ed. with intro. by A. M. Stewart (*STS*, 79), xxvii and lviii n. 72.
[247] *Vita, geste, costumi, discorsi, lettere di M. Aurelio Imperatore.*
[248] *Epistolas familiares.* 2 vols., *Libro aureo de Marco Aurelio.*
[249] Cf. e.g. Durkan and Ross, *ESL*, passim.
[250] *Commentaires . . . De la matiere medicinale.*
[251] *de anatomicis administrationibus, de compositione medicamentorum,* and *Epitome omnium rerum et sententiarum.*
[252] *De Historia et Causis Plantarum.*

were still of current value. The medieval authors, Bernardus de Gordoniis,[253] Guy de Chauliac,[254] Nicole Prévost[255] and the *Regimen Sanitatis Salernitanum*,[256] remained popular throughout the sixteenth century. Several of the works were practical compilations of specific remedies which a local apothecary would be capable of making up. The obvious interest in surgery is unusual and the works which he had were as many as one would expect in the working library of a surgeon practising at that time.[257] The awareness of contemporary medical knowledge is illustrated by works of Thomas Erastus,[258] Jean Fernel,[259] Conrad Gesner,[260] Ambrose Paré[261] and Andreas Vesalius[262] being in the library. All were leading medical men of that time.

Plants and their uses were given in the writings of most of the important contemporary descriptive botanists such as Valerius Cordus,[263] Rembert Dodoens,[264] Leonard Fuchs,[265] and Pietro Andrea Mettioli.[266] Thurneisser zum Thurn combined Bothwell's interests in astrology and botany in his *Historia sive descriptio plantarum omnium*,[267] although it was of no scientific value. Bothwell may have become acquainted with him when he was inspector of mines in Scotland.[268] The bishop did not neglect the more popular practical approach of *Le grand herbier en francoys*[269] and, in this connection, it should be remembered that there were possibilities of gaining practical knowledge about plants from herb gardens then in existence in Scotland.[270]

A knowledge of medicine and surgery was acquired by a large number of renaissance scholars and Bothwell was following in the tradition of a long line of churchmen who had a professional interest in such fields.[271] For example,

[253] *Lilium Medicinae.*

[254] *Chirurgia.*

[255] *Dispensarium.*

[256] Innumerable editions from 1480 onwards.

[257] In addition to identifiable authors he had *Chirurgia universalis, Chirurgica Opera*, etc.

[258] *De occultis pharmacorum potestatibus.*

[259] *De luis Venereae curatione perfectissima*, and *Therapeutices universalis.*

[260] *Thesaurus Evonymi Philiatri de Remediis Secretis.*

[261] *Opera chirurgica.*

[262] His revision of *Institutionum anatomicarum secundum Galeni sententiam.*

[263] *Dispensatorum, hoc est, pharmacorum conficiendorum ratio.*

[264] *Histoire de plantes.*

[265] *Commentarius de historia stirpium, Stirpium imagines L.F. in enchiridii formam contractae*, etc.

[266] His extensive commentaries on n 250 above.

[267] Berlin, 1578 or Cologne, 1587.

[268] Leonhard Thurneisser zum Thurn, *Allgemeine Deutsche Biographie* (Leipzig, 1894), xxxviii, 226–9.

[269] A. Arber, *Herbals, their origin and evolution in the history of botany 1470–1670.* rev. ed. (Cambridge, 1938).

[270] E.g. possibly at the preceptory of Torphichen (cf. the herbal printed in *The Complaynt of Scotland*, fl. 53r and v).

[271] P. Delaunay, *La médicine et l'Église, Contribution à l'histoire de l'exercice médical par les clercs* (Paris, 1948).

William Scheves, archbishop of St Andrews, was astrologer and court physician to James IV,[272] who himself showed a practical interest in medicine and surgery[273] and in the acquisition of books on 'alchemy'.[274] It was during his reign that the Guild of Surgeons and Barbers of Edinburgh developed from 1505 under the authority of the town council.[275] The guild had close relationships with the council and the court of session[276] both of which were part of the background to Bothwell's life from birth.

Nearer his time, Robert Gray was lecturer in medicine at Aberdeen[277] and the redoubtable Dr Andrew Boorde, a Carthusian, spent a year at the university of Glasgow, teaching and practising medicine.[278] The most likely person within this group whom Bothwell might have known was Girolamo Cardano, one of the most popular philosophers and fashionable physicians of the sixteenth century,[279] who came to Scotland in 1552 to assist the Spanish physician William Cassanate in the treatment of John Hamilton, archbishop of St Andrews. Cardano spent some months in Edinburgh and Monimail successfully treating Hamilton for asthma.[280] It is worth noting that Cardano met, on his journeyings, Jean Fernel in Paris, Conrad Gesner in Zurich and Jacobus Dubois, or Silvius, in London.[281] Bothwell had many of the works of Cardano and the other three.[282]

Cardano's influence may also have extended to furthering Bothwell's knowledge of mathematics, in which he was interested, for, although he did not possess Cardano's *The Book of the Great Art* which dealt with the problem of solving cubic equations, he did have a book of Tartaglia,[283] who had been the originator of the theories propounded by Cardano.[284] The Italian's interest in astrology, expressed in the provision of a horoscope for Archbishop Hamilton during his stay in Scotland, may also have left its mark on the bishop.[285] He had a respect for Cardano's general knowledge, as he has

[272] *TA*, i, 21, 28. He had also been the master of the hospital at Brechin. (*RMS*, ii, no. 1358). It is significant that he had a copy of N. Falcutius, *Sermones Medicinales* (Pavia, 1484). (*ESL*, 49) which summarised the whole of medieval medicine abounding in original citations from all the known authorities.

[273] J. D. Comrie, *History of Scottish Medicine to 1860* (London, 1932), i, 148–54.

[274] *James IV Letters*, 32.

[275] *Edinburgh Burgh Recs., 1403–1528*, 101–4.

[276] Ibid., 1557–71, 2, 155, 165–6.

[277] *Kinloss Recs.*, xix.

[278] R. C. Buist, 'Andrew Boorde' in *Caledonian Medical Journal*, xi, 292f.

[279] *Hieronymi Cardani opera omnia* (Lyon, 1663). Reprint with intro. by A. Buck (Stuttgart, 1966), 10 vols.; H. Morley, *The Life of Girolamo Cardano of Milan Physician* (London, 1854), 2 vols.

[280] H. Yule, 'Jerome Cardan's Travels in Scotland' in *The Geographical Magazine* (Sept. 1874), 240f.

[281] Morley, op. cit., ii, chaps. iv and v.

[282] Cf.

[283] D. E. Smith, 'Medicine and Mathematics in the Sixteenth Century' in *Annals of Medical History*, i (1917), 125f.

[284] N. Tartaglia, *La prima (-sexta) parte del general trattato di numeri et misure* (Venice, 1556–60), 2 vols.

[285] Reproduced in D. Guthrie, *A History of Medicine* (Philadelphia, 1946), plate 31.

his *de subtilitate*, a popular encyclopaedia which ran through many editions from 1550.

Thus, Bothwell was in every respect like Chaucer's Doctour of Phisík:

'Well knew he the old Esculapius,
And Deiscorides, and eek Rufus;
Old Ypocras, Haly, and Galien;
Sarapyon, Razis, and Avycen;
Averrois, Demascen, and Constantyn;
Bernard, and Gatisden, and Gilbertyn.'

However, he did not only have a wide reading knowledge of the best authorities, he was, like his contemporaries, fascinated by astronomy and astrology, prognosis and prognostications. Indeed,

'. . . was there non him like
To speke of phisik and of surgerye;
For he was grounded in astronomye.
He kepte his pacient wondrously and wel
In al houres by his magik naturel.
Wel coude he gesse the ascending of the star
Wherein his patientes fortunes settled were.'[286]

Thus the lingering medieval influence of the esoteric, in contrast to the growing rational approach of much of renaissance thought, held a fascination for a large proportion of the intellectuals, including those among the clergy.[287] While this outlook allied to the medieval interest in eschatology encouraged scholars to look again at the role of the apocalyptic in the Bible, it also was the motivating force in the study of all aspects of the occult, apparitions, prognostications and the higher astrological powers. Authors, such as Bodin,[288] Lavater[289] and Palingenius,[290] provided Bothwell with material on the subject but yet there may have been a streak of scepticism in his mind about the whole approach as he did not have Henry Cornelius Agrippa's *de occulta philosophia* but had his *de incertitudine et vanitate scientiarum* which shows Agrippa's progress from occultism to a refined scepticism.

Sixteenth century man saw the function of magic as being the imposition of 'the human will on nature, on man, or on the supernatural world in order to master them.'[291] It is only when this is borne in mind that the pan-European obsession with witchcraft[292] and the like[293] can be understood.

---

[286] *The Canterbury Tales*, The Prologue.
[287] E.g. in England, cf. *LP Henry VIII*, x, 804, 850, 891; xii, II, 1102; xiii, II, 815.
[288] *De Magorum Daemonomania*.
[289] *De Spectris, lemuribus et magis atque insolitis fragoribus* . . .
[290] *Zodiacus vite, hoc est de hominis vita, studio ac moribus* . . .
[291] E. M. Butler, *Ritual Magic* (Cambridge, 1949), 3.
[292] The whole of Europe experienced the self same trauma, e.g. A. Soman, 'The Parlement of Paris and the Great Witch Hunt (1565–1640)' in *Sixteenth Century Journal*, ix (1978), 31–44; J. Tazbir, 'Procesy o czary' in *Odrodzenie i reformacja w Polsce*, xxiii (1978).

Bothwell was no different to his contemporaries in this respect. He was well read in demonology and witchcraft, no doubt influenced, in accordance with contemporary humanism, by Horace's Canidia and Vergil's Sibyl. It may, however, have been a concern that was forced upon him late in life by the witchcraft trials in Scotland of 1590[294] and the obsessions of James VI.[295] He possessed, for example, a copy of Bodin's De magorum Daemonomania which was translated by Fischart and published in Basle in 1581. His Malleus Maleficarum was almost certainly the edition published in Frankfurt in 1582, revised and edited by Fischart. It is interesting to observe a senator of the College of Justice acquiring the latter volume which was written by the arch-inquisitors, Heinrich Institoris and Jacob Sprenger, who had been granted extraordinary inquisitorial authority over the greater part of Germany by Innocent VIII in 1484,[296] and, while he purchased Bodin who supported witch-hunting, he does not appear to have had Weier's De praestigiis daemonum which was completely sceptical of much of the contemporary beliefs about witches and, revealing the author's training as a physician, attempted to put the discussion on to a scientific basis. With such a volume missing from the library, it suggests that he may not have been aware of the broad debate and was prepared to conform to generally accepted views.

The influences which shaped attitudes and motivated criminal proceedings came from diverse sources, the continuing activities of the inquisition of the Church of Rome which owed much to a residual medieval outlook,[297] renaissance speculations,[298] and, in Scotland, a theology which owed more to Luther[299] and the late medieval German situation,[300] as far as this problem is concerned, than to Zwingli and Calvin, the concern of the latter was within the accepted jurisprudence of the period[301] although he believed, like

---

[293] E.g. J. Irvine Smith fails to appreciate the contemporary situation when he blandly states that the Scottish Parliament, 'under the influence of the Reformed Church, in 1563, c. 73, passed the only Statute on the subject, imposing the death sentence not only on users but on seekers or employers of sorcery or witchcraft.' (An Introduction to Scottish Legal History, ed. G. C. H. Paton, Stair Society (Edinburgh, 1958), 290.)

[294] H. G. Stafford, 'Notes on Scottish Witchcraft cases' in Essays in honor of Conyers Reid (Chicago, 1953), 96–118.

[295] Daemonologie (Edinburgh, 1597).

[296] Summis desiderantes.

[297] H. C. Lea, A History of the Inquisition in the Middle Ages (London, 1887), 3 vols.

[298] J. Burckhardt, The Civilisation of the Renaissance in Italy, trans. S. G. C. Middlemore (London, 1904), 524–33.

[299] H. Obendiek, Der Teufel bei Martin Luther, eine theologische Untersuchung (Berlin, 1931).

[300] N. Paulus, Hexenwahn und Hexenprozess vornehmlich im 16. Jahrhundert (Freiburg, 1910).

[301] O. R. Pfister rather ignores the need for an awareness of this dimension in his study, Calvins Eingreifen in die Hexer- und Hexen-prozesse von Peney 1545 (Zurich, 1947). However, the later neo-Calvinist developments as described by J. L. Teall, 'Witchcraft and Calvinism in Elizabethan England' in Journal of the History of Ideas, xxiii (1962) have little direct connection with the teaching of Calvin.

all his contemporaries[302] in the personal intervention of the devil in human affairs.[303]

As a prelate and a gentleman, he was eager to acquire the attributes and qualities of the society in which he moved. This has to be seen in the context of a renewed interest in chivalry[304] which began in the late middle ages[305] and developed in the renaissance.[306] It has to be remembered that James IV was a Knight of the Garter, of the Order of the Golden Fleece and of the Order of St Michael.[307] Yet, even against such a background, it may be a little surprising to find in his possession a copy of the rule of the military order of St James of the Sword.[308] However, the ideals of 'the courtier, who combined arms and letters, chivalry and learning, prowess in war with social grace, a welding of medieval knight to Renaissance humanist,'[309] as described by Baldassare Castiglione in *Il cortegiano* made it essential for him to have a copy of this work.

The various aspects of the life of a gentleman were studied by the bishop. There are three different books on the art of war[310] and one on military discipline.[311] All of this was not merely theoretical. He wore armour in the autumn of 1567 when he took part in the pursuit of John Hepburn, earl of Bothwell. The weight of it nearly caused him to drown when the *Unicorn*, commanded by James Kirkcaldy of Grange, was wrecked in Shetland.[312] His

[302] *Opera*, xii, 412f.

[303] *Chivalry*, ed. E. Prestage (London, 1928) and R. Barber, *The Age of Chivalry* (London, 1979). For the legal implications in England cf. G. D. Squibb, *The High Court of Chivalry* (Oxford, 1958).

[304] J. Huizinga, *The Waning of the Middle Ages* (London, 1924), chap. vi and vii. The mid-fifteenth century saw Gilbert Hay's translations into Scots of *L'Arbre de Bataille*, *Livre de Chevalerie*, and *Liber de Regimine Principum* from a French version. (*Gilbert the Haye's Prose Manuscript (A.D. 1456)* ed. J. H. Stevenson STS (Edinburgh, 1901).)

[305] For an account of a spectacular manifestation, cf. F. A. Yates, 'Elizabethan Chivalry: The Romance of Accession Day Tilts' in *Journal of the Warburg and Courtauld Institute*, xx, 1f. For a description of Scottish tournaments at the beginning of the sixteenth century cf. J. W. Baxter, *William Dunbar: a Biographical Study* (Edinburgh, 1952), 163–7.

[306] A. H. Dunbar, *Scottish Kings* (Edinburgh, 1899), 233.

[307] *Regula y Establecimentos, de la orden de la caualleria de Sanctiago de Espana* (Leon, 1555); cf. *Saint James, the Order of the Rule of the Spanish Military Order of St James 1170–1493*, ed. E. G. Blanco (Leiden, 1971).

[308] A. M. Kinghorn, *The Chorus of History: Literary-historical relations in Britain 1484–1558* (London, 1971), 251.

[309] Cf. *The Book of the Courtier*, trans. C. S. Singleton (New York, 1959) and J. Cartwright, *The Perfect Courtier, Baldassare Castiglione: his Life and Letters* (London, 1927), 2nd ed., 2 vols.

[310] Certainly, Flavius Vegetius, *De arte militari* (Paris, 1536 or 1553) (an English translation of which was in James VI's library (*James VI's Library*, lxvi), cf. D. Bornstein, 'The Scottish prose version of Vegetius's *De Re Militari*' in *Studies in Scottish Literature*, 8 (1971), 174–83, and possibly Robert Valturius, *De l'art militaire* (Paris, 1555) and *Le chevalier de la Tour et le Guidon des guerres* (Paris, n.d.).

[311] *Livre de discipline militeir* (unidentified).

[312] David Hume of Godscroft, *History of the House of Douglas and Angus* (Edinburgh, 1743), ii, 80.

interest in navigation[313] and the advice of experienced seamen[314] did not prevent Kirkcaldy of Grange from causing the shipwreck.

He was interested in horsemanship[315] and acquired a book on duelling.[316] Duelling was not merely connected with the martial arts but had a place within the processes of law as trial by combat was still recognised throughout Europe as a legitimate method of settling disputes. It belonged to the grand gestures of kings. Richard II, with his uncles the dukes of Gloucester, Lancaster and York, challenged Charles VI, with his uncles the dukes of Anjou, Berry and Burgundy.[317] While in Bothwell's time, Francesco Gonzaga offered to fight Cesare Borgia to rid Italy[318] of him and, on two occasions, Charles V proposed single combat with Francis I of France to settle their differences.[319] Thus it was in such a tradition that the earl of Bothwell offered to submit to trial by combat when suspected of implication in the murder of Henry Stewart, Lord Darnley.[320] Private duelling continued to be common during the sixteenth century in Scotland but it would appear that the last judicial combat took place in 1597.[321] James VI disapproved of it and attempted to have the practice stopped.[322]

Fine wines, good food, the number of courses at a meal and the worthy entertainment of guests were the hallmarks of a gentleman and an indication of his status. An act of parliament of 1552 'devised and ordained, that no archbishops, bishops nor earls, have at his meat but eight dishes of meat', the next group below in the hierarchy were allowed four and so on.[323] As would be expected, it was foreign sources which inspired the culinary arts in the bishop's household, Christoforo de Messburg's popular work[324] and *Livre de Taillevent, grant cuisinier du roy.*[325]

Some of the other accomplishments of a renaissance gentleman are revealed, such as his interest in art,[326] but, in spite of the important place given

---

[313] Probably, Pedro de Menida, *Arte de navegor* (Valladolid, 1545).

[314] Hume of Godscroft, op. cit.

[315] Federico Grisone, *L'Ecuirie du S.F.G. en laquelle est monstré l'ordre et l'art de choiser, compter . . . et manier les chevaux . . . aveques figures de diuerse sortes de mors de bride. n'aguières traduite d'Italien en François et nouvellement . . . augmentée, . . .* (Paris, 1579).

[316] Girolamo Muzio, *Ill duello* (Venice, 1550).

[317] T. Rymer, *Foedera, . . .* (London, 1727–35), vii, 407.

[318] F. von Bezold, 'Aus dem Briefwechsel der Markgräfin Isabella von Este-Gonzaga' in *Archiv für Kulturgeschichte,* viii, 396.

[319] H. Baumgarten, *Geschichte Karles des V* (Stuttgart, 1885–92), ii, 641. Feuter, *Geschichte des europäischen Staatensystems, 1492–1559,* 307.

[320] *APS,* iii, 76.

[321] Bruntsfield challenged Carmichael for murdering his brother; Carmichael was killed.

[322] D. H. Willson, *King James VI and I* (London, 1956), 305–8.

[323] *APS,* ii, 488.

[324] *Banchetti Messibugo, compositioni di vivande, et apparecchio generale.*

[325] Paris, n.d.; Ferrara, 1549 or subsequent Venice editions of 1556 or 1581.

[326] J. Cousin, *Livre de Perspectiue,* and 'Lart emamere des symmer' (unidentified).

to music at that time,[327] there do not appear to have been any books on the subject nor manuscript scores.

One intriguingly vague entry in the catalogue of the bishop's books is 'Warkis in Inglis'.[328] It is not possible to know how many books are concealed under this heading but it does indicate that they were not considered to be of any great importance. The library, like others in Scotland at that time, shows that Scotland was almost exclusively receiving its theological and intellectual impulses directly from the continent. The role of English books and printers on Scottish reformation and renaissance thought was not very significant and to a large extent any reformation literature coming from England was probably having its greatest circulation among those who could read no language but their own.[329] English influences and anglicisation were marks of the next century.

It is to be regretted that so few of the books from this library have been located as still being extant as the indications are, from those which have been identified, that some of the marginalia would add to our knowledge of the actual interests and accomplishments of the bishop.

Some of the extant books bearing marks of Bothwell's ownership do not appear on the list of 1594.[330] While some of these may have been lent by him and not returned, others may have been gifted. Several gifts of books to James VI are recorded,[331] but it would seem that he regretted parting with Munster's *Cosmographia* as the title is deleted in the catalogue of the King's library[332] and is on the 1594 list. This brief glance through the library gives some indication of the wide range of influences which were brought to bear on one of the figures who stands on the fringe of so many events of national importance and is a constant reminder of the ways in which attitudes were shaped and which can now only be fragmentarily appreciated.

The renaissance apperception of which Bothwell was so typical began to decline in Scotland, as elsewhere, towards the end of his life. Although there are indications of continuing minor renaissance influences within the Church in Scotland,[333] broad intellectual and cultural interests gave place to narrow confessional concerns brought about by the 'second reformation'[334] which was reinforced by neo-Calvinism, mainly of Dutch origin,[335] by the anti-intellectualism of the counter-reformation,[336] by nascent Anglican imperialism,[337] by the exclusive Calvinistic biblical theology within the

---

[327] D. P. Walker, 'Musical Humanism in the 16th and early 17th Centuries' in *The Music Review*, ii (1941), 1f., 111f., 220f., and Ibid., iii (1942), 55f.

[328] *Warrender Papers*, ii, 407.

[329] D. Davidson, 'Influence of the English Printers on the Scottish Reformation' in *RSCHS*, i, 75–87 and G. Christie, *The Influence of Letters on the Scottish Reformation* (Edinburgh, 1908).

[330] E.g. Durkan and Ross, *ESL*, 29, nos. 1, 2 and 9.

[331] *James VI Library*, xl, lxii, lxiii.

[332] Ibid., xlvii.

[333] J. K. Cameron, 'The Renaissance Tradition in the Reformed Church of Scotland' in *Renaissance and Renewal in Church History*, ed. D. Baker (Oxford, 1977), 251–69.

Scottish universities,[338] by confessional statements of an extreme neo-Calvinistic nature,[339] and the gradual growth of specialisation in various fields of intellectual and professional life.

Thus, in common with the whole of Europe, ecclesiastical introspection ensured that the unified outlook of the renaissance ebbed away. As a result, 'the new factor' – the scientific revolution – 'began to elbow at the other ones, pushing them out of their places – and, indeed, began immediately to seek control of the rest, as the apostles of the new movement had declared their intention of doing from the very start. . . . We know now that what was emerging towards the end of the seventeenth century was a civilisation exhilaratingly new perhaps, but strange as Nineveh and Babylon'.[340]

---

[334] This phrase has been used by many historians in relation to Scotland without an awareness of its continental origins and similar developments (cf. e.g. T. Klein, *Der Kampf um die Zweite Reformation in Kursachsen 1586-1591* (Cologne, 1962)). Samuel Hartlib, deeply concerned about a second reformation was committed to 'the reformation of the whole world'. (H. Dircks, *A Biographical Memoir of Samuel Hartlib* (London, 1865), 17.)

[335] H. A. E. van Gelder, *The Two Reformations in the Sixteenth Century*, trans. J. F. Finlay (The Hague, 1961).

[336] Reaching its height with the publication of the *Index librorum prohibitorum* in 1559 by pope Paul IV.

[337] Originating in the concepts of *translatio imperii* (cf. W. Goez, *Translatio Imperii: ein Beitrag des Geschichtsdenkens und der politischen Theorien im Mittelalter und in der frühen Neuzeit* (Tübingen, 1958) and F. A. Yates, *Astraea. The Imperial Theme in the Sixteenth Century* (London, 1974)) and of Elizabeth Tudor as the Protestant Constantine (*The Acts and Monuments of John Foxe*, ed. J. Pratt (London, 1853), i, 292–301 and 312) which has continued, even through the days of the Protectorate in, for example, the supra-European ecclesiastical views of Puritans such as Sir Samuel Moreland (*The History of the Evangelical Churches of Piemont* (London, 1658), sig. A 2v–3v), down to the present time.

[338] Cf. *The Statutes of the Faculty of Arts and the Faculty of Theology at the Period of the Reformation*, ed. R. K. Hannay (St Andrews, 1910), 71f., the marginalia of John Malcolm, regent in St Leonard's College, in Calvin's *Harmonia ex tribus euangelistis composita, . . .: adiuncto seorsum Iohanne, . . .* (Geneva, 1560) (St Andrews University Library, press no. Typ. SWG. B60.SB), and the signatures of several early post-Reformation students of St Andrews on the title and the marginalia in Calvin's *Commentarii integri in acta apostolorvm* (Geneva, 1560) which is in the writer's possession.

[339] E.g. The Confession of Faith of 1615 (*BUK*, 589–99).

[340] H. Butterfield, *The Origins of Modern Science 1300-1800* (London, 1950), 174.

DUNCAN SHAW

10

King James's Popish Chancellor

That the Scottish Reformation was vehemently anti-Catholic from its inception is an historical truism which hardly seems to require demonstration. John Knox declared that one Mass was more dangerous than ten thousand armed men, and lectured his sovereign on the iniquities of the Roman harlot whom she cherished. A generation later Andrew Melville found a large number of Anglopiscopapistical propositions in the writings of his sovereign, King James, who fell far short of Melville's ideal of a godly prince. A generation later still, in July 1637, the first use of a new prayer book alleged to be even more Popish than its English counterpart touched off the famous riot in Edinburgh which led to the civil war. All this is well known. Not so well known is the fact that for almost twenty years Alexander Seton, earl of Dunfermline, a man whom everyone believed to be a Roman Catholic, though he outwardly conformed, held the highest office in the king's gift, the lord chancellorship, and conducted himself in office in such a way that after his death men of all shades of religious opinion combined to praise him and his stewardship. The reasons for his success in overcoming the handicap of his putative Catholicism deserve closer examination; they provide a revealing insight into Jacobean politics and attitudes.

Seton was born in 1556,[1] the third son of George, 5th Lord Seton, a rather stupid man whose great virtue of loyalty, to the ancient faith and to Mary queen of Scots, created all sorts of problems for himself and his family. As a younger son Alexander was destined for the church. Queen Mary, his godmother, gave him the lands of the priory of Pluscarden as a godbairn's gift, and the title of prior was formally conferred on him at the age of nine. Many members of aristocratic families became commendators of monastic benefices in this period without any expectation that they would become clerics, but in this case it seems likely that Lord Seton genuinely intended Alexander for the church. In 1571, when the boy was about fifteen, he was sent off to Rome and became a student at the Jesuit-run German college, where he acquired that excellent classical education and enthusiasm for books

---

[1] The date usually given is 1555. When he died in June 1622, however, he was described as being in his sixty-seventh year, which would mean that he was born between June 1555 and June 1556. His portrait by Gheeraerts, dated 1610, gives his age as 53. These, taken together, indicate a birth date in the first half of 1556.

which is so apparent in his letters and which was to be of great help to him in his relations with his equally learned king. How long he stayed in Italy is not clear, but there is no evidence for the assertion that he took holy orders.[2] From Italy he went to France, where he studied law. He was absent from Scotland for almost a decade in all; he returned late in 1580, when the rise of the king's French cousin Esmé Stuart, who ultimately became duke of Lennox, held out the hope of better days for families like the Setons, doubly pilloried during the regency of the earl of Morton in the 1570s as Catholics and as followers of the fallen queen.[3] Seton managed to keep his footing amid the vicissitudes of Scottish politics in the early 1580s, though he was almost ruined in the spring of 1583 thanks to his father's habit of allowing the family house at Seton to be used almost openly as a headquarters for visiting Catholic priests. One of these, a Jesuit named William Holt, was seized as he was about to depart for France; among the letters he was carrying was one from Seton to his old schoolmaster in the seminary at Rome. The duke of Lennox, wrote Seton, had been so successful with the king that James's mind was alienated from the ministers. He expressed the hope that foreign aid would be available to restore the true faith, and reported that Holt's ministrations had provided 'great satisfaction and consolation'.[4] Unfortunately for Seton, Lennox had recently been driven from the country by the ultra-Protestant regime of the Ruthven Raiders. Seton underwent an interrogation, but avoided real unpleasantness when they in their turn fell from power in June 1583.

The overthrow of the Ruthven Raiders was no great help to Seton in other respects, however, because the man who came to dominate both king and government was that dazzling and greedy adventurer Captain James Stewart of Bothwellmuir, recently created earl of Arran. This title was regarded as the prerequisite of the Hamiltons; Seton's only sister was the wife of the Catholic Lord Claude Hamilton, one of the two effective heads of the family. Under these circumstances Seton could expect nothing from Arran; he therefore supported the coalition which overthrew Arran in November 1585 and received his reward in the form of a seat on the privy council and, in January 1586, an appointment as an extraordinary lord of session in place of one of Arran's supporters. This appointment was somewhat unusual, since the function of the extraordinary lord of session was to serve as a link between the fifteen ordinary lords, originally thought of as professional judges, and the privy council; the typical appointee to this office was an important aristocratic politician or an official like the lord treasurer, whose seat was virtually *ex officio*. Seton was neither of these things, but he was a lawyer who was

---

[2] George Seton, *Memoir of Alexander Seton, Earl of Dunfermline* (Edinburgh, 1882), 19; M. Dilworth, 'Scottish Students at the Collegium Germanicum' in *I.R.*, xix, 20–1.

[3] In 1577 Seton had been deprived of the temporalities of Pluscarden for failure to conform to the established Protestant church; the benefice was conferred on one of Morton's bastard sons. In 1581 Seton got it back again. *RMS*, iv, 717; *APS*, iii, 276, Calderwood, *History*, iv, 400.

[4] Calderwood, *History*, iv, 394, 430.

expected to be useful to the new administration and his appointment pending a vacancy among the ordinary lords of session may be seen in this light.

With Arran's downfall James VI, now nineteen years old, began to govern in fact as well as in name. The principal domestic political goal of the young king and his political mentor, John Maitland of Thirlestane, secretary of state in 1585 and lord chancellor from 1587 till his death in 1595, was to enhance the royal authority by curbing the independent power of the upper aristocracy and the kirk.[5] This entailed, among other things, the creation of a class of reliable government servants. Seton was just the sort of man they needed: a younger son of an aristocratic family, professionally trained, and with his way to make in the world, a man who would find government service rewarding in both a psychic and a material sense. He was also, like his cousin Maitland, one of those by whom James set great store: men who had been loyal to his mother and then transferred that loyalty to him. Seton had done just that, brushing aside the attempts of Mary's agents to involve him in their impractical scheming in the mid-1580s, and making himself as useful as he could. He was faithful in his attendance at council meetings, did his best to persuade Elizabeth's veteran ambassador Sir Thomas Randolph that he was friendly to England, and served on the committee of the articles at the parliament of 1587 which enacted the legislation Maitland devised to implement his policy.

But what of Seton's faith? He was, after all, a Roman Catholic, son of a Catholic father who in 1584 was writing to the Pope with more enthusiasm than sense of his hopes of James's conversion.[6] Seton knew very well that such hopes were chimerical; furthermore, by 1587 the direction of the government's policy was perfectly apparent. Bringing the aristocracy under control had priority; so the government would conciliate and compromise with the kirk in exchange for its support in that campaign – a policy which Maitland advocated and James adopted with some misgivings. Conciliating the kirk meant that no professed Catholic could expect to retain public office: sooner or later Seton would have to make a choice between his career and public acknowledgment of his faith. The moment came early in 1588, when James appointed him an ordinary lord of session. He took the oath of office, but his colleagues were understandably suspicious of his faith. There was no record of his having communicated according to Protestant rites; they insisted that he do so, and he agreed.[7] And from 1588 on there was no public backsliding: until his death he outwardly conformed to the church established by law.

This is not merely another case of a man's wrestling with his conscience and losing. The most powerful motives for his remaining publicly committed to the ancient faith no longer operated. Seton had been fond of his

[5] For Maitland see M. Lee, Jr., *John Maitland of Thirlestane* (Princeton, 1959).

[6] W. Forbes-Leith, ed., *Narratives of Scottish Catholics under Mary Stuart and James VI* (Edinburgh, 1885), 187.

[7] Seton, *Memoir of Alexander Seton*, 23, citing the books of *Sederunt* of the court of session.

quixotic father, and had been closer to him, in his later years, than any of his other children. But now his father was dead, and so was the queen whom he had served so faithfully. It was no longer possible to reconcile the two great principles of loyalty to the true faith and to the crown, as his father had, by working for either Mary's restoration or James's conversion. So Seton chose loyalty to his king. But he read that king aright: he saw that what James wanted of his servants was outward conformity. Like Elizabeth, James believed that it was neither possible nor desirable to make windows into men's souls. Open defiance he would not countenance; but if a person publicly conformed to the established church, what he, or she, chose to believe, or even practise in private, did not greatly concern him. So Seton became, and remained, what was known in England as a church papist. He continued to receive the occasional priest from foreign parts, though far more discreetly than his father had. In 1605, shortly after he became chancellor, he was visited by two Scottish Jesuits, whose reports to the general of their order summarize the situation well:

'He publicly professes the state religion, rendering external obedience to the king and the ministers, and goes occasionally, though rarely, to the sermons, sometimes to their heretical communion. He has also subscribed their confession of faith, without which he would not be able to retain peaceable possession of the rank, office, and estates with which he is so richly endowed. . . . Two or three times a year he comes to Catholic confession and communion with his mother, brother, sister, and nephews, who are better Catholics than himself!'[8]

'Lord Seton often said to me in Scotland, when I urged him to support the Catholic cause, "Be not eager to act before the time comes. I have to live in Scotland, and I must give way to circumstances. When the opportunity presents itself, and there is any hope of success, I shall not be sparing of my goods, my blood, or my life, for the restoration of the Catholic religion." He is now all powerful in Scotland, but he will attempt nothing until he sees a solid foundation for hope. Meanwhile he takes his portion in this life, though at the risk of that which is eternal.'[9]

There is no evidence that Seton ever made any effort to restore the old faith, or even to secure any kind of unofficial toleration for it beyond the sort that he himself enjoyed. But of course he was suspected of far worse. In 1585 the ministers called him 'this papistical prelate and pensioner of the Pope' who 'hath uttered not obscurely his practising against religion, and in one massacre to cut the throats of the professors thereof.'[10] His hypocritical pretence of conformity was only to be expected of one educated by the Jesuits. The grumbling continued as Seton's career prospered. In 1593 he became president of the court of session and the chairman of the committee to manage Queen Anne's Scottish property for her. This appointment was

[8] Forbes-Leith, *Narratives*, 278–9.
[9] Ibid., 282.
[10] Calderwood, *History*, iv, 430–1.

important because it led to a permanent friendship with Anne, who herself eventually became a Catholic and whose favourite lady-in-waiting, Lady Jean Drummond, was Seton's sister-in-law. Seton and his colleagues were so successful in managing Anne's property that in January 1596, three months after the death of Chancellor Maitland, James made them the nucleus of an eight-man committee entrusted with the considerable task of bringing order out of the chaos of the finances of the crown.

This committee was promptly dubbed the Octavians; Seton was its chairman, and its membership was alarming to the kirk: 'all almost either Papists known or inclining to Popery or malignancy', wrote the presbyterian minister and historian John Row.[11] The great fear of the ministers, and also of the English agents in Scotland, was that Seton, whose ambition for the post was no secret, would succeed Maitland as chancellor and as the king's *éminence grise*. 'If that man should prevail', wrote the English agent Roger Aston in November 1595, 'there were nothing to be looked for but a peril to the good cause'.[12] Aston need not have worried. In the first place, James had no intention of taking on a new *éminence grise*, and he in fact kept the chancellorship vacant for three years. Second, Seton wrecked his own chances by a series of miscalculations in 1596 which almost destroyed his career. His mistakes were not owing to the financial stewardship of the committee, which did a very good job of eliminating unnecessary expenditures and improving the king's revenues, though the courtiers whose pensions were cut naturally had no love for the Octavians and waited for the chance to ruin them. Seton's blunders were political.

The great public issue in 1596 was whether or not George Gordon, earl of Huntly, the most powerful Catholic noble in Scotland, would be allowed to return from the exile into which he had been driven the year before, an exile which symbolized the triumph of the policy of curbing the independent power of the higher aristocracy. Andrew Melville and the rest of the dominant faction in the church adamantly opposed Huntly's return. James, on the other hand, wanted him back. He liked the earl, he believed that Huntly had learned his lesson, above all he believed that gentle treatment of Huntly would smooth his path to the English throne by reducing the possibility of Catholic opposition, either domestic or foreign. Seton threw himself into this fray on the king's side, making an eloquent speech in the convention of estates in August 1596 calling for Huntly's return. This speech was a bad mistake; it convinced Huntly's enemies that there was a Popish plot afoot, and that Seton himself was the chief conspirator. Seton compounded his error by urging James to be firm in the matter of the punishment of David Black, the intemperate minister of St Andrews, who in October 1596 preached a series of outrageous sermons personally attacking James and Anne, and for good measure calling Queen Elizabeth an atheist. The result was, that the famous religious riot in Edinburgh in December 1596 was

---

[11] John Row, *The History of the Kirk of Scotland*, ed. D. Laing (Edinburgh, 1842), 165. Cf. Calderwood, *History*, v, 394.

[12] *CSP Scot.*, xii, 60.

directed principally against Seton, 'that Romanist president, a shaveling and a priest, more meet to say mass in Salamanca nor (than) bear office in Christian and reformed commonweals'.[13] Seton was not the only target; other suspected Papists among the Octavians were attacked too, and the riot was encouraged – perhaps even precipitated – by the courtiers whose pocket-books the Octavians' economies had pinched. James dealt with the riot easily enough, but he came to the conclusion that the Octavians, and particularly Seton, were more of a political liability than a fiscal asset. Within a month of the riot the Octavians' power was transferred to the most impeccably Protestant member of the group, Lord Treasurer Blantyre, who proved quite unable to handle it.

Given the embarrassment which his conspicuous advocacy of Huntly's return had caused the king, Seton's losses were not great. He retained the positions he had held before the appointment of the Octavians, and he did not lose the king's favour. In 1598 James made him a lord of parliament in his own right as Lord Fyvie and forced his election as provost of Edinburgh, an office he was to hold for ten years. But his chance for real political power had apparently vanished. Other suspected Catholics among the Octavians could become very influential, as the secretary, James Elphinstone, the future Lord Balmerino, did for a brief time between 1598 and 1600; but not Seton. Like Huntly, he had become a symbol, one who, if given real power, or even the appearance of power, would make James's task that much more difficult.

Seton concluded that he must change both his image and his tactics if he were ever to realize his political ambitions. He had badly underestimated the strength and depth of anti-Catholic feeling, and the suspicion and dislike which his sort of conformity generated. He had also learned that for a man in his religious situation the politics of confrontation were impossible: the advantage his opponents would gain by charging him with Romanism would be too great to overcome. Conciliation and the achievement of consensus would have to be his tactics henceforth, if he ever got another chance. In the meantime, the prudent thing to do was to detach himself somewhat from his allegedly Catholic associates on the Octavians and to cultivate Protestant grandees like the earl of Mar, whom he unsuccessfully supported for the chancellorship in 1598.[14] His second wife, whom he married in 1601, came from an impeccably Protestant family. Two public stands, both of which risked alienating James, were particularly helpful to him. One was his support in 1599 of the legal claim of the Edinburgh minister Robert Bruce to a pension out of the revenues of the abbey of Arbroath when the king, who disliked Bruce, tried to stop it. The second was a speech in the convention of estates in 1600 opposing the levy of a tax to raise an army to make good James's claim to the English throne by force if need be, a proposal whose chief advocate was Elphinstone.[15] Seton's tactics had some success. Mar became

[13] Calderwood, *History*, v, 548.
[14] 29 March 1598, George Nicolson to Lord Burghley, in *CSP Scot.*, xiii, 181.
[15] 16 March 1599, 29 June 1600, Nicolson to Robert Cecil, ibid., 427–9, 661–4. Calderwood, *History*, v, 733–5.

his permanent ally, and by 1599 the suspicious English agent George Nicolson was describing him as an 'honest councillor'.[16] He was also able to take advantage of his position as provost of Edinburgh to look after the town's interests in ways which ultimately earned him the citizens' affection and gratitude.[17]

All this activity made Seton potentially employable again in serious matters of state, but he might never have been so employed had James lived out his days in Edinburgh as a mere king of Scots. It was James's succession to the English throne and the consequent administrative changes which gave Seton a second chance. As president of the court of session he was the most highly placed lawyer in the Scottish government – the chancellor, the earl of Montrose, was an elderly aristocratic nonentity – and so James decided to appoint Seton as the chief Scottish negotiator for a treaty of union between England and Scotland which the king had so much at heart. Seton, who was not too enthusiastic about the king's plans – all the evidence indicates that he, like other Scottish officials, was both suspicious and fearful that the union would open the door to English domination over Scotland – seized his opportunity with both hands. He never uttered a word in public against the proposals, conducted the negotiations both rapidly and skilfully, and in the process made another valuable friend in the person of the chief English commissioner, Robert Cecil. In the event, the union did not come to pass, but Seton had already received the reward for his efforts in the form of an earldom and the office he had coveted for a decade. By the beginning of 1605 he had become earl of Dunfermline and lord chancellor and real power once again lay open to him, because whether or not the treaty was ratified it was apparent that a change in the way King James conducted Scottish affairs was in the offing. Ever since the death of Maitland in 1595 James had in effect been his own chief minister. Even in the first year or so after his removal to London James carried on much as he had before, paying attention to such details as the wardship of the earl of Athol and the settlement of a dispute between Edinburgh and Leith. Inevitably, however, the problems and distractions of the king's new situation in London increasingly occupied his attention, while absence blurred his memory for details. The proposals for union did not provide for any amalgamation of the machinery of the two governments; there would be separate administrations in England and Scotland, with the latter being divided between the king in London attempting to govern by his pen with the aid of his advisers there, and the privy council in Edinburgh, obligated to execute the royal orders without question but not in fact always doing so. It became increasingly obvious that someone would have to be entrusted with the conduct of Scottish affairs under the King's general supervision and Dunfermline in the light of his new found favour must have had high hopes of being chosen in this capacity.

[16] *CSP Scot.*, xiii, 542.

[17] Seton's career as provost can be followed in *Extracts from the Records of the Burgh of Edinburgh*, ed. M. Wood and others (London and Edinburgh, 1927–54), vols. v and vi.

Once again it was not to be, and once again it was a religious question which stymied Dunfermline. This time, however, his own faith was not at issue. The difficulty stemmed from the religious policy which King James had been following ever since 1600, when he decided to reimpose diocesan episcopacy because it was the only sure means of giving him control of the Scottish church.[18] This decision split the clergy between supporters of the king's policy and the once dominant presbyterians, who believed that episcopacy was unscriptural and that ultimate authority in the church lay in the General Assembly. Dunfermline obviously had no theoretical quarrel with episcopacy, and he was a good enough Erastian; but he had reservations about the king's policy. Part of this was personal: he disliked and distrusted James's chief ecclesiastical adviser, Archbishop Spottiswoode, who cordially reciprocated both sentiments. To Spottiswoode Dunfermline was a dangerous concealed papist, constantly intriguing on behalf of his co-religionists; to Dunfermline Spottiswoode, who had been one of his most active critics in 1596, was an opportunist who hungered for political power. The chancellor feared that once Spottiswoode and his crew were restored to power in the church, they would seek it in the state as well, not only for ambition's sake, but also to employ the powers of the government against their clerical opponents, with the inevitable consequence of political rows and confrontations which Dunfermline was anxious to avoid. The chancellor therefore adopted a conciliatory attitude toward the moderate wing of the presbyterian party, but not because he sympathized with their views on church government. Such a stance might lessen their hostility to him as an individual and persuade them of the genuineness of his Protestantism, but his principal aim was political: to blunt Spottiswoode's anticipated drive for influence in the state.

The most insistent complaint of the bishops' opponents in the church was that the General Assembly was not being allowed to meet. This, they argued, was illegal: the law mandated a meeting once a year at least. Not at all, replied the bishops. The law was clear that the king, or his commissioner, determined the time and place of meeting; if James chose repeatedly to postpone the meeting, he was within his rights. The Assembly had last met in 1602. The pending union negotiations provided a plausible pretext for the postponement of the Assembly of 1604, but even so, there had been protests, and later in that year the synod of Fife, dominated by the radical wing of the presbyterian party, flatly declared that the Assembly could legally meet without royal permission.[19] Dunfermline had every reason to believe that another postponement would cause serious trouble. In June 1605 the postponement came, with the king giving no very convincing reason for his action. The ministers complained; one of them, the moderate John Forbes,

---

[18] On this point see M. Lee, Jr., 'James VI and the Revival of Episcopacy in Scotland, 1596-1600, in *Church History*, 43 (1974), 50-64.

[19] Calderwood, *History*, vi, 264-7, 270-1.

whose account of the affair is the fullest we have,[20] sought out Dunfermline to
indicate his distress. Dunfermline did not want a confrontation on this issue,
and did what he could to meet objections which seemed not unreasonable.
The ministers would be allowed to gather, and would be requested rather
than ordered to disperse. Whether Dunfermline intended that the ministers
should actually constitute themselves an Assembly is unclear; the privy
council's letter was addressed to the ministers 'convened at their Assembly at
Aberdeen' but on the same day the letter was written the council issued
James's proclamation forbidding the meeting.[21] At all events the handful of
ministers who appeared at Aberdeen did constitute themselves an Assembly
and then dissolved, after setting a date for another meeting in violation of the
council's instructions. James was angry; and Dunfermline was in a very
awkward position. Not only had he dealt rather ambiguously with Forbes
before the Assembly, but also, after it was dissolved but, before James's
anger became known, he had, according to Forbes, expressed to three
ministers who had been there his satisfaction with the proceedings on
learning that there had been no attack on the bishops.[22] After the
conviction of Forbes and five of his colleagues on a technical charge of
treason early in 1606, Archbishop Spottiswoode, aided and abetted by the
earl of Dunbar, the lord treasurer and Dunfermline's chief rival for the
position of James's principal Scottish adviser, set out 'to procure the
Chancellor his disgrace, as suspected to be an enemy to the estate of
bishops'.[23] Once again Dunfermline's career hung in the balance.

For a time it looked as if the king might be angry enough to dismiss his
chancellor. He allowed Spottiswoode and Dunbar to press their charges by
means of a formal hearing before the privy council, and he was reportedly
ready to oust Dunfermline if he could be convicted of 'undutifulness'.[24] But
in the end he decided that Dunfermline's behaviour was owing to
miscalculation rather than disloyalty. His temporizing policy was due to a
serious overestimate of the backlash which postponing the General Assembly
would produce – the number of ministers gathered at Aberdeen had been
very small. He had partially redeemed himself by his useful work at Forbes's
treason trial; but the real hero of that occasion, in James's view, was Dunbar,
whose rapid and forceful methods James judged to be best suited for the
implementation of his religious policy. Dunfermline had qualms about such
tactics. 'I desire not his sacred Majesty to put us oft to such proofs', he wrote
to Salisbury after the trial, 'for I assure your Lordship in truth in this kingdom
the puritanism is very far predominant, and albeit this be done to his
Majesty's will and wish, it is not without a greater grudge and malcontent-

---

[20] John Forbes, *Certaine Records touching the Estate of the Church of Scotland*, ed. D.
Laing (Edinburgh, 1846), 383ff. Given the treatment meted out to Forbes, he is
remarkably fair-minded.
[21] Ibid., 388–9, 391–2; *RPC*, 1st series, vii, 62.
[22] Forbes, *Certaine Records*, 401–2.
[23] Ibid., 406.
[24] Ibid., 513.

ment nor (than) the consequence of it can be of avail. Such diseases in policy will neither so well nor so easily mend, by direct contrariety and opposition, as indirectly and by compass about, specially when the disease is inveterate and has taken hold, as this is here indeed.'[25] James did not agree with this plea for gradualism. He intended to reimpose diocesan episcopacy as rapidly as possible; for that purpose the ruthless Dunbar would be far more suitable than the conciliatory Dunfermline, who, James knew, would do what he was told.

So Dunfermline survived, at the price of acquiescence in both James's religious policy and Dunbar's domination of the Scottish political scene. But the somewhat paradoxical effect of his troubles was to make him much less unpopular with the presbyterian elements in Scottish society, both inside the church and out, because they perceived him as the enemy of their enemy, the bishops. This was enormously helpful to him, because these were precisely the groups that were most likely to criticize what they regarded as simulated conformity. David Calderwood, the presbyterian historian, who was exiled in 1617 for his opposition to the king's religious policy, tells in his *History* a number of what may well be *ben trovato* stories about Dunfermline: poking fun at Archbishop Gledstanes's lack of legal knowledge, grumbling about the councillors' having to play the bishops' hangmen.[26] Attacks on him as a papist after 1606 were not very numerous, were usually politically inspired, and could be safely ignored as long as he retained the king's favour, and this he was able to do. One weapon was flattery: he was effusive in his praise of James, and of Dunbar, whose work in repressing lawlessness on the borders he compared to the cleansing of the Augean stables.[27] Cooperation was another: he worked effectively with Dunbar on a number of issues, notably the ending of free trade between Scotland and England in 1610,[28] and where he was able to take some initiative, as, for instance, in highland matters, he was very successful.

The religious question would be the acid test, however, and here Dunfermline trod very warily. What he deduced for the near-disaster of 1606 was that he should not meddle in religious issues at all if he could possibly help it. For someone in his ambiguous personal position they were far too dangerous; his career had almost been ruined twice on account of them. But of course he could not avoid them altogether. So he worked to further the king's ecclesiastical policy when necessary – at the parliament of 1606, for instance, he strongly advocated the restoration of the temporalities of the bishops, which, according to Spottiswoode, he had previously opposed.[29] He would not, or could not, prevent the occasional harassment of his

[25] PRO, SP 14/18, no. 31.

[26] Calderwood, *History*, vi, 699–701, vii, 450.

[27] 12 Aug. 1609, Dunfermline to James, *Letters and State Papers during the Reign of King James the Sixth*, ed. J. Maidment (Edinburgh, 1838), 171–3.

[28] See their joint memorandum on this subject written in October 1610, BM Add. Mss. 24, 275, ff. 9–9b.

[29] John Spottiswoode, *The History of the Church of Scotland*, ed. M. Russell and M. Napier (Edinburgh, 1847–51), iii, 175.

relatives as suspected Papists, and only occasionally protested when he was himself abused, either by a bishop or at one of the rare meetings of the General Assembly.[30] About all he was willing to do was to try to minimize the influence of bishops, especially bishops like Spottiswoode, in the business of government,[31] to prevent them from using the privy council as an instrument of coercion of their opponents in the church, and occasionally to help those opponents as individuals. Among these individuals was his brother-in-law, John Moray, minister of Leith, who was ousted from his benefice on Spottiswoode's initiative for publishing an allegedly seditious sermon; Dunfermline's efforts could not save him. In only one area was Dunfermline willing voluntarily to involve himself: he was a key figure in the various commissions to improve clerical stipends, a matter on which he saw eye-to-eye with Spottiswoode and the king.[32]

So during Dunbar's years of power Dunfermline made himself as useful as he could, made no effort to unseat the lord treasurer, and mended his fences as carefully as possible. His careful cultivation of all the important individuals and groups in Scottish politics, with the exception of the irreconcilable archbishop, was eventually crowned with success. The all-powerful Dunbar, who was about Dunfermline's age, died in January 1611, at precisely the right moment for Dunfermline's political prospects. The work of restoring diocesan episcopacy had been completed in the previous year; a period of consolidation was now indicated, for which Dunfermline's conciliatory methods were ideally suited. Spottiswoode was eager to be Dunbar's successor, but James knew, if Spottiswoode did not, that the time was far from ripe to give an ecclesiastic that sort of political power. So Dunfermline became the king's *éminence grise* in Scottish affairs, and remained so until his death in 1622. The chancellor saw to it that there was, in fact, no real challenge to his position during his decade of control by following a cautious and conservative policy designed to upset no one, by using the knowledge gained during his decade as provost of Edinburgh to look after the economic interests of the burghs, and by continuing to avoid religious issues as much as possible – though now, by contrast with Dunbar's day, he was occasionally willing to protect Catholics from harassment, especially if his own household

---

[30] See, e.g., 3 Aug. 1608, Dunfermline to James, Maidment, *Letters and State Papers*, 142–4; 13 Oct. 1608, Sir William Seton to James, the bailies of Haddington to James, NLS. Denmilne Mss. II, nos. 84, 85; 1 Sept., 1610, Margaret Seton, Lady Paisley, to Queen Anne, *Original Letters Relating to the Ecclesiastical Affairs of Scotland . . . 1603–1625*, ed. D. Laing (Edinburgh, 1851), i, 257.

[31] Two exceptions to this generalisation should be noted: in Orkney, where Dunfermline's government used Bishop Law against the king's ruffianly cousin Earl Patrick, and in the western highlands, where the chancellor worked closely with Bishop Knox of the Isles in devising the policy which led to the statutes of Icolmkill of 1609. Knox was the one bishop with whom Dunfermline was really friendly.

[32] For the Moray episode see Calderwood, *History*, vi, 689–92, 699–702, vii, 19–20, and *RPC*, viii, 72–3, 270–1, 492–4, 496, 499–500, 563–4. On clerical stipends see W. R. Foster, 'A Constant Platt Achieved: Provision for the Ministry, 1600–1638', in D. Shaw, ed., *Reformation and Revolution* (Edinburgh, 1967), 124–40.

was involved.[33] Though he unhesitatingly conformed to the five articles of Perth, he was not keen on them and showed it – indeed, no one in authority in Scotland, not even Spottiswoode, shared James's enthusiasm for these innovations.[34] Dunfermline also shored up his position through the uses of matrimony. He married three times, always into noble families, and had a large crop of daughters; he was also responsible for the marriages of the children of his older brother Robert, earl of Winton, who died in 1603. Dunfermline arranged a series of politically and socially useful marriages for this brood which connected him with a large number of important families, Catholic and Protestant, aristocratic and official, with the notable exception of the Gordons: Dunfermline wanted no link with the most overtly Popish family in the kingdom. The result was, that there were so many important people with a stake in Dunfermline's continuance in office that James, even if he had so wished, would have found it politically awkward to remove him.[35]

Not that James wanted to. He had always valued the chancellor's intelligence, efficiency, and loyalty, and he found Dunfermline's cautious and conservative variety of consensus politics to his liking in most respects, though he never warmed very much to Dunfermline as a man. From the chancellor's portrait, and from the marvellous painted gallery at his home, Pinkie House, it is easy to see why. Dunfermline's face is that of a reserved, fastidious intellectual; the mottoes on the allegorical paintings in the gallery give evidence of an ironic, sometimes cryptic, sometimes self-deprecatory sense of humour.[36] He was a man who would attract, and be attracted by, the king's genuine intellectualism, but not by James's raffish vulgarity. So Dunfermline was an exception to the general rule that continuous personal access to the king is a *sine qua non* for a ministerial career. He did better at a distance, in part because he knew how to write letters which would please the king: learned, prolix, full of Latin tags and classical references, and of flattery.[37] So Dunfermline reached the height of his power as the agent of an absentee king, power he might never have achieved or retained in the bawdy, Byzantine, corrupt and disorderly surroundings of Jacobean Whitehall.

It is possible to argue that, after his decision to conform, Dunfermline

---

[33] For an example see 28 May 1613, Archbishop Gledstanes to James, Sir William Fraser, *Memoirs of the Maxwells of Pollok* (Edinburgh, 1863), ii, 68–71.

[34] For the five articles of Perth see I. B. Cowan's assessment in Shaw, *Reformation and Revolution*, 160–77, and P. H. R. Mackay, 'The Reception given to the Five Articles of Perth', in *RSCHS*, xix (1977).

[35] For a fuller discussion of Dunfermline's methods of government see M. Lee, Jr., *Government by Pen: Scotland under James VI and I* (Urbana, Ill., 1980), esp. chap. 4.

[36] A few examples of these paintings are reproduced in M. R. Apted, *The Painted Ceilings of Scotland 1550–1650* (Edinburgh, 1966). There is a full description of the gallery in George Seton, *A History of the Family of Seton through Eight Centuries* (Edinburgh, 1896), ii, 813–19.

[37] There is no collection of Seton papers as such. Most of Dunfermline's surviving letters to James are in the Denmilne Mss. in the National Library of Scotland. Many have been printed in Maidment, *Letters and State Papers* and in Laing, *Original Letters . . . Ecclesiastical Affairs*.

ceased to be a Catholic in any meaningful sense. No matter how one chooses
to define a genuine Catholic, however, his fellow countrymen believed
Dunfermline to be one. The significance of his remarkable career, therefore,
is that in an age of violent public hostility to the ancient faith, he succeeded in
overcoming the prejudice aroused by his putative Catholicism, so that
Calderwood could write of him in recording his death, 'howsoever he was
Popishly disposed in his religion, yet he condemned many abuses and
corruption in the Kirk of Rome. He was a good justiciar, courteous and
humane both to strangers and to his own country people, but no good friend
to the bishops.'[38] Dunfermline's achievement was considerable for a man
who had once been the target of a Protestant mob, but it was not an isolated
case. There were other suspected papists like himself, other Octavians
indeed, who conformed as he did and had highly successful careers, notably
his colleague for thirty years, Thomas Hamilton, the Edinburgh lawyer's
son, who died in the next reign, full of years and honours, as earl of
Haddington. Dunfermline's success made it easier for others, of course: if the
presbyterians refrained from attacking the most prominent church papist in
the land because he was the bishops' enemy, it was difficult for them to attack
any of the others. It is, of course, true that after the exile of Andrew Melville,
the restoration of episcopal power, and the erection of potential engines of
repression like the courts of high commission it was much more dangerous
for religious dissidents to attack anyone save overt papists like the marquis
of Huntly, but it is noteworthy that none of those critical of Dunbar's
high-handed tactics during the controversy over the imposition of constant
moderators on the presbyteries and synods in 1607–08 or of the five articles of
Perth aimed their shafts at Dunfermline. What his career shows is that
religious animosities may have run less deeply than has sometimes been
supposed,[39] that in the atmosphere provided by what has been called King
James's Peace[40] it was possible to defuse the religious issue, to arrive at that
sort of unspoken compromise and *de facto* toleration which might, given
time, have led to genuine religious peace. But time was not given. How
fatally easy it was to reawaken all the old fears and hatreds, King James's inept
son and his maladroit agents would discover to their sorrow.

[38] Calderwood, *History*, vii, 549.
[39] On this point see M. Sanderson, 'Catholic Recusancy in Scotland in the
Sixteenth Century', *Innes Review*, xxi (1970), 87–107.
[40] Donaldson, *James V–James VII*, ch. 12.

MAURICE LEE Jr

The Edinburgh Merchants in Society, 1570–1603; the Evidence of their Testaments

A great deal can be learned about the late sixteenth-century Edinburgh merchants from records other than their testaments which, after all, represent fewer than 300 of all those believed to have flourished in the second half of the century.[1] However, the registers of testaments contain details about the merchants as individuals, their circumstances and everyday business activities which if put alongside the information found in civic and public records, present an all-round picture of the Edinburgh merchant in the reign of James VI.[2]

The first impression is the wide range of substance of those known as merchants, from John McMorane's inventory of £21000 to the £26 of John Geichan.[3] The really rich men appear to have been a small minority in a trading community which consisted mostly of middling merchants and shopkeepers. If, as an English memorandum of 1580 claimed, a Scots merchant was reckoned wealthy if he was worth £1000 sterling, then only seven individuals were in that class when they died; John McMorane (c £3155), William Birny[4] (c £2422), Mr John Provand[5] (his wife's testament, c £1886), Janet Fockhart,[6] widow of William Fowler, (c £1872), John Dick[7] (c

---

[1] I am grateful to Dr Michael Lynch for allowing me to read his PhD thesis on Edinburgh and the Reformation, in which he considers the role of the merchants in some detail, drawing conclusions about their relative substance and influence similar to those expressed in the first five paragraphs of this article.

[2] Records of the Commissariot of Edinburgh, Register of Testaments; CC8/8. This record, on which this article is based, will be cited hereafter by reference number only, on the first mention of a merchant. Time has permitted close examination of only 205 registered merchant testaments out of a surviving 286, but while this may have meant leaving out a few big names, it has also resulted in the inclusion of many smaller and, as it appears, typical merchants.

[3] (John McMorane) Fraser Papers (S.H.S.) 226; CC8/8/29, fo. 240v, all sums are in Scots money unless otherwise stated.

[4] CC8/8/1, fo. 218.

[5] CC8/8/18, fo. 52v.

[6] CC8/8/29, fo. 399v; (William Fowler) CC8/8/3, fo. 360v.

[7] CC8/8/31, fo. 61v.

£1809), Hector Rae[8] (his wife's testament, c £1112) and Ninian McMorane,[9] brother of John, (his wife's testament, c £1052), these amounts being in sterling according to the exchange rate of 12 to 1 that pertained at the end of the century. All of these merchants excepting Birny died within the last decade. In the cases of Bailie McMorane, shot by a rebellious Edinburgh schoolboy in 1595, and Janet Fockhart, who practised money-lending, no debts by them are recorded, and it may be questioned whether the whole picture has been preserved. Even so, this handful were so far beyond their fellow-merchants in wealth as to be exceptional. Part-ownership of ships and shares in cargoes, money-lending, including advances to government officials, sub-letting of burgh property, the holding of land in security from debtors, selling merchandise to retailers, provisioning the households of nobles and lairds and the predominance in their stock of expensive cloths and wine, characterise them as a group, although not all of them were engaged in all these activities.

These elements also characterise, if to a lesser degree, many of the testaments of the next strata of merchants, taken to be the thirty-six who left free gear of over £3000 and under £12000. Only two of these merchants died before 1580; most early testaments examined were those of smaller men, William Birny being a notable exception, and suggest a certain growth in prosperity towards the end of the century in spite of short-term setbacks. A bonus of information on a merchant's fortunes occurs where the testaments of the merchant and his wife, who died several years apart, have both been recorded, as in the cases of William McMath,[10] James Ross[11] and Mungo Russell[12] in this middle group.

The great majority of the merchants under consideration, however, left less than £3000, almost one-third of them under £500. The typical Edinburgh merchant was not the money-lending owner or part-owner of ships, investing money in land and growing rich on the sale of luxury goods to the king's courtiers, but a much smaller, less influential figure.

The social background and connections of some individuals can be detected. In sixty-eight cases, where close family relationship to members of other social groups is revealed, the pattern is as follows:

Kinship with:

Other merchants	36
Proprietors, including lairds	12
Craftsmen	10
Professional groups (e.g. lawyers and clergy)	10
	68

Although this is a small sample the proportions are significant, indicating a high incidence of intermarriage among merchant families, some of whom

[8] CC8/8/34, 27 July 1600.
[9] CC8/8/29, fo. 15.
[10] CC8/8/25, fo. 271v.
[11] CC8/8/6, fo. 294v; 19, fo. 204.
[12] CC8/8/17, fo. 108; 25, fo. 186.

would be by then second- or even third-generation merchant burgesses. Many, however, would be more recent comers to trade. In the case of quite a number their geographical origins are suggested by direct references to relatives living to landward, by their bearing surnames particularly prevalent in a district or by the geographical emphasis in lists of debtors and creditors. Probable places of origin, outside the Lothians hinterland, include Aberdeen, Stirling, Ayr, Sanquhar, Dumfries, Glencairn, Biggar, Jedburgh, Douglas, Monkland in Lanarkshire and Glasgow.

Local connections were invaluable. Clement Edgar,[13] whose brother, Edward, was also a merchant in Edinburgh, had four debtors in Dumfries, where a third brother, Robert, was a merchant, and others in Wigtown, Minnigaff and Kirkcudbright. His cousin, Nicol Edgar, was made oversman of the testament of merchant, William Herries,[14] whose debtors included a Dumfries burgess and Robert Herries of Mabie, probably a relative. Matthew Jamieson, who died in Glasgow in January 1584/5, not only had debtors and relatives there, including 'my guid freind' sir Mark Jamieson, vicar of Kilspindie, whom he asked 'to be kynd to my barnis', but at the time of his death had just deposited a quantity of woad, some of it the property of another Edinburgh man, in the keeping of William Symmer in Glasgow, with the knowledge of Robert McIlwraith, a merchant there.

There is an impression, in these examples, of the more recently established merchants as outposts of families in rural areas and smaller burghs acting as suppliers of those at home, trying to extend the family fortunes further afield. Coming mainly from places on routes leading to Edinburgh from the Borders and Lanarkshire and from the Glasgow area with its access into the south-west, the merchants would also become outlets for the produce of their home localities. John McMath bought wool from John McMath in Auchensaugh and 'John McMath's barnis in Castilgirmur', in Lanarkshire,[15] James Graham bought 37 stones of wool from John Graham of Holylee, in Selkirkshire,[16] and Gilbert Lowrie quantities of it from his brother-in-law, James Henderson, and Michael Short in Lamington.[17] Doubtless, the many cadgers who appear as debtors and creditors helped to deliver the goods in this two-way traffic.

The query arises as to how many of these merchants were of recent rural origins. Only twenty testaments show clear indications of landed interests, in the possession of stock, crops and rents. The stock were usually sheep, often left with a steelbow tenant or in pasture with a farmer, and sold to local people or to the Edinburgh merchants and fleshers. James Martin, who was owed money by several people in Crawford, had sheep and cows in pasture with three people in Lanarkshire and with Adam Martin in Nisbet, probably a relative. He had sold wool to several people, and lambs and sheep to William

[13] CC8/8/30, fo. 269v.
[14] CC8/8/32, fo. 338v.
[15] CC8/8/29, fo. 316.
[16] CC8/8/29, fo. 16v.
[17] CC8/8/4, fo. 305v.

Gledstanes 'in the toun of Craufurde' and Alexander Weir in Glaspen, as well as 'auld sheep wol' to William Herries, burgess of Edinburgh, 'quha usit to travell with wol to Dunde', and 'schoirling' and 'fute faill' skins to the Edinburgh merchant, David Crosbie. He himself had bought 'nolt, sheep and wol', to the value of £500, from his brother, Thomas Martin in 'Polbudie'.[18] William Johnston, probably from Douglas parish, had some sheep in pasturing in the West toun of Douglas; the volume of his merchant business was small.[19] John Acheson a merchant living in the suburb 'under the Castle wall' of Edinburgh, sold twenty sheep to the laird of Auchindinny, Midlothian, and others to a Leith flesher and to John Miller 'merchand dwelland in the Drum'.[20]

Other merchants engaged in more serious farming. Andrew Stevenson had steadings on the East and West burgh muirs, where he had workhorses, oxen and sheep, and oats in the barn and barnyard. Further afield, he had tenants at Pittroddie, in Fife, who owed him about £140 in rents for 1587, and a steelbow tenant at Brotherton in Caldermure.[21] Robert Gillespie had bere worth £40 'standing unthreshin in Brochtoun',[22] and John Ainslie victual in his barnyard and maltbarn worth over £170, besides some stock.[23] Fermes were due to John Robertson from tenants at Auchtermuchty, in Fife, Broughton and the burgh muir of Edinburgh,[24] to David Morris from tenants at Currie and Restalrig, and from several individuals in the Canongate and Leith, for land which is not specified,[25] and to Robert Johnston from William Acheson in North Berwick.[26] David Morris had, in turn, sold victual to a number of people in Leith. Mungo Russell, who subfeued Dalry mills from George Carkettle, merchant, for £10, leased seven acres of Dalry Mains to a tenant and had himself sown grain to the value of £152 on the lands of Langlands. Patrick Cochrane, who probably came from the barony of Monkland in Lanarkshire, owed £30 'maill and teind' to the 'gudwyf of Haggs'.[27]

Significant as these examples are, the evidence for merchant involvement in farming and landholding is meagre in the 205 testaments examined. As far as the small men were concerned, close ties with their home country and access to its produce may have made the acquisition of land less necessary. Again, the 'small' Edinburgh merchant's turnover of overseas business was probably substantial enough, compared to that of provincial seaports, to render serious farming, even by remote control, time-consuming, whereas

[18] CC8/8/19, fo. 285v.
[19] CC8/8/19, fo. 47v.
[20] CC8/8/19, fo. 250.
[21] CC8/8/20, fo. 178v.
[22] CC8/8/23, fo. 300.
[23] CC8/8/32, fo. 160v.
[24] CC8/8/32, fo. 294v.
[25] CC8/8/18, fo. 164v; 21, fo. 149v.
[26] CC8/8/3, fo. 435.
[27] CC8/8/29, fo. 313v.

the merchant in a smaller or more remote burgh may have found it a valuable supplement to his comparatively small amount of overseas trade.

The bigger Edinburgh merchants were more interested in taking land and rents in security for loans. The wealthy William Birny, in addition to fermes from tenants on the lands of Grange and Barnhill, in Fife, to the amount of over £346, was due 150 bolls wheat and 1250 francs from George, 5th lord Seton, for which the latter had assigned Birny half the fermes of Tranent, Seton and Upcragy in 1567. Lord Seton, whose fortunes suffered from his support of Mary, queen of Scots, was still in debt to the merchants sixteen years later when he owed £300, on obligation, and his tenants of Upcragy £128, by their obligation, to the merchant, Mr John Provand. James Nicol was due 'byrin annualrents' from the lands of Polkemmet in West Lothian and Westfield in Moray, and others from the lairds of Craigmillar and Kinnear and lord Yester, the last-named also having wadset land to the merchant, George Wauchope.[28] Other wadsetters, with lairds in their pockets, included the merchant, Ninian Lowis, who held land in security belonging to Hector Munro of Foulis, Neil Munro of Swordell, John Munro of Lymlay, the laird of Brodie and David Dunbar of Durris.[29]

Straight money-lending was also a major source of income. Thomas Aitkenhead, probably the 'brother' mentioned in James Nicol's will as sharing the rents of lord Yester in security, who himself was a feuar of parts of the burgh muir, drew a number of 'annualrents' on financial loans: 100 merks from William Oliphant, advocate, £110 from Alexander Drummond of Midhope (also mentioned in Nicol's will as a debtor) and James Hamilton of Bridges, jointly, and £320 from Lord Lindsay of the Byres on a loan of 3000 merks. Aitkenhead, who made his will in 'this my auld aige' and had no stock in hand but over £900 in ready money and £400 of household goods, may have given up active trading for purely financial transactions.[30] There were dangers, of course, in too much lending. John Dick, who had Orkney connections, and who died in 1596 leaving free gear of £21717, looks on the surface like a rich man. In fact, his inventory amounted to only £314 and his own debts, based on obligations for many substantial sums, to over £7000. What altered the balance were the debts due to himself, on obligations, amounting to £29000, including the 39000 merks due him by Patrick, earl of Orkney. Dick's fortunes were, therefore, precarious.

The inherent dangers failed to deter many merchants from lending, as the constant references to 'lent' and 'borrowit' money make plain, although this could equally well be said of all kinds of people down to the peasant farmers. However, there is good evidence that, with merchants, lending was a deliberate occupation. The many large sums due 'on obligation' clearly do not all represent the price of goods bought, although some individuals were capable of running up huge bills. Mr John Provand, who was due a long list of sums, by obligation, from prominent people, which probably do

[28] CC8/8/25, fo. 192v.
[29] CC8/8/25, fo. 207.
[30] CC8/8/34, 26 July 1600.

represent bills for goods, was also owed £56 'byrin annualrent' by Adam Brown in East Monkrig and £141 6s 8d 'lent money' by John Scott in Falkirk, both 'by obligation'. On the same basis Alexander Walker in West Port of Edinburgh owed £10 'lent silver' to the merchant, John Watson.[31] The cases of Francis Napier and lord Hay of Yester who owed £1334 and £1000 respectively, by obligation, to Ninian McMorane, suggest borrowing rather than buying. The lawyers were sometimes among the borrowers; Andrew Lawson, writer, pledged a gold chain with Gilbert Dick for the loan of just over £39.[32]

An extensive money-lender, or at least exploiter of her debtors to the extent of taking substantial pledges, was the kenspeckle Janet Fockhart, widow of the merchant William Fowler, grandmother of the poet, William Drummond of Hawthornden. Janet's name occurs in the accounts of the Treasurer of Scotland as a lender to the government and her discharges, signed by herself, turn up in family archives. Her testament is *dative*, she died in May 1596, and no debts by herself are recorded and the picture may be incomplete. Nevertheless, her wealth was considerable. Her inventory of £7223 3s 4d includes what one suspects are many unredeemed goods, mostly jewellery and silver ware, household goods and utensils worth £733 6s 8d, her own 'silver work' to the value of £293 10s, 'ready money' amounting to £458 15s and over £68 'in hir purs'. The debts owing to her amounted to over £15000 and the list of debtors includes many prominent people, with a note of their respective pledges:

'lord Lindores, £600, pledged, a woman's gown of cloth of silver, 2 great gold pieces, gold buttons and a jewel; lady Orkney, £100, pledged, a diamond ring and a 'pointed' diamond ring; lord Spynie, 200 merks, pledged, a target of gold and 17 diamonds.'

Many others owed her large sums, on obligation, including Lady Gowrie (£636), Mr Andrew Lekprevik (£100), Sir Walter Ogilvy and James Ogilvy of Blairock (2100 merks), William Napier and David Hoppringle as cautioners for the earl of Orkney (1200 merks), the 'Auld Lady Justice Clerk' (£100), the master of Orkney (£100), lord Glamis (£1044), Robert Hudson (£10) and James Menzies and John Drummond as cautioners for the earl of Atholl (£40). The only reference in Janet's testament to overseas is the mention of 450 merks, owed by William Fowler, possibly her son, which was received by him in Flanders. It seems likely, although her husband had been a merchant in the conventional sense leaving £7900 when he died in 1575, that Janet was mostly concerned with finance.

Income might also be derived from burgh property, and property in Leith, apparent in the house, booth and cellar maill among debts due to merchants. George Ballantyne drew house maill from Leith, Andrew Craig from loft accommodation in the Luckenbooths.[33] David Morris drew nearly

---

[31] CC8/8/4, fo. 290v.
[32] CC8/8/21, fo. 57.
[33] CC8/8/27, fo. 226.

£130 a year from houses let to twelve people in Edinburgh and Leith, including the laird of Huttonhall, Mr Alexander Hamilton, doctor of medicine, and several saddlers cutlers and meal-makers. Many merchants bought up annualrents due from houses and ground. Others acted as factors in the financial and legal business of their customers. Ninian Lowis was due £133 6s 8d from Patrick Dunbar of Blarie, on obligations, for whom he had also paid £3 16s 8d for two 'letters of four forms' in pursuance of a legal action, 30s which he had given the laird's servant for his expenses and £123 6s 8d for silks supplied to Dunbar by the merchant's wife 'at the time of the laird of Grant's bridal'. John Coutts practised as a notary, leaving his 'haill prothogill bukis with minitis, scrollis and all uthir bukis, with (his) lettroun to put thame in', to John Ormiston, notary.[34] Robert Johnston had lead mines in Orkney, it is not stated precisely where, with ore to the value of 400 merks, 'laid upoun the hill of the lead mines', as well as creels, shovels, spades and gavels, and a 'sea boit' worth £20. When trading proper prevailed it is sometimes possible to tell where and from whom the merchants obtained the wool, sheepskins, hides and Scots cloth which they later exported. Predictably, these came from the Borders, Galloway and upper Lanarkshire and from the Lothians hinterland. John McMath, probably from Douglas parish, referred in his will to the wool he had bought 'this instant year', 1595, spending £2567 15s on 'the first buying'. His fifteen pokes of wool consisted of six 'of fyne galloway woll, thrie polkis of fyne woll of the Watterheid (received from the "gudeman" there), fyve pokis of forrest woll' and a poke of 'bona lana'. The wool was bought on the spot from the lairds of Watterhead and Smetoun, Andrew Macadam (127 stones), Mr James McMath, John McMath in Auchensaugh, Douglas parish, John McCall in Corsbank (40 stones 'with ane tar ruber') and others, the cost of transporting it to Edinburgh being £125 15s, with £45 for pack-sheets. It was still in the merchant's hands when he died but he had already shipped from Leith 'in Garye Dawson's ship', 8 'singill beddis of clayth' estimated to be 1600 Scots ells and worth £1163 15s 10d. More cloth (1300 ells) had gone on John Scott's ship and two 'cords' of skins on that of John Gray, the cloth worth £1026 13s 4d and the skins £495, the value of his total exports on that occasion just exceeding the amount paid for that year's first purchase of wool in Scotland. William Cockburn bought wool, hides and skins from a number of people in Dunsyre, in upper Lanarkshire. When he went to France he took with him 24 cwt wool, worth £181 6s 8d, with oncosts paid, 500 skins, 5½ daker hides and 2 white webs, at the same time sending a quantity of sheepskins and hides to Flanders in the charge of a factor. John Bawtie bought skins from William Hamilton, miller at Hamilton, for £34, the purchase probably consisting of about 125 skins, since the 500 shipped by him to Flanders were said to have cost him £140 in Scotland.[35]

The problem of storage for the raw materials and native cloth awaiting

[34] CC8/8/3, fo. 143.
[35] CC8/8/5, fo. 172.

shipment, and the imported goods destined for the home market but too bulky for the booth, was as acute as that of living space in the tall, narrow buildings of the crowded burgh where only the greatest merchants lived in houses or owned premises that could be described as commodious. Many merchants leased additional storage and all substantial importers wanted this at the port of Leith if possible. From the contents of cellars and lofts, some idea of the quantities of Scottish export goods a merchant might have on hand can be obtained. To supplement this information there are inventories of Scots goods lying unsold in Europe.

The testamentary material may not add to other available information on the overall trade figures but it does show some merchants sending a consignment of cloth, skins or hides to Europe which might fetch as much as some lairds could hope to realise from a year's rents. Of course, the money might take some time to come in; John Brown's 16 dakers of hides, worth £165, were said to have lain with his factor for three years.[36] Thomas McMichael's cellars in Edinburgh held 24 dakers hides, with 8 dakers of oxen hides, while his factor in Veere had 2300 sheepskins, in Flemish hundreds, estimated to be worth £1800.[37] Thomas Lothian shipped at one time to Flanders 2500 sheepskins worth £1125.[38] Ninian Lowis had 70 bolls great salt lying in Cromarty, 'in Mr Thomas Urquhart's house' where he rented a cellar for £5 a year, and 21 barrells of salmon with his factor in Rouen. William Burgess's Scots cloth in his Leith cellar consisted of linen, 'gled hewit cloth', black 'gray', 'gray mixit greene', white 'gray' and blue cloth.[39]

Transporting a cargo entailed owning a share of a ship – no cases of entire ownership have been found – or hiring the use of a ship or the services of the master to see the goods delivered. Thirty vessels are mentioned in this group of testaments, either by name or that of the master. Nine merchants owned shares, the others hired the services of the shipmaster. The value of the shares of most merchants, ranging from £140 to £1650, are put in perspective by those of John McMorane in nine vessels, amounting to over £4000. There were seven users of ships mostly belonging to Leith masters, with the addition of the *Daniel* of Burntisland, used by John McMath (1595), 'William Lambert's ship' of Kirkcaldy, used by Gilbert Dick, in addition to three others (1587), and the *Angel* of Bordeaux, used by Andrew Jowsie (1593/4).[40] The brothers Archibald and Cornelius Inglis used 'George Dawson's ship' jointly, and Archibald himself three others (1594).[41]

A merchant might accompany his cargo, or go abroad on business. Seven of the merchants under consideration died abroad; Ronald Paterson at Abbeville, in France, where he made his will,[42] witnessed by seven

[36] CC8/8/3, fo. 42v.
[37] CC8/8/27, fo. 204.
[38] CC8/8/23, fo. 103.
[39] CC8/8/22, fo. 373v.
[40] CC8/8/29, fo. 59v.
[41] CC8/8/28, fo. 296.
[42] CC8/8/26, fo. 125v.

fellow-Scots, James Lowrie in Calais,[43] William Birny in Veere, Elias Maxwell in Danzig,[44] Thomas Tait in Poland,[45] Thomas Henderson, 'quha wes slane in Ingland',[46] and Thomas Wright.[47] William Cockburn was in France when his wife died, in May 1573.

Goods, customarily sent abroad in relatively small consignments because of the high risk of loss at sea, were often sent 'in venture' with a factor, or agent, who not only saw them safely landed but, on the merchant's instructions, handled their sale and made purchases with the proceeds. Some merchants employed trusted near-relatives; William McMath sent salmon, wax and copper to the Biscay ports, in 1591, with his nephew, James, and his brother, Alexander, himself a merchant who rented a house from William and used the *Anna*, in which William owned a share, on a voyage to Norway six years later. Substantial merchants might use several factors, as they used several ships, for their cargoes, to lessen the effect of losses at sea; Alexander Udward ventured £700 to Dieppe, in 1596, among Moses Wallace, John Purves and William Paterson.[48] Cargoes entrusted in this way might be considerable – David Richardson sold salmon and wax for John McMorane estimated at £3938 2s 3d, or quite small – Harry Porteous sold 44 'buk skynnis callit schamois' in France for Christel Mayne for £105 12s.[49] Clement Russell, factor for his father, Mungo, had only just arrived home with a pack when his father died, while Clement's brother-in-law, Henry Nicol, was still in Danzig when his father, James Nicol, died.

There are references to 27 factors 'in Dieppe', 'in Camphier' and elsewhere, but it is difficult to decide whether these were residents in Europe handling the business of home-based merchants, as many undoubtedly were, or travelling factors who happened to be abroad when the merchant died. Apart from one factor in Rouen, one in Bordeaux and three in Danzig, the others were equally divided between Dieppe and Veere ('Flanders' usually indicating the latter) in this last quarter of the century. References to William Aikman and Harry Todd of Dieppe and to William Wallace and Thomas Cunningham of Veere cover 23, 13, 17 and 11 years respectively. Thomas Cunningham, from a Dumfriesshire family, settled in Veere in this period, his son, also Thomas, leaving records of his activities as Conservator of Scottish priviledges there in the seventeenth century. The four merchants whose testaments reveal their dealings with Cunningham, that is Thomas Copland,[50] Clement Edgar, James Johnston[51] and Thomas McMichael, also had Dumfriesshire connections so that the factor assumes the character of an even further outpost of the sheepfarmers of south-west Scotland. Scots-born

[43] CC8/8/27, fo. 216.
[44] CC8/8/29, fo. 201.
[45] CC8/8/35.
[46] CC8/8/18, fo. 245v.
[47] CC8/8/31, fo. 298v.
[48] CC8/8/30, fo. 158.
[49] CC8/8/29, fo. 19v.
[50] CC8/8/25, fo. 130.
[51] CC8/8/17, fo. 52v.

burgesses, or those of Scottish descent, turn up in lists of debtors and creditors in Europe; Alexander Cunningham and Thomas Armour, 'butterman', in Rouen, Robert Graham in Bordeaux, Sandy Weir, 'saipman', in Veere, James Richardson in Poland, James Reid, John Richardson, William Findlay, William Murray and James Fairservice in Denmark.

Space precludes a detailed examination of the mechanics of trade or the financial arrangements of the merchants, although the testaments shed a fair amount of light on these matters with regard to individuals. Only one case of the direct exchange of goods for goods was found, in the testament of William Birny who died in Veere in October 1568. Birny had left with his factor there, John Culper, not only coin amounting to £5106, but also 5 bolls madder and 3 puncheons alum, 'lowsit be him' to William for 4700 stones of lead worth £1905 6s 8d. The common method of exchange was by quasi-barter, in which exported goods were sold and the 'frie money' used to purchase goods for the home market, the money thus being a medium of exchange rather than an end in itself. Sometimes the free money and other cash in the factor's hands were put together to make a purchase, the cash providing makeweight in the bargain. Cornelius Cuthbert, burgess of Edinburgh, travelling factor to Flanders for William Geichan, had in his hands £200 Flemish, 'of coft money fra John Oustian burges of Edinburgh', and 1173 ells 'cuntrey claytht' worth £1122 10s Scots in 'frie money', these sums being employed by Cuthbert to buy 'orchart litt', soap, madder and pans, which merchandise when it came home to Scotland realised £2440 17s 6d when sold, all charges and oncosts being deducted; a profit of £1118 7s 6d on the whole transaction.[52]

There is evidence that money itself was often sent out of the country to purchase goods, in spite of prohibiting legislation. Gilbert Dick's factor in Dieppe, Thomas Fairlie, had received from another factor there, Harry Todd, in Dick's name 200 francs (£160 Scots) 'quhilk the defunct coft fra William Lamb in Kirkcaldy'. Robert Dougall sent £1466 13s 4d 'in venture to Bordeaux'.[53] Ninian McMorane sent in venture to the eastern seas with David Richardson, 'to be employit on wax', 500 crowns (£1500 Scots) and 500 crowns in venture to Boyen (? Bayonne) with Mungo McCall, 'to be employit on wine, cork and rosat'.

Trade with England is reflected in debts owed to merchants, mainly in London and Berwick. Robert Scott, in 1586,[54] and John Wood, in 1591,[55] owed £114 sterling and £25 sterling, respectively, to the London merchant, William Craven. In 1587 Gilbert Dick sent 'home' two packs of English stemming with William Lyndforde, London draper. Andrew Creich was also indebted to Lyndforde and to Robert Jackson in Berwick,[56] who also

[52] CC8/8/28, fo. 93v.
[53] CC8/8/34, 20 November 1599.
[54] CC8/8/24, fo. 214v.
[55] CC8/8/23, fo. 330.
[56] CC8/8/25, 13 July 1593.

supplied English cloth to Andrew Cairney[57] and James Masterton,[58] in the latter's case to the value of £1426 5s. Other English merchants include Christopher Morton in Berwick, to whom James Lowrie owed £1460, Thomas More and Thomas Hogg (? a Scot), also in Berwick, who supplied Mungo Russell, and William Parsons and Humphrey Hawkshaw, London merchants, who supplied John Ainslie. John Chalmers shared ownership of the *Thomas* with two Englishmen, Thomas Park and Robert Page.[59] John Ayton, a relative, possibly a brother of George Ayton of Inchderny, died at Chepstow while his ship was in harbour there.[60]

It is difficult to say whether the presence of debtors and creditors in other Scottish ports meant regular coastal trade or business dealings with individual merchants, in the nature of retailing. William Lamb, the Kirkcaldy burgess who changed money for Gilbert Dick which was destined for the latter's factor in Dieppe, himself owed Dick over £40. John Jackson and his wife were in Kirkcaldy when she died in October 1585, they may have left Edinburgh to escape the plague that year, where they had a quantity of imported merchandise with them.[61] Two Aberdeen burgesses owed Jackson large sums. Andrew Turnbull, who died in Dundee in 1590, had a considerable amount of merchandise there representing the usual mixture of stock.[62] Andrew Buk, Aberdeen merchant, owed William Birny two barrells of salmon, Robert Inglis of Aberdeen £15 to William Herries, and William Blair, whose stock consisted solely of wine, owed quantities of it to two Anstruther skippers and two Dundee burgesses.[63]

Customers in the home market, while they were mainly drawn from Edinburgh, Leith and the immediate neighbourhood, also came from farther afield, buying goods when they visited Edinburgh, in the case of nobles and lairds often through their servants, but also from the many chapmen and travelling merchants, who purchased from the merchants and retailed down into Lanarkshire, Dumfriesshire and Ayrshire, as well as in the Lothians. Chapmen and 'travelling merchants' were not only based in burghs but in landward areas, many of them along the south-western routes. The merchants who dealt with them ranged from Patrick Cochrane, who left over £8000 and was due money from three chapmen and a traveller in Cumnock, Mauchline, Galloway and Ayr, to Robert Gillespie, who left £889 and had no fewer than eleven among his debtors, five from Falkirk, three from Stirling and three from Linlithgow. John Ritchie 'travelor about Moffat' bought £16 10s of lint from Thomas Tweedie,[64] Thomas Cairns 'in the Bow' standing his cautioner for payment. The merchant John Danesoun

[57] CC8/8/18, fo. 81.
[58] CC8/8/28, fo. 9.
[59] CC8/8/3, fo. 235v.
[60] CC8/8/32, fo. 78v.
[61] CC8/8/20, fo. 281.
[62] CC8/8/22, fo. 71v.
[63] CC8/8/31, fo. 151.
[64] CC8/8/28, fo. 25.

was owed a small sum by 'the chopman that travels to John Hardie', a phrase that suggests a regular business arrangement.[65]

The members of the trading community were divided into 'outland' and 'inland' merchants, importers and shopkeepers. Dividing lines were blurred in practice, however, since those merchants mainly engaged in overseas trade also retailed to smaller merchants and individual customers while on the other hand the 'shopkeepers' greatly varied in the volume of their business, from fairly prosperous traders selling in bulk to the cramers and luckenbooth holders. It is difficult, therefore, to say what proportion was represented by the 'outland' men, but it is likely that they were a largish minority. Certain recurrent elements in the testaments, clearly indicative of overseas trade, account for just over 43 per cent of the merchants under consideration, these elements being ownership of ships or cargoes, resident or travelling factors, the employment of skippers, mention of overseas debtors and creditors, references to goods or money sent abroad, lying abroad or brought home, and the merchant travelling abroad himself.

It is, of course, impossible to say whether the remaining 57 per cent of the merchants were all 'inland' traders, since evidence of a man's overseas interests may have missed his testament, depending on the circumstances when he died. However, certain significant features are found in this larger group of testaments which suggest that it did contain most of the inland merchants and shopkeepers. To begin with, the great majority were small men, leaving estate of less than £1000. Secondly, although importers can be found owing money to one another, a number of these smaller merchants owed money to merchants on a scale that suggests buying in order to retail. William MacFadzean, who left free gear of £416, bought merchandise from six merchants, one of whom was in Stirling and other two were the brothers Edward and Clement Edgar; it is worth noting that not only were the Edgars originally from Dumfriesshire, but that a burgess and a chapman from Dumfries owed MacFadzean money, suggesting that he, too, may have had connections there.[66] Mr Michael Chisholm, who left £595, owed over £400 to nine Edinburgh merchants,[67] John Stevenson, leaving £1334, had spent the large sum of £1899 5s 8d on merchandise from seven merchants, and David Williamson, whose free gear amounted to £1364 9s 6d, owed over £1300 to three merchants, two of whom were kinsmen.[68] Thirdly, it is noticeable, from the inventories of many of these smaller merchants whom it may be surmised included the retailers, that their stock tends to consist of one type of goods, or of closely allied types – unlike the very mixed goods carried by the big importers – the most common types, or combinations, being cloth and haberdashery, or perishable goods and small hardware. John Stevenson stocked materials and trimmings, the majority of his debtors being tailors. Alexander Burnet, who left £407 when he died in March 1577/8, had a stock of

[65] CC8/8/1, fo. 178v.
[66] CC8/8/23, fo. 288.
[67] CC8/8/22, fo. 125v.
[68] CC8/8/22, fo. 224v.

sweetmeats, fruits, spices, sugar, honey and soap. His creditors consisted of fourteen merchants from whom he had bought goods, including raisins from William Nisbet, figs and raisins from William Napier, soap from Thomas Hall and William Rutherford and prunes (plumdames) from David Bassendean.[69] When his son's widow died thirteen years later her stock was of the same type, but was worth three times as much and her bills were paid up, no merchants appearing among her few creditors.[70] Alexander's grandson, Samuel, was still selling fruit and confectionery, with some wine, in the year 1600.[71]

Fourthly, the smaller merchants' testaments which show no clear overseas connections, often contain a stock of Scots goods, mainly cloth, which they sold at home. William Johnston, for example, who left free gear of only £140, carried a stock, at the time of his death, of 'black grayis' and harden. He had sold 'woven cloth' to an Edinburgh tailor, woven cloth and worsteds to John Dinwiddie in Duns, wool cards and cloth to John White in Wanlockhead and blue cloth to Michael White in Douglas. Thomas Andrew's widow's stock consisted of small linen, blue cloth, harden, scourings, plaiding, 'ane pair of hewit plaidis', a grey web and black wool; her debtors included many tailors and John Brown in Glasgow who had bought 12 ells of 'fyne blue'.[72] One undoubted shopkeeper was John Fleming, who left £94 10s 8d free gear. His inventory is headed, 'crame wairis in the hous', giving a good picture of a cramer's stock.[73]

Three individuals are designated 'tailor and merchant'; it would be easy, on building up a good tailor's business, to stock enough materials to be able to retail them to fellow-tailors, as Andrew Cairney,[74] Andrew Clark[75] and Thomas Muirhead did.[76] Although Cairney left only £482 free gear, he had loaned money to Andrew Lamb in Leith and counted the earl of Eglinton and a handful of advocates among his customers. Much of the cloth in his booth was English, some of it bought in Berwick; the 'new luiking glass in the buyth' was presumably for sartorial purposes.

Only cross-referencing of lists of debtors and creditors from all surviving testaments could begin to illuminate the business relations of the merchant community with the various social groups, yet, even then, it might be difficult to decide what kind of business was being done. Much of the connection was indirect, through the tailors and other craftsmen who bought materials from the merchants and supplied their customers with finished goods. Noblemen turn up as debtors and creditors – as the former, often in the persons of their wives or sons – but not in great numbers and it may be

[69] CC8/8/17, fo. 22v.
[70] CC8/8/23, fo. 266.
[71] CC8/8/29, fo. 289; 35, fo. 61.
[72] CC8/8/17, fo. 70v.
[73] CC8/8/22, fo. 256v.
[74] CC8/8/18, fo. 81.
[75] CC8/8/21, fo. 232v.
[76] CC8/8/19, fo. 285.

suspected that their business was often purely financial. There are very many lairds and smaller proprietors, as well as burgesses, husbandmen and rural craftsmen, often buying raw materials such as iron, timber, dyestuffs, lint and tar, and the home-produced goods and cloth which the merchants bought in the home market and resold.

Bills by royal servants may have been personal, but some are clearly 'official' debts by the king's master of works, comptroller and other officials. The royal 'comptrolleris and sumelairis' owed Hector McMath £405 for wine for 1581 and 1582 'according to the tounis pryce' and 'Jerome Bowyis tikkettis of receipt',[77] and Alexander Millar, the king's tailor, £224 6s 7d, on obligation, to Thomas Wright in 1598. William Birny was due £700 'upoun certane pledgis' from the regent Moray in 1568, and Mr John Provand £2100 9s 9d by the late regent Morton in 1583, which the latter's son, James Douglas, had promised to pay.

The advocates feature fairly prominently in the testaments, as debtors, creditors, relatives, tutors testamentar and oversmen; thirty-eight appear in those testaments examined. The daughters of merchants Ninian Lowis, John Murray and James Brown married advocates, Mr John Nicolson, Mr David Guthrie and Mr John Cramond respectively, and two daughters of the merchant Mr John Provand married Mr Oliver Colt and Mr Thomas Gilbert, advocates. James Ross's wife, the daughter of Hamilton of Priestfield, was a sister of Mr Thomas Hamilton, and the wife of James Wright was a close relative of Mr Thomas Craig.

The merchants' stock preserves its own picture of social life; the colours of the clothes, the variety of foodstuffs, at least at richer tables, the everyday necessities and the luxury and ready-made goods which those entitled by the sumptuary laws – and, one suspects, a good many who were not – purchased for themselves and their households. The goods fall into seven main categories: cloth, haberdashery, apparel, food, craft materials and implements, household goods and utensils, and weapons and sporting gear. Seventy-eight separate varieties of cloth are mentioned, both fine and serviceable, English, Flemish, Florentine, French, Lombard, Naples and Spanish, in black, blue, brown, 'cramoisie', 'glad-coloured', grey, 'mouse-coloured', orange, russet, 'sky-coloured', violet, purple and white. Haberdashery, although the word is not used, predominates in the stock of many small merchants who may have supplied the chapmen – it is open to speculation how much the rural housewife paid for her ribbons and pins at fourth hand. Apparel included headwear of all styles, for men, women and children, gloves, collars, points, sleeves, hose and shanks, bags, purses, belts and spectacles, some of which would be home-manufactured as well as imported. Merchants who stocked perishable goods often carried a preponderance of these, or combined them with hardware. Accompanying the fruits, sugar and spices was an enticing variety of 'sweetmeats', of which the Burnett family definitely had the best selection – the Justice Clerk's family

---

[77] CC8/8/20, fo. 120.

patronised three generations of Burnetts – from crystallised fruits and 'dragie muskies' to six boxes 'confusit gray confeittis and scrotchartis'.

Craft materials, in addition to large quantities of timber, iron and dyestuffs, included such implements as scissors, wool and clipping shears, shearing hooks, balances, packing sheets and rope, nails and fleshers' knives. There are many references to paper, of both the 'hand' and 'pot' watermarks, familiar in the period, the former costing 26s 8d and the latter 38s a ream, packing paper, Lombard paper and, in the testament of Mungo Russell, 'fyne paper of the best sort' at 52s a ream, 'of the secund sort' at 34s, 'gelt' paper at 9s a quire and 'prenting paper' at 30s a ream, for some of which the printer, Robert Waldegrave, owed Russell £254 13s 4d.

Weapons and armour and sports equipment included bow-strings, Jedburgh staff-heads, spurs, steel bonnets and bonnet cases (people often kept money in the latter), sword belts and blades, whingers, dog-leashes, golf balls, hawk bells and falconers' bags and gauntlets. The lists include small strings 'for barnis bowis', 'kniffis for barnis' and 'ane belt, bag and quhingar of blak velvot for ane barne'. It is sometimes difficult to separate a merchant's own effects from household items in stock but many of the latter, including cooking vessels and tableware, were certainly sold. For leisure hours there were dice, tables and chessmen, and strings for virginals and lutes.

Later wills record the circumstances of family life and give an idea of the merchants' standard of living, supplemented by the valuations of household goods and the sums of ready money in a merchant's possession, from William Johnston's £5 to the £5068 of John McMorane. Household goods are rarely detailed in the inventories, although sometimes included in bequests, but are usually valued as a whole. In this respect the merchants are at an advantage over some contemporary lairds in being obviously more comfortably provided with furniture, furnishings, napery, vessels and silver.

A constantly changing pattern of family life was as characteristic of the merchants' households as of those of their landward relatives; the almost customary remarriage on the death of a partner, the early age at which children left home to be fostered or apprenticed, the way in which, on a merchant's death, a relative or friend could become responsible overnight for the substance and welfare of his family, the gaps left in the household by plague, illness and death in childbirth, all of which made the stepfather, stepmother and 'bad uncle' of folklore realities in many families. At the same time, circumstances committed the merchant financially to an extended family of stepchildren, apprentices and dependent relatives, reflected in many bequests and arrangements for future provision.

While there were definitely merchant dynasties, concerned about the continuity of the businesses on which their fortunes and influence had been built, there were far more merchants who lived, as it were, from voyage to voyage, or market to market, some of whom, it appears, were giving merchandise a try, who were simply concerned that their families should survive rather than that their businesses as such should continue. To this end their resources were exploited realistically – profits and the money they left behind were to be 'laid out' on property and annualrents, put aside for daughters' tochers or the future prospects of sons. James Wright, whose wife had died in the plague of 1585, arranged for his plenishing and merchandise to be rouped for the benefit of his three children whom he allocated to three different relatives to be brought up. William Nisbet requested that even the heirship goods be sold on behalf of his son 'to mak him ane pak' and set him up in business anew on his own account.[78] On occasions widows are found carrying on the merchant business, there were other cases where the business must have broken up on the merchant's death; William Geichan left a son under 10 years old, arranging for him to be brought up by an older sister and leaving 50 merks a year for his upkeep. If a son was old enough and willing to carry on business, he would take on the burden of older dependent relatives of his father's generation; John Bawtie left his sister, Malie, 3 merks a year, 'hous maill frie', for her lifetime, 'and hir meit' as his son and she could agree upon;[79] Matthew Jamieson left his nephew, an apprentice cooper in Leith, £40, 'with meit and clayth in my hous all his prentischip'. There are a number of cases of provision for natural children. James Lowrie left £100 to his natural daughter, Marion, 'gottin upoun Isobel Penango', to be laid out on land or annualrents for her, and 40 merks to her mother. Here and there, too, is the plight of children unable to look after themselves: the wealthy William Birny was able to make provision for the future of his daughter, Margaret, 'that is naturally impotent in mind and bodie'.

James Nicol's will, written by himself in his own words, is one of those that almost carry the tone of the merchant's voice, business-like but human:

> 'And the Lord grant me ane good end and blyssed departure furth of this lyfe. I leave my soul to the eternal Lord my God from whom I receivit the samyn . . . I leif . . . (his second son, Henry) the quarter of the ship callit the Lyoun . . . a maser next best to the airschip and my haill claythis maid to my bodie . . . the Lord mak him thairwith ane honest man . . . my youngest daughter Marioun, 3,000 merkis, praying the Lord send hir sum honest and discreit husband, and that I may see the samin or I depart this lyf, gif it be His plesoure, as ane barne quhome of I have had ovirguid service, comfort and gude expectatioun . . .'

Marion had probably been housekeeping for her widower father; uncertain to whose care he should leave her, he left this matter

> 'to hir awin discretioun and mynd as to ane young lass quha as I onderstand myndis to be ane honest woman.'

Clearly, many merchants handled sufficient money to furnish a comparatively comfortable home and to provide clothes and other possessions for their families suitable to their position in the burgh community. Just as many wives of merchants, it would seem, as of lairds left jewellery to relatives and

---

[78] CC8/8/19, fo. 49.
[79] CC8/8/3, fo. 219.

friends, 'in token', and many middling merchants could leave bequests to children far greater than those of their rural relatives, the small proprietors and tenant-farmers.

Without a similar examination of the testaments of craftsmen it is difficult to have a clear picture of their relations with the merchants in everyday terms, but the impression is that there was little at personal level of the friction that existed publicly and on the town council between influential members of the two groups. Intermarriage, the interchange of apprentices from merchant and craft families, daily business dealings and living in close proximity minimised it. Many craftsmen, humble skinners and fleshers as well as prosperous tailors and prestigious goldsmiths, occur as witnesses, tutors and oversmen in the testaments of merchants whose relatives they often were. In many cases, a similarity of substance, resources and social background meant that the two groups had much in common, with personal and financial reasons for dependence on each other.

MARGARET H. B. SANDERSON

12

Shetland in the Sixteenth Century

Sixteenth century Shetland was a very individual region, with a small but homogeneous population of humble people bound together by long-standing traditions. They were a rural people, numbering probably between 10000 and 12000 souls, inhabiting islands totalling 550 square miles in area, mostly north of 60° latitude, opposite western Norway.[1]

The overseas connections were primarily with the mother country of Norway, through language, laws and customs, as well as communications; and secondarily with the continental countries of Germany and Holland, through trade with Hanseatic merchants and the great Dutch herring fishery which was operated every summer from the haven of Bressay Sound – later called Lerwick Harbour. The connection with Scotland was more tenuous than either of the other two connections until the last quarter of the century, when it became rapidly strengthened through changes in the administration of the islands.

Shetland had been pawned in 1469, as Orkney had been the previous year, to King James III of Scotland by the Dane, King Christian I of Denmark, Norway and Sweden, acting in his capacity as king of Norway[2]: he did not preside over a united kingdom, but held the three crowns simultaneously. With this help to eke out the dowry of his fifteen-year-old daughter Margaret, he got her married to the seventeen-year-old Scottish monarch. He thus secured a dynastic foothold in a fourth country, and made sure he would not have to fight on two fronts: he was at the time at war with the Swedish nobles.

According to a late sixteenth-century Danish historian, King Christian, at the time of the second impignoration, wrote to the inhabitants of both Orkney and Shetland telling them to pay their dues to the king of Scotland until they were redeemed – a natural command under the circumstances.[3]

---

[1] Gordon Donaldson, *Shetland Life under Earl Patrick* (Edinburgh and London, 1958), 136.

[2] In the documents of impignoration he repeatedly uses phrases such as: 'Nos et successores nostros Norwegie Reges'.

[3] A. Huitfeldt, *Historical Description of Life in Copenhagen under the most Potent and noble Lord, Christian I* (Copenhagen, 1599), 190, quoted by Barbara Hall or Crawford, 'The Earls of Orkney-Caithness and their Relations with Norway and Scotland,

Both mortgages were without time-limit and the sixteenth century was to see six offers made to redeem the two groups of islands, with another six to follow in succeeding centuries.[4] Christian I's grandson Christian III, who reigned from 1537 to 1559, at one time, after he had offered the redemption money in vain, seriously contemplated enforcing his claims by means of a great naval armament, which was to have been joined by a fleet sent by Queen Mary of England; but this ambitious plan did not materialise.[5]

Successive Scots governments simply ignored the various offers of redemption but in doing so acted illegally. It is not surprising, therefore, that they exercised great caution in their treatment of the islands. As late as 1567, practically a century after the impignorations, 'the Scottish parliament specifically "found" that both Orkney and Shetland should continue to enjoy their own laws and should not be subject to the common laws of Scotland'.[6] This held good beyond the end of the century till 'the Scottish Privy Council, in 1611, unequivocally decreed that the "foreign laws" within Orkney and Shetland were to be "discharged"'.[7]

The 'annexation' of Orkney and Shetland by the Scots parliament in 1472 was not a territorial annexation at all. It was an attachment by restriction to legitimate sons of the Scottish royal family, of the earldom of Orkney and lordship of Shetland which James III had procured for himself that year by exchanging lands at Ravenscraig in Fife for earldom property in the northern isles held by earl William Sinclair, the last independent earl of Orkney.[8] If the two groups of islands had been redeemed, the earldom would still have been held by the Scottish royal family.

In 1472 also James III got the pope to transfer the bishopric of Orkney, which included Shetland, from the Norwegian archiepiscopate of Nidaros, later called Trondhjem, to the newly established province of St Andrews.[9] Yet this ecclesiastical re-arrangement was unknown to the contemporary Norwegian church authorities and became forgotten for a long time at Rome

---

1158–1470' (unpublished thesis for the degree of Doctor of Philosophy, University of St Andrews, April, 1971), 364.

[4] Gilbert Goudie, *The Celtic and Scandinavian Antiquities of Shetland* (Edinburgh and London, 1904), 213–29.

[5] Frederick Schiern, *Life of James Hepburn Earl of Bothwell* (1863 and 1875), translated from the Danish by the Rev David Berry (Edinburgh, 1880), 344–5, quoting memoir, 12 April 1575, by the French Minister Charles Dancay, looking back on his first embassy to Denmark.

[6] W. Croft Dickinson, 'Odal Rights and Feudal Wrongs,' W. Douglas Simpson ed. *The Viking Congress* (Edinburgh, 1954), 147, quoting *APS*, iii, 41, c 48.

[7] Ibid., same page, quoting *RPC*, ix, 181.

[8] John Mooney, *The Cathedral and Royal Burgh of Kirkwall* (Kirkwall, 1943), 208, quoting 8 Act of Sc. Parl., Feby., 1472.

[9] Ludwig Daae, in lecture to the Union of Political Economy in Norway, 1894, 'About Contacts between the Orkneys and Shetland and the Motherland Norway after 1468' translated by E. S. Reid Tait in *Two Translations from the Dano-Norwegian* (Lerwick, 1953), 12.

itself.[10] In 1514 Christian II at his coronation in Oslo ordered a letter to be sent
to the Orcadians asking them to pay the traditional revenues to the newly
appointed archbishop of Nidaros. The letter was never sent but the original
survived. In 1520 Pope Leo X complained that the bishop of Orkney had
sent money to the archbishop of Nidaros which should have been sent to
him for the building of St Peter's church and which thereafter should be
sent to Rome. In 1522 the newly consecrated bishop of Skalholt in Iceland,
Ogmund Paalsson, at the request of the chapter of Trondhjem, carried out
an ecclesiastical visitation in Shetland from 21st June to the 11th or 12th of
July, on his way home from Norway to Iceland. The dean of the chapter of
Trondhjem, who became archbishop Olaf Engelbretsson, not satisfied
about statements regarding the island bishopric, commissioned a German
clergyman, Zutpheldus Wardenberg, to make enquiries in Rome. After a
prolonged search in the papal registers, Wardenberg at last in 1525 found
pope Sixtus IV's Bull of 1472, of which he sent a transcript to the
Norwegian archbishop along with advice on how to reclaim the sundered
diocese. That Engelbretsson did not take steps accordingly was almost
certainly due to the overthrow of the Catholic church in Norway which
took place soon after this incident.

Despite these changes life in Shetland remained different from that of
the mainland and even from that of Orkney. In 1194 King Sverri of
Norway had severed Shetland from the Norwegian earldom of Orkney,
and thereafter Shetland was administered direct from Norway, a change
which bound Shetland closer to that country and made its history follow a
different course from that of Orkney. This was reflected in the fields of land
tenure, law and government, language and custom, still in the sixteenth
century affecting the whole people of Shetland.

There was at that time not the least beginning of the town of Lerwick.
Standing on clay soil entirely unsuitable for agriculture, and by nature
separated from its hinterland by wide peat moors now traversed by roads,
Lerwick only arose in the seventeenth century, originally through intercourse and trade with the Dutch herring fishermen. In the sixteenth century
the centre of Shetland affairs was still, as it had been for centuries, in the fertile
valley of Tingwall, and at its foot there were possibly the beginnings of the
present village of Scalloway.

The Norwegian udal system of land tenure lasted in Shetland right
through and after the close of the sixteenth century. In contrast to the feudal
system, by that time long established in Scotland, the udal system required,
on the death of a proprietor, big or small, subdivision of the property among
sons and daughters, the daughters getting half the shares of the sons; or
alternatively, when, in order to keep a property intact, the whole of it was
assigned to the eldest son, he had to compensate his brothers and sisters.
When a big estate was subdivided, the eldest son in any case got the 'head buil'
or best farm.

[10] Ibid., 12–14.

This system did not preclude the accumulation of land in big estates and the creation of tenancies. On the contrary the constant pressure from heirs for subdivision sometimes led to impoverishment which in turn led many people to sell their holdings to estate owners and become tenants. It has been stated that in Norway 'by the mid-fourteenth century about three-fifths of the native population had been forced to become tenants'.[11]

By the sixteenth century the same thing had come about in Shetland in large measure, but with the difference that the big estates were all in possession of absentee landowners, most of them, though not all, in Norway.

The Orcadian and Scottish landlords were the bishop of Orkney, the canons of St Magnus Cathedral in Kirkwall, and the king of Scotland, who held earldom lands by inheritance and royal estates by virtue of the still continuing impignoration.

The most notable of the Norwegian landlords were the family descendants of Sigurd Jonsson til Giske, the richest man of his time in Norway, who when he died in 1453 owned as Shetland properties Papa Stour, Vaila, Noss, most of the parish of Sandness, the big farms of Stove in Haraldswick, Skea in Northmavine, Burwick in Tingwall, and much more, all administered for him by a chamberlain resident in Shetland.[12] As his only son and widow died not long after him, his estates were divided among his three sisters and their descendants, each of whom got some land in Shetland.[13]

Papa Stour in due course was inherited by Ingegerd Ottesdotter, who became very rich in Norway, and played a significant but not illustrious part in politics. Though Norwegian herself, she used her wealth and influence to help forward Danish domination over Norway.[14] She is immortalised as the principal character in Ibsen's play 'Østraat'.

Another inheritor of Jonsson estates owning land in Shetland was Gørvel Fadersdatter, who was born in Sweden in 1509, lived most of her life outside Norway, and died in Sweden in 1602. When in 1582 she carried out an exchange of properties with her king, she transferred all her estates in West and North Norway and Shetland, parting with 600 Norwegian farms or parts of farms, and at the time a roll of her Shetland lands showing the rents and the names of the farmers was delivered.[15]

The Shetland people of the sixteenth century were neither affluent nor poor, though there were individual cases of poverty. They were at one and the same time small farmers and fishermen, maintaining a balance of

[11] Brian Smith, now Archivist for Shetland, 'Scotsmen in Shetland, 1500–1700: a Re-interpretation'. Unpublished lecture to Shetland Archaeological & Historical Society early in 1976, quoting Foote & Wilson, *The Viking Achievement* (1970), 88.
[12] Ibid.
[13] Letter from S. Tveite, Department of Agricultural Economics and Farm Management, Agricultural University of Norway, to Prof. T. C. Smout, in possession of Brian Smith, Shetland Archivist.
[14] Hjalmar H. Boyesen, *A History of Norway* (London, 1900), 485.
[15] Letter from S. Tveite.

cattle and sheep on their agricultural holdings, most families owning at least one boat, in some cases several.

Examples of the balance of cattle and sheep are Paul in Houff, Whiteness, with 11 cattle and 21 sheep; Nicol Thomasson in Veensgarth, Tingwall, with 27 cattle and 45 sheep; James Strang of Vailzie in Fetlar with three oxen, 10 cows and the exceptionally high number of 30 sheep. In the same island at Funzie was a poor man, William Sutherland. He had only one 'yow' and a lamb, but he owned three cows. In the early seventeenth century a dozen households showed an average of nine cattle (oxen, cows and young animals) and 22 sheep. If that average is adopted over 2000 holdings (probably an over-estimate) totals are obtained of 18000 cattle and 44000 sheep, among a population of at most 12000.[16]

In the sixteenth century the ground was cultivated to provide food for man and beast, the sheep grazing on the pastures. A notable fact is that the soil was turned over by the plough, indicating sizeable holdings. In their capacity as fisherfolk the Shetland people had in addition a source of income in the trade they did annually with the German Hanseatic merchants, who every summer came supplied with salt with which to cure the fish sold to them by the Shetlanders, and carrying supplies of victuals, cloth, iron, hemp and luxury goods to sell to the people. There was probably also already some trade with Dutch fishermen by means of knitted goods made of Shetland wool.

It has been suggested that the absence of the Lords of Norway, as the Norwegian landlords were called, and of the few Scottish landlords, positively helped the Shetland people to retain intact the largely democratic system of government derived from Norway and adapted to Shetland needs. Another thing which no doubt helped in this respect was the fact that when the impignorations took place, Shetland was not rejoined to the Orkney earldom, but was kept as a distinct administrative entity and designated a lordship, being attached by the 1472 'annexation' to legitimate sons of the royal family side by side with the Orkney earldom, not as part of it. 'The royal estates in Shetland went directly into the hands of the Scottish crown (and if Shetland had been redeemed they would have reverted to the Danish crown)'.[17]

As in Norway and Iceland, the governmental system in Shetland rested on the local assemblies called *tings*, which were both legislative assemblies and courts of law for dealing with offenders and criminals. There were local district tings from which certain parish names in Shetland today have come down – Aithsting, Sandsting, Lunnasting, Delting. There was also the superior ting for the whole islands, which continued to meet in the open air at the head of the loch of Tingwall – the valley called after it – right to the very end of the sixteenth century. By contrast in Orkney, the resident earls bought up land in a big way, virtually taking control of the lawmaking process, and the law-ting had ceased to exist by about 1540.

[16] Donaldson, *Shetland Life*, 16 ff.
[17] Crawford, The Earls of Orkney-Caithness, 365–7; Smith, Lecture.

In Shetland the tings continued as representative assemblies. The elected officials in each case were the lawman, who kept track of the laws and was an authority on them, and the lawrightman, who had the responsibility of seeing, on behalf of the people, that just weights and measures were maintained for the payment of tax and the usage of trade.

Presiding over the tings were officials appointed by the king: the foud over the main ting at Tingwall, and the underfouds over the district tings. The fouds and underfouds were also the tax collectors. The one tax, which was paid in kind – cloth, fish, butter – was skat, a tax for national defence and maintenance of the king's establishment, obviously what Christian I had referred to in his letter of 1469. Though not a rent, skat was assessed on arable land. It was paid either by tenant or landlord, usually by the tenant. A neighbourhood comprising several townships was called a skattald. The inhabitants of skattalds were called 'skatt brethren' because they paid their skat together, and they used the pasture land outside their township dykes in common.[18] From 1469 not only was skat due to the king of Scotland, but he also came to appoint the fouds. By the sixteenth century this had become regular practice and constituted the first firm link with Scotland.

The ting officials played such important parts that some names preserved from the sixteenth century are of interest. Among the underfouds in 1545 were Andro Tollach for Northmavine and Willom in Brustedt for Delting; in 1575 Henrie Halcro for Tingwall, Olaw for Unst, Andro Giffurdo for Delting and Scatsta, Thomas for Northmavine, John Smyth and Gilbert Coupland for the large parish of Dunrossness, and James Sutherland for Fetlar; while in 1581 Walter Smyth and Vylzeam Mansone officiated in Unst. Lawrightmen included in 1545 Magnus Tollach for Northmavine, in 1558 Orme of Bw for Dunrossness, and in 1575 Nichole [in] Hardwall for Delting and Scatsta, Erling of Bw for Dunrossness, Erasmus of Kirkbustare for Bressay, David Tulloch for Northmavine and Christopher Laurenson for Walls, or Waas to give the true pronunciation.[19]

The courts in Norway continued to function as superior courts after 1469. In 1485 an agreement about land in Shetland was made in the court in Bergen with a lawrightman from Shetland present, and in 1538 a judgement given in a Shetland court according to Gulating law (i.e. the law of the west of Norway) was confirmed at Bergen.[20] The continuation of communications with Norway into the sixteenth century also suggests unchanged Norwegian connections and influence, and to this day one particular sea entrance to Bergen is called Hjeltefjord – Shetlanders' Fjord. A mid-sixteenth century memorandum regarding customs dues paid by the different nationalities at Bergen does not, however, include Orkney and Shetland ships, though they are included later in the same century.

The same undated document says: 'when ships come from Shetland they

[18] Rent was entirely separate, payable naturally only by tenants to their landlords, and not everyone was a tenant; Smith, Lecture.

[19] Goudie, *Celtic and Scandinavian Antiquities*, 232, 240.

[20] Dickinson, *Odal Rights*, 146.

are obliged to bring to the Castle (Bergenhus) all the unemployed working boys and girls whom they carry hither and of them the Commander of the Castle takes so many as he thinks suitable'.

In a letter dated 1530 the governor of Alershus, the castle in Oslo, writes to the governor of the castle in Bergen thus: 'Item it is my earnest request that you will procure for me 3 or 4 working lads from Shetland or Faroe. I have great need of workmen . . .'.

'These testimonies go to prove that there was in Bergen a constant influx of young people from the islands and that the governor of Bergenhus looked after them and disposed of them in a sort of patriarchal manner'.[21] At the same time it is evident from the foregoing that either there was full employment in Bergen and Oslo at the time, or the young islanders were found to be exceptionally 'suitable'. Twenty-nine Shetlanders in various capacities are recorded in Norwegian documents of the sixteenth century. In 1518 Shetlanders were being sent back to Shetland to bring lime to the castle of Bergen. Another Shetlander one Nils Hjelt was ordained as a clergyman in the diocese of Bergen in 1569.

Simultaneously with the islands' attachment to Scotland, Scots people were coming into Shetland to settle, as several of the names of ting officials quoted above show. The influx began later in Shetland than in Orkney, 'but in the second half of the sixteenth century a considerable number of Scots, especially from the Lothians, Fife and Angus, settled in the islands, and by 1600 about 25 per cent of the population had surnames which point to a Scottish origin'.[22] Highlanders, too, had been pursuing expansionist and aggressive tactics in the sixteenth century. Shetland, which was to be colonised by Lowlanders, complained again and again of raids by men from Lewis, who seem to have terrorised the islanders.[23] There is a mound in Dunrossness, near Spiggie, which is said locally to be a burial mound resulting from one of these Hebridean raids. These Scottish settlers – not the wild raiders – included people of modest means like the native Shetlanders. They quickly became integrated with the local population, intermarrying with them, and adopting the language and land-tenure customs of the islands. Some of them were elected as lawting representatives. One, Nicol Reid of Aith in Bressay, was in 1532 elevated to the highest elective office in Shetland, that of lawman-general at the principal ting at Tingwall, while the Tullochs of Northmavine more than once became lawrightmen in that parish.

At the same time Scotsmen became appointed by the king of Scotland as fouds. Shortly after Henry, lord Sinclair got a lease of the earldom of Orkney in 1485, Sir David Sinclair was appointed foud of Shetland. He became a past master at serving the king of Scotland and the Scandinavian king at the same time, as may be judged from the fact that he held simultaneously the two

[21] Daae–Tait, *Contacts between the Orkneys and Shetland*, 4.
[22] Gordon Donaldson, *The Scots Overseas* (London, 1966), 28.
[23] Ibid., 30.

offices of foud of Shetland and governor of the castle of Bergen.[24] He was apparently perfectly at ease in both the Scottish and Norwegian milieux.

Eventually the Sinclairs or St Clairs became in fact the hereditary and natural governors of Shetland. The last and most notable of them was Ola Sinclair of Havera. He maintained the old system, co-operating with the lawman Nicol Reid. He fought on the Orkney-Shetland side against the earl of Caithness at Summerdale in Orkney in 1527. He led local forces against Highland marauders and lost an eye leaping over Sumburgh Head to escape from a band of Lewismen. He gave a cordial reception to the earl of Bothwell in 1567 when he came north on his way to Scandinavia to seek military help for his spouse, Mary, queen of Scots, from king Frederick II, and he helped Bothwell on his way. When the great foud died in 1571 he divided his estates among his three sons in the old udal way.

It is not possible to get such direct evidence regarding the language, but the situation can be arrived at by deduction. In such an effort full allowance must be made for bilingualism and trilingualism. In 1700 the Rev John Brand, a Church of Scotland commissioner, visited Shetland and found that English was the common language, yet that many people spoke Norse, especially in the North Isles; some also spoke Dutch, and in some places Norse was the first language the children spoke, so ordinary was it.[25] As a visitor Brand may have got an exaggerated impression of the use of English. What he says could imply a form of Norse as the prevailing language among the people themselves, with English spoken to English- or Scots-speaking strangers.

The same conclusion is evident in the findings at the very end of the nineteenth century of the Faroese philologist Jakob Jakobsen, who in the course of three years' research all over Shetland, found in the speech of the people and the remembrance of obsolete words among the old people, a total of 10000 words of Norse origin, which he preserved and explained in his monumental *Etymological Dictionary of the Norn Language in Shetland.*

It is a fair deduction that in the sixteenth century, however much or little of other languages the people at that time understood and spoke, the Shetland variant of Norse later called Norn was the principal tongue for domestic conversation, with English spoken to visitors.

The situation regarding written material was a mixed one. On the one hand a number of legal documents in Norn ranging in date from 1516 to 1597, are still extant. Of two of the deeds, one executed in Shetland, the other in Bergen, it has been stated that 'both are in the ordinary Norse language then vernacular in the islands, as in Scandinavia generally . . . certain of the ancient grammatical forms are more distinctly exhibited in the composition of the native document than in the other framed in Norway'.[26] Nevertheless

---

[24] Barbara Crawford, 'Sir David Sinclair of Sumburgh: Foud of Shetland and Governor of Bergen Castle' in *Scandinavian Shetland: An Ongoing Tradition?* ed. John R. Baldwin (Edinburgh, 1978), 1–11.

[25] Rev John Brand, *A Brief Description of Orkney, Zetland, Pightland-Firth & Caithness* (pub. 1701), reprint (Edinburgh, 1883), 104.

[26] G. Goudie, *Celtic and Scandinavian Antiquities*, 78–131.

contemporaneously with these deeds there are others, 'expressed in good current Scots . . . significantly indicating the conflict then going on between the old and new systems and races'.

The change in written language was relatively rapid: 'The latest document written in the Norse tongue in Shetland belongs to the early seventeenth century'.[27]

The 1597 document is a mortgage of a very small property owned in Shetland by a Norwegian lady, Else Throndsdaughter, to whose sister Anna the earl of Bothwell was betrothed before he married Lady Jane Gordon. Else had a Shetland husband, Andrew Mowat of Hugoland in Eshaness, who settled with her in Norway, and their son Axel Mowat became in his time the greatest landowner in the west of Norway.[28] This illustrates vividly how the Shetland-Norwegian connection continued actively right to the end of the sixteenth century.

Evidence of social customs leads to the same conclusion. In 1774 the Rev George Low, a minister in Orkney, toured both Orkney and Shetland, and was handed a description of Unst, the most northerly island in Shetland, by its minister, William Archibald. In this description the following passage occurs:

> 'There is one species of dance which seems peculiar to themselves, in which they do not proceed from one end of the floor to the other in a figure, nor is it after the manner of a Scotch reel; but a dozen or so form themselves into a circle, and taking each other by the hand, perform a sort of circular dance, one of the company all the while singing a Norn Visick. This was formerly their only dance, but has now almost given entire way to the reel'.[29]

That could serve as an accurate if brief description of the ring dance performed to innumerable sung ballads, many of them of great antiquity, which is still carried on in the Faroe Islands, alongside modern dancing, but it gives no idea of the fire and the zest at times roused in the dancers, to whom the ballads themselves, and not the dance, are the main thing. The fact that the same kind of thing could be seen in Unst at the end of the eighteenth century strongly suggests that it was still ubiquitous in the Shetland of the sixteenth century. It is a tragedy that the whole corpus of the Shetland ballads, whatever they contained, was swept into oblivion by the change of language, instead of being preserved as is the case with the Faroese ballads.

All in all, it appears that for a whole century after 1469, life went on in Shetland much as it had done for a long time before that date. The old ways and the old speech remained; the intercourse with Norway and Norwegian ownership of property in Shetland both continued. Those Scotsmen who came into the islands, whether to high station or to low, became integrated

[27] Donaldson, *Scots Overseas*, 28.

[28] Letter to the writer, 9 October 1977, from Knut Robberstad, Emeritus Professor of Law, University of Oslo.

[29] Rev George Low, *A Tour through the Islands of Orkney and Schetland . . . in 1774* (Kirkwall, 1879), 163.

with the people and became Shetlanders in outlook and sentiment. The people paid their skat to the tax collectors, the fouds, as they had always done, so that the changed destiny of the tax did not affect them personally.

In Shetland the payment of skat, church tithes, rents, and trade with the Hanseatic merchants had for ever so long been governed by weights and measurements mutually agreed between the fouds and the lawwrightmen. The weighing instrument, the bismar (a miniature wooden steelyard) commonly bore the marks of both foud and lawrightman. Back in the thirteenth century Jan Tait in Fetlar had killed a Norwegian tax collector with his bismar for persistently accusing him of falsifying it.

As more money appeared in circulation in the sixteenth century Hanseatic merchants increased their prices, certain of the lords of Norway (for example, the daughters of Ingegerd Ottesdotter, and Gørvel Fadersdatter herself, at different times) farmed out their rents to local factors, while some new vicars farmed out their teinds in a somewhat similar way. To enable all this to be carried out, new weights and measures, not authorised by the lawting, were introduced.

The old co-operation between fouds and lawrightmen might have done something to stem this rising tide, but in 1564 Mary, queen of Scots, gave the lands of Shetland to her half-brother, lord Robert Stewart, an illegitimate son of her father, James V, thus investing him with the foudrie, and he immediately altered the weights and measures in the earldom estate, while four years later he got a feu of the bishopric lands in Orkney and Shetland in exchange for the abbacy of Holyrood in Edinburgh which he held. Then in May, 1571, when Ola Sinclair of Havera died, lord Robert conferred the office of foud on his half-brother Laurence Bruce of Cultmalindie in Perthshire, a son of lord Robert's mother by a marriage contracted after her association with King James V.

This appointment opened the floodgates. Bruce abolished the office of lawrightman and altered the ancient weights and measures. The reaction in Shetland was tremendous, and in 1576 Arthur Sinclair of Aith in Cunningsburgh drew up a comprehensive bill of complaint which he sent to the regent Morton. The regent and privy council were so impressed that they appointed William Mudie of Breckness in Orkney and William Henderson, Dingwall pursuivant, to proceed to Shetland as commissioners to conduct an enquiry.[30] In 1577 the two commissioners did their work thoroughly over a period of three weeks, taking evidence at Tingwall from nearly 800 Shetlanders in groups from all over the islands.[31] On receiving the report of the commissioners the regent and privy council deprived Bruce of his office of foud, banished him from Shetland and forbade him to return, while Lord Robert Stewart was imprisoned for similar conduct in Orkney. The relief for the islanders proved short-lived, however. The downfall and execution of the regent Morton occurred in 1581, and in the same year King James VI created his uncle lord Robert Stewart earl of Orkney and lord of Shetland.

[30] Francis Grant, *Zetland Family Histories* (Lerwick, 1907), 11.
[31] Smith, Lecture.

The sequel was the return to Shetland of Laurence Bruce, who increased his power so much that in 1598 he commenced in Unst the building of the castle of Muness.

In 1593 earl Robert died and was succeeded by his son Patrick, who set about following a course of his own which, if maintained, would have made a profound difference to the history of both Orkney and Shetland. He re-enunciated udal law, reinstated the lawrightmen, curbed the exploiting proclivities of the German merchants, and while reaping great benefit from the numerous fines imposed in the courts, revived the power and representative character of the lawting, going himself on circuit around the district tings. He also, in 1600, built Scalloway castle.

Earl Patrick's downfall and execution in 1615, and the simultaneous execution of his son Robert who had raised a strongly supported but unsuccessful rebellion in Orkney to help his father, had been preceded by the edict of 1611 already mentioned, whereby the 'foreign laws' of Shetland were 'discharged'.

In the midst of this late sixteenth century turmoil, the strongest of all the efforts to induce Scotland to return Orkney and Shetland to their owners was made. In June, 1585, an imposing embassy sailed from Denmark to Scotland in two ships and secured an interview with King James VI in Dunfermline, the court being away from Edinburgh on account of the plague. The embassy had two missions – to offer the money required to redeem the islands, and to propose a marriage between King James and the princess Anne of Denmark.

On the grounds that the plague in Edinburgh prevented him from examining his papers, 'the King besoght the ambassadors to tak patience for that tyme, for he suld send an ambassador of his awin, with the first commoditie, who sould give a resolute answer in that purpose' (and likewise as to the second point, the projected marriage). 'With these answers the ambassadors wer exceiding weill contentit, and departed from Scotland in the moneth of August with great joy',[32] to report to their monarch, Frederick II. Although he married Anne of Denmark in 1589, King James did not however, return the islands, and in 1614 persuaded Christian IV, who was visiting him in England, to let the matter stand over during their reigns.[33]

How the Catholic church served and was regarded by the people of Shetland, and how much interest was roused in the islands by Calvinism are unknown. Information exists, however, about the organisation of the ministry of the church in the islands.[34] Initially this was chiefly due to Bishop Adam Bothwell who was appointed bishop of the diocese of Orkney in 1559. When the Scots parliament in the following year abolished the authority of

[32] Goudie, *Celtic and Scandinavian Antiquities*, 222–3.

[33] Ibid., 228.

[34] Bishop Bothwell's organisation of the Reformed Church in Shetland was described in detail by Gordon Donaldson in a series of articles in the 'Shetland News' in 1943, 1946 and 1960, and in an additional article prepared some time between 1946 and 1960 but never sent for publication, although it is now available in the Shetland Archives, Lerwick.

the pope and forbade the mass, bishop Bothwell decided to support the reformation and thus became a protestant bishop.

'At first Bothwell could rely on only one of the Shetland clergy – Jerome Cheyne, the archdeacon, who in 1561 was already recognised as a minister. The second stage, in 1562, is marked by the acceptance of the vicars of Yell and Walls as readers. Meantime, as vacancies had arisen, the bishop had appointed new vicars to Northmavine, Fetlar and Dunrossness, with a view to their acting as ministers or readers, so that by 1562 or 1563 probably five or six parishes had been staffed. A further stage was the appointment of readers for the parishes of Bressay and Burra, Delting, Sandsting and Aithsting, Nesting, Dunrossness and Unst. After that appointments were made by stages till by 1567 Shetland had been provided with a complete staff of reformed clergy – two ministers and nine readers for the eleven parishes or "ministries". In eight cases out of eleven the reformed pastor seems to have had possession of the vicarage. . . . Partly, no doubt, because of a shortage of ministers, but partly because of a lack of the means to pay them, it was usual to combine two or more parishes under one minister, with readers to assist him. In 1574 there were four ministers, each with the oversight of two or three parishes, and eight readers acting under their supervision. With one certain and one possible exception, they are all men with Scottish names – Andrew Hill, James Fallowsdale, John Reid, John Denoon, Peter Maxwell, George Bellenden, are a few examples. The certain exception is Mons Norske, clearly a Norwegian, not merely from the appelation 'Norske' but because 'Mons' is the regular Norwegian contraction for Magnus, and he came to be known in Shetland as Magnus or Manss Norsk. The possible exception is the name Malcolmson, which, though built on the Scottish name Malcolm, seems to be peculiar to Shetland. Some of these men with Scottish names may have belonged to families long settled in Shetland, . . . it certainly looks as if the church in Shetland was staffed by Scotsmen or men of Scottish stock, increasingly before the Reformation, and practically speaking wholly after it. This is not surprising. There was probably a gradual loosening of the ties between Shetland and Norway though Shetlanders are recorded in Norway right to the end of the century. Only after 1600 was it usual to have a minister, with an adequate stipend, for every parish. Throughout this period stipends were still due in kind – the teinds or tithes of corn, wool, butter, lambs and so on – but it was usual for a vicar to set his teinds in tack, or lease, in return for a money payment'.

Two ministers and nine readers only seven years after the inauguration of the Reformation in Scotland was a most creditable achievement, every then existing parish being served in some way. Proper respect was also shown for the consciences of those priests who felt unable to join in the Reformation, and humane provision made for them, insofar as a vicar who did not serve in the reformed church was allowed to retain two-thirds of the vicarage for his lifetime. At the same time care was taken to provide religious ordinances for the population of some twelve thousand. The work of organisation involved the bishop in a lot of travelling through the roadless islands, between which the ferries, though well organised, were all open boats. It is not surprising that he claimed to have hazarded his life.[35]

Political activities also coloured those years of ecclesiastical activity and in 1567 the bishop married with protestant rites James Hepburn, earl of Bothwell to Queen Mary, who was a Catholic. The reformed church subsequently suspended the bishop for doing this and compelled him to make a public apology before reinstating him.

But before this occurred he made amends for his action by joining the expedition ordered by the regent Moray to pursue and arrest the earl after he had left the negotiations at Carberry Hill. The earl was being entertained ashore in Shetland by Ola Sinclair of Havera, the foud, when the pursuing squadron caught up with his ships anchored in Bressay Sound. These at once cut their cables and fled out the north mouth of the sound. Lured, it is said in Shetland by a local pilot on one of the earl's ships, the ship 'Unicorn' with Kirkcaldy of Grange and bishop Bothwell on board, struck and broke in pieces on a sunken rock not far to the north, and with others the bishop had a very narrow escape from drowning.

'The following year lord Robert Stewart compelled the bishop to hand over most, if not all, revenues in exchange for the abbey of Holyrood, and the bishop ceased to administer the church in Shetland.'[36] The bishop's duties in administering the church were transferred to a "commissioner"– an Orkney minister who was given the task of superintending the church in Shetland in addition to his own parochial duties. But the commissioner did not have the power to dispose of vicarages which the bishop had exercised, and the right to make appointments to them seems to have been disputed between Lord Robert and the crown. The general assembly of 1586 requested the king to cause the Lords of Session to declare whether the king or the earl had the right of patronage in Orkney and Shetland. There were quite clearly cases where Robert appointed creatures of his own to enjoy the vicarage revenues although they were not qualified to act as ministers or readers. In 1575 he was said to have disposed illegally of the vicarages of Unst, Scatsta (Delting), Nesting and 'Sands' (presumably Sandsting). Robert was also accused, in a complaint of 1575/76, of compelling beneficed men to set their revenues to him. In some cases Lord Robert and the crown seem both to have made appointments, so that there were rival candidates. But the crown itself was not free from blame, and some of its nominees were no more suited for pastoral work than were Robert's. There are certainly indications of a drive against inactive titulars, some of whom were deprived. ... Lord Robert created further difficulties for the Reformed Church by appropriating to himself half of the lamb teind and wool teind of all the parishes. The indications in the Court Book of 1602–4 are that church property was in tremendous confusion and that ministers were having a thin time against counter-claims.

[35] Gordon Donaldson, 'Bishop Adam Bothwell and the Reformation in Orkney', *RSCHS*, xiii (1959), 95.
[36] Donaldson, *Shetland Life*, 126.

Apart from the direct damage to the Church done by lord Robert, a particular effect of the bishop being withdrawn from the administration and being replaced by ministerial 'commissioners' from Orkney who had no power to make appointments was that 'from that point ecclesiastical administration in Shetland was seriously handicapped for a period of about forty years',[37] that is to say, into the beginning of the seventeenth century.

In consequence there were no kirk sessions in Shetland at any time in the sixteenth century. Accordingly discipline for moral offences was carried out by the ting courts: the courts under earl Patrick dealt with slander, assault on parents, witchcraft, adultery and fornication, yet, 'like any kirk session, commonly ordered the slanderer to ask forgiveness in church in face of the congregation'.[38] It is of interest to note that earl Patrick and his courts 'merely fined witches, just as he fined swearers and quarrellers' and that it was not till 1612, three years after Patrick's imprisonment and a year after the islands' 'foreign laws' had been 'discharged', that the first witch was strangled and burnt in Shetland.[39] Assimilation in other respects was equally slow and in some respects could be measured in centuries rather than years.

[37] Ibid., 126.
[38] Ibid., 128.
[39] Gordon Donaldson, 'The Early Ministers of the North Isles' *Shetland News*, 2, 9 and 16 September, 1943.

T. M. Y. MANSON

13

Literacy in the Highlands

The sixteenth century is the earliest for which a seriously researched statement as to the incidence of literacy in the Highlands can be made. But, even so, no statistical precision should be expected, for the evidence is unevenly distributed in geographical terms and, when it does exist, is sometimes obscure. Thus, the area that was dominated by the Lords of the Isles in the fourteenth and fifteenth centuries is easily the most productive,[1] while it is often a matter of some uncertainty as to how far an individual signature should be used as evidence of literacy.

In the Highlands of the sixteenth century three written languages, Gaelic, Latin and Scots were utilised. None was strictly speaking a vernacular. Written Gaelic was a literary dialect removed from the everyday speech of the people, while Latin and Scots were the languages of government. Only in peripheral areas where a bi-lingual situation was likely to obtain might Scots be classed as a vernacular.[2] Scots and Latin were normally written in forms of the current secretary hand[3] and Gaelic normally in what may be called Gaelic script. This last is simply a modified version of the Latin semi-uncial script that can be seen as far back as the second half of the sixth century in the extant copy of the psalter known as *Cathach Choluim Chille* which, it has been suggested, may have been the work of Columba himself.[4] Finally, it should be said that, because Gaelic Scotland and Ireland formed a single culture-province in the sixteenth century, many of the present conclusions could be more copiously illustrated in a contemporary Irish context, but this has been deliberately eschewed, though the Irish dimension is always present.

In Scotland, legal documents in Latin or Scots began to be signed by laymen from about the middle of the fifteenth century. The appended

[1] K. A. Steer and J. W. M. Bannerman, *Late Medieval Monumental Sculpture in the West Highlands* (Edinburgh, 1977), 203–6.

[2] For the purposes of this article, Scots and English are not distinguished except where a primary source specifically mentions English or is written in that language. The increasing assimilation of Scots to English in the sixteenth century, especially at documentary level, makes any formal distinction unnecessary.

[3] Grant G. Simpson, *Scottish Handwriting 1150–1650* (Edinburgh, 1973), passim.

[4] Brian Ó Cuív, 'The Changing Form of the Irish Language', in *A View of the Irish Language*, ed. Brian Ó Cuív (Dublin, 1969), 24; Francoise Henry, *Irish Art in the Early Christian Period to A.D. 800* (London, 1965), 58–60 and pls. 9, 12.

signatures of nobles, lairds and even burgesses became increasingly common and the custom received official approval in 1540 when parliament enacted that writs must be signed as well as sealed.[5] It has been estimated that, by 1500, at least 60 per cent of the greater nobility were able to sign their names in Scots.[6] Such was not the case in the Highlands and many of the remaining 40 per cent belonged to this area. With some exceptions, like the Campbell earls of Argyll, examples of heads of kindreds, great and small, able to sign their names in Scots were few before 1500. This is evident despite the paucity of relevant sources. There was a time lag of at least fifty years between Lowlands and Highlands in this matter. Indeed, the custom of signing legal instruments in Latin or Scots was itself slower to catch on in the Highlands.

The *Statutes of Iona*, drawn up on that island on 23 August 1609, read

> 'it is inactit that everie gentilman or yeoman within the said Ilandis, or ony of thame, haveing childreine maill or famell and being in goodis worth thriescore ky, sall put at the leist thair eldest sone, or haveing no childrene maill thair eldest dochter, to the scuillis on the Lawland, and interteny and bring thame up thair quhill thay may be found able sufficientlie to speik, reid, and wryte Inglische'.[7]

The implication of this is that a knowledge of Scots (or English) was not widespread in the Western Isles and the adjacent mainland among people of substance far less among the commonality. It follows also that literacy in Scots was likely to be even less common than the ability to speak the language. In 1632 it was reported with specific reference to the written word that Sir Ruairi MacLeod, chief of the MacLeods of Dunvegan and Harris from 1597 until his death in 1626, and one of the signatories of the *Statutes of Iona*, was 'unversit in the Scottis language'.[8]

Where, however, there was a bilingual situation, it was to be expected that the incidence of literacy in Scots among Gaelic speakers would be higher. The difficulty is to establish the line of demarcation between the two cultures in the sixteenth century. For instance, in the province of Lennox, Gaelic was certainly spoken well to the south and east of the physical Highland line. George Buchanan, the famous Latin scholar, born in Killearn in 1506 and probably schooled there and in Dumbarton, was a native Gaelic speaker according to his contemporary Ninian Winzet.[9] He was, of course, literate in Scots and in 1567 so too apparently were the heads of two Lennox kindreds, including his own, located to the west of Killearn and Dumbarton and therefore on the Gaelic side of the cultural divide. They were George

[5] *APS*, ii, 377.

[6] Simpson, *Scottish Handwriting*, 10–11.

[7] *RPC*, 1 ser. ix, 29.

[8] MacLeod of Dunvegan Papers, box 43, no. 5. At present in the SRO.

[9] P. Hume Brown, *George Buchanan, Humanist and Reformer* (Edinburgh, 1890), 11–12; *Velitatio in Georgium Buchananum* (Ingolstadt, 1582), 197. See also John Bannerman, 'The Lordship of the Isles', in *Scottish Society in the Fifteenth Century*, ed. Jennifer M. Brown (London, 1977), 210.

Buchanan of that Ilk and Walter MacAulay of Ardencaple, who appended their signatures to a bond of association pledging support for the infant James as king of Scots.[10] It is interesting to speculate whether James' frequently expressed disenchantment with his Gaelic speaking subjects in later life was in any way inspired by his dislike of George Buchanan who was his tutor for much of his early youth.[11] Whatever the case its outward expression was the education policy formulated in the *Statutes of Iona* in 1609 and made much more explicit in reinforcing legislation seven years later which stated

> 'that the vulgar Inglishe toung be universallie plantit, and the Irishe language, whilk is one of the cheif and principall causis of the continewance of barbaritie and incivilitie amongis the inhabitantis of the Ilis and Heylandis, may be abolisheit and removit'.[12]

Coupled with this was the first formal expression by central government of the Reformers' aim to establish a school in every parish. While some progress had been made in the Lowlands, all the evidence suggests that very little had been achieved in the Highlands and Islands.[13]

Nevertheless the second half of the sixteenth century saw an increase in the numbers of Gaelic speakers able at least to append their signatures in Scots to legal documents. In this respect, the evidence for literacy in Scots is not only less in the far west but it is also later in time. Thus, John Grant of Freuchie was able to sign his name in 1514, while a century later Donald, chief of Clan Ranald, a more powerful and numerous kindred, signed in 1616 'with my hand at the pen led by the notar'.[14] In 1582 no less than fourteen out of twenty-seven named 'principal men' of Clan Grant signed with their own hands an obligation to defend their chief against encroaching neighbours.[15] There is no apparent evidence from the sixteenth century of a *duin-uasal* or gentleman of the Clan Ranald literate in Scots. However, this westward progression is not invariable. It has already been noted that the Campbell chiefs had begun to sign legal documents before 1500, but in 1565 a notary public is found signing on behalf of Alexander MacNaughton of Dunderawe and Dugall MacDougall of Dunollie, chiefs of kindreds located to the east and north of the main Campbell territories respectively. This was a Campbell document and, besides Argyll himself, four of five lesser Campbells signed it with their own hands.[16] It seems likely that the attitude of the head of the kindred was a factor in determining the incidence of literacy in Scots within the kindred.

[10] James Anderson, *Collections relating to the History of Mary, Queen of Scotland*, ii (Edinburgh, 1727), 235.

[11] Brown, *George Buchanan*, 253–63.

[12] *RPC*, 1 ser. x, 671–2.

[13] Donaldson, *James V – James VI*, 263–5.

[14] William Fraser, *The Chiefs of Grant* iii (Edinburgh, 1883), 60; A. MacDonald and A. MacDonald, *The Clan Donald*, ii (Inverness, 1909), 770.

[15] Fraser, *The Chiefs of Grant*, iii, 157–8.

[16] *The Black Book of Taymouth*, ed. C. Innes (Bannatyne Club, 1885), 212.

Kenneth MacKenzie of Kintail, chief from 1561 to 1568 of the most powerful kindred in the North of Scotland, was apparently not literate in Scots but Colin, his son and successor, was.[17] Thereafter literacy was maintained at this level and lesser MacKenzies were increasingly able to sign their names. However, it is also true that Ruairi MacLeod of Dunvegan could not write Scots, yet his grandfather, William, who succeeded to the chiefship c 1546, was able to sign a contract of marriage in 1540 between himself and Agnes Fraser.[18]

To this contract Agnes appended her own signature alongside that of her father Hugh Fraser of Lovat. This was an unusual accomplishment for women in the Highlands of the sixteenth century, and what slight evidence there is for literacy in Scots among women suggests that a similar decline from east to west prevailed.

The Iona statute of 1609 bore fruit in Dunvegan at least, for Ruairi Mór MacLeod saw to it that his four sons went to Glasgow University, John, the eldest and his eventual successor, matriculated in 1624, Ruairi in 1625, Donald in 1627 and Norman in 1631.[19] John and Ruairi may even have attended school in Glasgow before going on to university for there is extant a discharge of 13 November 1623 by James Finlay, merchant burgess of Glasgow, and Agnes Stewart, his wife, acknowledging payment of debts incurred by Ruairi MacLeod for the board and entertainment of his sons.[20] But it has been suggested that the MacLeod boys received tuition in Scots before they left Dunvegan for Glasgow, and so too probably did their sister, Mór, who signed her own marriage contract on 15 February 1613,[21] thereby giving us the earliest known autograph signature of a woman from the Western Isles.

Their tutor was probably Toirdhealbhach Ó Muirgheasáin, one of two chief scribes employed by Ruairi MacLeod of Dunvegan.[22] The Ó Muirgheasáins were a well-known hereditary bardic family attached to the court of MacLean of Duart as well as to that of MacLeod of Dunvegan during the sixteenth and seventeenth centuries.[23] The bardic families were at the apex of the professional orders in Gaelic Ireland and Scotland. Almost as important were churchmen and, perhaps particularly in Scotland, the hereditary medical families, but there were also musicians – harpists and pipers, while hereditary families practising the law of the kin-based society

[17] *The Book of the Thanes of Cawdor* (Spalding Club, 1859), 169; Fraser, *The Chiefs of Grant*, iii, 157.

[18] R. C. MacLeod, *The Book of Dunvegan*, i (Aberdeen, 1938), 51–2.

[19] *Glas. Mun.*, iii, 77, 78, 81, 84.

[20] MacLeod of Dunvegan Papers, box 16, no. 34.

[21] John Bannerman, 'Gaelic Endorsements of Early Seventeenth Century Legal Documents', *Studia Celtica*, xiv–xv (1979–80), 20; MacLeod of Dunvegan Papers, box 2, no. 28.

[22] Bannerman, 'Gaelic Endorsements', 20–1.

[23] Ronald Black, 'Poems by Maol Domhnaigh O Muirgheasain', *SGS*, xii (1976), 195–6; N. M. Bristol, 'The O'Muirgheasain Bardic Family', *Notes & Queries*, vi (1978), 3–7. See also William Matheson in *Notes & Queries*, vii (1978), 24–5.

survived into the sixteenth century.[24] Nor should craftsmen be forgotten, for medieval Gaelic society did not differentiate between a craft and a profession. The culture that they shared and professed was mainly orientated towards Gaelic and this was, of course, particularly true of the bardic profession. At first glance they are not the most likely people in the area to profess literacy in Scots. However, they were also competent Latinists and as such they already represented the nobility as scribes and servitors in their dealings with a government, which, at both central and local levels, relied heavily on the written word. For long, of course, the written language of government had been Latin but in the Highlands by the sixteenth century, somewhat less rapidly than in the Lowlands, it was being superseded by Scots. If the professional classes wished to retain access to this no doubt lucrative area of employment in face of competition, which there clearly was from Lowland Scots,[25] they had no choice but to make themselves as proficient in Scots as they already were in Latin. Although perhaps not until after the *Statutes of Iona* were promulgated might they be expected also to tutor in Scots.

Thus, Toirhealbhach Ó Muirgheasáin at Dunvegan can be matched with his contemporary Cathal MacMhuirich, generally recognised to be the greatest exponent of bardic verse in Scotland since his ancestor Muireadhach Albannach. The latter seems to have been attached for a time in the early thirteenth century to the court of the mormaers or earls of Lennox. Since then the MacMhuirichs had been chief poets to the Lords of the Isles and from about the middle of the sixteenth century they were employed, although not exclusively, by the MacDonalds of Clan Ranald.[26] In an elegy to Catriona, daughter of Donald Gorm Òg, chief of the MacDonalds of Sleat from 1617 to 1643, Cathal reveals that he had been her tutor in her youth.[27] As servitor to Ranald MacDonald of Benbecula by 1634, he wrote and signed documents in Scots.[28] His signature, of which a number of examples exist, is in a fine italic script which was only rarely in evidence in Scotland before the middle of the sixteenth century.[29]

In 1614, Toirdhealbhach Ó Muirgheasáin drew up and signed thus a Gaelic contract of fosterage for Ruairi Mór MacLeod but in Scots he was called *Charles Morison*, the accepted Scoticised form of his Gaelic name.[30] His

[24] William Matheson, 'The Morisons of Ness', *TGSI*, l (1976–8), 3–23.

[25] Mr William Bowie, author of *The Black Book of Taymouth* written in Scots in the month of June 1598, dedicated his work to Sir Duncan Campbell of Glenorchy, whose servitor he was. John Auchinross, who bore an Ayrshire surname, was scribe and servitor to Lachlan Mór MacLean of Duart in 1595 (*CSP Scot.*, xi, 567–691).

[26] Derick S. Thomson, 'The MacMhuirich Bardic Family', *TGSI*, xliii (1960–3), 276–304.

[27] Ronald Black, 'The Genius of Cathal MacMhuirich', *TGSI*, l (1976–8), 334.

[28] SRO Clanranald Papers GD 201/1, nos. 40A, 43; RS 37/5/186–7. I am indebted to Mr James Stewart for drawing my attention to these documents.

[29] Simpson, *Scottish Handwriting*, 19–25.

[30] SRO RH 9/17, no. 35; *Facsimiles of National Manuscripts of Scotland*, iii (Edinburgh, 1871), no. LXXXIV; Bannerman, 'Gaelic Endorsements', 21.

colleague and the second of the two chief scribes employed by Ruairi Mór MacLeod, wrote and signed documents in Scots as Thomas Donaldson. But he almost certainly also endorsed a number of these documents and others in the Dunvegan muniments in the Gaelic language and script and was therefore a member of the Gaelic learned orders, probably a Beaton of Husabost who were employed as physicians by the MacLeods of Dunvegan from at least as early as the first half of the sixteenth century. He was using his translated patronymic as a suitable surname in a Scots context in place of his Gaelic surname *MacBeatha* or a Scoticised form thereof.[31]

Another demonstration of the role of interpreter between cultures in which members of the Gaelic professional orders of Scotland were sometimes engaged comes from Ireland. In 1587 attention is drawn to 'a young man, a Scot, being named Davies Omey, that attendeth upon Turlough Lynagh, writeth for him, and keepeth his seal'.[32] It is further recorded that a Gaelic letter from Turlough Lynagh or Sir Toirdhealbhach Luineach ÓNeill, intended to be the 'ground' for a letter in Latin to Queen Elizabeth of England, had been translated into English by Davies[33] or Duncan Omey for the benefit of Sir John Perrot, the English lord deputy in Ireland. The Omeys were located in Kintyre in the sixteenth century. According to tradition they were originally brought there from Ireland 'to teach and practise weaving' but by this period they were exhibiting the propensity for free movement between professions and crafts so marked a feature of the Gaelic learned orders in late medieval Scotland.[34] Thus, Mr Duncan Omey was appointed 'principall cirurgiane' to the king in 1526, and in 1542 his son, James, was presented to the parsonage of Kilchoman in Islay.[35] Mr Cornelius Omey was made parson of the Islay parish of Kildalton in 1548, and he went on to become dean of Kintyre between c 1550 and c 1577.[36] The church continued to provide openings for members of the family into the seventeenth century.[37]

Indeed the church, orientated as it was to the Lowlands of Scotland, especially after 1560, is the most obvious profession in which to find Gaelic speakers literate in Scots. And since churchmen frequently doubled as notaries public, there is no lack of evidence as to their competence, for they were responsible for much of the legal documentation that oiled the wheels of

[31] Bannerman, 'Gaelic Endorsements', 21–4.

[32] *CSP Ireland* (1586–8), 390.

[33] Probably a mistranscription of *Denis* used in Ireland as an equivalent for Gaelic *Donnachadh* (Patrick Woulfe, *Sloinnte Gaedeal is Gall* (Dublin, 1923), 47). *Donnchadh* or *Duncan* was a characteristic Omey name in the sixteenth century (see below).

[34] Andrew McKerral, *Kintyre in the Seventeenth Century* (Edinburgh, 1948), 171; A. E. Anderson, 'Kilbrandon and Kilchattan Session Records, 1753-1773', *TGSI*, xxxv (1929-30), 269; Derick S. Thomson, 'Gaelic Learned Orders and Literati in Medieval Scotland', *SS*, xii (1968), 66–8.

[35] *RSS*, i, no. 3416; ii, no. 4739.

[36] *RSS*, iii, no. 2586; *AT*, passim.

[37] McKerral, *Kintyre*, 171.

local government. About twenty notaries can be identified in the Argyll muniments between 1530 and 1560.[38] The most notable of these was Mr John Carswell, who was one of two notaries licensed by the diocese of the Isles, the other being sir Archibald MacGillivray, vicar or Killean in Kintyre, who drew up the document of 1545 appointing the commissioners from Donald Dubh, Lord of the Isles, and his Council, to treat with Henry VIII of England.[39] Later in that year Carswell accompanied Donald Dubh to Ireland. By July 1553 he was parson of Kilmartin and perhaps his close association with the Campbell earls of Argyll began at this point. Sometime before June 1562 he had been appointed Superintendent of Argyll and in 1567 he was formally presented to the bishopric of the Isles and commendatorship of Iona.[40] As well as notarial instruments there is a letter of May 1564 written by him in fluent Scots to Robert Campbell of Kinzeancleuch in Ayrshire.[41]

Another churchman of note and exact contemporary of John Carswell with a similar career was sir Donald Munro from Kiltearn in Easter Ross. In 1526 he was presented to the vicarage of Snizort and Raasay in the diocese of the Isles and he became archdeacon of the Isles in 1548. In 1563 the General Assembly made him commissioner for the diocese of Ross.[42] Seven years later one of his ministers was appointed to 'assist' him 'because the said Commissioner was not prompt in the Scottish tongue'.[43] But although his spoken knowledge of Scots may have been wanting, he was literate in the language as his description of the Western Isles written in Scots c 1550 amply indicates.

Finally, and paradoxically perhaps, one of two central Gaelic documents of the sixteenth century, the *Book of the Dean of Lismore*,[44] is itself important evidence for literacy in Scots. Quite apart from the considerable passages of prose and poetry in that language, the many thousand lines of Gaelic poetry are without exception written in a spelling based on Scots. The secretary hands of sir James MacGregor, vicar of Fortingall and dean of Lismore (d. 1551), of his poet brother, Duncan, and of their father, Dugall, can be identified. Since the dean and his father were notaries public, it is not surprising that the Scoticisation of the Gaelic in the *Book of the Dean of Lismore* bears some resemblance to the Scoticisation of Gaelic surnames and placenames in contemporary legal documents.[45] The MacGregors were

[38] Donald E. Meek and James Kirk, 'John Carswell, Superintendent of Argyll, a reassessment', *RSCHS*, xix (1975), 5.

[39] *L.P. Henry VIII*, xx (pt 1), no. 1298.

[40] Ibid., xx (pt 2), no. 42; John Bannerman, 'Two early post-Reformation inscriptions in Argyll', *PSAS*, cv (1972–4), 308.

[41] *Miscellany of the Wodrow Society*, ed. D. Laing, (Wodrow Society, 1844), i, 285–6.

[42] R. W. Munro, *Monro's Western Isles of Scotland and Genealogies of the Clans 1549* (Edinburgh, 1961), 11–25.

[43] *Acts and Proceedings of the General Assemblies of the Kirk of Scotland* (Maitland Club, 1839), i, 175. See also A. Matheson, review in *SHR*, xlii (1963), 50.

[44] NLS 72. 1. 37.

[45] Steer and Bannerman, *Monumental Sculpture*, 91–2.

natives of Fortingall in Perthshire and, since the only other identifiable hand among the many who had a part in bringing together this collection over a period which spanned the years 1512 to 1542, was William Drummond, curate in Fortingall, it can be assumed that there was a considerable group of Gaelic speakers in the area who were literate in Scots in the first half of the sixteenth century.[46]

The material in Scots in the *Book of the Dean of Lismore* is matched by that in Latin. This is no more than might be expected in scribes who were pre-Reformation clergy and notaries public, particularly the latter, a notary unable to write Latin would not be very effective in a period when that language was still being extensively used in legal documentation. The other central document in the Gaelic canon of the sixteenth century is the translation of and additions to the *Book of Common Order* or *Knox's Liturgy* as it is sometimes known.[47] Mr John Carswell claimed that he translated in part from the Latin, presumably the version known as *Ratio et Forma* published in 1556. In fact it probably owes more to the English edition of 1564 but there can be no doubt of Carswell's expertise in Latin.[48] Not only was he a notary public but he attained the level of BA and graduated MA at St Andrews University in 1542 and 1544 respectively.[49] Literacy in Latin was a prerequisite of a university education and most of those who can be identified as attending university from the Gaelic speaking areas of Scotland in the sixteenth century did so as a preliminary to a career in the church. It has been estimated that half of the forty parish priests identified in the diocese of Argyll in the thirty years or so before the Reformation of 1560 were graduates in Arts.[50] So were no less than seven of the eight incumbents of, or candidates for, the bishopric of the Isles and commendatorship of Iona in the sixteenth century who were natives of the area,[51] indicating that higher education was a factor in ecclesiastical preferment in the Highlands whether before or after 1560.

Nor before 1560 were the regular clergy to be outshone in this respect. Duncan MacArthur, prior of Ardchattan, from c 1508 to 1538 was a graduate in Arts from St Andrews and, at about the same time, a prior of Iona was a bachelor of decreets.[52] In 1532 a Latin charter was signed in Latin and in their own hands by six members of the community of Iona. The seventh, and only one who claimed to be unable to write bore the Lowland surname of *Lathom* or *Lethom*.[53]

But the church, university and local government, all orientated towards

---

[46] I am indebted to Mr Ronald Black for giving me access to the catalogue of Gaelic manuscripts in the National Library of Scotland which he is in the process of compiling.

[47] *Foirm na n-Urrnuidheadh*, ed. R. L. Thomson, (SGTS, 1970).

[48] Ibid., lxviii; Meek and Kirk, 'John Carswell', 18.

[49] *St A. Acta*, ii, 396, 400.

[50] Meek and Kirk, 'John Carswell', 7.

[51] Steer and Bannerman, *Monumental Sculpture*, 116–17.

[52] Ibid., 135; *St A. Acta*, ii, 264; Steer and Bannerman, *Monumental Sculpture*, 115–16.

[53] *The Book of the Thanes of Cawdor*, 158; George F. Black, *The Surnames of Scotland* (New York, 1962), 425–6.

Lowland Scotland, were not the only avenues through which the Gaelic speaking Scot might become proficient in Latin. There was a native tradition of literacy in the language. A royal letter of 1544 states that Mr Roderick MacLean, bishop of the Isles (d. c 1553), was 'educated in the islands' and 'sufficiently learned according to the custom of [his] people'. In 1534 he matriculated at the German university of Wittenberg and doubtless graduated from there as a Master of Arts.[54] He could hardly have proceeded there without a previous and competent knowledge of Latin.

The fact is that the professional orders of Gaelic society, side by side with their devotion to Gaelic culture, maintained a continuing interest in Latin learning. This manifested itself particularly in terms of the bardic and medical professions, but the inscription on the cross at Ardchattan carved by John ÓBrolchán in 1500 suggests that a master mason might also be literate in Latin.[55] That the poets' interest was primarily a literary one is shown by the frequent allusions to classical Latin literature in bardic poetry. This goes back to a pre-twelfth century situation when the vernacular poets were closely associated with a church which prided itself on its Latin scholarship. But it must have been heavily reinforced when Latin became the language of government in the twelfth century, and for exactly the same reasons that a knowledge of Scots had become something of a necessity by the sixteenth century. Since Latin and Scots shared this role throughout the sixteenth century, it points to members of the Gaelic professional orders literate in both languages. Duncan Omey was probably responsible for the Latin version of the original Gaelic letter from Toirdhealbhach ÓNéill to Elizabeth of England. At any rate it was his knowledge of the contents, which apparently included material derogatory to Sir John Perrot, the lord deputy, and not in the Gaelic original, that induced the latter, after 'some devices were wrought to convey him (Omey) out of the way', to find him, interrogate him, and have him translate the Gaelic letter into English.[56]

Cathal MacMhuirich was literate in Latin and indeed he frequently signed a Latinised form of his forename even when the text of the document was in Gaelic or Scots.[57] His contemporary, John Beaton (1594–1657), signed documents written in Scots in an equally fine italic hand as follows: *Johannes Bettonus testis.* He was head of the well-known medical family of Pennycross in Mull and as such, *ard ollamh*, 'chief physician', to MacLean of Duart.[58] Mr John MacLean, minister of Kilninian in Mull from 1702 to 1756, wrote of the Beatons of Pennycross that 'they were expert scholars both in Irish and Latine

[54] *Epistolae Jacobi Quarti, Jacobi Quinti et Mariae Regum Scotorum,* ed. T. Ruddiman (Edinburgh, 1722–4), ii, 221; J. Durkan, 'The Cultural Background in Sixteenth-century Scotland' in *Essays on the Scottish Reformation,* ed. David MacRoberts (Glasgow, 1962), 320.

[55] Steer and Bannerman, *Monumental Sculpture,* 134–5.

[56] *CSP Ireland* (1586–8), 390.

[57] TCD 1337/2 (H. 3. 18, pt ii), 696–9; SRO Clanranald Papers GD 201/1, no. 40A, GD 201/2, no. 2.

[58] MacLeod of Dunvegan Papers, box 14C, 30 June 1633, 25 July 1635; John Bannerman, 'The Beatons', *SGS* (forthcoming).

but had English ne'er a word'.[59] John MacLean was a friend of Mr John Beaton who was his predecessor as minister of Kilninian and second son of John Beaton, the physician.[60] While the assertion that the Beatons of Pennycross had no English can probably be attributed to a form of linguistic nationalism on the part of John MacLean, their devotion to Latin scholarship cannot be in doubt. For John Beaton and his immediate descendants, this is evidenced by the lengthy Latin inscription, that includes a verse of poetry, on his grave-slab, still to be seen on Iona, which his grandson, Donald, commissioned in 1674, more than a century after Latin inscriptions on stone had ceased to be the fashion in the area.[61] But for the Beatons in general and for all other hereditary medical families, the most obvious evidence of their literacy in Latin is to be found in their own medical manuscripts which are mainly translations of and commentaries on thirteenth and fourteenth century Latin treatises emanating from the medical schools of such southern universities as Salerno, Padua and Montpellier.[62]

Lack of evidence makes it difficult to tell how far the professional classes, particularly the hereditary bardic families, imparted their Latin learning to the laity. Bishop Roderick MacLean was a member of a lay family, the MacLeans of Kingairloch, and he, as noted, apparently received a Latin education locally. It is perhaps not without significance in this context that the Latin work published by him in Rome in 1549 was a book of poetry.[63] But there is every likelihood that the later tutelage in Scots provided by bardic families was mirrored in Latin at an earlier period. Until 1560 the nobility were accustomed to commissioning funereal monuments in stone bearing Latin inscriptions.[64] This included women and Katherine, daughter of Hector Mór MacLean of Duart, whose public career began with her marriage to Archibald, 4th Earl of Argyll, sometime before January 1547, was noted for her linguistic accomplishments 'beyng not unlernyd in the Latyn tong, speckyth good French, and as is sayd, som lytell Italyone'.[65] Finally, a master stone-mason like Mael-Sechlainn O'Cuinn, who renovated the priory of Oronsay at the beginning of the sixteenth century felt it worth his while to record this fact in a Latin building inscription.[66]

Mael-Sechlainn's name and professional designation are carved in impeccable Gaelic orthography of the period both in the building inscription and in an inscription on the great cross at Oronsay which relates that it was

[59] J. L. Campbell and Derick Thomson, *Edward Lhuyd in the Scottish Highlands 1699–1700* (Oxford, 1963), 33.

[60] Ibid., 12–36.

[61] Steer and Bannerman, *Monumental Sculpture*, 91; Bannerman, 'The Beatons'.

[62] Donald MacKinnon, *A Descriptive Catalogue of Gaelic Manuscripts* (Edinburgh, 1912), 5–71, 275–7, 283–5, 295, 298–9, 324; Francis Shaw, 'Irish Medical Men and Philosophers' in *Seven Centuries of Irish Learning*, ed. Brian ÓCuív (Dublin, 1961), 93–4.

[63] *Essays on the Scottish Reformation*, xvi and opp. 224.

[64] Steer and Bannerman, *Monumental Sculpture*, 87–163.

[65] *CSP Ireland* (1509–73), 172.

[66] Steer and Bannerman, *Monumental Sculpture*, 120.

also his work.[67] John Carswell implies that writing Gaelic was commonplace in his lifetime and what he laments is the lack of printed works in the language. He singles out 'the history of our ancestors' for special mention.

> 'It is great labour to write that by hand, when one considers what is printed in the press, how smartly and how quickly each work, however great, is completed thereby'.[68]

Nor was literacy in Gaelic a new thing in the sixteenth century or necessarily even on the increase. Indeed, it is possible that the decline in the ability to write Gaelic, evident towards the end of the following century, had already begun by the end of this period.[69]

The strong and continuing oral character of much Gaelic literature has tended to obscure the fact that there was, until the eighteenth century, a parallel scribal tradition which in many ways sustained and complemented the former. The history of Gaelic as a written language goes back at least to the fourth century A.D. in terms of Ogam inscriptions on stone and wood. By the seventh century the monks of the recently established monastic church, recruited as they were in large measure from the existing native learned orders and spurred on by the ascetic intellectualism that they had inherited from the desert origins of their church, had begun to commit to writing the Gaelic learned tradition more or less as it stood. As time went by they Christianised this tradition and the church became closely identified with certain branches of it, particularly, manuscript illumination and work in stone and metal but also with the literary profession. The vernacular poet might even be the *fer-léginn* or master of the monastic school and scriptorium in which both Gaelic and Latin were studied and written. When, with the twelfth century reorganisation of the church along continental lines, the poet and the church parted company, the ability to write the vernacular was not abandoned. The extremely conservative society of Scotland and Ireland was not likely in any case to let go a part of its cultural tradition to which it had become accustomed over such a long period of time. But the survival of literacy in Gaelic was put beyond doubt by the fact that it was to play a more important role than hitherto in the maintenance of that society.

From the twelfth century onwards the poet had to rely entirely on lay patronage for his livelihood and consequently greater emphasis was laid on panegyric – eulogy and elegy. Panegyric always had been an important part of the literary output of the *fili* or learned poet of the Dark Ages but thereafter, more generally known as the *bard*, he specialised therein and became such a ubiquitous and prominent element in the kin-based society of Ireland and Scotland that the word *bard* was eventually borrowed into the English language. The *oes dána* or learned orders as a whole were accorded the status of nobles in the seventh and eighth century law tracts and the court poet was ranked with the highest in the land. He maintained his position in the

[67] Ibid., 119.
[68] *Foirm na n-Urrnuidheadh*, 10-11, 179-80.
[69] Bannerman, 'Gaelic Endorsements', 26.

medieval period, becoming even more indispensible in terms of society itself, for in his panegyric poetry he was concerned to maintain and preserve it in all its pristine glory. He praised the chief and his kindred and burnished the image of their ancestors from whose sterling example they must not deviate. It is not surprising therefore that the poets were frequently to be found playing a decisive role in the political events of their time as mentors, confidants and plenipotentiaries of their noble employers.

Cathal MacMhuirich wrote a verse epistle to Colla Ciotach MacDonald of Colonsay c 1615 in which he undertook to advise him to follow a more peaceful course in the Hebrides than hitherto, suggesting further that he might pay a visit to Ireland and 'allow the Islesmen a respite'. Cathal concluded what may have been the original draft of his letter with a request to Colla Ciotach to give on his behalf 'a thousand blessings' to Donald MacMhuirich and his wife.[70] Colla Ciotach and Donald MacMhuirich signed a Gaelic letter to Rome dated 1 April 1629 in which the progress so far made by the Franciscan mission to Scotland was commended.[71] Clearly Donald was another member of the hereditary bardic family to which Cathal belonged who, although an employee of Colla Ciotach, was wholly in his confidence. More especially so, since Colla Ciotach was a Catholic, while the Irishman who may have translated the letter into Latin noted that Donald was a 'heretic'. Finally, the ambassadorial function of the bard is well illustrated by a statement made to the English authorities in Ireland in 1594 to the effect that 'one of the M'Cleries, a scholar and agent for O'Donnell was in Scotland' on what amounted to a recruiting drive. The family of ÓCléirigh had been poet-historians to the ÓDomhnaills since the fourteenth century.[72]

The important position that the bard occupied in society is reflected in the statute of Iona which states that

'na vagabound, baird, nor profest pleisant pretending libertie to baird and flattir, be ressavit within the boundis of the saidis Yllis be ony of the saidis speciall barronis and gentilmen'.[73]

The bards, even those who had permanent patrons, made frequent circuits of noble houses and bardic schools in both Ireland and Scotland and it is to this aspect that the statute specifically refers. There is no evidence that any real notice was taken and there is perhaps no more telling illustration from the area of the high regard in which travelling poets and their poetry continued to be held than Cornelius Ward's own account of how, in 1624, his first year in the field as a Franciscan missionary, he gained access to Sir John Campbell of

[70] R. Black, 'A Manuscript of Cathal Mac Muireadhaigh', *Celtica*, x (1973), 193–209; David Stevenson, *Alasdair MacColla and the Highland Problem in the Seventeenth Century* (Edinburgh, 1980), 61, n. 86.

[71] Cathaldus Giblin, *Irish Franciscan Mission to Scotland 1619–1646* (Dublin, 1964), 125.

[72] *CSP Ireland* (1592–6), 217; Paul Walsh, *The ÓCléirigh Family of Tír Conaill* (Dublin, 1938), 1–3.

[73] *RPC*, 1 ser. ix, 29.

Cawdor, a person of great influence but 'an obstinate heretic'. Ward, who was a member of the well known bardic family of that name from Donegal, composed the customary bardic eulogy and then, pretending to be a visiting Irish poet and accompanied by a harpist, he betook himself and his poem to Sir John who, we are told, received him graciously. After three days entertainment as a poet, he revealed who he was and he eventually persuaded Sir John to profess Catholicism. The latter, who was Laird of Islay by this time, was recognised by the mission to be the most influential convert that they made during their stay in Scotland.[74]

Sir Ruairi Mór MacLeod of Dunvegan may have sent his sons to university at the behest of the *Statutes of Iona* but he did not cease to offer permanent employment to members of the bardic families. Toirdhealbhach ÓMuirgheasáin, his servitor in 1606, was certainly still so in 1616 and probably continued to serve him until his death in 1626.[75] Eoin Òg ÓMuirgheasáin, perhaps of that branch of the family employed by Hector Òg MacLean of Duart (d. c 1623), another signatory of the *Statutes of Iona*, composed an elegy for Ruairi which is still extant.[76] In it Ruairi's past generosity to poets is even more than usually emphasised.

This elegy is composed in the bardic tradition that had evolved some four hundred years before. The bardic metres, based on syllable counting, derived ultimately from pre-Christian metrical forms, influenced by Latin hymn metres of the fifth and sixth centuries.[77] By the end of the twelfth century the numbers of possible metres in use were much reduced, but there was a greater insistence on metrical ornament, particularly, rime and alliteration. A parallel and more striking development was the evolution in the second half of the twelfth century of a standard literary language based on what has been called 'a normative or prescriptive grammar'.[78] This language was adopted by all branches of the professional orders but the surviving manuscript material suggests that it was the hereditary bardic families who were ultimately responsible for its creation. Nowhere is this more clearly demonstrated than in the grammatical tracts, most of which in their present form derive from the sixteenth century. It has been pointed out that the tract on declension is illustrated by 2000 citations in verse, partly so that the form of each word studied might be fixed by the metre and partly because the language was being studied and taught in terms of its use in poetry.[79] It is interesting that the latest and one of the fullest copies of the tract on verbs is a paper manuscript of

[74] Giblin, *Franciscan Mission*, 54–5, 80, 124.

[75] Bannerman, 'Gaelic Endorsements', 20–1.

[76] J. MacDonald, 'An Elegy for Ruaidhri Mór', *SGS*, viii (1958), 30–52; Ronald Black, 'Maol Domhnaigh O Muirgheasain (1)', *SGS*, xii (1976), 195–6; William Matheson, 'The O'Muirgheasain Bardic Family', *Notes & Queries*, vii (1978), 24–5.

[77] Calvert Watkins, 'Indo-European Metrics and Archaic Irish Verse', *Celtica*, vi (1963), 194–249.

[78] Brian Ó Cuív, *The Linguistic Training of the Mediaeval Irish Poet* (Dublin, 1973), 3–4.

[79] O. Bergin, 'The Native Irish Grammarian', *PBA*, xxiv (1938), 210. The tract on declension was edited by O. Bergin in a supplement to *Eriu*, viii–x (1916–28).

seventeenth century date 'procured from the Highlands of Scotland' with many grammatical comments and verse citations added by two later hands,[80] all of which is illustrative of the fact that training in the composition of bardic poetry continued in Scotland into the eighteenth century. John Carswell, praising the 'standard of diction or propriety laid down for Gaelic by the poets', was in no doubt as to who were the arbiters of linguistic taste in his day and he felt that his own command of the literary dialect 'wants the polish of the poets'.[81]

The student-poet had much to learn, not only literature, history, genealogy and the rules of versification but also 'matters pertaining to phonetics, phonology, morphology, syntax and vocabulary'.[82] It is not surprising that he might spend between seven and twelve years in a bardic school training to attain the highest rank of poet.[83] There is no certain contemporary reference to a specific school in Scotland but plenty to schools in general and it is inconceivable that such important bardic families as the MacMhuirichs and the ÓMuirgheasáins did not conduct such schools.[84] Indeed, attention has already been drawn to the possible tutorial functions of Cathal MacMhuirich and Toirdhealbhach ÓMuirgheasáin in the context of literacy in Scots. On the mainland, the MacEwens were poet-historians and genealogists to the MacDougals of Dunollie and the Campbells of Argyll in the sixteenth century, while as late as 1700 Donald MacMharcuis, a member of a family of poets located in Kintyre since 1500 at least, wrote and signed a letter written in English as 'professor of Gaelic'.[85]

The act of bardic composition retained its essentially oral character and the most detailed, if somewhat hostile, account comes from a native of Skye, Martin Martin, who published his description of the Western Isles in 1703.[86] As soon as the poem was completed, however, it was committed to writing by the bard. Its first public airing was normally also in a purely oral contest, in the form of a recitation accompanied by harp music in the hall of the person eulogised, but thereafter it was written into the *duanaire* or song-book possessed by the ruling family of each important kindred. On occasion, however, the recitation may have been accompanied or even replaced by a presentation manuscript copy of the poem. This must surely be the

[80] Thomas Astle, *The Origin and Progress of Writing* (London, 1803), 123, 125; Bergin, 'The Native Irish Grammarian', 213–14. The tract on verbs was edited from three manuscript versions by O. Bergin in a supplement to *Eriu*, xiv (1946). This is the third version, now in the Royal Irish Academy, E. iv. 1. (no. 751).

[81] *Foirm na n-Urrnuidheadh*, 12, 112, 180, 182.

[82] Ó Cuív, *The Linguistic Training*, 4.

[83] J. E. Caerwyn Williams, 'The Court Poet in Medieval Ireland, *PBA*, lvii (1971), 36–7.

[84] William J. Watson, 'Classic Gaelic Poetry of Panegyric in Scotland', *TGSI*, xxix (1914–19), 204.

[85] *Foirm na n-Urrnuidheadh*, 183–6; *Early Letters of Robert Wodrow, 1698–1709*, ed. L. W. Sharp (SHS, 1937), 76–7. See also Colm ÓBaoill, 'Domhnall MacMharcuis', *SGS*, xii (1976), 183–92.

[86] Martin Martin, *A Description of the Western Islands of Scotland circa 1695* (Stirling, 1934), 176–7; Williams, 'The Court Poet', 35–7.

explanation for the elaborately written and ornamented parchment copy of an elegy to Sir Duncan Campbell of Glenorchy (d. 1631), probably composed, written and presented to his successor by Neill MacEwen.[87]

However, the important place that literacy held in the bardic ethos is best seen in the training of the bard. The voluminous metrical and grammatical tracts in manuscript which are heavily annotated make it clear that literacy in the standard literary dialect of the medieval period was an absolute requirement and they have been described as the text books of the bardic schools. Even if literacy in Gaelic had not been a longstanding cultural feature of the prevailing society by the twelfth century, it is difficult to see how it could have been avoided thereafter considering that bardic poetry, the central part of the native literary output, was in terms of metrics heavily dependent on a knowledge of the rules of spelling and in terms of language was based on a newly constructed and highly scholastic prescriptive grammar. The apparent rapidity with which this last was effected sometime towards the end of the twelfth century is itself a mark of literacy. It could be argued that bardic poetry would not have evolved in quite this way if literacy had not already been a feature of the existing cultural scene.

It has already been noted that other branches of the learned orders adopted the literary dialect for their own purposes. Particularly, the medical profession who used it to translate and comment on the Latin tracts that they apparently found so necessary to maintain their medical mystique, if not their medical skill. It is perhaps a commentary on the importance placed on literacy by this profession in a purely Scottish context that more manuscripts which once belonged to hereditary medical families have survived than for any other profession in the sixteenth century. Indeed, the manuscripts of the Beatons reveal that their interests went far beyond medicine to include history and genealogy and they may have complemented the bardic families in their role as educators.[88]

Nor did Mr John Carswell write in a vacuum. He clearly expected to have an audience for his translation of and additions to the *Book of Common Order* in the current literary dialect of which, despite his protestations to the contrary, he is an acknowledged master. How far he hoped to draw his readership from the laity is conjectural but there can be no doubt that he intended his book to be of practical use to the churchmen of his day and in 1574 we find Colin, 6th Earl of Argyll, urging 'ministreis and rederis at ilk paroche Kirk' in his territories to adopt

> 'the prayaris, ministratioun of the sacramentis and forme of discipline after the ordour of Genevay translatit out of Englis in the Erische toung be Maister Jhone Carsuale, lait beshope of the Ylis'.[89]

---

[87] *The National Manuscripts of Scotland*, iii (Edinburgh, 1871), No. XCVI; William J. Watson, *Marbhnadh Dhonnchaidh Duibh* (Glasgow, 1917), 1–16; Donald MacNicol, *Remarks on Dr Samuel Johnson's Journey to the Hebrides* (London, 1779), 245–6; Brian Ó Cuív, *The Irish Bardic Duanaire or "Poem-Book"* (Dublin, 1973), 28.

[88] Bannerman, 'The Beatons'.

[89] *CSP Scotland*, v, 34.

Clergymen of this century had already shown their practical interest in classical Gaelic literature in the persons of James MacGregor, dean of Lismore, and William Drummond, curate in Fortingall, both scribes of the *Book of the Dean of Lismore*, and that collection contains a bardic poem on the murder of Angus Òg in 1490 composed by John MacMhuirich, who was dean of Knoydart by 1506×1510 and a member of the famous bardic family of that name.[90]

The key to literacy in Gaelic among the laity lies in bardic poetry. There had to be an audience for this poetry and it is inconceivable that it was not intended to be fully intelligible. If the poet required training to become proficient in his art, so did his audience to fully appreciate the results thereof. Because literacy was an integral part of that training, it could be assumed, even if no other evidence existed, that the ability to write Gaelic was likely to be relatively common, at least in the upper levels of lay society to whom the bard addressed the bulk of his output, and it is worth noting that the ability to write has a place among the traditional attributes of a chief worthy of bardic praise.[91] But it can be reasonably assumed that a layman who composed a bardic poem was also literate in Gaelic. Noteworthy, therefore, is the number of poems attributed to poets who were not members of the professional orders in the *Book of the Dean of Lismore*. Included therein is a poem by Finlay MacNab, chief of the MacNabs of Glendochart (d. 1525), urging the compilation of such a collection which he called a *duanaire* and suggesting that on completion it should be brought to Argyll for his judgement of its merits: 'Bring unto MacCailein no poem lacking artistry to be read'.[92] Since the collection was begun by 1512, this is probably Archibald, 2nd Earl of Argyll, who was killed at Flodden in 1513. One of the poems, a *brosnachadh catha*, 'an incitement to battle', before Flodden is addressed to him.[93] Another was composed by 'MacCailein, Earl of Argyll', and this may be Colin, Archibald's son and successor, for elsewhere in the manuscript two verses are attributed to 'MacCailein Mór, id est, Callein Math'.[94] Colin was one of two Campbells whose help was acknowledged by Hector Boece in the preface to his *Scotorum Historiae*, published in 1527, the other was Colin's kinsman, John Campbell, treasurer of Scotland.[95] It is worth noting that they represented a direct link between Boece and the MacEwen bardic family, who were historians in the classical tradition of Gaelic learning, and who doubtless gave the youthful Colin formal training in the composition of

---

[90] W. J. Watson, *Scottish Verse from the Book of the Dean of Lismore* (SGTS, 1937), 96–8; Thomson, 'The MacMhuirich Bardic Family', 287–8.

[91] John MacInnes, 'The Panegyric Code in Gaelic Poetry and its Historical Background', *TGSI*, l (1976–8), 454.

[92] Watson, *Scottish Verse*, 2–4.

[93] Ibid., 158–64.

[94] NLS 72, 1. 37., 73, 271. But see William Gillies, 'Some Aspects of Campbell History', *TGSI*, l (1976–8), 287, n. 3.

[95] Hector Boece, *Scotorum Historiae* (Paris, 1527), f. iii.

bardic poetry. Another Campbell, who may have been tutored by them and whose output of poetry recorded in the *Book of the Dean of Lismore* is the largest of any Scottish author, professional or lay, was Duncan Campbell of Glenorchy, *an Ridire Math*, 'the Good Knight', who fell with his chief at Flodden.[96]

Women too might receive training in bardic composition. Thus, two poems in the *Book of the Dean of Lismore* are attributed to Isobel *ní Mheic Cailéin*, 'daughter of MacCailein', either of Colin, 1st earl of Argyll (d. 1493), or of his successor, Archibald, already mentioned.[97] Another was composed by *Contissa Ergadien Issobell*, presumably Isobel (d. 1510), daughter of John Stewart, Lord of Lorn, and wife of Colin, 1st earl of Argyll.[98]

The connection with the ruling family of the Clan Campbell is striking and it includes Duncan Campbell of Glenorchy who was a first cousin of Colin, 1st earl of Argyll. They belonged to the uppermost echelon of society in the area and it is difficult to know how far down the social scale literacy in Gaelic extended. But there are other Scottish poets named in the *Book of the Dean of Lismore* who were not members of the professional orders. One whose first name was Eoghan and whose title *an barún*, 'the baron', clearly identifies him as a layman may have been a chief of the MacEwens of Otter, who were habitually described as barons at an early period.[99] Another, Robert Lamont of Ascog in Cowal, on record between the years 1477 and 1520, was a *duin-uasal* or gentleman of the Clan Lamont,[100] while Fearchar, son of Patrick Grant, also bears the surname of a territorial kindred, but cannot be identified as a member of the ruling family.[101] One of the best known poems in the *Book of the Dean of Lismore* is a lament for Neill MacNeill of Gigha (d. 1455×72) by Oighreag MacCorquodale, apparently his wife and presumably also a MacCorquodale of Phantilands in Lorn, an identifiable but minor kindred of the time.[102]

Donald Gorm, chief of the MacDonalds of Sleat from 1585 until his death in 1617, was, according to tradition, a noted wit and composer of epigrammatic verse, and he was perhaps the author of the bardic quatrain on folio 231 of the only surviving manuscript to contain James I's well known poem *The Kingis Quair*. At any rate Donald Gorm wrote it down and signed

[96] William Gillies, 'The Gaelic Poems of Sir Duncan Campbell of Glenorchy (1)', *SGS*, xiii (1978), 18–45.

[97] NLS 72. I. 37., 285, 292. See also Watson, *Scottish Verse*, 307–8.

[98] NLS 72. I. 37., 251. There seems to be no good reason to assume with Professor J. C. Watson (Watson, *Scottish Verse*, 307) that Isobel *ní Mheic Cailéin* and Isobel, Countess of Argyll, were one and the same person. See John Bannerman and Ronald Black, 'A Sixteenth-century Gaelic Letter', *SGS*, xiii (1978), 64, n. 10, and Gillies, 'Some Aspects of Campbell History', 286–7, n. 3.

[99] NLS 72. I. 37., 179; R. MacEwen, *Clan Ewen* (Glasgow, 1904), 6. But see Steer and Bannerman, *Monumental Sculpture*, 206, n. 7.

[100] NLS 72. I. 37., 170; *An Inventory of Lamont Papers*, ed. Norman Lamont (SRS, 1914), 24, 32; Hector McKechnie, *The Lamont Clan* (Edinburgh, 1938), 403–4.

[101] NLS 72. I. 37., 88, 170.

[102] Watson, *Scottish Verse*, 60–4.

it probably in or shortly before the year 1592.[103] His elegant Gaelic hand is sufficient indication of his training in the classical tradition.

Donald Gorm signed legal documents in the current secretary script,[104] but by the turn of the century it is possible to point to people who signed such documents, whether written in Scots or Latin, in the Gaelic language and script. Pressure to sign personally may have begun to count for more than a signature by proxy in the language and script in which the body of the text was written. At any rate there are many examples, comparatively speaking, of the Gaelic signature of Ruairi Mór MacLeod of Dunvegan. Its appearance on a number of occasions in the *Register of the Privy Council* indicates that a Gaelic signature was acceptable at the highest government levels.[105] His contemporary and neighbour, Lachlan MacKinnon of Strathordle, also invariably signed in Gaelic.[106] So too did Donald Gorm MacDonald of Borrodale, nephew of Donald, chief of Clan Ranald (d. 1618).[107] It was still possible for a layman, namely, Allan, son of Roderick MacDonald of Glenalladale, to sign a discharge in the Gaelic language and script in 1699.[108]

It has been noted that Ruairi Mór MacLeod could not read Scots and was therefore probably unable to sign his name in secretary hand. This may also be the explanation for Lachlan MacKinnon's Gaelic signature. Until they were knighted,[109] their signatures consisted simply of their styles, *MacLeoid* and *MacFhionguine* respectively, which was how heads of kindreds frequently identified themselves in Gaelic. In contemporary Scots, the signatures of those who could write the secretary script normally consisted of first name and surname as was usual elsewhere in Scotland. Ruairi Mór and Lachlan were both signatories of the *Statutes of Iona* on 23 August 1609. Although the original of that document is no longer extant, it was copied on 27 July 1610 into the *Register of the Privy Council*. It is recorded therein that the signatories signed with their own hands, and forms of their signatures were written into the *Register*.[110] Those of Ruairi Mór and Lachlan consist of their styles only, and, although they are present in a Scoticised form, it can be assumed that they appended their usual Gaelic signatures to the original. It is interesting therefore that four of the other seven signatories, namely, Hector Òg MacLean of Duart, Lachlan MacLean of Coll, Hector MacLean of Lochbuie and Gill-easbuig MacQuarrie of Ulva apparently did not include their personal names in their signatures. It may be that all nine signed the

---

[103] Bannerman, 'Gaelic Endorsements', 26.

[104] MacLeod of Dunvegan Papers, box 7, August 1609.

[105] Ibid., box 1, 9 April 1623; box 7, August 1609, 24 August 1616; *RPC*, 1 ser. xiii, 362, 745, 824.

[106] MacLeod of Dunvegan Papers, box 7, August 1609; box 8, 15 February 1613; SRO Lord MacDonald Papers GD 221/106, 9 June 1625.

[107] MacLeod of Dunvegan Papers, box 1, 18 July 1626; box 16, no. 28.

[108] SRO Clanranald Papers GD 201/1, no. 168.

[109] *S. R. Macleoid* (MacLeod of Dunvegan Papers, box 1, 9 April 1623); *sir lachloinn mac fionguine* (SRO Lord MacDonald Papers GD 221/106, 9 June 1625).

[110] *RPC*, 1 ser. ix, 30.

Statutes of Iona in the Gaelic language and script, perhaps as a gesture of defiance against the implied denigration of their language in the body of the text.

What has gone before suggests that when a sixteenth century Gaelic speaker signed a document with his hand led by a notary public 'because he could not write', this should not be taken as proof of illiteracy *per se* but merely of his inability to write his name in the current secretary hand. This is how the councillors of the Isles signed the commission appointing plenipotentiaries to treat with Henry VIII of England in 1545. The signatories, who were eighteen in number, included Donald Dubh, Lord of the Isles, and most of the heads of important kindreds in the Lordship. It is inconceivable that they were all illiterate in Gaelic. They were at the apex of society in the area and at once the employers and the audience of the bards. Indeed, one of them, Hector Mór MacLean of Duart, was himself a poet in the bardic tradition.[111]

The writing and receiving of letters is perhaps the real test of literacy in lay society. And although the texts of only two letters written in Gaelic by laymen of the sixteenth century have survived, there are sufficient contemporary references to letter writing in that language to indicate that it was common enough, at least in the second half of that century. The first of the two extant letters was a casual note of instruction written c 1595 by Lachlan Mór MacLean of Duart to his physician, Malcolm Beaton of Pennycross; the other, probably dating to 1604, was almost certainly by Sir James MacDonald of Islay.[112] It is addressed to unnamed 'friends and kinsmen' warning them against attempting to rescue him from Edinburgh Castle where he was currently incarcerated by central government.

From 1579 there has survived also the texts of three Gaelic letters to kinsmen of Sir James MacDonald, namely, Ranald of Colonsay, Alexander Ciotach, probably the same as Alexander, son of Somhairle Buidhe, who was killed in 1585, and Ùisdean, perhaps he who died in 1588. The letters, sent by James Fitzmaurice, grandson of the 14th Earl of Desmond, urged these MacDonalds to support him in his projected rising against the English in Ireland.[113]

The verse epistle to Colla Ciotach MacDonald of Colonsay, nephew and successor of Ranald, composed by Cathal MacMhuirich c 1615 and the Gaelic letter to Rome written in 1629 on behalf of the Franciscan mission to Scotland and signed by Colla Ciotach and his employee Donald MacMhuirich have already been mentioned. Colla Ciotach's description in a marginal note to the

---

[111] *L.P. Henry VIII*, xx (pt 1), no. 1298; A. MacDonald and A. MacDonald, *The MacDonald Collection of Gaelic Poetry* (Inverness, 1911), ix, 30.

[112] Bannerman and Black, 'A Sixteenth-century Gaelic Letter', 56–65; Angus Matheson, 'Documents connected with the Trial of Sir James MacDonald of Islay', *TGSG*, v (1958), 211–12.

[113] *The Annals of Loch Cé*, ed. William M. Hennessy (London, 1871), ii, 468, 486; *CSP Ireland* (1574–85), 173.

surviving records of the mission as a *vir bellicosissimus*[114] bears out the general impression of his career given by other contemporary sources, not to mention later tradition. That he should be associated with letter writing in Gaelic is perhaps itself some measure of the prevalence of literacy in the language at this time.

From 1629 there has survived Latin translations of another two Gaelic letters whose purpose was to bear witness to the success of the Franciscan mission. The first, like that of Colla Ciotach, was sent from Colonsay by Donald MacDonald, probably a relative, who tells that he had been a captain in the army of the king of Spain at Naples. The second letter, written on Islay, was signed by three men and a woman bearing Islay surnames, namely, Gillacriosd Mcgiolla Mhicheil (Carmichael), Niall Mcgiollachriosd (MacGilchrist), Giollacriosd Mc a ghobhann (MacGowan) and Maria nic astocair (MacStalker).[115]

Other Gaelic letters on record include one sent jointly by Donald Gorm and Alexander Carrach, sons of James MacDonald of Islay (d. 1565), to Sir Richard Byngham, the English governor of Connaught, about a month before they were both killed at the battle of Ardnaree on 23 September 1586. In 1589 Somhairle Buidhe MacDonald of the Glens wrote to Hugh ÓNéill, earl of Tyrone, to inform him that the MacLeans were proposing to mount an expedition to Ireland, and in 1593 Sir Hugh Maguire enquired of Angus MacDonald of Islay about the possibility of hiring MacDonald mercenaries.[116]

The fact that the majority of the letters on record can be shown to have been sent or received by members of the Clan Donald of Islay[117] is a reflection of the main source from which the evidence is drawn, namely, the English state papers relating to Ireland and of the close involvement of the Islay MacDonalds in Irish affairs. But the earliest known record of a Gaelic letter received by a Scot, which, as it happens, is derived from the same source, is that sent by Seán ONéill, Lord of Tyrone, to Archibald Campbell, earl of Argyll, in 1560, proposing an alliance between them to be cemented by the

[114] Giblin, *Franciscan Mission*, 61, n. 9.
[115] Ibid., 122–4. For Islay surnames, see list of converts, 40–1.
[116] *CSP Ireland* (1586–8), 153–4; (1588–92), 227; (1592–6), 114.
[117] Clan Donald of Islay.

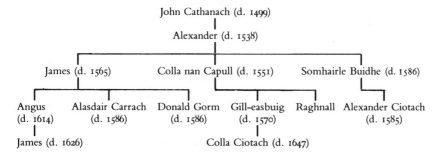

John Cathanach (d. 1499)
Alexander (d. 1538)

James (d. 1565)   Colla nan Capull (d. 1551)   Somhairle Buidhe (d. 1586)

Angus (d. 1614)   Alasdair Carrach (d. 1586)   Donald Gorm (d. 1586)   Gill-easbuig (d. 1570)   Raghnall   Alexander Ciotach (d. 1585)

James (d. 1626)   Colla Ciotach (d. 1647)

marriage of ÓNéill himself to Archibald's sister.[118] This is the same Campbell chief between whom and ÓNéill's enemy, An Calbhach ÓDomhnaill, Lord of Tyrconnell, a confirmation in 1560 of a bond of alliance made five years earlier was drawn up in Gaelic.[119] It was to him too that John Carswell dedicated his Gaelic translation of the *Book of Common Order* in 1567, not to mention the recently built castle of Carnasserie, of which Carswell was the keeper, in an inscription carved above the door in the Gaelic language and script.[120]

The evidence from the sixteenth century indicates that in terms of the written word there were Gaelic speaking Scots who operated at the interface of three languages, Gaelic, Latin and Scots, and, although the survival rate has been poor, there are contemporary documents extant and records of others that bear witness to this fact. Of the latter, one of the most interesting, because it is the most precise, is the Gaelic letter of 1587 to Elizabeth of England which had a Latin and an English version, all three of which were probably written by the young Scottish scribe, Duncan Omey.

But perhaps John Carswell must rank as the most notable practitioner of the three cultures in the sixteenth century. He used literacy in the conservative literary dialect of the day as a tool to promote understanding of the Reformed Faith and this only some six years after the Reformation Parliament of 1560 had given it its blessing, producing thereby the first book printed in Gaelic in either Scotland or Ireland. He showed himself to have been aware of the radical nature of his enterprise when he wrote:

> 'Therefore we have desired to begin now something that we have not heard was done before, namely to translate into Gaelic the form and substance of prayers and of the holy sacraments.'[121]

It is perhaps a measure of his innovatory achievement that some sixty-three years were to elapse before the next Gaelic book was printed in Scotland.[122]

Nor should the *Book of the Dean of Lismore* be forgotten. Its considerable band of named and unnamed scribes seems to move easily between all three languages, even to the extent of writing one of them in the orthography of another. The unanimity and consistency with which this was done is perhaps the most remarkable feature of all.

With the approach of the quatercentenary year of his death in 1582, it would be pleasant to be able to claim George Buchanan also. His output in Latin and Scots is there for all to see but, although a Gaelic speaker, and

---

[118] *CSP Ireland*, 160. A contemporary translation of this letter into Scots survives, as does that of another Gaelic letter, sent by ÓNéill to an Irishman in Scotland in 1567 (Roland M. Smith, 'Shane O'Neill's Last Letter', *The Journal of Celtic Studies*, ii (1958), 131–3).

[119] John MacKechnie, 'Treaty between Argyll and O'Donnell', *SGS*, vii (1951–3), 94–9.

[120] *Foirm na n–Urrnuidheadh*, 1; Bannerman, 'Two early post-Reformation inscriptions', 309.

[121] *Foirm na n–Urrnuidheadh*, 8, 177.

[122] *Adtimchiol an Chreidimh*, ed. R. L. Thomson (SGTS, 1962), xiv.

interested enough to be the first scholar on record to recognise the linguistic relationship between the different branches of Celtic, which included the Gaelic language,[123] there is no apparent evidence that he could write the literary dialect common to late medieval Scotland and Ireland. But his origins in what was by this time a peripheral area of the Gaelic world makes it less likely that he would profess the classical Gaelic learning current in a metropolitan region like the former Lordship of the Isles. There the supportive role of the bard and of his highly literate panegyric poetry in the very maintenance of the prevailing kin-based society may have required a greater degree of literacy in the vernacular among the laity than was common in other contemporary societies. Indeed, there was probably a greater pressure on lay people to be literate in Gaelic than in either of the two languages of government in the sixteenth century and this must have been even more the case in preceding centuries when the authority of the crown was less pervasive. The ruling grade of society, that is, the heads of important kindreds and their immediate families, cannot easily have avoided being literate in the language and there is some evidence that literacy therein might extend downwards to include lesser people, specifically perhaps the *daoin-uaisle* or gentlemen of individual kindreds.[124]

[123] George Buchanan, *The History of Scotland*, trans. James Aikman (Glasgow, 1827), i, 64–129; T. G. E. Powell, *The Celts* (London, 1958), 17–19; Arthur H. Williamson, *Scottish National Consciousness in the Age of James VI* (Edinburgh, 1979) 123–4.

[124] I wish to thank Mr Ronald Black and Mr Donald Meek, who kindly read this paper in a first draft, for help and advice.

JOHN BANNERMAN

Bibliography of Works by Gordon Donaldson

1938   Story of the Parish of South Yell, 1838–1938, in collaboration with the Reverend Douglas Beck. *The Shetland Times*, Lerwick, 10, 17 and 24 December.

1940   The relations between the English and Scottish presbyterian movement to 1604. PhD thesis summary in *Bulletin of Institute of Historical Research (IHR)*, xvii, 39–41.

1942   *St Andrews Formulare, 1514–1546*, with C. Macrae. Stair Society, vol. i.
        The attitude of Whitgift and Bancroft to the Scottish Church.
        Transactions of the Royal Historical Society, Fourth Series, xxiv, 95–115.

1943   The Early Ministers of the North Isles. *The Shetland News*, 2, 9 and 16 September.

1944   *St Andrews Formulare, 1514–1546*, Stair Society, vol. ii.
        Sources for the study of Scottish ecclesiastical organisation and personnel, 1560–1600. *Bulletin of IHR*, xix, 188–203.

1945   The Scottish Episcopate at the Reformation. *EHR*, lx, 349–64.

1946   The Archdeaconry of Shetland in the Sixteenth Century. *The Shetland News*, 3 and 24 October and 7 November.

1947   List of official records acquired 1905–1946, appended to W. Angus, Accessions of Public records to the Register House since 1905. *SHR*, xxvi, 30–46.
        Alexander Gordon, Bishop of Galloway (1559–1575) and his work in the reformed church. *TDGAS* (3rd series), xxiv, 111–28.

1948   Origins of the Diocese of Edinburgh. *Edinburgh Diocesan Gazette*, January and May.
        'The Example of Denmark' in the Scottish Reformation. *SHR*, xxvii, 57–64.
        Scottish Service Books since the Reformation. *The Scottish Guardian*, 4, 11, 18, 25 June and 2 July.

1949   *The Prayer Book in Scotland, 1549–1949*, Dundee, privately printed.
        The Prayer Book in Scotland, 1549–1949. *Edinburgh Diocesan Gazette*, May.
        Life in Yell under Earl Patrick. *The Shetland News*, 27 July.
        'Plus ça change', *Edinburgh Diocesan Gazette*, October and September 1950.

1950   *A Handlist of Manuscripts in the British Isles relating to Malta*. (Compiled for the Historical Archives of Malta Committee.) *Bulletin of IHR Malta*, no. 7.
        The Scottish Communion Office of 1637 ed.
        The Pope's Reply to the Scottish Barons in 1320. *SHR*, xxix, 119–20.

The Bishops and Priors of Whithorn. *TDGAS*, 3rd series, xxvii, 127–54.

A notice of *Some Aspects of later Seventeenth–Century Scotland*, by H. W. Meikle. *History*, xxxv.

'Eighteenth Century Family Letters'; A review of *The Seven Sons of the Provost*, ed. H. Taylor. *SHR*, xxix, 188–94.

Reviews of *The Life and Times of James Kennedy*, by A. I. Dunlop and *Veterum Laudes*, ed. J. B. Salmond. *Edinburgh University Journal (EUJ)*, xv, 197–8.

1951   Forty Years Since. *Edinburgh Diocesan Gazette*, April.

Lord Chancellor Glamis and Theodore Beza. *SHS Misc.*, viii, 89–113.

South-East Scotland, 1500–1951. *A Scientific Survey of South-East Scotland*, 61–4.

The Norwegian Coast. *The Shetland News*, 18 and 25 October, 1, 8, 15 and 22 November.

A review of *Scottish Pageant, 1625–1707*, ed. A. M. Mackenzie. *SHR*, xxx, 86–7.

A review of *John Knox in Controversy*, by H. Watt. *SHR*, xxx, 182–6.

A review of *The College of St Salvator*, by R. G. Cant. *EUJ*, xv, 261.

1952   *A Source Book of Scottish History*, ed. with W. C. Dickinson and I. A. Milne, vol. i.

Letters of Exemption from Military Service. *SHR*, xxxi, 97–8.

The Cistercian Nunnery of St Mary Haddington. *Trans. East Lothian Antiquarian Society*, v, 2–24.

Texts and translations of Documents. *Charters and Other Records of the City and Royal Burgh of Kirkwall*, ed. J. Mooney.

A review of *Map of Monastic Britain*. North Sheet. *SHR*, xxxi, 84–6.

A review of *Scottish Pageant 1707–1802*, ed. A. M. Mackenzie. *SHR*, xxxi, 87–9.

A notice of *Bibliography of British History, the Eighteenth Century, 1714–1789*, edd. S. Pargellis and D. J. Medley. *SHR*, xxxi, 91.

A review of *John Knox*, by J. D. Mackie. *SHR*, xxxi, 165–7.

A review of *The Episcopal Church in Scotland from the Restoration to the Present Day*, by F. Goldie. *Scottish Journal of Theology (SJT)*, v, 444–6.

A notice of *Selected Cases from Acta Dominorum Concilii et Sessionis*, ed. I. H. Shearer, Stair Society. *EHR*, lxvii, 440.

A notice of *Supra Crepidam*, by Rt. Hon. Lord Cooper. *EHR*, lxvii, 462–3.

A notice of *The Times, Life, and Thought of Patrick Forbes, bishop of Aberdeen, 1618–1635*, by W. G. S. Snow. *EHR*, lxvii, 601–2.

1953   *A Source Book of Scottish History*, ed. with W. C. Dickinson and I. A. Milne, vol. ii.

Whithorn and Kirkmadrine, Wigtownshire, with C. A. Ralegh Radford.

Post-reformation church of Whithorn, with C. A. ·Ralegh Radford, *PSAS*, lxxv, 117–30.

The 'New Enterit Benefices', 1573–1586. *SHR*, xxxii, 93–8.

The Galloway Clergy at the Reformation. *TDGAS*, Third Series, xxx, 38–60.

A review of *The Domestic Life of Scotland in the Eighteenth Century*, by Marjory Plant. *EUJ*, xvi, 277.

A notice of *The Royal Burgh of Ayr*, ed. A. I. Dunlop. *EUJ*, xvii, 59.

A review of *English Monasteries. Medieval Religious Houses: England and Wales*, by D. Knowles and R. N. Hadcock. *The Scotsman*, 27 August.

James IV's Letters. A review of *The Letters of James IV, 1505–1513*, by R. K. Hannay, edd. R. L. Mackie and A. Spilman. *The Scotsman*, 17 December.

A notice of *Orkney Farm-Names*, by H. Marwick. *EHR*, lxviii, 468–9.

A notice of The Administration of Justice in Medieval Scotland, by W. C. Dickinson. *Aberdeen University Review (AUR)*, xxxiv, 338–51. *SHR*, xxxii, 195.

1954   *The Story of Christ Church, Trinity.*
The Scottish Church, from Queen Margaret to the Reformation.
The Making of the Scottish Prayer Book of 1637.
A Source Book of Scottish History, ed. with W. C. Dickinson, vol. iii.

St James's, Leith. *Edinburgh Diocesan Gazette*, viii, no. 2, 10–12.

Northern History in Scottish Records. *Orkney Miscellany*, 2, 72–8.

Scottish Ordinations in the Restoration Period. *SHR*, xxxiii, 169–75.

A review of *The Register of the Privy Seal*, iv. *SHR*, xxxiii, 40.

A review of *James Stewart, Earl of Moray*, by M. Lee. *SHR*, xxxiii, 139–44.

A notice of *Monasticon Praemonstratense, id est Historia Circariarum atque Canoniarum Candidi et Canonici Ordinis Praemonstratensis*, by N. Backmund, vol. ii. *SHR*, xxxiii, 164.

A notice of *Orkney Miscellany*, i. *SHR*, xxxiii, 164–5.

A review of *The University of Glasgow, 1451–1951*, by J. D. Mackie. *Saltire Review*, i, no. 2, 90–1.

A review of *The Letters of James the Fourth 1505–1513*. Calendared by R. K. Hannay, edd. R. L. Mackie and A. Spilman. *EHR*, lxix, 439–42.

The Celtic Church. A review of *The Celtic Church in Dunblane*, by J. H. Cockburn. *The Scotsman*, 18 November.

The Norman Conquest in Scotland. A review of *The Normans in Scotland*, by R. L. Graeme Ritchie. *The Scotsman*, 17 December.

1955   *Court Book of Shetland 1602–4. SRS.*

Scottish Bishops' Sees before the Reign of David I. *PSAS*, lxxxvii, 106–17.

The Polity of the Scottish Church, 1560–1600. *RSCHS*, xi, 212–26.

Guisborough and the Annandale Churches. *TDGAS*, xxxii, 142–54.

Why January the First? *The Quest*, no. 21, 11–12.

A review of *Rival Establishments in Scotland, 1560–1690*, by A. M. Mackenzie. *SJT*, viii, 104–5.

A notice of *Orkney Miscellany*, ii. *SHR*, xxxiv, 76–7.

A notice of *Two translations from the Dano-Norwegian*, by E. S. Reid Tait. *SHR*, xxxiv, 79.

A review of *The Viking Congress*, ed. W. D. Simpson. *SHR*, xxxiv, 150–3.

A review of *The Normans in Scotland*, by R. L. Graeme Ritchie. *EUJ*, xvii, 258.

1956 Text and Translation of Foundation Documents in *King's College, Aberdeen, its fittings, ornaments and ceremonial in the sixteenth century*, ed. F. C. Eeles.

Common Errors in Scottish History, ed.

The Office of the Superintendent in the Reformed Church. *Common Errors in Scottish History*, 13–15.

Accidental Homicide in Perth in 1571. *SHR*, xxxv, 182.

A review of *The Presbyterian College, Belfast, 1853–1953*, by R. Allen. *SHR*, xxxv, 69–71.

Notices of *Scotland under Charles I*, by D. Mathew; *The Catholic Church in the Hebrides, 1560–1760*, by J. L. Campbell. *The Tablet*, ccvi, no. 6032.

Notices of *A Quarter of a Millenium of Anglo-Scottish Union*, by R. Pares, *History*, xxxix, no. 137, *SHR*, xxxv, 153, 179–80.

A notice of *Devotional Pieces in Verse and Prose*, ed. J. A. W. Bennett. *EUJ*, xviii, 130.

1957 *Register of the Privy Seal of Scotland, 1556–1567*, ed. with J. Beveridge, v, 2 parts.

The Scottish Province – History. *Pan-Anglican*, viii, 12–16.

A review of *King James VI and I*, by D. H. Willson. *EHR*, lxxii, 117–20.

From the Vatican's Archives. A review. *Scottish Supplications to Rome 1423–1428*, ed. A. I. Dunlop. *The Scotsman*, 14 March.

A notice of *The Maladies of Mary, Queen of Scots and her Husband*, by M. H. Armstrong Davison. *Report of the Proceedings of the Scottish Society of the History of Medicine, 1955–56*. *SHR*, xxxvi, 78.

1958 *Shetland Life under Earl Patrick.*

Inter-diocesan and inter-provincial communication before and after the Reformation. *RSCHS*, xxii, 73–81.

Scottish Worship: the heritage of the past and the needs of the present. *Church Service Society Annual*, 3–14.

The Church Courts. *An Introduction to Scottish Legal History*. Stair Society, 363–73.

A review of *The James Carmichaell Collection of Proverbs in Scots*, ed. M. L. Anderson. *EUJ*, xix, 52–3.

A notice of *Montrose*, by J. Buchan, a reissue. *SHR*, xxxvii, 88.

The cloistral life. A review of *Adam of Dryburgh*, by James Bulloch. *The Scotsman*, 21 May.

Why George Buchanan wrote partisan history. A review of *The*

Tyrannous reign of Mary Stewart, by W. Gatherer. *The Scotsman*, 24 July.

A review of *The Wisest Fool in Christendom*, by W. McElwee, *The Scotsman*, 9 August.

A notice of *Prince Charles's Puritan Chaplain*, by I. Morgan. *History*, xliii, 236.

A review of *The Christian Scholar in the age of the Reformation*, in *The Student World*, no. 4, 414–16.

1959   *A Source Book of Scottish History*, Second Edition, i and ii.

A Reformation Chronology. *The Scotsman*, 20 May.

A review of *A profest papist; Bishop John Gordon*, by T. F. Taylor. *EHR*, lxxiv, 161–2.

A review of *Bishop and Presbytery; the Church of Scotland 1661–1688*, by W. R. Foster. *EHR*, lxxiv, 354–5.

The Queen's Commissioner. A review of *The Office of the Lord High Commissioner*, by S. Mechie, in *Manse Mail*, February.

A review of *The Medieval Bishops of Dunblane and their Church*, by J. H. Cockburn. *The Scotsman*, 23 April.

Secretary to a successful Stewart King. A review of *John Maitland of Thirlstane*, by M. Lee. *The Scotsman*, 15 August.

Mary Stuart and Elizabeth. A review of *The Reign of Elizabeth*, by J. B. Black. *The Scotsman*, 15 September.

Life of the Cloister. A review of *A Monastery in Moray*, by P. Anson. *The Scotsman*, 5 December.

A notice of *King James IV of Scotland*, by R. L. Mackie. *EUJ*, xix, 213–14.

A review of *The History of Trinity House of Leith*, by J. Mason. *SHR*, xxxviii, 153–4.

1960   *Scotland, Church and Nation through Sixteen Centuries.*

The Scottish Reformation.

The Parish Clergy and the Scottish Reformation. *Innes Review*, x, 5–20.

The Reformation in Shetland. *The Shetland News*, 31 March.

David Lindsay. *Fathers of the Kirk*, ed. R. S. Wright, 27–37.

'Flitting Friday', the Beggars' Summons and Knox's Sermon at Perth. *SHR*, xxxix, 175–6.

What the Reformation did for Education. *Life and Work*, New Series, xiii, 107–8.

Sources for Scottish agrarian history before the eighteenth century. *The Agricultural History Review*, viii, 82–90.

Bishop Adam Bothwell and the Reformation in Orkney. *RSCHS*, xiii, 85–100.

A review article: Reformations. *Spectator*, 9 December.

A notice of *The sources for the life of St Kentigern*, by K. H. Jackson. *Studies in the early British Church*, ed. N. K. Chadwick. *SHR*, xxxix, 82–3.

A notice of *York metropolitan jurisdiction and papal judges delegate*, by R. Brentano. *SHR*, xxxix, 155–6.

A review of *Scotland Past and Present*, by J. M. Reid. *Scottish Studies*, iv, 104–5.

A review of *The MacLeods: the History of a Clan*, by I. F. Grant. *History*, xlv, 193–4.

A notice of *The Story of Scotland*, by J. Glover. *History*, xlv, 299–300.

1961   *A Source Book of Scottish History*, with W. C. Dickinson, revised and enlarged, 2nd ed., iii.

Foundations of Anglo-Scottish Union. *Elizabethan Government and Society, Essays presented to Sir John Neale*, ed. S. T. Bindoff *et al.*, 282–314.

Episcopalian Pedigree. *Church of England Newspaper*, 29 September.

A review of *The Church and Scottish Social Development*, by S. Mechie. *Journal of Ecclesiastical History (JEH)*, xii, 133–4.

A notice of *The Holy Communion in the Reformed Church of Scotland*, by G. B. Burnett. *EHR*, lxxvi, 727–8.

A notice of *Elizabeth I and the Unity of England*, by J. Hurstfield. *SHR*, xl, 164.

A notice of *The Faith of John Knox*, by J. S. McEwen. *Church of England Newspaper*, 24 November.

1962   *A Short History of Scotland*, by R. L. Mackie, revised.

Scottish Presbyterian Exiles in England, 1584–8. *RSCHS*, xiv, 67–80.

A notice of *Wigtownshire Charters*, ed. R. C. Reid. *EHR*, lxxvii, 136–7.

A notice of *Letters of Thomas Wood, Puritan*, ed. P. Collinson. *JEH*, xiii, 127–8.

A notice of *The Buik of the Kirk of the Canagait*, ed. S. Wright. *Archives*, v, 175–6.

New Order in the North. A review of *The Court Book of Orkney and Shetland 1612–1613*, ed. R. S. Barclay. *The Scotsman*, 26 May.

1963   *Register of the Privy Seal of Scotland, 1567–1574*, vi.

A review of *The Court Book of Orkney and Shetland 1612–1613*, ed. R. S. Barclay. *SHR*, xlii, 77.

1964   *Scottish History and the Scottish Nation.*

A Historian looks at Scotland's Future. *Scots Magazine*, new series, lxxxi, 501–10.

Obituary: E. W. M. Balfour-Melville. *SHR*, xliii, 88.

Wandering Scholars. A review of *The Letters of John Johnston and Robert Howie*, ed. J. K. Cameron. *Times Literary Supplement (TLS)*, 27 February.

A review of *Sir Henry Killigrew, Elizabethan Soldier and Diplomat*, by A. C. Miller. *SHR*, xliii, 53–4.

1965   *Scotland: James V to James VII.*

A review of *Irish Franciscan Mission to Scotland*, by C. Giblin. *JEH*, xvi, 130–1.

The Community of the Realm. A review of *Robert Bruce and the Community of the Realm of Scotland*, by G. W. S. Barrow. *Library Review*, cliv, 139–40.

1966   The Scots Overseas.
Northwards by Sea.
Register of the Privy Seal of Scotland, 1575–1580, vii.
A Scottish Liturgy of the Reign of James VI. *SHS Misc.*, x, 87–117.
The Rights of the Scottish crown in Episcopal Vacancies. *SHR*, xlv, 27–35.
Map of the Siege of Leith, 1560. *Book of Old Edinburgh Club*, xxxii, 1–7.
The National Factor in Scotland. *Faith and Unity*, x, 104–5.
Scotland's Conservative North in the Sixteenth and Seventeenth Centuries. *Trans. Royal Historical Society*, 5th series, xvi, 65–79.
A notice of *Images of a Queen*, by J. E. Phillips. *EHR*, lxxxi, 161–2.
A notice of Deutsche Schottenklöster, Schottische Reformation, Katholische Reform und Gegenreformation in West- und Mitteleuropa. *Zeitschrift für bayerische Landesgeschichte*, xxvi, 131–255. *EHR*, lxxxi, 164.
A notice of *An Elizabethan Problem: some aspects of the careers of two exile-adventurers*, by L. Hicks. *EHR*, lxxxi, 589–90.
A review of *A History of Scotland*, by J. D. Mackie and *A New History of Scotland*, 2nd ed., by W. C. Dickinson. *SHR*, xlv, 203–5.

1967   Scottish Kings.
The Stewarts and the Reformation, and Under British Rule. *The Shetland Book*, ed. A. T. Cluness, 72–8.
Unity and the National Factor in Scotland, *Scan*, August.

1968   The Attitude of Whitgift and Bancroft to the Scottish Church (a reprint). *Essays in Modern History*, ed. I. R. Christie, 56–74.

1969   The Memoirs of Sir James Melville of Halhill, ed. for Folio Society.
The First Trial of Mary, Queen of Scots.
John Knox: *New Edinburgh Review*, No. 3, 20–3.
The Earlier Gunpowder Plot. *Folio*, July, September, 58–65.
Introduction to Scotland and Scandinavia in *SHR*, xlviii, 1–5.
Scottish Devolution: The Historical Background, with others: *Government and Nationalism in Scotland: An Enquiry by Members of the University of Edinburgh*, ed. J. N. Wolfe, 1–16.

1970   Scottish Historical Documents.
Scotland before Flodden; Scotland and the Stuarts; Kirk and Covenant; and Scotland since 1660. *The History of the English-Speaking Peoples*, ed. R. Humble, 1058–63, 1371–7, 1516–19, 1828–31.

1971   Worship in Scotland in 1620. *Liturgical Studies*, November.

1972   Scotland: James V to James VII. Japanese edition.
The Scottish Reformation. 2nd impression.
Scotland: Church and Nation through Sixteen Centuries, 2nd ed.
The emergence of schism in seventeenth-century Scotland. *Studies in Church History*, ix, 277–94.

James VI and Vanishing Frontiers. *The Scottish Nation*, ed. G. Menzies, 103–17.

John Knox: Reformer Reassessed. *The Scotsman*, 25 November.

1973   Scotland's Earliest Church Buildings. *RSCHS*, xviii, 1–9.

The Scottish Church, 1567–1625. *The Reign of James VI and I*, ed. A. G. R. Smith, 40–56.

The Age of the Moderates. A review of *The Scottish Church 1688–1843*, by A. L. Drummond and J. Bulloch. *Life and Work*, 26–7.

1974   *Who's Who in Scottish History*, with R. S. Morpeth.

The First Trial of Mary, Queen of Scots, paperback edition.

Mary, Queen of Scots.

Scotland: The Shaping of a Nation.

Aberdeen University and the Reformation. *Northern Scotland*, i, 129–42.

The Foundation of Elgin Cathedral. *Elgin Cathedral and the Diocese of Moray*, 1–2.

Stewart Builders: the descendants of James V. *The Stewarts*, xiv, 116–22.

The significance of genealogy to the Scottish historian. *Scottish Genealogist*, xxi, 59–64.

Westminster need not be the model. *Glasgow Herald*, 30 October.

The Second World War: Further Adventures of the Records. *SHR*, liii, 211–19.

A review of *Scottish Parish Clergy at the Reformation*, by C. H. Haws. *SHR*, liii, 83–6.

1975   Knox the Man. *John Knox: A Quatercentenary Reappraisal*, ed. D. Shaw, 18–32.

Hopes Fulfilled: the Grey Book. *Liturgical Review*, v, 21–8.

Leighton's Predecessors. *Journal of the Society of the Friends of Dunblane Cathedral*, xii, pt. 2, 7–16.

A comment. British History. *Journal of Modern History*, xlvii, 623–5.

A notice. *David Livingstone and Africa. SHR*, liv, 105.

1976   Historic Sites – Introduction. *National Trust for Scotland Guide.*

Viking Tracks in Scotland. *Proceedings of the Conference on Scottish Studies*, ed. C. Haws, no. 3, 3–10.

The Legal Profession in Scottish Society in the sixteenth and seventeenth Centuries. *Juridical Review*, 1–19; reprinted in *Lawyers in their Social Setting*, ed. D. N. MacCormick, 152–70.

The origins of the burgh. *Edinburgh: A Symposium, for Dr J. B. Barclay*, ed. B. C. Skinner, 1–7.

A notice of *South African Liturgy. Liturgical Review*, 67–8.

A review of *Scotland from the Eleventh Century to 1603*, by B. Webster. *SHR*, lv, 74–6.

Myths Old and New. A review of *John Knox*, by H. MacDiarmid *et al.* and *The Scottish Covenanters*, by I. B. Cowan. *Scottish Review*, i, pt. 4, 28–32.

1977 *Scottish Kings*, 2nd revised ed.
A Dictionary of Scottish History, with R. S. Morpeth.
Withdrawing realistically. A review of *The University of Glasgow*, by J. Durkan and J. Kirk. *TLS*, 9 September.
Propaganda in Stone. A review of *The Medieval Church of St Andrews*, by David MacRoberts. *TLS*, 14 October.

1978 *Northwards by Sea*, 2nd rev. enlarged ed.
Scotland: James V to James VII, paperback ed.
The Sources of Scottish History. privately printed.
Norse and Scottish Law in Shetland. *The Shetland Report*, i, 136–50.
Introduction to *The Pirate Gow*, by D. Defoe.
Bachelors All. A review of *A Biographical Dictionary of Scottish Graduates to A.D. 1410*, by D. E. R. Watt. *TLS*, 28 April.
Kings and their crises. A review of *Scottish Society in the Fifteenth Century*, ed. J. M. Brown. *TLS*, 8 September.
Fifteenth Century Scotland. A notice of *Scottish Society in the Fifteenth Century*, ed. J. M. Brown. *Books in Scotland*, no. 2, 35.
A review of *Scandinavian Shetland: an Ongoing tradition?*, by J. R. Baldwin. *SHR*, lvii, 208–9.
A notice of *Medieval Manuscripts in British Libraries*, by N. R. Ker, ii. *SHR*, lvii, 206.

1979 Admiral Cochrane. A review of *The Sea Wolf: The Life of Admiral Cochrane*, by Ian Grimble. *Books in Scotland*, no. 4, 20–9.
Life in the Islands. A review of *The Northern Isles: Orkney and Shetland*, by A. Fenton. *Books in Scotland*, no. 4, 37.
The Politicians and the Union. A review article on *King William and the Scottish Politicians*, by P. W. J. Riley, *The Union of England and Scotland*, by P. W. J. Riley, and *1707: The Union of Scotland and England*, by P. H. Scott. *Books in Scotland*, no. 5, 19–20.

1980 *The Scottish Reformation*, third impression.
Scotland: The Shaping of a Nation, 2nd edn.
Fletcher of Saltoun. *The Scottish Review*, no. 17, 21–6.
A review of *The best of our owne: Letters of Archibald Pitcairne, 1652–1713*, ed. W. T. Johnston, *The Scottish Review*, no. 18, 42–3.
Holyrood and its Port. *Scottish Genealogist*, xxvii, no. 2, 66–72.

1981 *Surnames and Society in Scotland*. privately printed.
Historiography. *A Companion to Scottish Culture*, ed. D. Daiches, 165–9.
Renaissance and Reformation. *The Scottish World*, ed. H. Orel *et al.*, 87–118.
Stair's Scotland: The Intellectual Inheritance. *Juridical Review*, xxvi (N.S.), 128–45.
Reviews of *The Records of the Synod of Lothian and Tweeddale*, ed. J. Kirk, and *Edward I and the Throne of Scotland*, ed. E. L. G. Stones and G. G. Simpson, *Juridical Review*, xxvi (N.S.), 89–99.

Donors and Subscribers

D. M. Abbott
David G. Adams
James Tait Aitken
Nicolas Allen
Per Sveaas Andersen
James Anderson
Peter D. Anderson
Hubert Andrew
Miss Catherine Armet
Mrs Joan Auld
Miss M. M. Baird
John H. Ballantyne
J. B. Barclay
G. W. S. Barrow
Mrs John Barrows
Mrs Caroline Batt
Gibson K. Boath
Gerald C. N. Bramley
Andrew M. Broom
James Brown
Gerrard A. Burnett
David G. C. Burns
J. H. Burns
J. B. Caird
The Hon Lord Cameron
James K. Cameron
Mrs A. D. H. Campbell
I. M. Campbell
R. H. Campbell
Ronald G. Cant
Miss Cecilia C. Cavaye
J. W. Chambers
Mrs Ann Chapman
Mrs G. Charles-Edwards
Hugh Cheape
Thorkild Lyby Christensen
Tristan Clarke
Ronald Francis Coghill
Lin Collis
Ernest Cormack
D. S. F. Couper
Winifred K. Coutts

Ian B. Cowan
Miss A. S. Cowper
Barbara E. Crawford
Mrs Kathleen Gray Crosbie
James Darragh
Frank W. Darroch of Mulmorich
Christopher J. Davey
J. W. S. Dearness
W. G. Dey
W. G. and Lesley Diack
William Dickson
Mark Dilworth
Vernon Donaldson
Marjorie J. Drexler
Peter Drummond-Murray
David Dumville
Michael D. Dun
A. A. M. Duncan
A. Ian Dunlop
Alastair M. Dunnett
John Durkan
Wm. S. Dykes
Gerald and Margaret Elliot
Alexander Fenton
William Ferguson
Iain Flett
Eric Malcolm Forrester
Ian L. Forrester
Denton Fox
Ronald Fyfe
William Gillies
Alistair R. Gordon
Thomas W. Graham
Douglas Grant
Ian D. Grant
Ian R. Grant
John G. Gray
Ivor R. Guild
Jean R. Guild
R. T. Halliday
W. Fergus Harris
Charles H. Haws

Denys Hay
Marion C. C. Hay
M. J. Henderson
Alasdair I. C. Heron
Christian Lady Hesketh
George R. Hewitt
Colin F. Hogg
Mrs E. Isobel Humphrey
Miss G. B. Hunter
Mrs Margaret S. Hunter
B. J. Iggo
William Inglis
Malcolm R. Innes of Edingight
Mrs Annie Jack
Kenneth H. Jackson
Christine Johnson
George M. Johnson
Gordon M. Johnston
W. Gerald Jones
Ian Keillar
Charles Kelham
Puk Kyong Kim
Miss C. M. Kinnear
James Kirk
Harold Kirkpatrick
A. Douglas Lamb
Brian Lambie
Christina Larner
Alexander Law
J. J. Lawrie
Bruce Lenman
The Hon John Leslie
Gottfried W. Locher
Kenneth J. Logue
F. P. Lole
Niall Lothian
R. Stuart Louden
Michael Lynch
Alexander C. McAulay
John F. McCaffrey
Ian McCraw
Mrs Ailsa F. McCullough
A. A. MacDonald
Mrs J. D. B. MacDonald
Norman Macdougall
Andrew B. W. MacEwen
Allan I. Macinnes
Farquhar Macintosh
P. H. R. Mackay
Catherine B. Mackechnie

Miss Mary E. Mackenzie
Allan Maclean of Dochgarroch
Nicholas Maclean–Bristol
Annabel MacLeay of Linsaig
    (Mrs H. Imrie-Swainston)
John McLintock
James F. McMillan
D. J. McNeill
Ian R. Macneil of Barra
Peter G. B. McNeill
Alan Macquarrie
Hector L. MacQueen
John Macqueen
Ruth McQuillan
Walter H. Makey
R. J. and E. E. Malden
T. M. Y. Manson
James S. Marshall
Rosalind K. Marshall
Mrs Irene W. Matthew
Stuart Maxwell
M. H. Merriman
A. Taylor Milne
Edwin Morgan
C. M. Morrison
David Morrison
R. W. and Jean Munro
Athol L. Murray
Mrs A. E. Nimmo
Geoffrey Parker
R. M. Pinkerton
Mrs K. M. Pollard
Thomas I. Rae
David C. G. Reckord
Charles T. Reid
G. D. Richardson
Felicity J. Riddy
J. D. M. Robertson
James J. Robertson
W. J. Robertson
W. I. S. Robson
Angus W. Rodger
P. C. Rodger
Anthony Ross
A. W. and E. R. Russell
Margaret H. B. Sanderson
William W. Scott
B. Sedberg
Henry R. Sefton
David Sellar

Brian J. Sharp
Duncan Shaw
Frances J. Shaw
Moira Simmons
Grant G. Simpson
John Simpson
Cecil J. Sinclair
H. Gordon Slade
James E. Smail
Mrs Aileen Smart
Kiki Smiler
Annette M. Smith
Brian Smith
David B. Smith
John A. Smith
T. C. Smout
Malcolm Sinclair
David M. G. Stalker
Margaret Steele
B. A. Stenhouse
David Stevenson
Alasdair M. Stewart
Miss Marion M. Stewart
Miss M. V. Stokes
Miss M. Tait
J. A. F. Thomson
John M. Todd
John R. Todd
Thomas F. Torrance
E. P. D. Torrie
James A. Troup
Hans H. Uyl
David M. Walker
David F. Ward
J. Steven Watson
Margot N. Watson
D. E. R. Watt
The Earl of Wemyss & March
D. H. Whiteford
Donald Whyte

Janet Elizabeth Hadley Williams
W. W. Williams
Samuel R. Williamson
Mrs Virginia Wills
Miss Isabel J. T. Wilson
William J. Windram
C. W. J. Withers
Jenny Wormald
Ian Wotherspoon
Ronald Selby Wright
Margaret D. Young

Aberdeen City Libraries
Aberdeen University Library
Borthwick Institute of Historical Research
Christ's College, Aberdeen
Dollar Academy
Edinburgh University Library
Edinburgh University School of Studies Library
Edinburgh University Scottish History Department
Glasgow University Library
Huntington Library
Leeds University Library
Liverpool University Sydney Jones Library
National Library of Wales
National Museum of Antiquities of Scotland Library
New College Library
Oslo University Institute of History
Perth and Kinross District Libraries
Queen's University Library
St Peter's College Library
Scottish Episcopal Theological College Library
Scottish Genealogy Society
Scottish Record Office
Society of Writers to H.M. Signet

Index

Only Scottish names and places in articles apart from the Appreciation have been indexed.